# Communications in Computer and Information Science 401

Jinshu Su Baokang Zhao Zhigang Sun
Xiaofeng Wang Fei Wang Ke Xu (Eds.)

# Frontiers in Internet Technologies

Second CCF Internet Conference of China, ICoC 2013
Zhangjiajie, China, July 10, 2013
Revised Selected Papers

Volume Editors

Jinshu Su
Baokang Zhao
Zhigang Sun
Xiaofeng Wang
Fei Wang
National University of Defense Technology
Changsha, China
E-mail:{sjs, sunzhigang, bkzhao}@nudt.edu.cn

Ke Xu
Tsinghua University, Bejing, China
E-mail: xuke@tsinghua.edu.cn

ISSN 1865-0929 e-ISSN 1865-0937
ISBN 978-3-642-53958-9 e-ISBN 978-3-642-53959-6
DOI 10.1007/978-3-642-53959-6
Springer Heidelberg New York Dordrecht London

Library of Congress Control Number: 2013956747

CR Subject Classification (1998): C.2, J.1, J.4, K.4.4, D.4.6, K.6.5



*Typesetting:* Camera-ready by author, data conversion by Scientific Publishing Services, Chennai, India

Printed on acid-free paper

Springer is part of Springer Science+Business Media (www.springer.com)

# Preface

As the flagship conference organized by the Internet Technical Committee of China Computer Federation, the Second Internet Conference of China (CCF ICoC 2013) was hosted by the National University of Defense Technology in Zhangjiajie, Hunan Province, on July 10, 2013. The conference focused on the latest advances in research on Internet-related theory and technology.

ICoC 2013 invited authors to submit full papers representing original, unpublished work in all areas of Internet communication and computing. Topics include but are not limited to the following areas: future Internet architecture, Internet routing, network security, network management, data center networks, green networks, wireless networks, P2P networks, mobile Internet and Internet of Things.

ICoC 2013 received 63 papers from 36 universities. After an extensive peer-review process involving more than 42 reviewers, the Program Committee chairs went through all the reports and ranked the papers according to the reviewers' comments. Each paper was evaluated by at least three reviewers. The top 24 manuscripts were finally selected for inclusion in these proceedings and for presentation at the conference. This represents an acceptance rate of 38%, which guarantees that ICoC will continue to be one of the most respected conferences for researchers working on networks around the world.

July 2013

JinShu Su
Baokang Zhao
Zhigang Sun
Xiaofeng Wang
Fei Wang
Ke Xu

# Preface

# Organization

**The Second CCF Internet Conference**

**of China**

**——CCF ICoC 2013——**

**ZhangJiaJie, China**

**July 10–11, 2013**

*Hosted by*

**China Computer Federation**

*Organized by*

**Internet Technical Committee of the China Computer Federation**

**National University of Defense Technology**

**Fuzhou University**

*Edited by*

**Jinshu Su, Baokang Zhao, Zhigang Sun,**

**Xiaofeng Wang, Fei Wang, Ke Xu**

# Organizers

## General Chair

| | |
|---|---|
| Jinshu Su | National University of Defense Technology, China |

## Program Chairs

| | |
|---|---|
| Mingwei Xu | Tsinghua University, China |
| Zhigang Sun | National University of Defense Technology, China |
| Guojun Wang | Central South University, China |

## Publicity Chair

| | |
|---|---|
| Guolong Chen | Fuzhou University, China |

## Publication Chairs

| | |
|---|---|
| Baokang Zhao | National University of Defense Technology, China |
| Ke Xu | Tsinghua University, China |

## Organization Chair

| | |
|---|---|
| Xiaofeng Wang | National University of Defense Technology, China |

## Program Committee

| | |
|---|---|
| Baokang Zhao | National University of Defense Technology, China |
| Chunhe Xia | Beijing University of Aeronautics and Astronautics, China |
| Dongliang Xie | Beijing University of Posts and Telecommunications, China |
| Fu Chen | Beijing Foreign Studies University, China |
| Guang Cheng | Southeast University, China |

| | |
|---|---|
| Guolong Chen | Fuzhou University, China |
| Hao Ma | Peking University, China |
| Hua Li | Inner Mongolia University, China |
| Jian Gong | Southeast University, China |
| Jingsong Wang | Tianjin University of Technology, China |
| Jun Bi | Tsinghua University, China |
| Kan Li | Beijing Institute of Technology, China |
| Ke Xu | Tsinghua University, China |
| Libing Wu | Wuhan University, China |
| Lijun Wu | University of Electronic Science and Technology of China, China |
| Mingwen Wang | Jiangxi Normal University, China |
| Shiyong Zhang | Fudan University, China |
| Teng Jiang | Heilongjiang University, China |
| Wei Yan | Peking University, China |
| Wenzhong Guo | Fuzhou University, China |
| Xianghan Zheng | Fuzhou University, China |
| Xiaofeng Wang | National University of Defense Technology, China |
| Xin Wang | Fudan University, China |
| Xingwei Wang | Northeastern University, China |
| Yaohui Jin | Shanghai Jiao Tong University, China |
| Yong Tang | University of Electronic Science and Technology of China, China |
| Yuzhong Chen | Fuzhou University, China |

# Table of Contents

# A Prediction Algorithm for Real-Time Video Traffic Based on Wavelet Packet

Yingyou Wen[1,2], Zhi Li[1,2], Jian Chen[1], and Hong Zhao[1]

[1] Northeastern University, Shenyang, 110003, China
[2] Laboratory of Medical Image Computing, Shenyang, Liaoning, 110179, China

**Abstract.** Long-term prediction is a key problem in real-time video traffic applications. Most of real-time video traffic belong to VBR traffic and has specific properties such as time variation, non-linearity and long range dependence. In this paper, feature extraction method of real-time video traffic based on multi-scale wavelet packet decomposition is proposed. On this basis, LMS algorithm is adopted to predict wavelet coefficients. Through reverse wavelet transforms of the predicted wavelet coefficients, the long-term prediction of real-time video traffic is realized. Numerical and simulation results show that this long-term prediction algorithm can accurately track the variation trend of video signal and obtain an excellent prediction result.

**Keywords:** real-time video traffic, wavelet packet, multi-scale decomposition, long-term prediction, LMS.

## 1 Introduction

In recent years, the proportion of video traffic transmission in network is gradually increased. Prediction of video traffic in coming period will do much help to improve the quality of video transmission [1-3]. Therefore, study of real-time video traffic prediction algorithm has important significance considering the requirements of efficient bandwidth allocation. Traditional bandwidth analysis method for pre-encoded video is not suitable for the analysis of real-time video traffic because signal encoding method can not be obtained in advance.

Self-similarity and long-range dependence are essential to accurately traffic prediction [4]. Related studies have shown that the broadband network traffic and video traffic both have nature of long-range dependence and self-similarity in addition to short-range dependence [5, 6]. Some traffic prediction algorithms have been proposed [7, 8], most of which belongs to short-term prediction (1 to 10 frames), such as ARX and ARMA etc. Long-term prediction is one of the most difficult problems in the area of video traffic prediction. In this paper, we proposed an optimal multi-scale decomposition method of real-time video traffic and realize a long-term prediction of decomposed video traffic based on LMS algorithm.

J. Su et al. (Eds.): ICoC 2013, CCIS 401, pp. 1–8, 2013.

## 2 Optimal Multi-scale Decomposition of Real Time Video Traffic

Multi-scale decomposition of signal comes from the wavelet theory [9], and wavelet packet decomposition is based on wavelet decomposition. Combined with a rigorous mathematical theory and numerical calculations, wavelet packet decomposition can be used to conduct multi-level signal decomposition in different frequency bands.

### 2.1 Analysis of Video Traffic Wavelet Packet Decomposition

Prediction commonly use linear time series analysis and nonlinear time series analysis method. The former assumes that the sequence is a linear correlation structure, the latter assumes that the series has chaos characteristic. For signals with long-range dependence, wavelet decomposition is an important method to change its long-range dependence. In this paper, we adopt α/β traffic model to describe the video traffic [10]. Alpha components of traffic is highly non-Gaussian and entirely responsible for the bursty behavior, β component is a aggregation of low-rate traffics, and has a long-range dependence, its marginal distribution can be well approximated with a Gaussian distribution, so β traffic can be expressed using a fractal Gaussian approximation. An aggregate traffic can be decomposed into[10]:

$$Total_{traffic} = \alpha_{traffic} + \beta_{traffic} \tag{1}$$

Literature [11] mentioned that for a video traffic expressed with α/β traffic model, if β traffic obey fractal Gaussian distribution and α traffic obey the Gaussian distribution, wavelet transform coefficients is short-range dependence in the same scale after wavelet transform. Thus, if we predict wavelet transform coefficients with short-range dependence using traditional series prediction method, we will be able to predict both the variation trend of video traffic and the bursty behavior of video traffic.

### 2.2 Optimal Wavelet Packet Decomposition of Video Traffic

The quality of signal decomposition and time-frequency analysis is heavily dependent on the choice of the fundamental function, so it is necessary to solve two problems, one is how to evaluate the pros and cons of a basis, the second is how to find the optimal basis in a wavelet library quickly. According to the selection principle of optimal basis [12], the cost function of video signals is defined as the Shannon entropy of wavelet packet coefficient sequence $u = \{u_j\}$, which is generated by decomposition of video signal $x(t)$ using an orthogonal wavelet basis.

**Definition 1:** set sequence $u = \{u_j\}$, $P_j = |u_j|^2 / |u|^2$, if $P = 0$, $P_j \log P_j = 0$, shannon entropy of $u$ is defined as:

$$M(u) = -\sum_j p_j \log p_j \tag{2}$$

The cost function should have additivity, namely $M(0)=0$, $M(\{u_i\})=\sum_i M(u_i)$, and values of $M(u)$ should reflect the concentration of the coefficient.

**Definition 2**: let $M(u)$ be the cost function, $u=\{u_j\}$ is a vector in space $V$, $B$ is an orthogonal basis selected from the library, $B_u$ is expansion coefficients of $u$ with basis B. $\forall$ $u \in V$, if $M(B_u)$ is the smallest, then $B$ is the optimal basis.

This orthogonal basis library is a binary tree structure if it meet the following conditions. First, subset of basis vectors is equivalent to a interval of non-negative integer set $N$, namely $I_{n,k} = \left[2^k n, 2^k(n+1)\right]$, where $k \in Z$, $n \in N$. Second, each basis in the library corresponds to a disjoint covering composed of $I_{n,k}$ in $N$. Thirdly, if $V_{n,k}$ is equivalent to $I_{n,k}$, then $V_{n,k+1} = V_{2n,k} \oplus V_{2n+1,k}$. If the library is a tree, optimal basis can be found by induction of $k$. Let $B_{n,k}$ be a basis of corresponding vector $I_{n,k}$, $A_{n,k}$ is the optimal basis of $u$ subject to $B_n$. To $k=0$, there exists a single basis, namely $I_{n,0}$, to be the optimal one, and formula $A_{n,0} = B_{n,0}$ holds for all $n \geq 0$. Let $k \geq 0$, $n \geq 0$, $V = I_{0,k}$, we can use the following formula to generate $u$'s optimal orthogonal basis related with cost function $M$.

$$A_{n,k+1} = \begin{cases} B_{n,k+1} & \text{if } M(B_{n,k+1}(u)) < M(A_{2n,k}(u)) + M(A_{2n+1,k}(u)) \\ A_{2n,k} \oplus A_{2n+1,k} & \text{otherwise} \end{cases} \tag{3}$$

As to real-time video traffic sequence, using the bottom-up search algorithm, we can find a wavelet packet sequence which makes the cost function minimum, and then we can find the optimal basis. This algorithm is shown as follows:

- Step 1: calculate each node's cost function $M(u)$ in every step of the wavelet packet decomposition;
- Step 2: mark all nodes from the lowest layer, take their cost value as an initial value and calculate the sum of pair wise, then compare with parent node' value in upper layer;
- Step 3: if cost value of parent node is lower than that of child node, parent node should be marked. Otherwise, calculate the sum of two child nodes' cost function value and replace the cost value of parent node, and so forth, until the top level;
- Step 4: check and record all the marked nodes. When the upper node is marked, the mark of corresponding child nodes is deleted, after $o(N \log N)$ operations, all marked nodes of top level is selected, these marked nodes compose of non-overlapping coverage in $L^2(R)$ space, then coefficients are extracted from the optimal basis and output.

## 3 Video Traffic Prediction Based on Wavelet Packet

As mentioned above, frequency division of real-time video signal can be determined if we can find the optimal orthogonal wavelet packet basis in $L^2(R)$. This section gives video traffic prediction algorithm based on optimal wavelet packet decomposition.

LMS algorithm is a linear filtering method; it uses a linear combination of historical data to predict. This algorithm is more adaptive, simple and effective, does not need to know the autocorrelation structure of time series and able to achieve satisfactory online prediction results of real-time signal [13]. Real-time prediction accuracy of the LMS algorithm is close to the long memory model prediction accuracy when the signal has lower Hurst parameter and do not show very long correlation [14].

For prediction problem in the wavelet domain, LMS algorithm can be described as follows : there exists two sets of variables $d(i)$ and $p(i)$, where $d(i)$ is a known set of wavelet coefficients, $p(i)$ is a set of wavelet coefficients need to be predicted, namely, $p(i)$ is a function with an input set $\{d(i),\ d(i-1),\ \cdots,\ d(i-M+1)\}$. Assume that this function is linear and we have:

$$p(n+k)=\sum_{l=0}^{M-1} w(l)\cdot d(n-l) \tag{4}$$

Where, $W=[w(0),w(1),\cdots,w(M-1)]^T$ are coefficients of the prediction filter, $D(n)=[d(n),d(n-1),\cdots,d(n-M+1)]^T$ is the input sequence and $p(n+k)$ is the estimates of $k$ step. Prediction error is given as follows:

$$e(n)=p(n+k)-d(n+k)=p(n+k)-W^T D(n) \tag{5}$$

Optimal linear prediction on mean squared error sense should make the mathematical expectation of mean square error $\xi=E[e^2(n)]$ to obtain the minimum. LMS algorithm is a gradient search algorithm, the prediction coefficients $W$ alters over time, of which the adjustment process depends on the feedback of error $e(n)$. When prediction initiate, we first estimate to set the coefficient of the initial value $w(0)$, then update coefficient $W$ using equation (6) and use the updated coefficients for the next prediction.

$$W(n+1)=W(n)+\frac{\beta\cdot e(n-k)\cdot D(n-k)}{\left\|D(n-k)\right\|^2} \tag{6}$$

Where $\left\|D(n-k)\right\|^2=D(n-k)^T\cdot D(n-k)$, $\beta$ is step adjustment factor meet $0<\beta<2$ , if $\beta$ is greater, the prediction convergence is quicker and response to the signal changes is more rapid, but the fluctuations after the convergence is greater too. On the contrary, if $\beta$ is smaller, the prediction convergence is slower, but the fluctuations after the convergence is smaller too. As to the wavelet coefficients $d(k)$ at time $k$, $\{p(k+1), p(k+2), \cdots, p(k+i)\}$ need to be estimated. We adopt an iterative prediction method, the iterative relationship is given as following:

$$\begin{cases} p(k+1) = f(d(k), d(k-1), \cdots, d(k-i+1)) \\ p(k+2) = f(p(k+1), d(k), \cdots, d(k-i+2)) \\ \quad \cdots\cdots \\ p(k+i) = f(p(k+i-1), p(k+i-2), \cdots, d(k)) \end{cases} \tag{7}$$

Where $f(x)$ is the LMS prediction operator.

With wavelet packet decomposition, original video traffic with complex properties of long-range and short-range dependence can be transformed into a sequence in wavelet domain with short correlation. On this basis, by utilizing LMS algorithm to achieve approximate prediction of the wavelet coefficients after the wavelet packet transform, we can realize the real-time video traffic prediction algorithm, which is described as followings:

- Step 1: conduct wavelet packet decomposition on each group of video frames acquired and output sequence of wavelet coefficients;
- Step 2: use LMS algorithm to predict the next set of wavelet coefficients in the wavelet domain with the new acquired wavelet coefficients;
- Step 3: conduct inverse wavelet transform with predicted wavelet coefficients, then the prediction of video traffic in the next time window is realized;
- Step 4: every time new video frame traffic is acquired, traffic data should be recorded, then repeat step 1, 2, 3.

## 4 Simulatioin and Analysis

In this paper, experimental video "StarWars" and "News" are chosen from the MPEG4 video trace database of Berlin university. These Video adopt MPEG-I compression standard , with QCIF format, frame rate set to 30fps, and quantitative parameters is fixed at 10, 14 and 18.

First of all, NMSE (Normalized Mean Squared Error ) is introduced to evaluate performance of our algorithms. NMSE is defined as follows:

$$NMSE = \frac{1}{\sigma^2}\frac{1}{N}\sum[x(t) - \overline{x}(t)]^2 = \frac{1}{N}\sum[x(t) - \overline{x}(t)]^2 / Var(x(t)) \tag{8}$$

Where $x(t)$ is the actual frames at time $t$, $\overline{x}(t)$ is the prediction of $x(t)$. N is the number of predict test, $\sigma^2$ is the variance of the observed sequence, 1024 frames are randomly extracted from "Star Wars" and "News". Prediction is conducted on follow-up continuous 200 frames, and the prediction performance is studied.

In order to reduce the prediction time and avoid constantly modify of the model, we adopt an iterative prediction method and video traffic signal is decomposed with *db*1 wavelet and wavelet packet. The optimal wavelet decomposition tree expansion is given below.

$$S = AAAA4 \oplus DAAA4 \oplus ADAA4 \oplus DDAA4 \oplus DA2 \oplus D1 \tag{9}$$

When the length of video traffic prediction is set to 256 frames, the length of each wavelet coefficient need to be predicted is shown in Table 1.

**Table 1.** Wavelet Coefficients Information

| Wavelet level | coefficient Length of wavelet | Coefficient Length of wavelet to be predicted |
|---|---|---|
| AAAA4 | 64 | 16 |
| DAAA4 | 64 | 16 |
| ADAA4 | 64 | 16 |
| DDAA4 | 64 | 16 |
| DA2 | 256 | 64 |
| D1 | 512 | 128 |

Figure 2 shows wavelet packet decomposition and coefficients prediction of "News" frame sequence. Figure 1(a) indicates prediction result of AAAA4 wavelet packet coefficients. This wavelet packet coefficient reflects the trend of signal change. Prediction performance of wavelet packet coefficients DAAA4, ADAA4, DDAA4, DA2 and D1 are shown respectively in Figure 1(b), 2(c), 2(d), 2(e), 2(f).

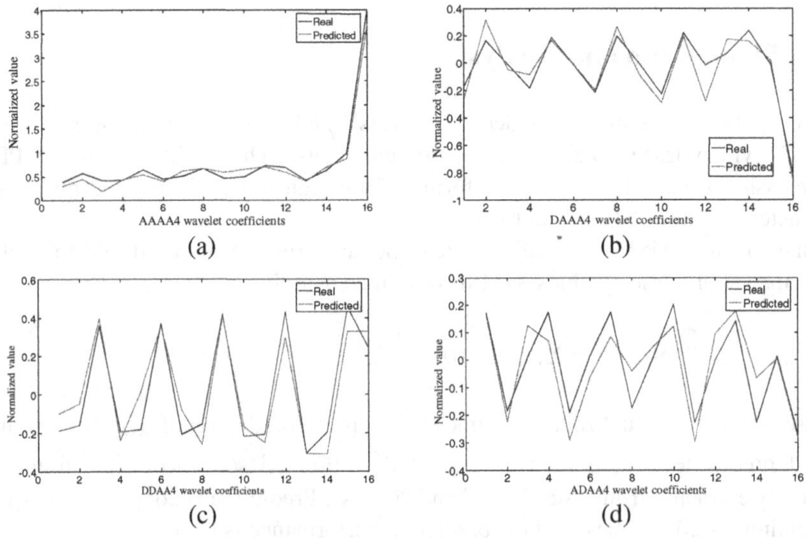


**Fig. 1.** Wavelet packet decomposition and coefficients prediction

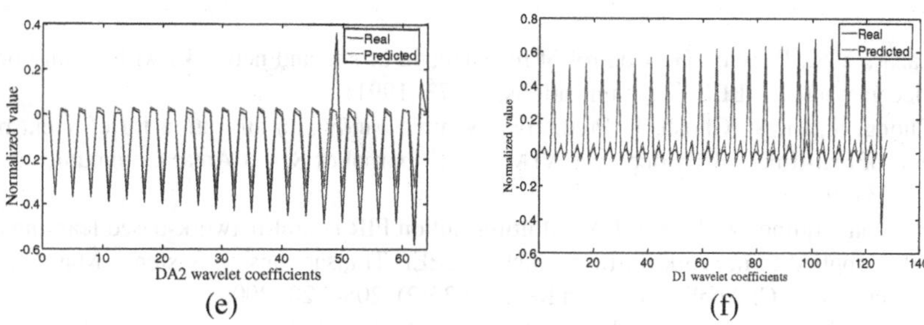


**Fig. 1.** *(Continued)*

Figure2 shows prediction of "News" traffic after inverse wavelet transform.

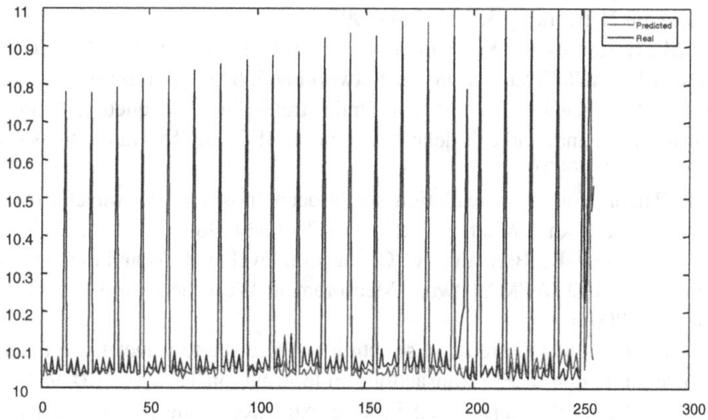


**Fig. 2.** Prediction of "News" traffic after inverse wavelet transform

From Figure 1 and Figure 2, we can see that prediction of the wavelet coefficients based on wavelet packet decomposition can accurately predict both the variation trend and the bursty behavior of video traffic, which verifies the validity of this algorithm on the long-term prediction.

# 5 Conclusions

In this paper, we propose a real-time video traffic prediction algorithm based on wavelet packet decomposition. Compared with conventional video traffic prediction method, the proposed algorithm greatly improves the accuracy of long-term prediction. Owing to the ability of following the trend of the video traffic variation accurately and the capability of capturing bursty traffic of real-time video signal, this video traffic prediction algorithm provide a new method to realize bandwidth resource management in a network with long delay and constrained bandwidth.

## References

1. Lazar, A.A., Pacifici, G.: Control of resources in broadband networks with quality of service guarantees. IEEE Communications, 66–73 (1991)
2. Chong, S., Li, S., Ghosh, J.: Predictive dynamic bandwidth allocation for efficient transport of real-time VBR video over ATM. IEEE Journal of Select Areas Communication 13, 12–23 (1995)
3. Alarcon-Aquino, V., Barria, J.A.: Multiresolution FIR neural-network-based learning algorithm applied to network traffic prediction. IEEE Transactions on Systems, Man, and Cybernetics-Part C: Applications and Reviews 36(2), 208–220 (2006)
4. Leland, E., Taqqu, M.S., Willinger, W., et al.: On the self similar nature of Ethernet traffic (extended version). IEEE/ACM Transactions on Networking 2, 1–15 (1994)
5. Beran, J., Sherman, R., Taqqu, M.S., Willinger, W.: Long-range dependence in variable-bit-rate video traffic. IEEE Transactions on Communication 43, 1566–1579 (1995)
6. Paxson, V., Floyd, S.: Wide-area traffic: the failure of possion modeling. IEEE/ACM Transactions on Networking 3, 226–244 (1995)
7. Crovella, M., Bestavros, A.: Self similarity in world wide web traffic: Evidence and possible causes. IEEE/ACM Transactions on Networking 5, 835–846 (1997)
8. Tsybkov, B., Georganas, N.D.: On self-similar traffic in ATM queues: definitions, overflow probability bound, and cell delay distribution. IEEE/ACM Transactions on Networking 5(3), 397–409 (1997)
9. Mallat, S.: Theory for multi-resolution signal decomposition: the wavelet representation. IEEE Trans. Pattern Anal. Machine Intell. 11, 674–693 (1989)
10. Sarvotham, S., Riedi, R., Baraniuk, R.: Connection level analysis and modeling of network traffic. In: Proc. IEEE/ACM Network Measurement Workshop, pp. 99–103. ACM Press, San Francisco (2001)
11. Tewfik, A.H., Kim, M.: Correlation structure of the discrete wavelet coefficients of fractional brownian motion. IEEE Transactions on Information Theory 38(2), 904–909 (1992)
12. Wang, S.Y., Zhu, G.X., Tang, Y.Y.: Feature extraction using best wavelet packet transform. Acta Electronica Sinica 31(7), 1035–1038 (2003)
13. Adas, A.: Using adaptive linear prediction to support real-time VBR video under RCBR network service model. IEEE Transactions on Networking 6(5), 635–644 (1998)
14. Iera, A., Molinaro, A., Marano, S.: Call admission control and resource management issues for real-time VBR traffic in ATM-satellite networks. IEEE Journal on Selected Areas in Communications 18(11), 2393–2403 (2000)
15. Su, X.X., Chang, S.J., Xiong, T., et al.: Online VBR video traffic prediction using neural network. ACTA Electronica Sinica 33(7), 1163–1167 (2005)
16. Mao, G., Liu, H.: Real time variable bit rate video traffic. International Journal of Communication System 20(4), 491–505 (2006); Akyildiz, I.F., Su, W., Sankarasubramaniam, Y., Cayirci, E.: A survey on sensor networks. IEEE Communications Magazine 40(8), 102–114 (2002)

# The Evaluation of Online Social Network's Nodes Influence Based on User's Attribute and Behavior

Xiushuang Yi, Yeting Han, and Xingwei Wang

College of Information Science and Engineering Northeastern University Shenyang, China
xsyi@mail.neu.edu.cn

**Abstract.** Objective and accurate assessment of each node influence is a vital issue to research social networks. Many algorithms have been developed, but most of them use of single metric, which is incomplete and limited to evaluate node influence. In this paper, we propose a method of evaluating node influence based on user's attribute and behavior. We study the quantification of nodes influence. The thought of PageRank is used to explore the effect of behavior. Then the method proposed is applied to Sina micro-blog. Experiment results show that method has a good and reasonable value.

**Keywords:** social networks, node influence, PageRank, node attribute.

## 1 Introduction

In last ten years, the numbers of online social networks like Facebook, MySpace and Twitter gained considerable popularity and grown at an unprecedented rate. The emergence of online social networks has brought great convenience to people's life. One of the main applications of online social networks can help manufacturers to promote their products, and to utilize the lowest investment cost to achieve the maximum effectiveness of marketing. Therefore, online social networks have also attracted many scholars to study it. A part of scholars focus on the influence of online social networks nodes, more and more interests have been made in obtaining information from social networking websites for analyzing people behaviors. These researches are focusing on identifying the influential social network users, so it can help to increase the marketing efficiency, and also can be utilized to gather opinions and information on particular topics as well as to predict the trends [1-3].

Micro-blog is a typical online social network, it not only has the social network characteristics but also has the media characteristics, so it can be analyzed from social networks and news dissemination, how to find influential micro-blog is a basic problem in the research and application of microblog.A lot of micro-blog application use "micro-blog numbers", "number of fans", "attention", "forward", as the ranking basis. These indicators can only measure the nodes from one aspect. These indexes not only can't help the user to find the influence of micro-blog quickly, but also can not truly reflect the actual influence of micro-blog users in the network. In order to overcome these shortcomings, we try to present a new method to evaluate node influence.

J. Su et al. (Eds.): ICoC 2013, CCIS 401, pp. 9–20, 2013.

In this paper we take the micro-blog for example, put forward the method of evaluating node's influence of online social networks. This paper is organized as follows: Section 2 we give an overview of related work. We introduce the basic idea of our method in Section 3. Section 4 we introduce the method of this paper in a great detail. The analysis of experiment in Section 5. We draw conclusions of this paper in Section 6.

## 2 Related Work

In earlier research, the people according to the method of system science use indexes like node degree, betweenness, closeness, information, eigenvector, the network diameter and so on to measure the influence. In some recent studies of influence people gradually combine the methods of social network analysis and methods of Internet search [4].

There are a lot of study of micro-blog mainly focus on the Twitter. Efforts have been made to evaluating influence of online social network [5-19]. Leila [5] investigates the power of retweet mechanism and findings suggest that relations of “friendship” at Twitter are important but not enough. Sun [6] proposes a graph model to represent the relationships between online posts of one topic, in order to identify the influential users.Jianshu Weng [7] proposed TwitterRank which measures the influence taking both the topical similarity between users and the link structure into account.Meeyoung analyzed Propagation characteristics of Twitter, micro-blog forwarding and uses three parameters, by the study of a large number of Twitter data [8]. So they found effects of the user in the topic in the process of communication. Pal performed an extensive study about Twitter follower-following topology analysis [18].

Wu [10] utilize power multiplication iterative to calculate Markov matrix, by optimizing and improving the PageRank algorithm. Yang [11] Starting from the two angles of active users and blog quality, constructed the evaluation index of the blogger influence, introduced the blogger communication ability factor, using the idea of PageRank algorithm to design a new influence ranking algorithm to evaluate the blogger influence.Guo [12] proposed the quantitative definition of user information dissemination scope, and gives the method for calculating the influence.

## 3 The Basic Ideas of Algorithm

As we know, every micro-blog users in the network corresponding to individual or unit of reality. User can enhance his own prestige by publishing micro-blog, forwarding and commenting of others, concern for others. The attribute in the micro-blog included two parts e.g. user attributes and micro-blog properties. The user itself includes the user ID, user type, attention number, number of fans , number of micro-blog, number of mentions, and micro-blog attributes including number of micro-blog, publish time, the forwarding numbers, numbers of comments. Micro-blog network and online community network, the user can according to their own preferences selectively use "forward", "collection", "comment" on a piece of information or micro-blog do corresponding operations.

Node’s attribute is the basic characteristic of node. If the user measure the node's influence only by itself or micro-blog attribute to measure the node's influence is relatively one-sided, they should also be take the direct effect on node influence which is given by behavior between nodes in account. The behavior of forward and comment can change the size of the impact of a user. Therefore, when measure of influence of nodes we should fully consider the interaction between the nodes that play an important role for influence.

We proposed model of influence rank (model of IR).The method in this paper proposed by combining the interactive behavior between nodes and node's attributes. Firstly we need to give a node attribute's quantification. Node attribute has many factors; these factors will influence effect of node. We should select some main influence factors, and then we use analysis hierarchy process to give the weight of every factor of influence, using the weighted to calculate the quantification of node attribute value. Secondly we introduce the thought of PageRank [13] algorithm to study the node interaction behavior. The PageRank algorithm is based on the assumption: the webpage is more important when it link to more webpage; webpage is more important when it linked to the more important webpage. Similarly, for online social networks, when the user is more commented by others, its influence will be greater; when the user is forward comments by more important users; its influence will be greater. Finally the user attributes and user behavior as the node influence factor synthesis node's influence in online social networks.

# 4 The Evaluation of Node's Influence

## 4.1 Measuring Node Attributes

There are lots of node's attributes in online social network; we select some attributes which have more obvious role: user type, numbers of fans, numbers of forwarded, numbers of attention, numbers of micro-blog, and numbers of comments. The numbers of fans, numbers of forwarding, and the numbers of comments can reflect the influence of nodes from different aspects. The analytic hierarchy process to solve the weight problem of each influence factor, and then use the weighted and calculate the quantization node attribute value. Calculation steps as follows:

**Step1:** Construction of index matrix **X** and normalization, so we get new matrix **A** as follows:

$$X = \begin{bmatrix} x_{11} & x_{12} & \cdots & x_{1m} \\ x_{21} & x_{22} & \cdots & x_{2m} \\ \cdots & \cdots & \cdots & \cdots \\ x_{n1} & x_{n2} & \cdots & x_{nm} \end{bmatrix} \qquad A = \begin{bmatrix} a_{11} & a_{12} & \cdots & a_{1n} \\ a_{21} & a_{22} & \cdots & a_{2n} \\ \cdots & \cdots & \cdots & \cdots \\ a_{m1} & a_{m2} & \cdots & a_{mn} \end{bmatrix}$$

We can use the standard 0-1 transform to normalize:

$$a_{ij} = \frac{x_{ij} - x_j^{\min}}{x_j^{\max} - x_{ij}} \tag{1}$$

Where $x_j^{\max}$ the maximum value in the j column is, $x_j^{\min}$ is the minimum value in the $j$ column.

**Step2:** Using analysis hierarchy process to calculate the index weight.

(a) Constructing a judgment matrix **B**, we use Table I to determine the value of **B**.

**Table 1.** The Reference Values of Elements in Matrix **B**

| Relative importance | Definition | Meaning |
|---|---|---|
| 1 | Equally importance | Two attributes are equally importance |
| 3 | Slightly importance | One attribute is more slightly importance |
| 5 | Considerable importance | One is considerable importance |
| 7 | Obvious importance | One is more obvious than another |
| 9 | Absolutely importance | One is more absolute importance |
| 2、4、6、8 | Compromise | Compromise of two grades |

$$B = \begin{bmatrix} b_{11} & b_{12} & \cdots & b_{1m} \\ b_{21} & b_{22} & \cdots & b_{2m} \\ \cdots & \cdots & \cdots & \cdots \\ b_{m1} & b_{m2} & \cdots & b_{mm} \end{bmatrix}$$

The elements $b_{ij}$ are scale of $b_i$ relative to $b_j$ in matrix **B**.

(b) To determine the weight of different indexes and check consistency:

(i) Multiplication element of B in a row:

$$b_i = \prod_{j=1}^{m} b_{ij} \quad j = 1, 2, \cdots, m \tag{2}$$

(ii) Calculating product to the $m^{th}$ roots:

$$c_i = \sqrt[m]{b_i} \quad i = 1, 2, \cdots, m \tag{3}$$

(iii) Weight calculation:

$$w_i = \frac{c_i}{\sum_{j=1}^{m} c_j} \quad i = 1, 2, \cdots, m \tag{4}$$

(iv) Checking consistency: we compute the latent root of **B** and calculate coincidence index denoted by *CI*.

$$CI = \frac{\lambda_{\max} - m}{m-1} \quad (5)$$

If $CI < 0.1$ ,we can accept the weight of different indexes. Otherwise, we need to recalculate the **Step2.**

**Step3:** Calculating AR according to the weight of each index $w_j$ and the index value of each node $a_{ij}$ :

$$AR(i) = \sum_{j=1}^{m} a_{ij} w_j \quad i = 1, 2, \cdots, n \quad (6)$$

### 4.2 Behavior Measurement

In this process, we use PageRank algorithm to solve the problem of interaction between nodes.PageRank is one of the core technology of Google, its basic idea is to determine the importance of using webpage hyperlink structure webpage, The PageRank generates represent each page importance value becomes the PR value, a page's PR value not only depends on the number of connected to the page, but also be influenced by the quality and importance of the page, but the page's PR value will be evenly distributed to its chain of the page[14].The calculating formula of PageRank as follows:

$$PR(p_i) = d + (1-d) \sum_{p_j \in M(p_i)} \frac{PR(p_j)}{L(p_j)} \quad (7)$$

Where $L(P_j)$ is number of $P_j$ links to other page, where $M(P_i)$ is numbers of chain into $P_i$ , $d$ is damping coefficient.

Then extract the relationship of forwarded or comments in online social network, a directed graph of forward comments relationship could be constructed. In the following simple diagram, the direction of the arrow represents the object forwarding comments. Because of the large scale network, the analysis is difficult; we can start from a node to consider. Observation of the following figure, for example the user a forward or comment of user e、 f and g. Of course, there are also have other users will forward information of user a. The user e and g may also go forward or comment on other user, this part of the forward or comment leave out in Fig.1.We consider only the relationship between local forward or comments, and then further promotion.

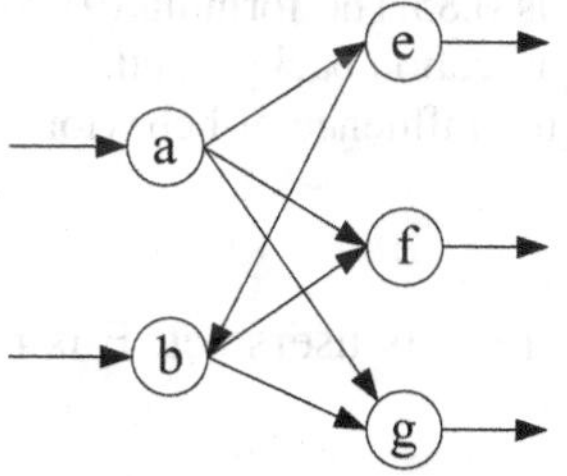


**Fig. 1.** Schematic diagram of forwarding

For example, user a and user b have forwarded f, and the user a also forwarded user e. $N_{af}$ is the number of a forwarded f, $N_{bf}$ is the number of b forwarded f, $N_{ae}$ is the number of a forwarded e. $BR(a)$ and $BR(b)$ are important degree. We can make conclusion as following (I) if the number of a forwarded f is more i.e. $N_{af} > N_{bf}$. It is suggest that user a make a larger contribution to f. (II) if user a is more important than b i.e. $BR(a) > BR(b)$ .The user a will make a larger contribution to f. (III) The user a forwarded e and f, but if $N_{af} > N_{ae}$, it suggest that user a make a larger contribution to f.

These three conclusions obtained above are consistent with the idea of PageRank algorithm; the interactive behavior can change the node influence. Forwarding can be as the voting behavior, the more number of forwarding equivalent to more votes, "the greater support to other users", such as the above conclusions (I) (III); if it is an important vote, the "support" will be greater, likes the above conclusion (II). Unlike the original PageRank algorithm, the node "contribution" in this paper is not the average distribution, in the conclusion (III) have illustrated this point. Distribution of the "contribution" is related to the number of forward or comments; the more forward the more "contribution". For the general case, If the relationship of forward or comment between nodes v and u is existed, the node v forward node u, then use the following formula to express the v to u "contribution" ratio:

$$p_{vu} = \frac{N_{vu}}{\sum_{x \in O(v)} N_{vx}} \tag{8}$$

The $N_{vu}$ stand for number of $v$ forward u, $O(v)$ is the set of $v$ forwards, $N_{vx}$ is $v$ forwards others, where $p_{vu}$ represents the probability of v forward u.

The core idea of PageRank is to calculating the PR value of each node value according to the number of back links, uniform "flow" to all nodes. Each node's PR value is the total of "contribution" of node's PR value. We borrowed this idea. Then we revised the problems of "contribution" average distribution, and put forward the calculating formula evaluation node behavior influence:

$$BR(u) = (1-d) \times BR(u) + d \sum_{v \in I(u)} p_{vu} BR(v) \tag{9}$$

This is an iterative formula. The initial value of *BR* is related to *AR* refer to formula (6), and where $p_{vu}$ is distribution probability, where $I(u)$ is set of pointed to $u$ in directed graph. The value of d is 0.85.The formula (9) combines the characteristics of online social network and its application background.

The value of BR represents the influence of behavior; the calculation process of BR is following:

Calculation of the value of BR

Get data set G=(V,E),where V is users set, E is relationship set, initial AR, BR, $N_{vu}$, $P_{vu}$, d, ε, σ

```
for each user v, u ∈ V  do
    update value of Nvu
end for
for each user v, u ∈ V  do
    Pvu ⇐ N_vu / Σ_{x∈o(N)} N_vx
    update value of Pvu
end for
i ⇐ 1, BR_1 ⇐ AR, ε ⇐ 0.0001, σ ⇐ 1
while σ ≥ ε do
    BR_{i+1} ⇐ (1−d)×BR_i + d×P×BR_i
    σ ⇐ ‖BR_{i+1} − BR_i‖
    i ⇐ i + 1
end while
return BR
```

### 4.3 To Establish the Model of IR

The first two chapter studied effects on influence of nodes from aspect of node attributes and interaction behavior. According to the above algorithm, the two aspects will be integrated. We use them as nodes influence factor synthesis in online social networks influence.

After a lot of observation and analysis: node attribute is a basic condition determines the influence of nodes, if the node attribute value AR is weak, the node will not influence overall strong. At the same time, the interactive behavior between the nodes can also change the node influence; this kind of behavior is equivalent to the influence in the network spread, similar to the random walk model. The interaction behavior between nodes and the attributes of the nodes combined in accordance with the appropriate weight, a formula to calculate the influence of nodes:

$$IR(i) = \alpha AR(i) + (1-\alpha)BR(i) \quad i = 1, 2, \cdots, n \tag{10}$$

In formula (10) $\alpha$ is regulatory factor, it can regulate the weight of AR and BR. This formula is a linear combination of AR and BR. When $0.5 < \alpha < 1$, it is shown that the node attribute is more importance. When $0 < \alpha < 0.5$, it shown that we more emphasis on interactive behavior between nodes to measure the influence.

## 5 Experiments

The paper selects the Sina micro-blog as the data source, the data obtained by Sina open API.The data set is part of Sina micro-blog user information in December 2012. It contains 60290 users. Every user includes a user ID, user type, numbers of fans, numbers of micro-blogs, numbers of attention, forwarding numbers, the number of comments.

Firstly, we construct matrix of the influence factor, and utilize analysis hierarchy process to determine the weight of each node, and then calculate node's *AR*.According to the network relationship of micro-blog, and the matrix of transition probability, we can get the node's *BR*.Finally, and we calculate the node of the *IR* value through Influence Rank model proposed in this paper.

**Table 2.** The Calculation Results of Top 10 Users

| UserID | AR | BR | IR |
|---|---|---|---|
| 1266321801 | 1.0000 | 0.4409 | 0.6086 |
| 1192329374 | 0.7045 | 0.3538 | 0.4590 |
| 1656809190 | 0.5305 | 0.4265 | 0.4577 |
| 1087770692 | 0.5508 | 0.3814 | 0.4322 |
| 1192515960 | 0.3304 | 0.3977 | 0.3775 |
| 1752467960 | 0.3249 | 0.3390 | 0.3347 |
| 1742727537 | 0.1000 | 0.4233 | 0.3263 |
| 1730336902 | 0.1331 | 0.4046 | 0.3231 |
| 1212812142 | 0.2137 | 0.3683 | 0.3219 |
| 1854283601 | 0.0601 | 0.4126 | 0.3069 |

Because the data set is large, we list the influence of top ten users. In the process of calculation, we assumed $\alpha$ is 0.3.Node's *IR* value is not only closely related with the *AR* and *BR* values, but also with the relevant to the value of $\alpha$. In general, if the influence of node is greater, the *AR* and *BR* will be greater.

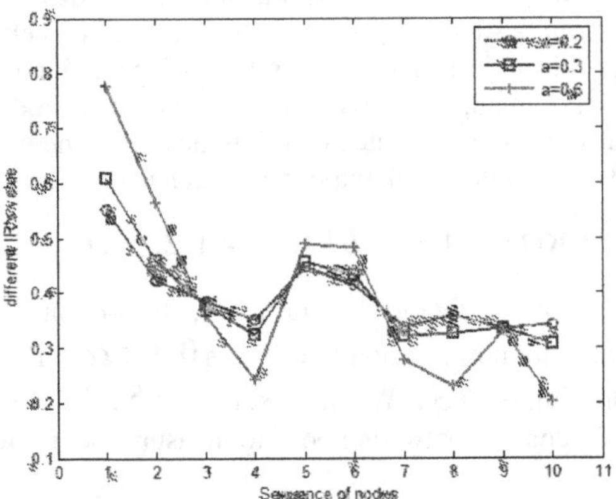


**Fig. 2.** Comparison of different IR

Like formula (10), when $\alpha$ taking different values, the results of IR are different. As is shown in Figure2 the node's IR value is closely related to regulatory factor $\alpha$. The regulatory factor represents the weight of AR.As is shown in TABLEII, the 10th node's AR is very small, when $\alpha$ is larger the IR will be smaller as shown in Figure2. Therefore, $\alpha$ is used to balance of AR and BR according to need.

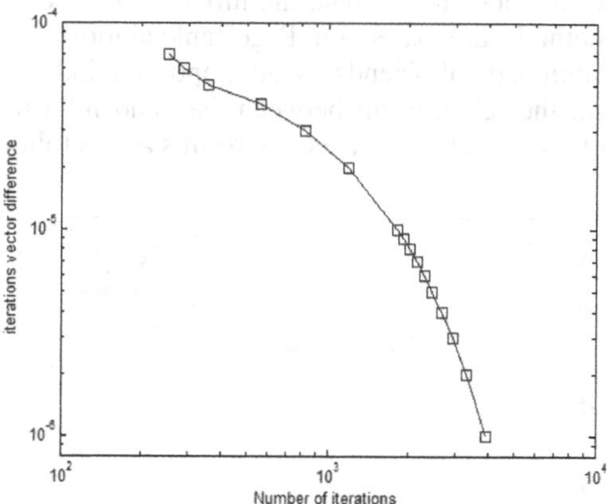


**Fig. 3.** Convergence analysis of BR

According to the core idea of PageRank, the calculation results of BR have nothing to do with initial value. As is shown in the Figure3, after 3928 times of computation, the difference vector is close to 0. It shows that the value of BR gradually trends a stable value. Therefore, the value of BR is convergence. According to formula (10), the value of IR also trends a stable value. So that the IR' value of each node can be calculated.

As is shown in the Figure4, we use three methods to calculate the influence of node. This shows that our method is closely related with the number of fans and the number of micro blogs. Observed from the curve of fans, fans of the 3rd node are larger than the 4th node. But 3rd node's IR is less than 4th node's IR, from another perspective, the 4th node's interactive behavior is greater than 3rd node's, this shows that the 4th node is involved in more social behavior which can bring greater influence. Observed from the curve of comments, the 5th node's comments is less than 6th node's but 5th node's *IR* is about as same as 6th node's *IR*. It is shows that 5th node's AR is larger. The experimental results have shown that IR is related to user's attribute and user's behavior.

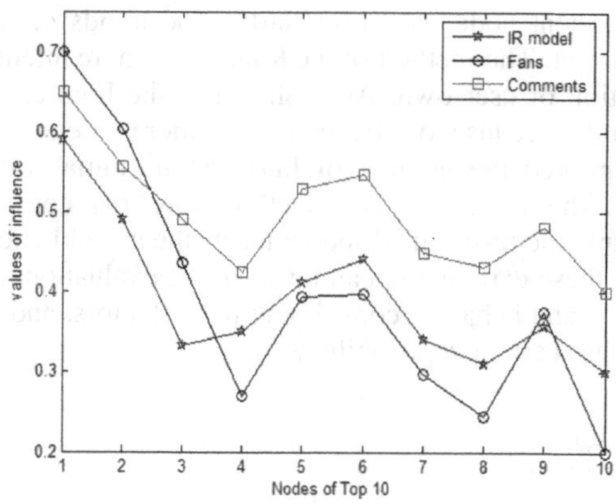


**Fig. 4.** The relation between IR model and Fans as well as that between IR model and Comments

We use the other two methods to evaluate the influence of node: UserRank [9] and TURank [15].These methods are based on PageRank algorithm. The core idea of UserRank is that the numbers of friends is an important index of influence. The TURank could to reveal the relationship between user and information and obtain a more accurate result of ranking. The experimental results are as follows.

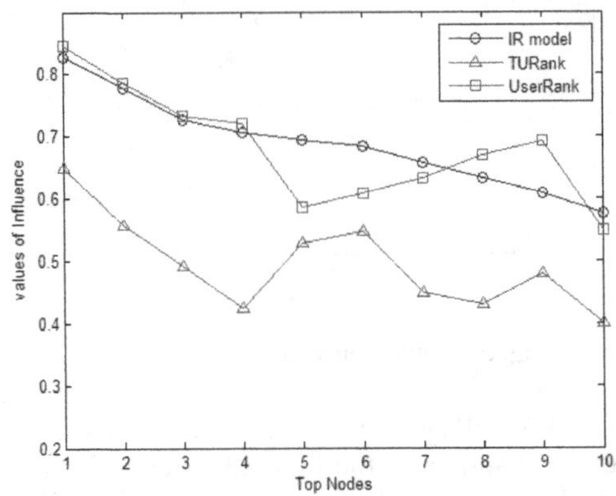


**Fig. 5.** Comparision of three methods

We selected the top ten users as shown in TABLEII. The value of IR gradually decreased from node 1 to node 10. Observed from the curve of UserRank, the first four nodes' influence is decreasing, but the influence of subsequent node is increasing, the influence of node 9 is very large. Why trends of the two curve is not consistent? The most important reason is that the two methods considering the problem from different angles. The method of UserRank focuses more on the number of friends. For example, the experiment shows that node 9 has 876 friends so that its influence is larger. Because of the existence of zombie fans, the node has a lot of friends and its influence unnecessarily large. Compared with IR model, UserRank is not considered comprehensively, the result of UserRank is not very accurate.

Observed from the curve of TURank, the first four nodes' influence is decreasing, the influence of subsequent node vary irregularly. The trends of the IR model and TURank are not consistent. The method of TURank pays more attention to interactive behavior and information of user own. As is shown in the Figure5, the node 6 has a large value of TURank; because of the node has more interactive behavior. The method of TURank ignored the number of fans and its initial value should be set artificially. Therefore, the results of two methods are not completely consistent. Compared with TURank, the result of IR model meets the actual better.

From the results of these experiment can be seen, the evaluation of nodes influence based on user's attribute and behavior considering many factors, and the result is more realistic. This method has certain applicability.

## 6 Conclusion

This paper proposes the model of IR; it can be comprehensive consideration attributes and interactive behavior. Firstly, we calculate the node attribute value AR, and then calculate the node's BR according to the principle of PageRank.The model avoids the defects caused by using of single factor to evaluate node's influence. Experiments show that node's IR has no direct relationship with fans and numbers of micro blog. Theory analysis and example of real network experiment show that the new proposed method can effectively evaluate the node influence of the online social network.

**Acknowledgment.** This work has been supported by the National Natural Science Foundation of China under Grant No.61070162 and No.60903159; the National Science Technology support Project of China under Grant No.2008BAH37B05;the National High Technology Research and Development Project of China under Grant No.2007AA041201;the Project of Fundamental Research Funds for Central-affiliated University of China under Grant No.N110216001.

## References

1. Xu, Z., Lu, R., Xiang, L.: Discovering User Interest on Twitter with a Modified Author-Topic Model, pp. 422–429 (2011)
2. Ghosh, S., Viswanath, B., Kooti, F.: Understanding and combating link farming in the twitter social network. In: Proceeding of the 21st International Conference on World Wide Web, pp. 61–70 (2012)
3. Benevenuto, F., Rodrigues, T., Cha, M.: Characterizing user behavior in online social networks. In: Proceedings of the 9th ACM SIGCOMM Conference on Internet Measurement, pp. 49–62 (2009)
4. Sun, R., Luo, W.: Review on evaluation of node importance in public opinion. Application Research of Computer 29(10), 3606–3608 (2012)
5. Weitzel, L., Quaresma, P.: Measuring node importance on Twitter microblogging. In: Proceedings of the 2nd International Conference on Web Intelligence, Mining and Semantics, vol. (11) (2012)
6. Sun, B., Ng, V.T.: Identifying Influential Users by Their Postings in Social Networks. In: Proceeding of the 3rd International Workshop on Modeling Social Media, pp. 1–8 (2012)
7. Weng, J., Lim, E.-P.: TwitterRank:Finding Topic sensitive Influential Twitterers. In: Proceedings of the Third ACM International Conference on Web Search and Data Mining, pp. 261–270 (2012)
8. Meeyoung, C.: Measuring user influence in twitter: The million follower fallacy. In: Proceedings of International Conference on Weblogs and Media (2010)
9. Jun, L., Zhen, C., Jiwei, H.: Micro-blog Impact Evaluation. Information Network Security (3), 10–13 (2012)
10. Jialin, W., Yongji, T.: The optimization and improvement of PageRank algorithm. Computer Engineering and Applications 45(16), 56–59 (2009)
11. Changchun, Y., Kefei, Y., Shiren, Y.: New assessment method on influence of bloggers in community of Chinese microblog. Computer Engineering and Applications 48(25), 229–233 (2012)
12. Hao, G., Yuliang, L., Yu, W.: Measuring user influence of a microblog based on information diffusion. Journal of Shandong University (Natural Science) 47(5), 78–83 (2012)
13. Xiaofei, C., Yitong, W., Xiaojun, F.: An Improvement of PageRank Algorithm Based on Page Quality. Journal of Computer Research and Development 46(suppl.), 381–387 (2009)

14. Shenjun, Z., Xiongkai, S.: An Improved N-PageRank Algorithm which Considers the User Behavior. Computer Technology and Development 21(8), 137–140 (2011)
15. Yamaguchi, Y., Takahashi, T., Amagasa, T., Kitagawa, H.: TURank:Twitter User Ranking Based on User-Tweet Graph Analysis. In: Chen, L., Triantafillou, P., Suel, T. (eds.) WISE 2010. LNCS, vol. 6488, pp. 240–253. Springer, Heidelberg (2010)
16. Ye, S., Wu, S.F.: Measuring Message Propagation and social Influence on Twitter.com. In: Bolc, L., Makowski, M., Wierzbicki, A. (eds.) SocInfo 2010. LNCS, vol. 6430, pp. 216–231. Springer, Heidelberg (2010)
17. Sun, B., Ng, V.T.: Lifespan and Popularity Measurement of Online Content on Social Networks. In: Social Computing Workshop of IEEE ISI Conference, pp. 379–383 (2011)
18. Ilyas, M.U., Radha, H.: A KLT-inspired Node Centrality for Identifying Influential Neighborhoods in Graphs. In: Conference on Information Sciences and Systems, pp. 1–7 (2010)
19. Pal, A., Counts, S.: Indentifying topical authorities in microblogs. In: Proceedings of the Fourth ACM International Conference on Web Search and Data Mining, pp. 45–54 (2011)

# A Bayesian Investment Model for Online P2P Lending*

Xubo Wang, Defu Zhang, Xiangxiang Zeng**, and Xiaoying Wu

Department of Computer Science, Xiamen University, Xiamen, China
xwang@stu.xmu.edu.cn, {dfzhang,xzeng}@xmu.edu.cn,
wuxiaoying0720@126.com

**Abstract.** P2P online lending is an emerging economic lending model. In this marketplace, borrowers submit requests for loans, and lenders make bids on them. It has put forward new challenges to investors about how to make effective investment decisions. Bayesian network is a probabilistic graphical model that represents a set of random variables and their conditional dependencies. In the paper, we calculate the mutual information of every two variables to measure their mutual dependence and build a Bayesian network model to select loans that would pay back with high confidence. We perform abundant experiments on the data from the world's largest P2P lending platform Prosper.com. Experimental results reveal that Bayesian network model can significantly help investors make better investment decisions than other investment models.

**Keywords:** P2P lending, Classification, Bayesian network, Tree Augmented Naïve Bayesian.

## 1 Introduction

P2P lending , also called online social lending, allows direct lending and borrowing between individuals on an Internet-based platform, without the participation of traditional financial intermediaries such as banks (Wang, 2009). In this way, it provides convenient online services for reallocating small funds in credit transaction. There are more than 30 online P2P lending markets in more than 10 countries in the world, such as Zopa in UK and Prosper in the US. In recent years, advances in P2P lending marketplaces have provided new research opportunities with the availability of massive amounts of P2P transaction data. In this study, we focus on Prosper (http://www.prosper.com), the largest online P2P lending market in US, which has helped its 1.26 million members receive over $314 million loans. In this marketplace, borrowers submit requests for loans (called listing), and then lenders make bids on them. Prosper handles the aggregation and disbursement of funds to borrowers and then services the loans, collecting and distributing payments and interest back to the loan investors.

---

* The work was supported National Natural Science Foundation of China (61202011 and 61272385).

** Corresponding author.

J. Su et al. (Eds.): ICoC 2013, CCIS 401, pp. 21–30, 2013.

P2P lending, as a novel economic model, has been studied extensively in recent years, and is mainly focused on borrowers' social networks and personal information, loan attributes, lenders' decisions and so on. As for social networks, Freedman & Jin (2008) have investigated whether they solve the information asymmetry problem in peer-to-peer lending. They found that loans with friend endorsements and friend bids have fewer missed payments, but the estimated return of group loans is lower than those of non-group loans due to lender's learning and the elimination of group leader rewards. Lin et al. (2009) distinguished between structural and relational aspects of networks, and found the relational aspects are consistently significant predictors of the funding probability, interest rates, and ex-post default. Collier and Hampshire (2010) built a theoretical framework for the evaluation and design of community reputation systems. Sergio (2009) also built a model-based clustering method to measures the influence of social interactions in the risk evaluation of a money request.

To help the lenders make better decision, Luo et al. (2011) proposed a data driven investment decision-making framework, which exploits the investor composition of each investment for enhancing decisions making in P2P lending. They revealed that following some investors who have good investment performance in the past will make more correct investment decisions. Katherine & Sergio (2009) examined the behavior of lenders and find that, while there exists high variance in risk-taking between individuals, many transactions represent sub-optimal decisions on the part of lenders. Klafft (2008) showed that following some simple investment rules improves profitability of a portfolio. Kumar (2007) empirically proves that lenders mostly behave rationally and charge appropriate risk premiums for antecedents of loan default. Iyer (2009) also find that lenders are able to use available information to infer a third of the variation in creditworthiness that can be captured by a borrower's personal information. Puro et al. (2010) developed a borrower decision aid system, which helps the borrowers quantify their strategic options, such as starting interest rate, and the amount of loan to request. Wu & Xu (2011) proposed a decision support system based on intelligent agents in P2P Lending to help borrowers getting loan more efficiently, by providing borrowers with individual risk assessment, eligible lender search, lending combination and loan recommendation.

On Prosper, loan transactions between borrowers and lenders are conducted in an information-rich environment. When posting a listing, borrowers also submit their personal portfolios, such as Amount-Requested, Credit-Score, Homeowner, Category (or purpose), debt information and so on. All these information have influence on investors' decision. Li & Qiu (2011) displayed that borrower' decisions, e.g., loan amount, interest rate will determine whether successfully fund loan or not. Herzenstein et al (2008) also explored the determinants of funding successfully, found that borrowers' financial strength and efforts after they post a listing are major factors. The role of financial intermediaries on the P2P online market was analyzed by Berger & Gleisner (2009), which demonstrates that the recommendation of a borrower significantly enhances credit conditions, and the intermediary's bid on a credit listing has a crucial impact on the resulting interest rate. Pope & Sydnor (2008) analyzed discrimination in Prosper, found that loan listings with blacks in the attached picture are 25 to 35 percent less likely to receive funding than those of whites with similar credit profiles. Badunenko et al. (2010) observed that female borrowers pay on average higher interest rates than males at the largest German P2P lending platform, due to female borrowers deliberately offer higher interest rates in anticipation that they would be otherwise discriminated.

The above researches mainly focus on one or part of information of loans. In this paper, we try to investigate all the loan information in a uniform framework. Specifically, we develop a Bayesian network model with all the information in table listing, including the amount of loan to request, interest rate, category of loan, borrowers' credit score, homeowner, dept-to-income-rate, month-loan-payment. Using a large sample of paid or default loan data of Prosper from 2008 to 2011, we construct a Tree Augmented Naïve (TAN) Bayesian network model. Then we experimentally tested this model, using the data in 2012, and compared them to logistic regression, and Luo's method (Luo et al, 2011). Experimental results reveal that TAN Bayesian network can significantly help investors make better investment decisions than other models.

The rest of this paper is organized as follows: The base knowledge of TAN Bayesian network model is provided in Section 2. In Section 3, a Bayesian network model for P2P lending is built and compared to other investment models. Finally, we conclude the work in Section 4.

## 2 Bayesian Networks

Tree Augmented Naïve (TAN) Bayesian network algorithm (Chow & Lui, 1968) is used mainly for classification. It efficiently creates a simple Bayesian network model, allowing for each predictor to depend on another predictor in addition to the target variable. Its main advantages are its classification accuracy and favorable performance compared with general Bayesian network models. As for the paper, the target variable loan status will be simplified as 1=paid or 0=default two classes, then a listing with portfolios can forecast to classified as 0 or 1 by the Bayesian network model constructed by the past loans.

### 2.1 TAN Classifier Learning Procedure

Let X = (X1, X2, … , Xn) represent a categorical predictor vector and Y represent the target category, The learning procedure is summarized in Fig. 1 and illustrated in more detail below.

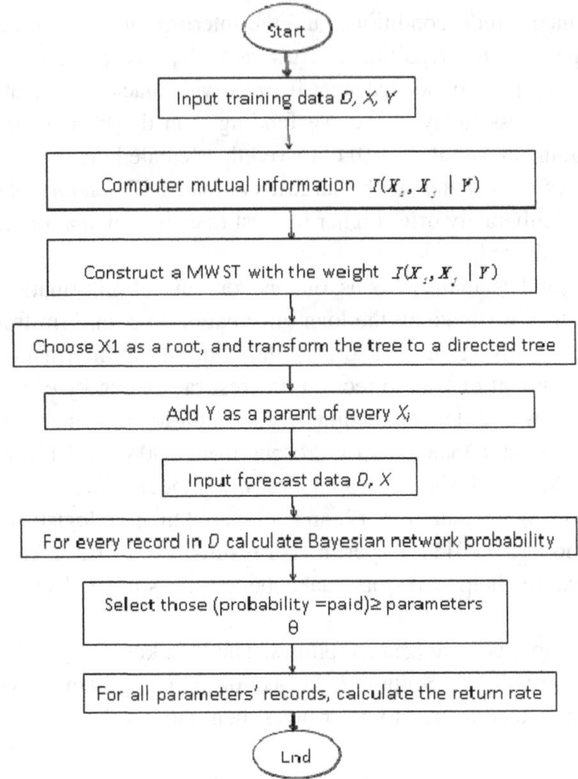


**Fig. 1.** Bayesian Network Algorithm

1. Take the training data *D* as input.
2. Compute the conditional mutual information[21] by

$$I(X_i, X_j \mid Y) = \sum_{x_i, x_j, y_k} P(x_i, x_j, y_k) \times \log\left(\frac{p(x_i, x_j \mid y_k)}{p(x_i \mid y_k) p(x_j \mid y_k)}\right) \tag{1}$$

In probability theory and information theory, the mutual information of two random variables is a quantity that measures the mutual dependence of the two random variables. Learning a tree-like network structure over D by using the structure learning algorithm outlined below.

3. Using Prim's algorithm (Prim, 1957) to construct a maximum weighted spanning tree with the weight of an edge connecting $X_i$ to $X_j$ by $I(X_i, X_j \mid Y)$.
4. Transform the resulting undirected tree to directed one by choosing $X_1$ as a root node and setting the direction of all edges to be outward from it.
5. Add *Y* as a parent of every $X_i$ where $1 \le i \le n$.

### 2.2 Probability Calculating

The Bayesian network classifier is a simple classification method, which classifies a case by determining the probability of it belonging to the i-th target category Yi. As investors, we main concern is the loans that will pay back with high probability. These probabilities are calculated as

$$\begin{aligned} &P(BStatus = 1 \mid X_1 = x_1^j, X_2 = x_2^j, \ldots\ldots, X_n = x_n^j) \\ &= \frac{P(BStatus = 1, X_1 = x_1^j, X_2 = x_2^j, \ldots\ldots, X_n = x_n^j)}{P(X_1 = x_1^j, X_2 = x_2^j, \ldots\ldots, X_n = x_n^j)} \\ &= \frac{P(BStatus = 1)\prod_{k=1}^{n} P(X_k = x_k^j \mid parrent(X_k))}{P(X_1 = x_1^j, X_2 = x_2^j, \ldots\ldots, X_n = x_n^j)} \end{aligned} \quad (2)$$

## 3 Experiment Results and Comparison

### 3.1 Dataset

The dataset used in our experiments is from Prosper.com. Prosper includes six relational data tables, which are Members, Groups, Credit Profile, Listings, Loans and Bids data tables. The Listing table is the most important for our modeling. A Listing is created by a Borrower to solicit bids by describing themselves and the reason they are looking to borrow money. If the Listing receives enough bids by Lenders to reach the Amount Requested then after the Listing period ends it will become a Loan.

In our experiments we use seven attributes from the Listing table, which are described in details below.

**AmountRequested** The amount that the member requested to borrow.

**BorrowerRate** The rate is computed as the LenderRate + GroupLeaderRewardRate (if applicable) + BankDraftFeeAnnualRate (if applicable).

**CreditScore** The credit score of the borrower at the time the listing was created

**Category** The Category is one of the following numerical values : 0 Not available, 1 Debt consolidation, 2 Home improvement, 3 Business, 4 Personal loan, 5 Student use, 6 Auto, 7 Other.

**DebtToIncomeRatio** The debt to income ratio of the borrower at the time the listing was created.

**IsBorrowerHomeowner** This attributes specifies whether or not the member is a verified Homeowner.

**BidCount** The total number of Bids.

### 3.2 Data Preprocessing

Bayesian nodes deal with discrete data, however, only category (0~7) and IsBorrowerHomeowner (0=false, 1=true) are discrete, the others are continuous values.

Therefore, we digitize these data by width-fixed method. For an attribute, assume that the maximum value of the attribute be $V_{max}$, and the minimum value of the attribute be $V_{min}$, we set the separation width to be $d = (V_{max} - V_{min}) / 5$, then the attribute is digitized to be 0, 1, 2, 3, 4, 5, when the value belongs to $\{V_{min}, V_{min}+d\}$, $\{V_{min}+d, V_{min}+2d\}$, $2\{V_{min}+2d, V_{min}+3d\}$, $3\{V_{min}+3d, V_{min}+4d\}$, and $\{V_{min}+4d, V_{max}\}$, respectively.

### 3.3 Forecast of Return Probability

The data to construct a Bayesian network is selected from the duration from 2008 to 2010. The network aims at predicting the return rate from Jan 1st, 2011 to April 30th, 2011. As we just concern about the people who would pay back as the model classified. The accuracy is calculated as follows:

$$R = \frac{f_{11}}{f_{11} + f_{01}} \tag{3}$$

Where $f_{11}$ is the number of Status=1 and B-Status=1, $f_{01}$ is the number of really Status=0 but B-Status=1. When the Bayesian network model is built, we can calculate the Bayesian probability with the information input. The Bayesian network algorithm is described as Figure3.

Specifically, we select the data from 2008.1 to 2010.1 to build model and use the data of 2011.1 to check the model. Next, add the 2010.2 data to the learning data while the check data is 2011.2, and by this analogy. With the TAN Bayesian method and model, we calculate the Bayesian probability of all the check data. Then the return rate of different probabilities can be calculated, that is, select those B-Status=1 loan that its Bayesian probability is higher than parameter$\theta$and compare with the really Status. The result is shown by Table1 and Figure 2.

**Table 1.** Return Rate of Different Bayesian Network Probability

| θ | Real Return Rate | 0.5 | 0.6 | 0.7 | 0.8 | 0.9 |
|---|---|---|---|---|---|---|
| 2011.1 | 0.74 | 0.78 | 0.81 | 0.79 | 0.90 | 1.00 |
| 2011.2 | 0.84 | 0.85 | 0.86 | 0.88 | 0.95 | 1.00 |
| 2011.3 | 0.79 | 0.81 | 0.82 | 0.84 | 0.89 | 1.00 |
| 2011.4 | 0.75 | 0.75 | 0.76 | 0.78 | 0.91 | 0.95 |

In P2P lending, our investment decision model ranks loans, from the best to the worst, according to the probability by Bayesian network. Investors can choose the top ones as the candidate set. We find empirical evidence to show the effectiveness of our model and the influence of different parameters. From Figure 3, the paid loans' distributions of Bayesian network probability is markedly higher than the default loans.

In Figure 4, we compare the rate of return by our model against three baselines, the average rate of return by investing on all loans, logistic regression model, investor composition method by Luo et al.(2011).We can find that, the higher $\gamma$ we choose, the higher return rate of the candidates chosen by our model has than others, where$\gamma$is the top probability loans to invest on.

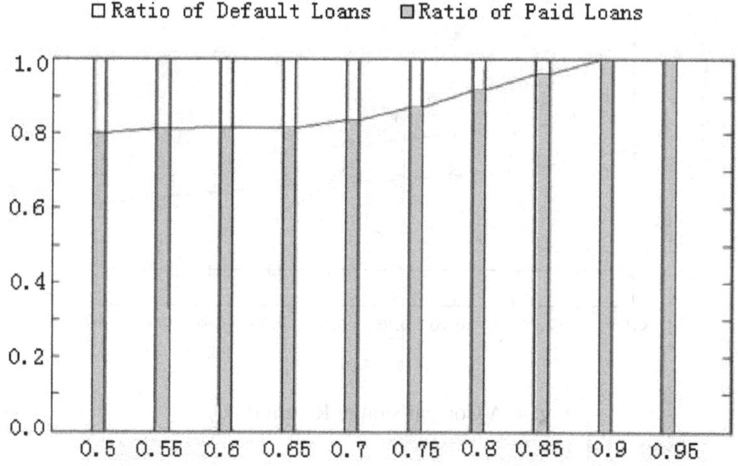


**Fig. 2.** Ratio of Loans Status by Bayesian Network Probability

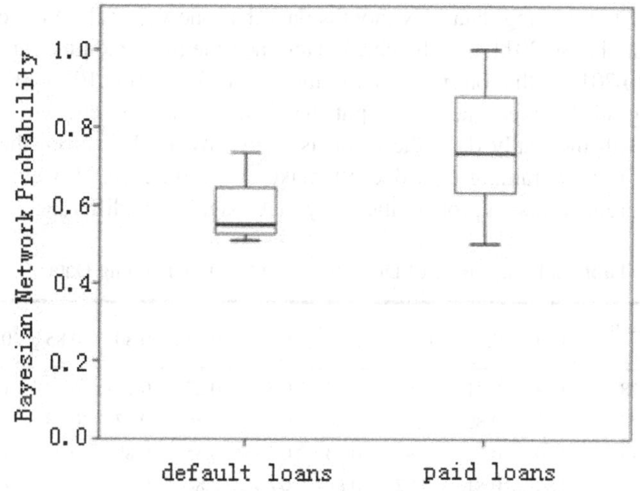


**Fig. 3.** Distributions of Bayesian Network Probability by Loans Status

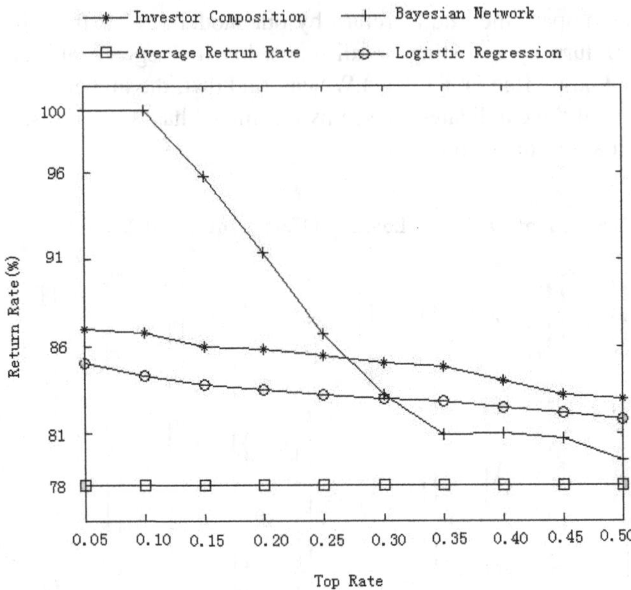


**Fig. 4.** A Comparision of Return Rate

### 3.4 Different Time Span of Training Data as an Indicator

Bayesian probability is learning from experiment data and expert knowledge. Whether the larger the learning data is the better? We choose the data from 2011.1 to 2011.4 as check data, and the training data is N months data that one year before the check data. That is, we first choose 2011.1 as the check data, then the three months training data is from 2009.11 to 2010.1, the four months training data is from 2009.10 to 2010.1, and so on. After doing all the experiments, we put the all three months' check data together, and compare with the really data, the result is shown by Table2. From the table, the different time span of training data doesn't make any difference. However, the table shows that different Bayesian probabilities may make significant different.

**Table 2.** Return Rate of Different Time Span of Training Data

| Training data | Return Rate | 0.50 | 0.55 | 0.60 | 0.65 | 0.70 | 0.75 | 0.80 | 0.85 | 0.90 | 0.95 |
|---|---|---|---|---|---|---|---|---|---|---|---|
| 3months | 0.78 | 0.79 | 0.81 | 0.82 | 0.84 | 0.84 | 0.87 | 0.91 | 0.92 | 1.00 | 1.00 |
| 4months | 0.78 | 0.82 | 0.82 | 0.82 | 0.84 | 0.84 | 0.86 | 0.87 | 0.89 | 1.00 | 1.00 |
| 5months | 0.78 | 0.80 | 0.82 | 0.83 | 0.83 | 0.83 | 0.85 | 0.89 | 0.91 | 1.00 | 1.00 |
| 6months | 0.78 | 0.80 | 0.81 | 0.82 | 0.82 | 0.84 | 0.86 | 0.88 | 0.90 | 1.00 | 1.00 |
| 7months | 0.78 | 0.79 | 0.81 | 0.82 | 0.82 | 0.83 | 0.87 | 0.88 | 0.91 | 1.00 | 1.00 |
| 8months | 0.78 | 0.79 | 0.81 | 0.83 | 0.84 | 0.87 | 0.87 | 0.90 | 0.91 | 1.00 | 1.00 |
| 9months | 0.78 | 0.79 | 0.80 | 0.81 | 0.83 | 0.84 | 0.86 | 0.91 | 0.92 | 1.00 | 1.00 |

### 3.5 The Newest Bayesian Network Model

With those experiments, Bayesian network model is proved as an effective model for P2P lending loan. We use all the information and data in table loan since 2008 to build a new model. The model is shown in Fig. 5.

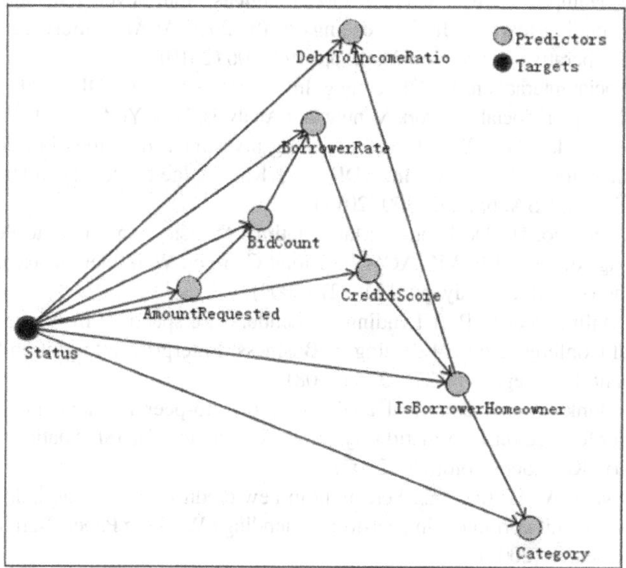


**Fig. 5.** A Bayesian Network Model

## 4 Conclusions

In this paper, we build Bayesian network model with all the borrower information and loan information in the table listing. First, we calculate the mutual information of every two variables and create a maximum weighted spanning tree (MWST) with them. When the weight matrix is created, the MWST algorithm gives an undirected tree that can be oriented with the choice of a root. A Bayesian network model is built when we add Status as the parent of every node. Then we check the model by the data a year later, if the Bayesian probability is higher, the rate of return is higher too. Experimental results reveal that Bayesian network model can improve investment performances.

## References

1. Wang, H., Greiner, M., Aronson, J.: People-to-People Lending: The Emerging E-Commerce Transformation of a Financial Market. Value Creation in E-Business Management 36, 182–195 (2009)
2. Prosper Marketplace, http://www.prosper.com

3. Freedman, S., Jin, G.: Do social networks solve information problems for peer-to-peer lending? Evidence from prosper.com, NET Institute Working Papers No. 08-43, Indiana University (2008)
4. Lin, M., Nagpurnan, R.P., Viswanathan, S.: Judging Borrowers By The Company They Keep: Social Networks and Adverse Selection in Online Peer-to-Peer Lending, Western Finance Association 2009 Annual Meeting Paper, University of Maryland, College Park, MD (2009)
5. Collier, B., Hampshire, R.: Sending mixed signals: multilevel reputation effects in peer-to-peer lending markets. In: Proceedings of the 2010 ACM Conference on Computer Supported Cooperative Work, New York, pp. 197–206 (2010)
6. Sergio, H.: Social interactions in P2P lending. In: Proceeding SNA-KDD 2009 Proceedings of the 3rd Workshop on Social Network Mining and Analysis, New York, Article No. 3 (2009)
7. Luo, C., Xiong, H., Zhou, W., et al.: Enhancing investment decisions in P2P lending: an investor composition perspective. In: KDD 2011(Knowledge Discovery in Databases), San Diego, California, USA, pp. 292–300 (2011)
8. Krumme, K., Sergio, H.: Do Lenders Make Optimal Decisions in a Peer-to-Peer Network? In: Proceedings of the IEEE/WIC/ACM Int'l Joint Conf. on Web Intelligence and Intelligent Agent Technology, Milan, Italy, pp. 124–127 (2009)
9. Klafft, M.: Online Peer-to-Peer Lending: A Lenders' Perspective. In: Proceedings of the International Conference on E-Learning, E-Business, Enterprise Information Systems, and E-Government, Las Vegas, pp. 371–375 (2008)
10. Kumar, S.: Bank of one: empirical analysis of peer-to-peer financial marketplaces. In: Americas Conference on Information Systems, Association for Information System Electronic Library, Keystone, Colorado (2007)
11. Iyer, R., Khwaja, A., Luttmer, E.: Screening in new credit markets: Can individual lenders infer borrower creditworthiness in peer-to-peer lending? Working Paper, National Bureau of Economic Research (2009)
12. Puro, L., Teich, J., Wallenius, H., Wallenius, J.: Borrower decision aid for people-to-people lending. Decision Support System 49, 52–60 (2010)
13. Wu, J., Xu, Y.: A Decision Support System for Borrower's Loan in P2P Lending. Journal of Computers 6(6) (June 2011)
14. Li, S., Qiu, J.: Do Borrowers Make Homogeneous Decisions in Online P2P Lending Market? An Empirical Study of PPDai in China. In: Service Systems and Service Management (ICSSSM), Tianjin, China, pp. 1–6 (2011)
15. Herzenstein, M., Andres, R., Dholakia, U., Lyandres, E.: The Democratization of Personal Consumer Loans? Determinants of Success in Online Peer-To-Peer Lending Communities. Working Paper, University of Delaware (2008)
16. Berger, S., Gleisner, F.: Emergence of financial intermediaries in electronic markets: The case of online p2p lending. BuR Business Research Journal 2(1), 39–65 (2009)
17. Pope, D., Justin, S.: What's in a picture? Evidence of discrimination from Prosper.com. Working Paper, University of Pennsylvania (2008)
18. Badunenko, N.B., Schäfer, D.: Are women more credit-constrained than men?– Evidence from a rising credit market. JEL Classification: G21, J16 (2010)
19. Chow, C., Lui, C.: Approximating discrete probability distributions with dependence trees. IEEE Trans. on Info. Theory 14, 462–467 (1968)
20. Prim, R.: Shortest connection networks and some generalisations. Bell System Technical Journal 36, 1389–1401 (1957)
21. Friedman, N.: Learning belief networks in the presence of missing values and hidden variables. In: Proceedings of the 14th International Conference on Machine Learning, pp. 125–133. Morgan Kaufmann (1997)

# Sub-channel and Power Allocation for Multiuser OFDM Systems with Proportional Rate Constraints Based on Genetic Algorithms

Weihai Li, Yunxiao Zu, and Yue Jia

School of Electronic Engineering
Beijing University of Posts and Telecommunications
Beijing, China
{liweihai,zuyx}@bupt.edu.cn, jiayue1@vip.qq.com

**Abstract.** This paper considers sub-channel and power allocation based on genetic algorithms to maximize the overall system capacity using proportional rate constraints in multiuser orthogonal frequency division multiplexing (OFDM) systems. The proposed algorithm first performs sub-channel allocation using a rough rate constraint under the premise of equal power allocation among the sub-channels. Then power allocation proceeds based on the sub-channel allocation scheme to implement proportional fairness and maintain maximum system capacity. Owing to the separation of sub-channel and power allocation, the computational complexity can be reduced from exponential to linear. Additionally, both the sub-channel allocation and power allocation are based on genetic algorithms, so the computational complexity of the proposed resource allocation algorithm can be further reduced. Simulation results show that the proposed algorithm achieves about 95% of the maximum capacity in an eight-user system and that the ratio of data rates among users can be set freely.

**Keywords:** sub-channel allocation, power allocation, multiuser OFDM, proportional fairness, system capacity, genetic algorithm.

## 1 Introduction

Orthogonal frequency division multiplexing (OFDM), which is a key technique in 4G mobile communication systems, has recently attracted a great deal of attention owing to its ability to combat multiple path interference. The basic idea is to divide the available bandwidth into N orthogonal sub-channels [1-3]. Meanwhile, the associated resource allocation has also become a key research focus. There are two types of resource allocation schemes, fixed resource allocation and dynamic resource allocation. The former scheme allocates independent dimensions of sub-channels and power to each user. This is obviously not optimal, since channel conditions are not considered. Instead, dynamic resource allocation adaptively adjusts the allocation scheme according to the changing wireless channel environment to make full use of the limited system resource [4] [5].

In a previous resource allocation study, Jang and Lee proposed an optimized algorithm to maximize total capacity by assigning each sub-channel to the user with the

J. Su et al. (Eds.): ICoC 2013, CCIS 401, pp. 31–39, 2013.

best channel gain [6]. However, if the channel gain differences among users are large, users with higher channel gain will occupy nearly all the resource causing other users to receive no data. The max-min problem was studied in [7] to ensure that all users generate a similar data rate. However, this study ignored the fact that different users may require different data rates. The authors in [8] proposed a suboptimal allocation scheme whereby a sub-channel is first allocated to the most suitable user based on a proportional rate parameter by assuming equal power distribution, and then power allocation is employed to maintain fairness. However, the sub-channel scheme algorithm has large computational complexity.

In this paper, we focus on a new optimization problem to achieve both proportional fairness and maximum system capacity. As before, the sub-channel is first allocated using a rough rate constraint to maximize capacity under the premise of equal power allocation. Then, the power allocation algorithm is employed to maintain maximum total capacity and ensure that each user has the required proportional rate. To reduce the computational complexity, we introduce genetic algorithms to both the sub-channel allocation and power allocation.

The rest of this paper is organized as follows. Section 2 introduces the multiuser OFDM system model and derives the optimization objective function. Sub-channel allocation and power allocation based on genetic algorithms are discussed in Section 3 with simulation results presented in Section 4. Conclusions are drawn in Section 5.

## 2 System Model

Fig. 1 depicts a multiuser OFDM system. It is assumed that instantaneous channel information is available at the base station, and all channel information is sent to the resource allocation algorithm through feedback channels from all the users. Then, the resource allocation algorithm formulates the related allocation schemes and forwards these to the OFDM transmitter. The transmitter selects a different number of bits from each user to form an OFDM symbol. The resource allocation schemes change adaptively according to variation in the wireless channel.

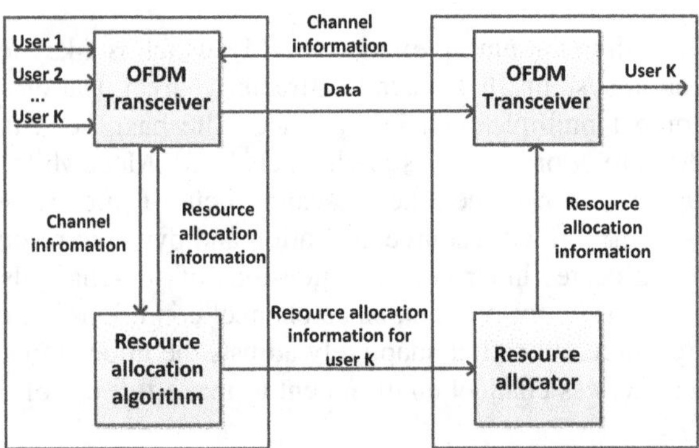


**Fig. 1.** Block diagram of multiuser OFDM system

In this paper, we consider a system with $K$ users sharing $N$ sub-channels. The objective function in the system aims to optimize sub-channel and power allocation to maximize system capacity under an aggregate power constraint. Meanwhile, owing to the introduction of proportional fairness, each user should also satisfy the related proportional rate. The benefit is that different users can achieve their expected data rate based on their different services.

Mathematically, the optimization problem discussed in this paper is formulated as

$$\max_{p_{k,n},\rho_{k,n}} \sum_{k=1}^{K}\sum_{n=1}^{N}\frac{\rho_{k,n}}{N}\log_2\left(1+\frac{|h_{k,n}|^2 p_{k,n}}{N_0\frac{B}{N}}\right)$$

subject to $$\sum_{k=1}^{K}\sum_{n=1}^{N} p_{k,n} \le P_{total} \quad p_{k,n} \ge 0 \text{ for all } k \text{ and } n$$

$$\sum_{k=1}^{K}\rho_{k,n} = 1,\ \rho_{k,n} = \{0,1\} \text{ for all } n$$

$$R_1 : R_2 : \ldots : R_K = \gamma_1 : \gamma_2 : \ldots : \gamma_K$$

where K is the number of users, N is the number of sub-channels, and $h_{k,n}$ and $p_{k,n}$ are the channel gain and power allocated to user k in sub-channel n, respectively. Further, $\rho_{k,n}$, which is either 0 or 1, indicates whether sub-channel n is assigned to user k, $N_0$ is the power spectral density of additive white Gaussian noise (AWGN), and B is the available bandwidth and $P_{total}$ is the total power. Here, $\{\gamma_i\}_{i=1}^{K}$ is a set of values indicating the data rate ratio among users.

## 3 Sub-channel Allocation and Power Allocation

### 3.1 Sub-channel Allocation

The sub-channel is first allocated under the assumption of equal power allocation to all the sub-channels based on a genetic algorithm to maximize system capacity using a rough rate constraint. A genetic algorithm is an evolutionary intelligent search technique that has been successfully used to solve many troublesome optimization problems. Fig. 2 depicts the flow chart, while each of the procedures is described below.

1) The number in each cell denotes which user is occupying the associated sub-channel. For example, in the chromosome shown in Fig. 3, cell number 3 contains the number 5, which means that sub-channel 3 is assigned to user 5. Different sub-channel allocation schemes can be represented by different chromosomes. Initially, W chromosomes are randomly generated.

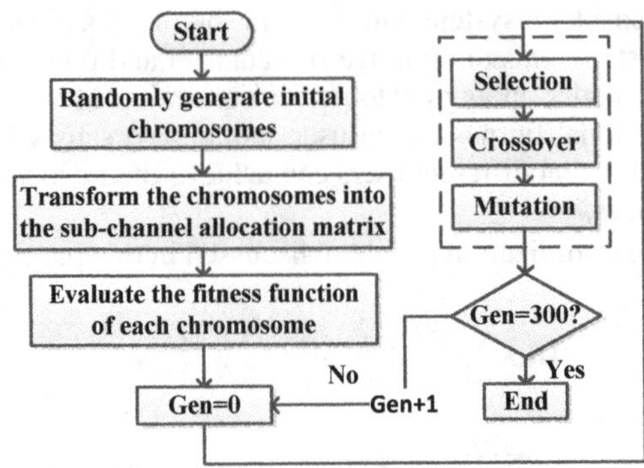


**Fig. 2.** Flow chart for sub-channel allocation

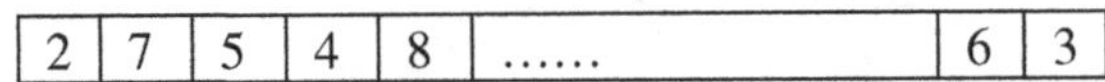


**Fig. 3.** A chromosome

2)Transform the chromosomes into a sub-channel allocation matrix: Since the generated chromosome cannot be used directly to evaluate the fitness function, it must first be transformed into an allocation matrix. The chromosome shown in Fig. 2 can be represented as a $8\times64$ matrix, with the elements in the matrix set to 0 or 1. Rows represent user numbers, while each column represents a sub-channel number. For example, if the element in the 5th row and 12th column is 1, it means that sub-channel 12 is assigned to user 5.

3)Evaluate the fitness function of each chromosome: The fitness function used is given by (1) and the target is to achieve maximum system capacity and a rough rate constraint for each user. Thus, the fitness of chromosomes is ranked based on the value of the fitness function. A larger value has a higher rank while the chromosome beyond the rate constraint requirement has the lowest rank.

4)Generate a new population by the following steps:

a)Selection: In the first generation, W chromosomes are randomly generated and assigned a fitness rank by step 3. In this step, the chromosomes with the lowest fitness ranks based on the selection probability Ps are abandoned; in other words, W*Ps chromosomes with the lowest fitness ranks are discarded.

b)Crossover: The remaining chromosomes are randomly grouped into pairs. For each pair, two new chromosomes are created using one-point crossover with crossover probability Pc, and the new individuals are called children.

c)Mutation: The mutation operator is used to alter one or more genes in the chromosome from its initial state to maintain individual diversity with mutation probability Pm. By following the above steps, a new generation with W chromosomes is formed.

5)Gen=300?: Gen defines the maximum number of generations. If the number of cycle operations satisfies the predefined number, the genetic algorithm terminates and returns the optimal solution.

Applying the above procedures will generate an optimal sub-channel allocation scheme with a rough rate constraint. The simulation results are presented in Section 4.

### 3.2 Power Allocation

After sub-channel allocation, the system has an optimal sub-channel scheme. Next, power allocation is carried out to ensure proportional fairness. The basic strategy is to assign power to the users according to the optimal solution, while power for the sub-channels owned by each user is allocated equally. The basic process flow, shown in Fig. 4, is similar to that depicted in Fig. 3. The optimization problem can be simplified as follows:

$$\max_{p_{k,n}, p_{k,n}} \sum_{k=1}^{K} \sum_{n \in A_K} \frac{1}{N} \log_2 \left(1 + \frac{|h_{k,n}|^2 p_{k,n}}{N_0 \frac{B}{N}}\right)$$

$$\text{subject to} \quad \sum_{k=1}^{K} \sum_{n \in A_k} p_{k,n} \le P_{total},\ p_{k,n} \ge 0 \text{ for all } k \text{ and } n$$

$$R_1 : R_2 : \ldots : R_K = \gamma_1 : \gamma_2 : \ldots : \gamma_K$$

where $A_k$ is the sub-channel distribution for the k-th user.

Compared with sub-channel allocation, power allocation is a multiple object optimization problem that includes maintaining system capacity, ensuring that the total power is consumed, and achieving proportional fairness.

Randomly generate initial chromosomes: A series of K elements, representing the power values for the users, with values ranging from 0 to 1 is randomly generated.

Evaluate the fitness function of each chromosome: There are two fitness functions: one is for system capacity, and the other is for proportional fairness. The chromosomes should, therefore, be divided into two groups, to which the respective fitness function is applied. The number of chromosomes allocated to each group is based on the weight. Here, the process focuses on the realization of proportional fairness. The specific method first calculates the user rates according to the power and sub-channel distributions. Next, it generates the user proportional rate by dividing the user rate by the proportion $\gamma_k$. Finally, the difference between the maximum and minimum user proportional rates is obtained, and if the absolute value of the difference is optimized to 0, proportional fairness has been achieved. So, the principle of ranking fitness considers the maximum system capacity and the minimum of the absolute value of the difference between the maximum and minimum user proportional rates.

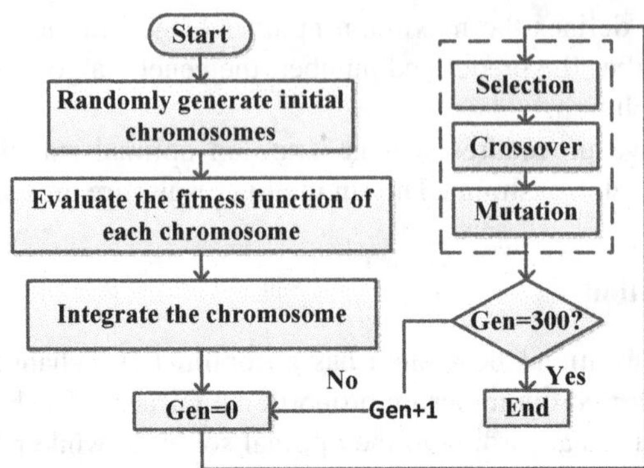


**Fig. 4.** Flow chart for power allocation

Integrate the chromosome: Owing to the separation of the fitness function calculation, the chromosome must be integrated after the evaluation terminates, to be included in the next procedure.

This step is the same as that for sub-channel allocation, including the operations of selection, crossover, and mutation.

When the algorithm terminates, system power has been rationally allocated among the users and the allocation scheme satisfies proportional fairness among users and maximum system capacity. The simulation results are presented in Section 4.

## 4 Simulation Results

In this section, we present our simulation results to validate the effectiveness of the proposed resource allocation strategy. A system with 64 sub-channels and 8 users was used. The wireless channel was modeled as a 6-tap frequency-selective Rayleigh channel employed in [8], and the total power $P_{total}$ and available bandwidth were set to 1 Watt and 1 MHz, respectively. The power spectral density for noise was set to -80 dB/Hz. The parameters in the genetic algorithms for sub-channel allocation and power allocation were the same, that is, W=100, Ps=0.9, Pc=0.7, Pm=0.035, and Gen=300.

Fig. 5 shows the total system capacity in terms of sub-channel allocation, power allocation, and maximum capacity. Owing to the fact that the sub-channel and power are both assigned to the user with the best channel gain, the maximum capacity method achieves maximum capacity. However, it also results in other users in the system having a zero data rate as shown in Fig. 6. The method with sub-channel allocation achieves slightly less than maximum capacity, but it introduces a rough rate constraint that ensures that all users can acquire sub-channels. The system capacity after power allocation is close to the sub-channel allocation. Since the method needs to realize proportional fairness at the expense of capacity loss, it has little effect on system capacity performance.

Fig. 6 shows the normalized ergodic capacity distribution among users for the different methods. Here, the data rate ratio is $\gamma_1 = \gamma_2 = 4$ and $\gamma_3 = \gamma_4 = ... = \gamma_8 = 1$. It can be seen that the method with maximum capacity assigns all the resource to user 1. Static TDMA tends to allocate equal capacity to each user based on the principle that all users have the same opportunities to transmit. However, this method does not satisfy the requirement of proportional fairness owing to the lack of a fairness control mechanism. Meanwhile, consider the method using only sub-channel allocation. Although the user rate distribution has no strict regulation, it satisfies a rough rate constraint and the total system capacity is close to maximum capacity. Using the proposed sub-channel and power allocation algorithms, the capacity is distributed fairly among users according to the rate ratio.

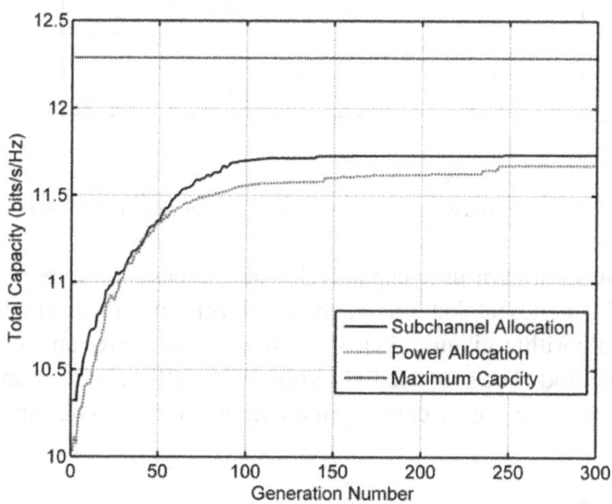


**Fig. 5.** Total system capacity for different numbers of generations

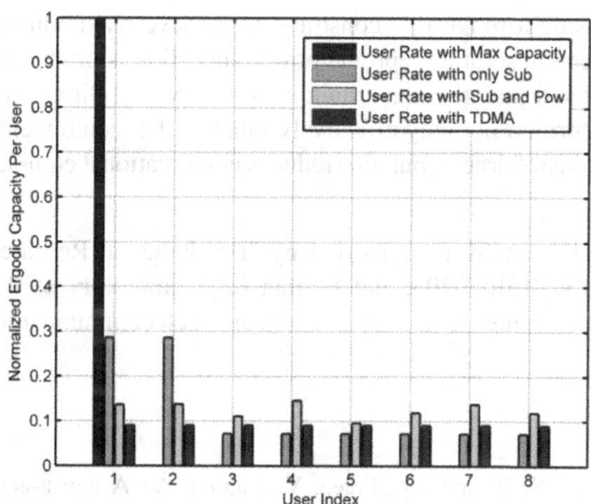


**Fig. 6.** Table 1. Fig. 6 Normalized ergodic capacity among users

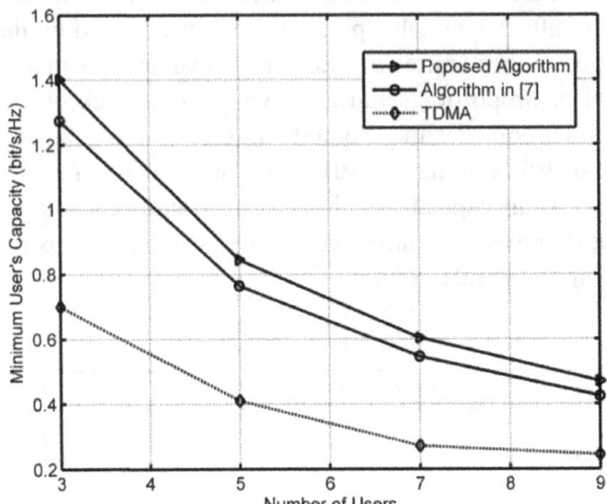


**Fig. 7.** Minimum user capacity with a different number of users

Fig. 7 shows the minimum user capacity for an increasing number of users in an OFDM system. We can see that the adaptive algorithms, including the proposed algorithm and the algorithm given in [7], show significant improvement over the non-adaptive TDMA method. The proposed algorithm with optimal sub-channel and power allocation achieves even higher capacity than the method proposed in [7].

# 5 Conclusion

In this paper we presented an algorithm based on genetic algorithms for adaptive resource allocation in a multiuser OFDM system. The algorithm first carries out sub-channel allocation using a rough rate constraint to achieve maximum capacity. Using the sub-channel allocation solution, optimal power allocation is implemented to achieve proportional fairness and maintain maximum system capacity. Simulation results show that the proposed algorithm not only effectively satisfies the requirements of maximum capacity and proportional fairness, but also reduces computational complexity.

**Acknowledgment**. This study is supported by "Fundamental Research Fund for he Central Universities"(2013RC0203, and Beijing Key Laboratory of Work Safety Intelligent Monitoring (Beijing University of Posts and Telecommunications).

# References

1. Sampath, H., Talwar, S., Tellado, J., Erceg, V., Paulraj, A.: A fourth-generation MIMO-OFDM broadband wireless system: Design, performance, and field trial results. IEEE Commun. Mag. 40(9), 143–149 (2002)

2. Rappaport, T.S., Annamalai, A., Buehrer, R.M., Tranter, W.H.: Wireless communications: Past events and a future perspective. IEEE Commun. Mag. 40(5), 148–161 (2002)
3. Huang, W., Letaief, K.B.: A cross-layer resource allocation and scheduling for multiuser space-time block coded MIMO/OFDM Systems. IEEE ICC 4, 2655–2659 (2005)
4. Liu, G., Liu, X., Zhang, P.: QoS oriented dynamical resource allocation for eigen beamforming MIMO OFDM. IEEE VTC 3, 1450–1454 (2005)
5. Choi, J.M., Kwak, J.S., Lee, J.H.: Adaptive subcarrier, bit and power allocation algorithm for MIMO-OFDMA system. IEEE VTC, 1801–1805 (2004)
6. Jang, J., Lee, K.B.: Transmit power adaptation for multiuser OFDM systems. IEEE J. Sel. Areas Commun. 21(2), 171–178 (2003)
7. Rhee, W., Cioffi, J.M.: Increasing in capacity of multiuser OFDM system using dynamic subchannel allocation. IEEE VTC 2, 1085–1089 (2000)
8. Sheng, Z., Andrews, J.G., Evans, B.L.: Adaptive resource allocation in multiuser OFDM systems with proportional rate constraints. IEEE Tran. Wireless Commun. 4, 2726–2737 (2005)

# On the Spatial-temporal Reachability of DTNs

Cheng Zhang[1], Chunhe Xia[1,2], Haiquan Wang[2,3], and Xiaojian Li[2,4]

[1] Beijing Key Laboratory of Network Technology, Beihang University, Beijing, China
[2] State Key Laboratory of Virtual Reality Technology and Systems, Beihang University, Beijing, China
[3] College of Software, Beihang University, Beijing, China
[4] College of Computer Science & Information Technology, Guangxi Normal University, Guilin, China

zc850717@gmail.com, {xch,whq}@buaa.edu.cn, xiaojian@mailbox.gxnu.edu.cn

**Abstract.** As traditional "Connectivity" concept from the Internet ignores the possibility of opportunistic contacts in DTNs, this paper brings time dimension into consideration, proposes Spatial-Temporal Path, Spatial-Temporal Reachability and K-Reachability in order to better describe the whole communication process and "Eventual Transportability" of DTN. Analytical and simulation results are given to show the correctness of our approach. Furthermore, Spatial-Temporal Reachability and K-Reachability, which tell a network's robustness in a quantitative fashion, are proved to be suitable for analyzing efficiency and routing performance of DTNs.

**Keywords:** DTN, Connectivity, Spatial-Temporal Reachability.

## 1 Introduction

Delay/Disruption Tolerant Networks, known as DTNs[1, 2] and DTMNs[3] are some typical cases of challenged network[4, 5], which is defined as a network that possesses one or more of the following characteristics: high end-to-end path latency, intermittent connection between nodes, or the absence of an end-to-end path from sources to destinations. In such situations, TCP, usually used in traditional Internet communication, faces great challenges when dealing with DTNs' highly dynamic fashion[6]. Therefore, in a set of new protocols called Bundle, researchers came up with a "store-carry-forward" strategy[1, 2, 7-9]. A forwarding node carries messages before getting the "opportunity" to forward them. This strategy enables the message to be delivered successfully in a given time in a DTN environment. By using Spatial-Temporal routing[10], the communicating process of DTNs is characterized as opportunistic contacting[11].

Traditional "Connectivity" concepts in relation to the Internet focus on the end-to-end path between a pair of nodes for an instant time. In order to better understand

J. Su et al. (Eds.): ICoC 2013, CCIS 401, pp. 40–49, 2013.

the "Eventual Transportability" of a communication process in DTNs, we can see from Fig 1: node0, node1, node2 are fixed nodes, while node3 moves clockwise. Node3 establishes wireless communication links with node 0,1,2 separately during times 1, 2, 3.

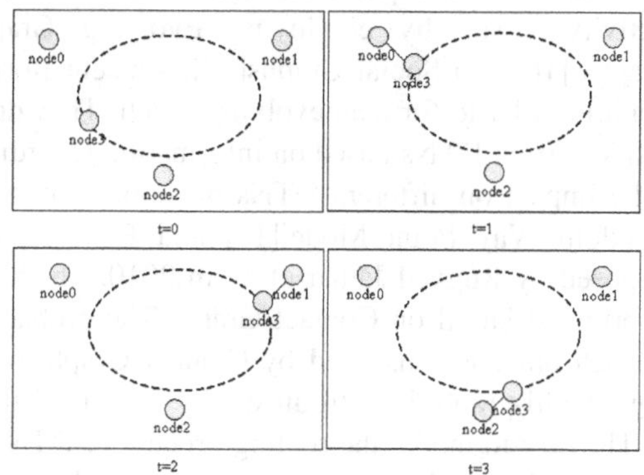


**Fig. 1.** A typical communication process in DTN

In above communication process, a message "path" is established for any node pair. Through this path, a message can be successfully transferred between any two nodes during a given time. This communication process tells us that the traditional "connectivity" concept mainly focuses on the static topological graph, while a static graph is not enough for describing the whole communication process and the "Eventual Transportability" of DTNs.

To our knowledge, the store-carry-forward fashion of challenged networks cannot be well described by known graph theory or other mathematical tools. In this paper, we bring time dimension into graph theory in order to form a Spatial-Temporal graph. "Spatial-Temporal Reachability" is proposed to describe the probability of a message reaching its destination in a given time in DTNs. Spatial-Temporal Reachability is a key concept of studying a communication system's delivery ratio, robustness and efficiency.

The rest of this paper is organized as follows: Section 2 gives the related works on both multi-hop networks and DTNs; Section 3 presents environment and definitions for the key elements of Spatial-Temporal Reachability; Section 4 gives the Spatial-Temporal Reachability analysis process and results; in Section 5, we compare the simulation results with the analytical results; some discussions and conclusions are given in Section 6.

## 2 Related Works

In this section, recent works on "connectivity" regarding both multi-hop wireless networks and DTNs are introduced. In the area of traditional multi-hop networks, Christian Bettstetter[13, 14] et al. have studied a basic concept of Ad Hoc networks: its

K-connectivity. The probability for the K-connectivity of an Ad Hoc network is derived using only local information such as node numbers, the radio transmission range and node density. "Connectivity" in DTNs is more challenging owing to its intermittent connection and absence of end-to-end paths between nodes. Some researchers investigated the "connectivity" issue by employing Evolving Graphs[14], Contact Graphs[15], Multi-graphs [16] and Social Graphs[17]. Vincent Borrel et al.[18] proposed a space-time path in order to form an evolving graph. They developed an algorithm which can classify current DTNs based on information regarding node contacts. They also analyzed the impact on different DTNs of mobility parameters using two mobility models: Random Way Point Model[19] and Random Walk Model[20]. Contact Graph is proposed by Rugved Jathar et al. in 2010. The author developed a probabilistic routing protocol based on Contact Graph. The probability of nodes acquiring contact with each other is illustrated by Contact Graph in order to enhance efficiency of routing. Multi-graph is introduced by Kevin Fall et al. in ACM SIGCOMM in 2004. They try to model the routing process of DTNs as a multi-graph with time t as a variable. Multi-graph brings time t as a variable in order to describe a communication process. Social Graph is proposed by T Hossmann et al. in INFOCOM 2009. The authors argue that in most current challenged networks, connections of nodes are not entirely random.

## 3 Environment and Definientia

We introduce a Spatial-Temporal Graph to describe DTN and its "store-carry-forward" communication fashion. By bringing time dimension into consideration, a sequence of graphs labeled by time is proposed. With this approach, a dynamic DTN can be described as a sequence of static graphs changing over time.

**Definition 1:** The Spatial-Temporal Link $e_{v_i,v_j}(t_n)$ between node $v_i$ and $v_j$ at time $t_n$ is,

$$e_{v_i,v_j}(t_n)=\langle v_i,v_j,t_n\rangle;i,j,n\in N;$$

**Definition 2:** The Spatial-Temporal Path $Path^T_{v_i,v_j}$ is a sequence of Spatial-Temporal Links within the Message Life Time T. The store-carry-forward technology passes a message along a Spatial-Temporal Path in order to complete a communication process,

$$Path^T_{v_i,v_j}=\langle e_{v_i,v_j}(t_n)\rangle;i,j,n\in[0,N],t_n\leq T;$$

**Definition 3:** The Spatial-Temporal Reachability $Reachability(G(t),T)$ denotes the property of a Spatial-Temporal Graph being Spatial-Temporal reachable, which means a Spatial-Temporal Path between any pair of nodes always exist in Message Life Time T,

$$\begin{cases} Reachability(G(t),T)\rightarrow\forall i\forall j\exists Path^T_{v_i,v_j}\wedge t\leq T; \\ i,j\in N,i\neq j; \end{cases}$$

**Definition 4:** Spatial-Temporal Reachability Degree $K-Reachability(G(t))$ is the degree of a Spatial-Temporal Graph being Spatial-Temporal reachable. If there exist K path-disjoint Spatial-Temporal paths between any node pair, we call the Spatial-Temporal Graph to be K-Reachable,

$$K-Reachability(G(t)) \rightarrow$$
$$(\forall i \forall j \exists Path^{T}_{v_i,v_j}) \wedge Number(Path^{T}_{v_i,v_j}) = K;$$
$$i, j, K \in N, i \neq j.$$

With the definitions on Spatial-Temporal Reachability and Spatial-Temporal Reachability Degree, we bring time-dimension into the analysis of the Eventual Transportability for messages. Spatial-Temporal Reachability tells that a DTN is "Connected" in the time of validity, and Spatial-Temporal Reachability Degree tells how well a DTN is "Connected". Spatial-Temporal Reachability is a better concept of studying a communication system's delivery ratio, robustness and efficiency rather that traditional "Connectivity".

## 4 Spatial-temporal Reachability analyses

In analyzing Spatial-Temporal Reachability, we intend to get the overall message reachability of a set of mobility models of DTNs. Using Random Direction Model as an example, we adapt a method to get the probability of a Spatial-Temporal Graph being K-Reachable from some local information such as node transmitting range, mobility model and speed of node movement.

### 4.1 Overall Ideas

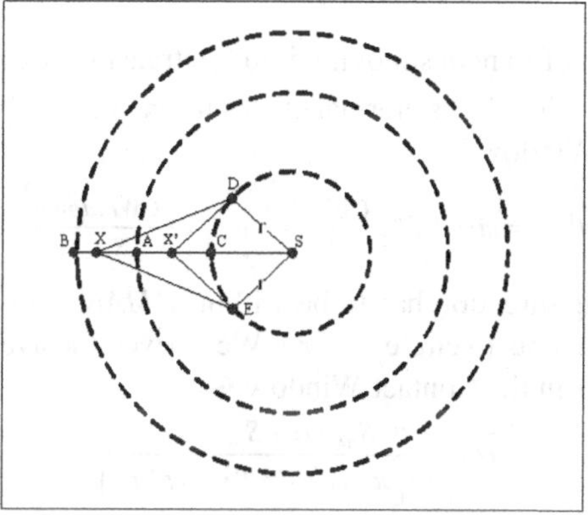


**Fig. 2.** Analysis of a two-dimensional random direction model

We use Random Direction Model[14, 22] as the mobility model for our analysis. V is the speed of movement for all the nodes in mobility model; r is the transmitting range for nodes; Message Life Time is set to T; total number of nodes is N. The number of neighbors (node degree) is a critical metric for a network. C. Bettstetter[12] gave a detailed analysis on the relationship between node degree and overall connectivity for a mobile network. He argues that a graph is said to be k–connected (k =1, 2, 3,...) if for each node pair there exist at least k mutually independent paths connecting them. In this paper, we follow this idea to calculate the paths each node has in order to get the overall Spatial-temporal Reachability for a DTN.

We first calculate the area size of the Contact Window ( $CWindow$ ). In this window, nodes have the opportunity to move into the transmitting range of a certain node S within Message Life Time T; secondly, the probability for n of m nodes moving into S's transmitting range is acquired; while $n \le m \le N$, we get the probability for n nodes having Spatial-Temporal links with S in Message Life Time T , $P(X = n)$, and the probability for all the nodes having at least n Spatial-Temporal links in Message Life Time T, $P(X \ge n)$.

## 4.2 Spatial-temporal Reachability in a Two-Dimensional Mobility Model

The space distribution of a Random Direction Model in any time is uniform[13]. For a square map with area of $S_{map}$ and a certain node S, we set pause time and reset time 0. The area size of ring BA and ring AC is $S_{BA}$ and $S_{AC}$.

As shown by Fig. 2, we follow the analysis steps,

**Step 1:** Calculating the area of the Contact Window.

For any node A, it has to be located in the circle $S-(|V*T|+r)$ to get the opportunity of contacting S within time T. We firstly put nodes within circle $S-r$ out of consideration, and get the area of contact window,

$$CWindow = \pi\left(|V*T|+r\right)^2 - \pi r^2$$

**Step 2:** Probability of n of m nodes moving into S's transmitting range.

As Random Direction Model fits normal distribution, the probability for m nodes located in the Contact Window is

$$P(U^* = m) = C_N^m * \left(\frac{CWindow}{S_{map}}\right)^m * \left(1 - \frac{CWindow}{S_{map}}\right)^{N-m}$$

For node A, the moving direction has to be within $\angle MAN$ in order to get a contact with S (AM, AN are tangents to circle $S-r$). We derived the average angle for all the nodes that can contact S in the Contact Window,

$$\overline{\alpha} = \frac{S_{BA} * \alpha + S_{AC} * \alpha'}{2*\left[\pi*(r+V*T)^2 - \pi*r^2\right]}.$$

Through the average angle, we get the probability for n of m nodes moving into S's transmitting range in the Contact Window.

$$P(U=n)= C_N^m * \left(\frac{CWindow}{S_{map}}\right)^m * \left(1-\frac{CWindow}{S_{map}}\right)^{N-m} * C_m^n * \left(\frac{\alpha}{\pi}\right)^n * \left(1-\frac{\alpha}{\pi}\right)^{m-n} \tag{1}$$

We go back for nodes that were originally located in circle $S-r$. These nodes can contact S from time 0, so the probability for q of N nodes that communicate with S is

$$P(V=q)=C_N^q * \left(\frac{\pi * r^2}{S_{map}}\right)^q * \left(1-\frac{\pi * r^2}{S_{map}}\right)^{N-q} \tag{2}$$

**Step 3:** Probability for n nodes having Spatial-Temporal links with S

Based on (1) and (2), we get the probability for n nodes having Spatial-Temporal links with a certain node S,

**Theorem 1:**

$$P(X=n)=\sum_{i=0}^{n}\left(\left(\sum_{m=i}^{N} P(U=i)\right) * P(V=n-i)\right)=$$

$$\sum_{i=0}^{n}\left(\sum_{m=i}^{N}\left(\begin{array}{l} C_N^m * \left(\frac{CWindow}{S_{map}}\right)^m * \left(1-\frac{CWindow}{S_{map}}\right)^{N-m} \\ * C_m^i * \left(\frac{\alpha}{\pi}\right)^i * \left(1-\frac{\alpha}{\pi}\right)^{m-i} \end{array}\right) * C_N^{n-i} * \left(\frac{\pi * r^2}{S_{map}}\right)^{n-i} * \left(1-\frac{\pi * r^2}{S_{map}}\right)^{N-n+i}\right)$$

From Theorem 1, we get the probability distribution of n nodes having Spatial-Temporal link with a certain node S within Message Life Time T:

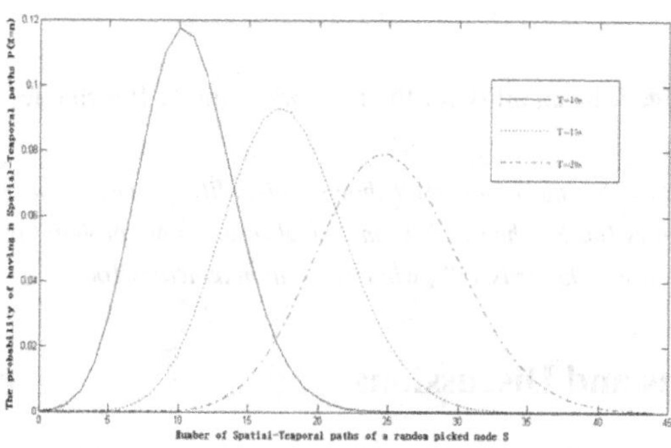


**Fig. 3.** Probability for all the nodes having n Spatial-Temporal links with a certain node S

1. *It shows that in T=15s, probability for all the nodes having 18 Spatial-Temporal links with a certain node S is 9% in analytical results;*
2. *When T=20s, analytical result shows probability for all the nodes having 26 Spatial-Temporal links with a certain node S is 8%.*

**Step 4:** Probability for the network being K-Reachable

Our goal is to get the overall reachability for the whole network. In Theorem 1 we acquired the probability for n nodes having Spatial-Temporal links with a certain node S. In a large scale network, events can be seen as independent from each other[13, 14]. As a result, when $N >> 1$, we finally get the probability for all the nodes having at least n Spatial-Temporal links, which means the network being K-Reachable:

$$P(X \geq n) = \left(1 - \sum_{j=0}^{n} P(X = j)\right)^{N} = \tag{3}$$

$$\left(1 - \sum_{j=0}^{n} \sum_{i=0}^{j} \left( \sum_{m=i}^{N} \left( C_N^m * \left(\frac{CWindow}{S_{map}}\right)^m * \left(1 - \frac{CWindow}{S_{map}}\right)^{N-m} * C_m^i * \left(\frac{\alpha}{\pi}\right)^i * \left(1 - \frac{\alpha}{\pi}\right)^{m-i} \right) * C_N^{j-i} * \left(\frac{\pi * r^2}{S_{map}}\right)^{j-i} * \left(1 - \frac{\pi * r^2}{S_{map}}\right)^{N-j+i} \right)\right)^N$$

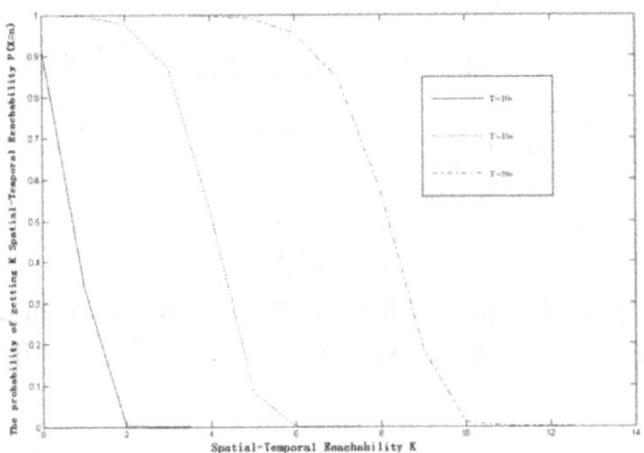


**Fig. 4.** Probability for the network being K-Reachable

*With Message Life Time T=15s, analytical result shows probability for the network being 3-Reachable is 92%, while simulation shows 100%; when T=20s, analytical result shows probability for the network being 3-Reachable is 95%, while simulation indicates 100%.*

## 5 Simulations and Discussions

In our simulation, we use C++ to build a Random Direction Model as an example for DTN simulation environment. For Random Direction Model, we set node number 1000, map size 2000m*2000m, node moving speed 20m/s, transmitting range 100m. We run the simulation 1000 times so that we can get the statistical distribution of n nodes having Spatial-Temporal links with a certain node S within Message Life Time T:

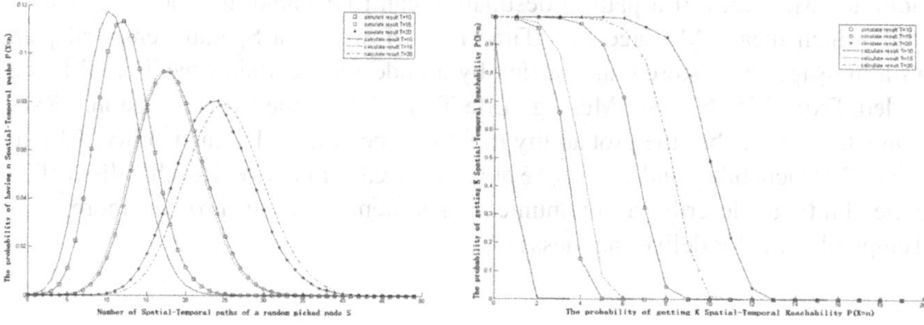


**Fig. 5.** Comparison for simulation results and analytical results

Fig. 5 shows that simulation results fit well with the analytical results. Probability for all the nodes having 18 Spatial-Temporal links with a certain node S is 9% in both analytical and simulation results; when T=20s, analytical results show that the probability for all the nodes having 26 Spatial-Temporal links with a certain node S is 8%, while simulation indicates 7%.

Fig. 5 also shows the probability for all the nodes having at least n Spatial-Temporal links (K-Reachability) in the two-dimensional Random Direction Model. We see that there are some differences between the analytical results and the simulation, the reason is that in our analysis process, we ignored the border effect, which can increase Spatial-Temporal Reachability when nodes bounce back to regain Spatial-Temporal links with other nodes. With Message Life Time T=15s, the analytical results show that the probability for all the nodes having at least 3 Spatial-Temporal links is 87%, while the simulation shows 100%; when T=20s, analytical results show that the probability for all the nodes having at least 6 Spatial-Temporal links is 95%, while the simulation shows 100%.

With the analysis above, we can get the probability of a network being at least K-Reachable for each Message Life Time.

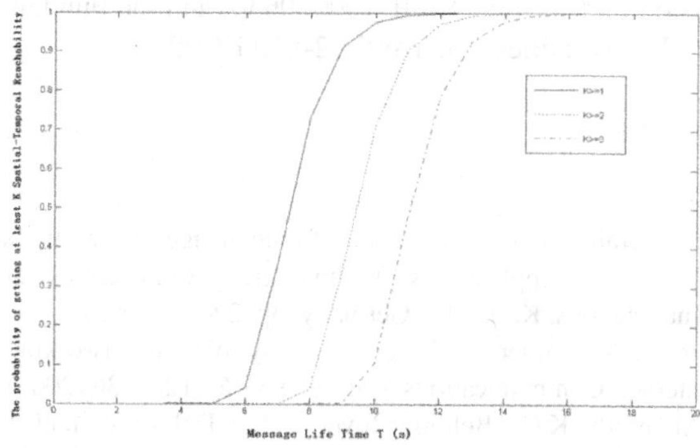


**Fig. 6.** Probability of a network being K-Reachability for each Message Life Time

In traditional MANETs, if a path to destination can't be found, the message will be dropped, which means Message Life Time is 0. However, a Spatial-Temporal path allows a message to be stored and carried by a node for a certain time T until being forwarded. From Fig. 6, when Message Life Time T=10s, the two-dimensional Random Direction Model has the probability of 97% to be at least 1-Reachability, 70% to be at least 2-Reachability and 10% to be at least 3-Reachability. K-Reachability offers more flexibility to describe a communication system, and can provide more Spatial-Temporal paths for delivering messages.

## 6 Conclusions

In this paper, we bring time dimension into graph theory to build a Spatial-Temporal graph. "Spatial-Temporal Reachability" is proposed to describe the probability of a message reaching its destination in time of validity in DTNs. Through mathematical analysis, we get K-Reachability for a network from some basic local information such as Message Life Time T, node moving speed V and transmitting range r. Simulations are also done to prove the correctness of our analytical results. By bringing time-dimension into consideration, we argue that Spatial-Temporal Reachability is a better concept of studying a communication system's delivery ratio, robustness and efficiency rather than traditional "Connectivity". Furthermore, we get the probability of a network being at least K-Reachable for each Message Life Time. Therefore, K-Reachability tells a network's robustness in a quantitative fashion, giving guidance to constructing high performance challenged networks. In the future, we plan to utilize our analytical approach in different mobility models, further applications of Spatial-Temporal Reachability are also considered.

**Acknowledgements.** This work is supported by following projects: The National Natural Science Foundation Project under Grant No. 61300173 and 61170295; National Foundation Research Project; The Project of Aeronautical Science Foundation of China under Grant No.2011ZC51024; The Co-Funding Project of Beijing Municipal education Commission under Grant No.JD100060630; and the Fundamental Research Funds for the Central Universities No. YWF-12-LXGY-001.

## References

1. Fall, K.: A delay-tolerant network architecture for challenged internets. In: Proceedings of the 2003 Conference on Applications, Technologies, Architectures, and Protocols for Computer Communications, Karlsruhe, Germany, pp. 27–34 (2003)
2. Burleigh, S., Hooke, A., Torgerson, L., et al.: Delay-tolerant networking: an approach to interplanetary Internet. Communications Magazine 41(6), 128–136 (2003)
3. Harras, K.A., Almeroth, K.C., Belding-Royer, E.M.: Delay Tolerant Mobile Networks (DTMNs): Controlled Flooding in Sparse Mobile Networks. In: Boutaba, R., Almeroth, K.C., Puigjaner, R., Shen, S., Black, J.P. (eds.) NETWORKING 2005. LNCS, vol. 3462, pp. 1180–1192. Springer, Heidelberg (2005)

4. Daly, E.M., Haahr, M.: The challenges of disconnected delay-tolerant MANETs. Ad Hoc Networks 8(2), 241–250 (2010)
5. de Cola, T., Ernst, H., Marchese, M.: Data Communication over Challenged Networks: Application of Error Control Schemes in the Delay Tolerant Network Architectures. In: Proceedings of 2nd International Symposium on Wireless Communication Systems, Siena, Italy, pp. 790–794 (2005)
6. Farrell, S., Cahill, V., Geraghty, D., et al.: When tcp breaks: Delay-and disruption-tolerant networking. IEEE Internet Computing 10(4), 72–78 (2006)
7. Yang, G., Chen, L., Sun, T., et al.: Ad-hoc Storage Overlay System (ASOS): A Delay-Tolerant Approach in MANETs. In: Proceedings of IEEE International Conference on Mobile Ad Hoc and Sensor Systems (MASS), Vancouver, BC, Canada, pp. 296–305 (2006)
8. Chuah, M.C., Ma, W.: Integrated Buffer and Route Management in a DTN with Message Ferry. In: Proceedings of IEEE Military Communications Conference (MILCOM), Washington, DC, USA, pp. 1–7 (2006)
9. Lu, R.X., Lin, X.D., Zhu, H.J., et al.: Pi: A Practical Incentive Protocol for Delay Tolerant Networks. IEEE Transactions on Wireless Communications 9(4), 1483–1493 (2010)
10. Merugu, S., Ammar, M.H., Zegura, E.W.: Routing in space and time in networks with predictable mobility. In: Technical report GIT-CC-04-07, Georgia Institute of Technology (2004)
11. Demmer, M., Brewer, E., Fall, K., et al.: Implementing delay tolerant networking. In: Technical report: IRB-TR-04-020, Intel Research Berkeley (2004)
12. Wang, L.: Modeling mobile ad hoc communication networks on two-dimensional square lattice. Frontiers of Physics in China 4(4), 556–560 (2009)
13. Bettstetter, C.: On the connectivity of ad hoc networks. The Computer Journal 47(4), 432 (2004)
14. Bettstetter, C.: On the minimum node degree and connectivity of a wireless multihop network. In: Proceedings of the 3rd ACM International Symposium on Mobile Ad Hoc Networking & Computing, pp. 80–91. ACM Press, New York (2002)
15. Ferreira, A.: Building a reference combinatorial model for MANETs. IEEE Network 18(5), 24–29 (2004)
16. Jathar, R., Gupta, A.: Probabilistic routing using contact sequencing in delay tolerant networks. In: Proceedings of Second International Conference on Communication Systems and Networks (COMSNETS), pp. 1–10 (2010)
17. Jain, S., Fall, K., Patra, R.: Routing in a delay tolerant network. ACM SIGCOMM Computer Communication Review 34(4), 145–158 (2004)
18. Hossmann, T., Legendre, F., Spyropoulos, T.: From Contacts to Graphs: Pitfalls in Using Complex Network Analysis for DTN Routing. In: INFOCOM 2009 Proceedings of the 28th IEEE International Conference on Computer Communications Workshops, NJ, USA, pp. 1–6 (2009)
19. Borrel, V., Ammar, M.H., Zegura, E.W.: Understanding the wireless and mobile network space: a routing-centered classification. In: Proceedings of the Second ACM Workshop on Challenged Networks, Montreal, Quebec, Canada, pp. 11–18 (2007)
20. Johnson, D.B., Maltz, D.A.: Dynamic source routing in ad hoc wireless networks. Mobile Computing, 153–181 (1996)

# Research on Efficient Non-slotted Tree Structures for Advance Reservation

Libing Wu, Ping Dang, Tianshui Yu, and Lei Nie*

School of Computer, Wuhan University, Wuhan, China
{wu,lnie}@whu.edu.cn, {dana_Job,ytswhucs}@163.com

**Abstract.** Resource reservation is a widely used mechanism in distributed systems and high-performance networks, and the optimization of its performance has been greatly concerned. Data structure is used to store summary information of reservation requests to provide direct basis for the admission control, so it is important to optimize the performance of data structure. In this paper, the existing data structures for resource reservations are analyzed and two new data structures—the resource clue tree and the resource binary tree—are proposed to solve the problem of low performance of non-slotted tree structures. The description performance, processing performance and store performance of several data structures are analyzed and compared with the timeslot array by experiments. The results show that the resource clue tree can achieve better performance than the timeslot array in some cases.

**Keywords:** resource reservation, data structure, resource clue tree, resource binary tree.

## 1 Introduction

The traditional internet provides the best-effort service for applications and resources are allocated when really needed. However, with the development of the multimedia and network technology, especially, the promotion of high-performance distributed applications such as grid computing and cloud computing, higher quality of service is required, which leads to the emergence of resource reservation [1-3].

Distributed systems are built on the basis of existing networks and many distributed applications are real-time tasks. At the same time, resources are dynamic, heterogeneous and autonomous, so the resource scheduling is more complex. In order to make sure that all kinds of resources for distributed applications can be provided on request, QoS guarantee is needed. Reservation mechanism is an important part of network quality of service, so resource reservation is a widely used mechanism in distributed systems and high-performance networks.

Data structure is used to store summary information of reservation requests and to provide direct basis for admission control in the process of resource reservation. Therefore, data structure must be able to provide quick access to the information and deal with it efficiently. About 60 percent of the total processing time is for the

* Corresponding author.

J. Su et al. (Eds.): ICoC 2013, CCIS 401, pp. 50–61, 2013.

processing of data structure, 8 percent for the selection of appropriate resources, and the remaining 32 percent for the management of resource extraction in resource reservation [2]. If an application request is for the whole potential advance reservation services, it will cost more time. For example, during the interval of scanning and detecting resources, the processing time of data structure is up to 90% of the total time.

The optimization of data structure can greatly improve the speed of processing in the resource advance reservation. The key issues to be resolved for data structure of advance reservation are to reduce the data redundancy and use of storage space, and to improve the processing and search speed. Two new non-slotted data structures—a resource clue tree and a resource binary tree—are proposed in this paper to solve the previous problem. Compared with the traditional timeslot array, the resource clue tree shows better description, processing and store performance.

## 2 Reservation Request and Reservation Procedure

Resource reservation is divided into immediate reservation and advance reservation. The first one is a quick way to respond to reservation requests. The applicant immediately starts using the resources after the reservation request is accepted. The advance reservation is a way of using the reserved resources a period of time after the reservation is made. Advance reservations include two stages: negotiation and use phase.

The resource reservation request (*req*) is represented by a triple $(bw, ts, te)$ in this paper. The parameters *ts* and *te* represent the start time and the end time respectively. The parameter *bw* represents the amount of requested resources (bandwidth). The method of generating reservation requests will be described in section 6.1.

Resource reservations are usually required to handle a large number of requests in a short time. One important task is the admission control-as long as there is a new request, the service provider must check whether there are sufficient resources available for it. So it needs some data structures to store the summary information of all reservation requests. Figure 1 indicates the situation of a resource reservation in some time, which is the virtual representation of information stored in a data structure. The amounts of idle resources can be clearly seen at any time and it is not difficult to infer the results of the admission control for a new reservation request.

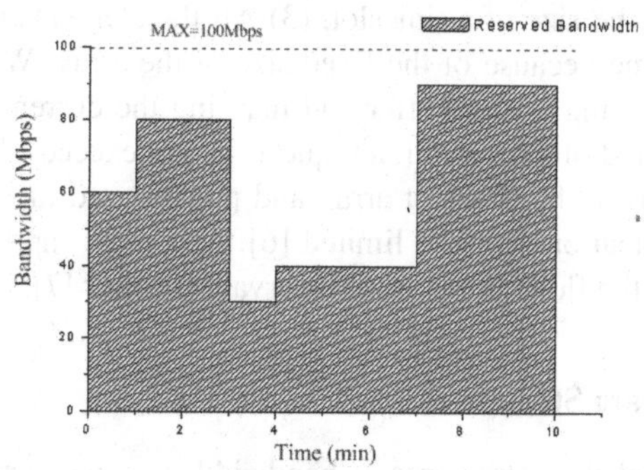


**Fig. 1.** Schematic diagram of a resource reservation

# 3 Related Work

Data structures in advance reservations are divided into two categories: slotted data structures and non-slotted data structures. Their inherent characters will be introduced in detail later.

## 3.1 Slotted Data Structures

Generally, a slot is the smallest time unit for the allocation of resources and each timeslot represents a fixed length of time such as one second, one minute, one hour, or even one day. There are two typical slotted data structures—the timeslot array [4] and the segment tree [5]. The comparison results show that the timeslot array is better than the segment tree in the consumption of time and storage space. An example of a timeslot array is showed in figure 2.

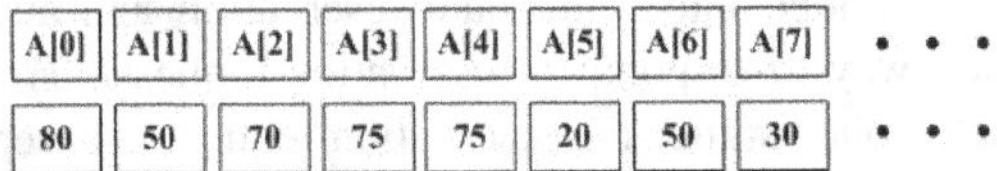


**Fig. 2.** A timeslot array

In figure 2, each array element represents a timeslot and its value represents the amount of allocated resources. The timeslot array must have an appropriate length (LEN) which should not be exceeded by the time bound of reservation requests and save storage space at the same time. A balance between these two points must be built.

The admission control of the timeslot array is very simple. For any arriving reservation request—*req*(*bw*, *ts*, *te*), it only needs to modify the value of each array element between the start time(*ts*) and the end time(*te*) (A[i] = A[i] + *bw*). There are still many drawbacks in the timeslot array: (1) if a reservation request covers a long period of time, a large number of array elements must be used to store the reserved information with the result of wasting a lot of memory; (2) each array element represents a fixed time period rather than an arbitrary time value, so the precision does not depend on actual demand but on the size of a timeslot. (3) All the elements in the array will still be overlapped over time because of the fixed size of the array. We can partially solve this problem through using a ring buffer and marking the current timeslot, which ensures that the time bound of a reservation requestwill not exceed LEN.

Mugurel et al. analyze the timeslot array and put forward the concept of time slot groups, but their application scope is limited [6]. And they improve the segment tree so that it can adapt to the flexible resource reservation better [7].

## 3.2 Non-slotted Data Structures

Among the non-slotted data structures, a bandwidth tree was proposed based on resource reservation [8]. However, simulation results [9] show that the bandwidth tree is worse than the timeslot array both in the consumption of time and storage space. Olov et al. propose a binary search tree, but the experimental results also show the performance of this data structure is worse than the segment tree [10]. QingXiong et al. proposea data structure based on the single linked list and the experimental results show that the storage consumption of the single linked list is far less than that in the timeslot array[9]. If the amount of requests is not large, the time consumption of the single linked list will be better [11-13]. The single linked list is optimized and improved to increase the processing and search speed with slightly higher cost of storage space [14-17].

In summary, the timeslot array has certain advantages in performance as a classical data structure whereas the performance of non-slotted data structures (the bandwidth tree, the binary search tree) is not satisfactory [18-22]. The description, processing and store performance of several data structures will be analyzed and compared with the timeslot array by experiments later.

# 4 Resource Clue Tree

## 4.1 Introduction

A resource clue tree is a data structure combining the binary search tree and the linked list, in which the list pointers (*tag*) link the nodes in sequence. In this way, it can combine the fast search speed of the binary search tree with the efficient traversal of the linked list to avoid recursion and improve the performance. A simple resource clue tree is shown as figure 3.

In Figure 3, the solid line pointers represent for the pointers of the tree (left and right) and the dashed pointers for the pointers of the list (*tag*). The pointer root and start stand for the root of the tree and the head node of the list, respectively. The node is defined as follows:

```
struct  node
{
   intbw;      //the value of resources(bandwidth)
   intts;      //start time
   struct node* tag;
   struct node* left;
   struct node* right;

   };
```

The tree is built according to the values of the key word *ts*. Any node p stores the value of *bw* during a period of time (*p.ts*, *p->tag.ts*). During this period, *bw* is a constant and the values of the adjacent nodes are different. The start time of the next node in list order (*p->tag*) represents for the end time of *p* in order to save storage space. The value of *bw* in the last node is 0 and identifying the end time of the previous node.

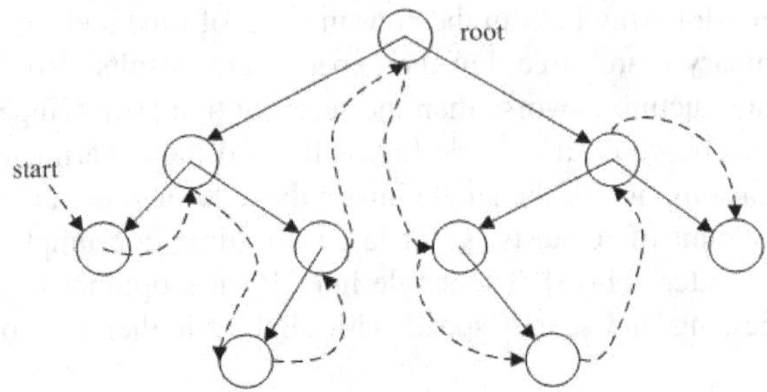


**Fig. 3.** An example of the resource clue tree

## 4.2 Algorithms of Request Processing

**The Algorithm to Insert the Start Time Node.**
The insertion of the start time node *p1* is similar to that of a binary search tree but it has a higher efficiency for search. During the insertion process it needs to handle the *tag* and start pointer.The algorithm is as follows:

```
Inserts(p, req)
Input: p;req
Explain: pre is the precursor of p
if  p == NULL   //not exist
      /*create new node 'p'*/
      if  pre != NULL
            /*handle the pointers */
      else
            p->tag = start;
            start = pre = p;
      end if
else if  req.ts == p->ts
            pre = p;
end if
else if  req.ts< p->ts
            p->left = insertts(p->left, req);
      else
            pre = p;
            p->right = insertts(p->right, req);
      end if
end if
return p;
```

**The Algorithm to Insert the End Time Node.**
The insertion of the end node *p2* makes use of the high traversal efficiency of the linked list. It traverses in the list order from *p1* to *p2* and deals with the values of *bw*. This process needs to correctly handle the pointers. The algorithm is shown in figure 4.

It is easy to update the values of *bw* and *tag*. But the pointers of the tree are more complicated to handle and they can be divided into two cases: (1) *p* is the precursor node of *p2* and when *p-> right == NULL*, it is indicated that *p* is the parent node of *p2* and *p2* is the right child of *p*; (2) when *p->right != NULL*, *p2* is the leftmost node of a subtree whose root is *p->right*.

## 4.3 Performance

There are still several performance issues in the resource clue tree. Firstly, there will be more and more nodes over time and all nodes will expire. If the current time now is big than the end time of a node, it will be meaningless. The expired nodes still occupy the storage space and result in the waste of storage resources. We define the pruning function to solve this problem. The main idea for that algorithm is to find all of the expired nodes periodically and remove them from the tree in order to eliminate redundancy and save storage. The process of the pruning algorithm is shown in figure 5.

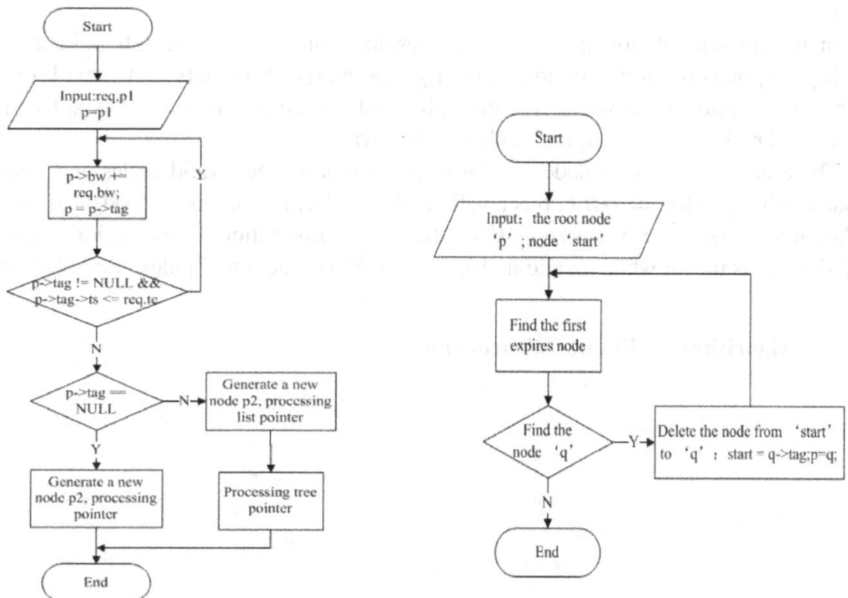


**Fig. 4.** The algorithmic process to insert the end time node

**Fig. 5.** The process of the pruning algorithm

Frequent usage of the pruning function will degrade the overall performance of the data structure because the function itself will also consume resources. Therefore, periodical pruning is reasonable. Experimental results show that the effect of the pruning function is obvious. Each pruning can remove 10% to 20% of the nodes to make the total number of nodes maintain a relatively stable level.

# 5 Resource Binary Tree

## 5.1 Introduction

The definition of the resource binary tree is similar to that of the resource clue tree. In a resource binary tree, each node stores the allocated values of *bw* within a time period (*l*, *r*). There is only a root node root (0, 0, +∞, *NULL*, *NULL*) in the initial tree. The definition of a tree node is shown as follows:

```
structtreenode
{
    intbw;  // the value of resources(bandwidth)
    int l;     //start time
    int r;     //end time
    structtreenode* left;
    structtreenode* right;

};
```

In the implementation process of the resource binary tree, the left pointer of a node(*left*) points to its first child and the right pointer(*right*) points to its next brother. When reservation requests arrive, the valid node meeting the conditions splits into new valid nodes and the original node will be invalid.

There are two types of nodes in the resource binary tree—valid nodes and invalid nodes. When *p->left==NULL*, p is a valid node, or else, it is an invalid node and has no relation with the value of *p->right*. Only the useful information of reservation stored in valid nodes is useful while invalid nodes only have the function of index and judgment.

## 5.2 Algorithms of Request Processing

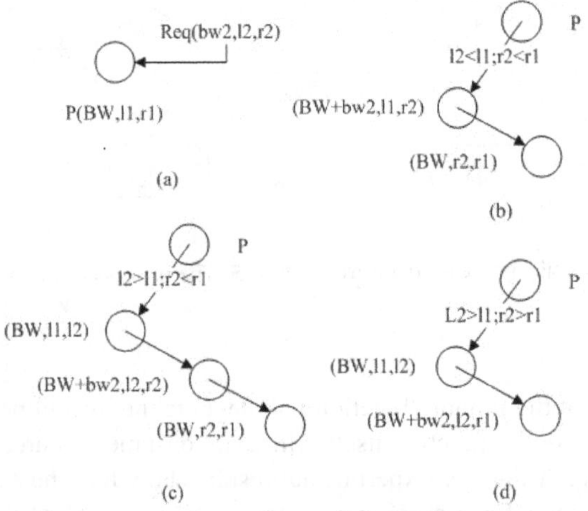


**Fig. 6.** Three methods of splitting

**Splitting Algorithm.**
If node *p* (*bw1, l1, r1, NULL, NULL*) is a valid node, when*req*(*bw2,l2,r2*) arrives, if *l2<l1 && r2>r1*, the value of *bw* in node *p* is consistent with value(*bw1+bw2*) and it does not need to split. If *p.bw* needs to change, the node *p* will be split. Three methods of splitting are shown in Figure 6.

**Insertion Algorithm.**
In the building process of the resource binary tree, the most important is the node insertion algorithm except for the splitting algorithm. The insertion algorithm is to convert a reservation request into a node and then insert it into the tree. The main idea is indicated as follows:

```
Addnode(req, p)
Input : req; the root of a subtreep
Stackin(p);  //let the eligible node into the stack
q = top;
while  q != NULL
    if   q->left == NULL
            Leaves(req, q) //valid node
    else
            Stackin(q);  //invalid node
    end if
    q = --top;
end while
```

# 6 Performance Measurements

## 6.1 Experimental Environment

The reservation request—*req*(*bw*, *ts*, *te*)—has been introduced in section 2. Qing-Xiong et al. provide a method to generate random values for each field[9].

$ts \sim U[20,100]$;

$td \sim \text{Exponential}(0.01)$;

$te = ts + td$.

Time units are seconds. The framework of experimental platform is shown in figure 7 and this paper focuses on the admission control and the data structure.

The establishment of the experimental platform and the implementation of data structures are completed by C language. The server is running on Ubuntu 10.10 and deployed on the mobile platforms of Intel core i3M390. All the experimental data below are derived based on this hardware and software environment.

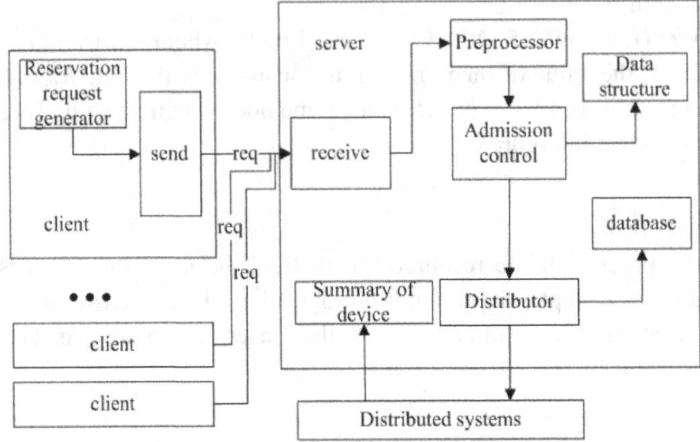


**Fig. 7.** The framework of experimental platform

## 6.2 Description Performance

The description performance refers to the ability of a data structure to describe resources. The non-slotted data structures can accurately describe the relationship between resources and time, while the slotted data structures can't.

A timeslot is the smallest unit to allocate resources. It is a fixed time period and the timeslot array cannot accurately represent moments smaller than it. In other words, the method based on timeslots cannot start and stop at any time it like, while it can only do it at some timeslots. Dividing the time into slots will lead to fragmentation and the reduction of available bandwidth [4].

This is the inherent defect of slotted data structures. To define a reasonable slot is very difficult. Long slots will reduce the accuracy and waste bandwidth, and short slots will waste time and storage space. Therefore, the size of time slots closely depends on the characters of reservation requests.

In our experimental environment, one second is chosen as the timeslot unit and the array length (LEN) is 1000. The elements of the array will be reused. So the timeslot array can describe the resources accurately, reduce bandwidth waste and avoid timeout thus working better.

## 6.3 Processing Performance

**Analysis.**
The processing performance means the speed to convert reservation requests and insert them into the data structure. The processing algorithms of the timeslot array is to deal with the array elements involved in turn and its time complexity is $O(td)$. The processing algorithms of the resource clue tree consist of one search procedure and the following linear processing and its time complexity is $O(logn)+O(m)$. The parameter $n$ is the number of nodes in the tree and $m$ is the number of nodes in

*p->ts* ∈[*ts,te*]. The processing algorithms of the resource binary tree involves one recursive operation and its time complexity is *O (logn) * O (m)*.

In summary, the processing performance of data structures is affected by many factors. The processing algorithm of the resource binary tree is poor. It is difficult to determinewhich is better between the resource cluetree and the timeslot array because it depends on the parameters of reservation requests.

**Experiment.**
The results support our analysis well. The processing performance of three data structures is measured as shown in Figure 8.

Figure 8 shows that the performance of the resource clue tree is slightly better than the timeslot array and much better than the resource binary tree. It is mainly because there are a large number of redundant nodes in the resource binary tree and the processing operation involves a lot of recursions which seriously affect the processing speed.

Two kinds of tree structures are less affected by reservation requests whereas the timeslot array is directly affected by the parameter *td*. Figure 9 indicates the processing performance of the timeslot array when the parameter $\lambda$ is 0.01, 0.1 and 1. As $\lambda$ increases, *td* increasingly concentrates to smaller values and the processing performance of the timeslot array improves significantly. At this point, its performance is far better than the resource clue tree. However, it is more sensitive to fluctuations of *td*, so it has more vigorous fluctuations under different conditions of reservation requests.

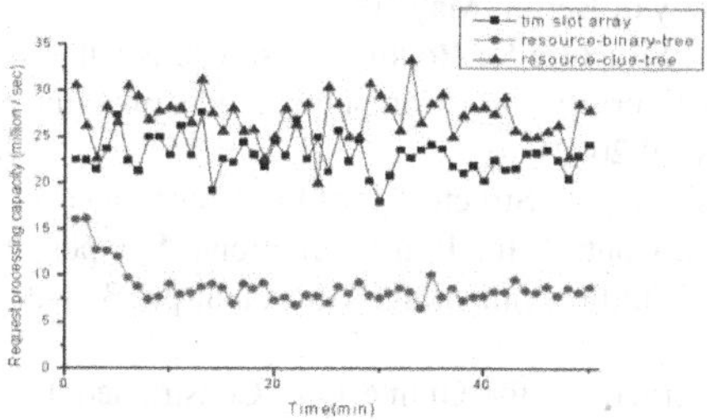


**Fig. 8.** The performance of processing algorithm

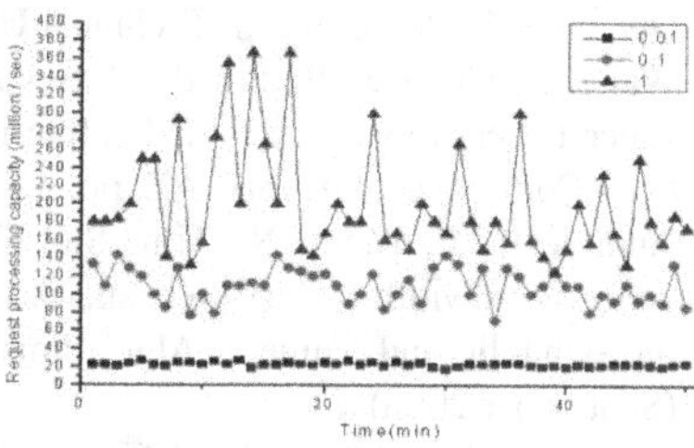


**Fig. 9.** The performance of the timeslot array under different conditions of reservation requests

## 7 Conclusion

In this paper, two new data structures—the resource clue tree and the resource binary tree—are proposed to solve the problem of low performance of non-slotted tree structures. The algorithms for establishment and performance improvement of the two data structures are introduced in detail. The description performance, processing performance and store performance of several data structures are analyzed and compared with the timeslot array by experiments.Experimental results show that resource clue tree can achieve better performance than the timeslot array in some cases and the resource binary tree has relatively poor performance.

The performance of data structures will be different under different values of reservation requests. Our next step is to do the experiments in real situations and minimize the impact of reservation requests to get a more flexible resource reservation.

**Acknowledgment.** This work is supported by National Science Foundation of China (No. 61070010, 61272112), the Natural Science Foundation of Hubei Province and Science and Technology Plan of Wuhan city.

## References

1. Reinhardt, W.: Advance Resource Reservation and its Impact on Reservation Protocols. In: Proc. of Broadband Islands 1995, Dublin, Ireland (September 1995)
2. Burchard, L.-O.: Analysis of Data Structures for Admission Control of Advance Reservation Requests. IEEE Transactions on Knowledge and Data Engineering 17(3), 413–424 (2005)
3. Xiong, N., Vasilakos, A.V., Yang, L.T., Song, L., Pan, Y., Kannan, R., Li, Y.: Comparative Analysis of Quality of Service and Memory Usage for Adaptive Failure Detectors in Healthcare Systems. IEEE Journal on Selected Areas in Communications 27(4), 495–509 (2009)
4. Burchard, L.-O., Heiss, H.-U.: Performance Evaluation of Data Structures For Admission Control in Bandwidth Brokers, Technical Report TR-KBS-01-02, Communications and Operating Systems Group, Technical University of Berlin (May 2002)
5. Wang, T., Chen, J.: Bandwidth Tree - A Data Structure for Routing in Networks with Advance Reservation. In: 21st IEEE International Performance, Computing, and Communications Conference, Phoenix, AZ, pp. 37–44 (April 2002)
6. Andreicaf, M., Ţăpuş, N.: Time Slot Groups - A Data Structure for QoS-Constrained Advance Bandwidth Reservation and Admission Control. In: 10th International Symposium on Symbolic and Numeric Algorithms for Scientific Computing, Timisoara, pp. 354–357 (September 2008)
7. Andreicaf, M., Ţăpuş, N.: Efficient Data Structures for Online QoS-Constrained Data Transfer Scheduling. In: International Symposium on Parallel and Distributed Computing, Timisoara, pp. 285–292 (July 2008)
8. Brodnik, A., Nilsson, A.: An Efficient Data Structure for Advance Bandwidth Reservations on the Internet. In: Proc. of the 3rd Conference on Computer Science and Electrical Engineering, pp. 1–5 (2002)
9. Xiong, Q., Wu, C., Xing, J., Wu, L., Zhang, H.: A Linked-List Data Structure for Advance Reservation Admission Control. In: Third International Conference, ICCNMC 2005, Zhangjiajie, China, pp. 901–910 (August 2005)
10. Bn, O., Nilsson, A., Norrgkd, J., Pink, S.: Performance of QoS Agents for Provisioning Network Resources. In: Seventh International Workshop on Quality of Service (IWQoS 1999), London, pp. 17–26 (1999)
11. Wu, L., Yu, T., He, Y., Li, F.: A index linked list suited for resource reservation. Journal of Wut (Information & Management Engineering) 33(6), 904–908 (2011) (in Chinese)

12. Berson, S., Lindell, R., Braden, R.: An Architecture for Advance Reservations in the Internet, Technical report, USC Information Sciences Institute (July 1998)
13. Xiong, N., Jia, X., Yang, L.T., Vasilakos, A.V., Pan, Y., Li, Y.: A Distributed Efficient Flow Control Scheme for Multi-rate Multicast Networks. IEEE Transactions on Parallel and Distributed Systems 21(9), 1254–1266 (2010)
14. Xiong, N., Vasilakos, A.V., Yang, L.T., Pan, Y., Wang, C.-X., Vandenberg, A.: Distributed Explicit Rate Schemes in Multi-input Multi-output Network Systems. IEEE Transactions on Systems, Man, and Cybernetics, Part C 40(3), 1–12 (2010)
15. Burchard, L.-O.: On the Performance of Computer Networks with Advance Reservation Mechanisms. In: Proc. 11th IEEE International Conference of Networks (ICON 2003), pp. 449–454 (2003)
16. Burchard, L.-O., Droste-Franke, M.: Fault Tolerance in Networks with an Advance Reservation Service. In: Jeffay, K., Stoica, I., Wehrle, K. (eds.) IWQoS 2003. LNCS, vol. 2707, pp. 215–228. Springer, Heidelberg (2003)
17. Burchard, L.-O., Hovestadt, M., Kao, O., Keller, A., Linnert, B.: The Virtual Resource Manager: An Architecture for SLA-aware Resource Management. In: Proc. IEEE International Symposium on Cluster Computing and the Grid (CCGrid 2004), pp. 126–133 (April 2004)
18. Sulistioa, A., Cibejb, U., Prasadc, S.K., Buyyaa, R.: GarQ: An Efficient Scheduling data Structure for Advance Reservations of Grid Resources. International Journal of Parallel, Emergent and Distributed Systems 24(1), 1–19 (2009)
19. Krzysztof, K., Ariel, O., Jan, W.: Multicriteria, Multi-user Scheduling in Grids with Advance Reservation. Journal of Scheduling 13(5), 493–508 (2010)
20. Kannan, R., Sanjay, R., Ye, X.: Advance Reservations and Scheduling for Bulk Transfers in Research Networks. IEEE Transactions on Parallel and Distributed Systems 20(11), 1682–1697 (2009)
21. Xiong, N., Vasilakos, A.V., Yang, L.T., Wang, C.-X., Kannan, R., Changf, C.-C., Pan, Y.: A Novel Self-Tuning Feedback Controller for Active Queue Management Supporting TCP Flows. Information Sciences 180(11), 2249–2263 (2010)
22. Chongyang, X., Hamad, A., Nasir, G.: Routing and Scheduling in Distributed Advance Reservation Networks. In: IEEE Global Telecommunications Conference, Miami, FL, pp. 1–6 (December 2010)

# A PSO-Optimized Nash Equilibrium-Based Task Scheduling Algorithm for Wireless Sensor Network

Jiaye Chen and Wenzhong Guo*

College of Mathematics and Computer Sciences, Fuzhou University, Fuzhou 350108, PR China
cjy_fzu@126.com, guowenzhong@fzu.edu.cn

**Abstract.** For the dynamic load characteristics of Wireless sensor network, we propose the idea of parallel Coalition and introduce the game theory into the solving of dynamic task allocation problem. In this paper, we design the model of multiple task allocation based on Nash equilibrium, and use runtime of task, Transmission energy consumption and Residual energy to design the utility function of Games. Then we use PSO to find to the point of Nash equilibrium. By using this method, guarantee the task execution effectiveness and improve the utilization rate of networks. Simulation results prove the validity of the algorithm, and can effectively prolong the lifetime of the network.

**Keywords:** WSN, task allocation, PSO, Game Theory, Nash equilibrium.

## 1 Introduction

Wireless sensor network (WSN) which includes a large number of sensor nodes is a wireless self-organizing and data-centric network [1]. The biggest drawback of wireless sensor network is that nodes have very limited energy, storage space and computing ability. Task scheduling is a classic problem of extensive research in the field of high-performance computing, and is also the core issues in the area of operating system research. In the operation of parallel and distributed computing systems, In order to effectively use the system resources, an application is usually decomposed into multiple tasks. Systems allocate resources to each task and determine the ordering of tasks execution. Task management is an important module in WSN, and it works together with the mobile management and energy management to monitor energy consumption, dynamic change and the role of task allocation of the sensor nodes in the entire network [1].

Many native and foreign scholars have done much research work on task allocation of WSN during the past several years. Yang et al propose an energy-balanced allocation of a real-time application onto a single-hop cluster of homogeneous sensor nodes connected with multiple wireless channels [2]. An epoch-based application consisting of a set of communicating tasks is considered. Each sensor node is equipped with discrete dynamic voltage scaling (DVS). The time and energy costs of both computation

* Corresponding author.

J. Su et al. (Eds.): ICoC 2013, CCIS 401, pp. 62–73, 2013.

and communication activities are considered. Liu et al propose a method based on elastic neural network to reduce energy consumption under the background of tracking aerial flying targets with the aim of the task allocation of collaborative technique in wireless sensor network [3]. In order to prolong the lifetime, reduce the energy consumption and balance the network load effectively, CHEN et al propose a dynamic Coalition model and its corresponding algorithm of task assignment in wireless sensor network (WSN) [4]. This method describes a cost function according to the execution time, energy consumption and load balance. Particle swarm optimization (PSO) is used to optimize task allocation. And on this basis propose a multi-agent-based architecture for WSNs and construct a mathematical model of dynamic Coalition for the task allocation problem [5].

Since Maynard Smith and Price introduced the ideas of evolutionary into game theory, learning from the analysis method of biological theory of evolution became a new way to calculate Nash equilibrium points and had been obtained abundant outcomes[6~8]. As in [9], the solution of the Nash equilibrium been shown to belong PPAD problem completely. Thomas et al solves the Nash equilibrium by using the genetic algorithms [10]. YI et al built a Grid model of m*n type grid using M/ M/ 1 queue system, and promoted the concept of task scheduling Nash equilibrium among multi-schedulers. The optimal objective of each scheduler is mean complete time per task [11].

This paper also based on the mechanism of dynamic coalition, and PSO was adopted to design a WSNs task allocation algorithm based on game theory. PSO is simple and easy to implement, and with no gradient information and with other advantages, which can be used to solve many complex problems. Our algorithm is able to adapt to the dynamic change of network load and adjust the network running status in time. This paper defines the utility function with the goal of reducing the execution time, reducing transport energy consumption and balancing network energy distribution, and using PSO to obtain the Nash equilibrium of tasks allocation. The results of experiment show its dependability and feasibility. The following will detail description of the problem as well as the specific algorithm implementation.

## 2 Model of Dynamic Task Allocation

### 2.1 Parallel Coalition

Coalition formation is a key problem in multi-agent systems. Parallel Coalition [12] is a concurrent generation problem of multiple dynamic coalitions. Parallel Coalition consists of two cases: Crossed Coalition and multi-task Coalition. Crossed Coalition means that an agent to join multiple coalition s or a task can be performed by multiple Coalitions.

Due to the limitations of WSNs such as resource availability and shared communication medium, parallel processing among sensor nodes is a promising solution to provide the demanded computation capacity in WSNs. Considering many points of similarity between WSNs and multi-agent systems, this paper introduces the complicated coalition into WSNs. As shown in Figure 1, a coalition consists of a number of nodes, and tasks are assigned to the selected coalition structure. Using this method we can take full advantage of the core capacity of member nodes, which can lead to finishing the tasks more efficiently and is more suitable for the application environment of WSNs.

### 2.2 The Concept of Mixed Nash Equilibrium

Game theory is a mathematical decisive approach aiming to solve the problem between competition and cooperation. If there is a competing or collaborative behavior among bodies in the environment, they will tend to adopt some effective strategies to maximize the utility of the individual of group. Generally, game body, strategy and utility are three main elements of game theory. The game body also acts as the player for the game. In general, a game requires at least two players. Besides, the game strategy is the actions of each body which is defined in advance, and each body has their own strategy set. In additional, each player of the game has a utility function to estimate the utility obtained from a certain strategy of the body. Assuming an $n$-person non-cooperative game, the pure strategy of player $p_i$ is defined as $S^i= (s^i_1, s^i_2, \cdots, s^i_{mi})$, where $m_i$ denotes the number of the pure strategy of $p_i$. The corresponding mixed strategy of the pure strategy $S^i$ is defined as $x^i= (x^i_1, x^i_2, \cdots, x^i_{mi})$, where $x^i$ meets $x^i_j \geq 0$ and $x^i_1+x^i_2+\cdots+x^i_{mi}=1$. i.e., the player selects the pure strategy $s^i_j$ $(1 \leq j \leq m_j)$ with probability $x^i_j$. Then the mixed situation of the game theory can be defined as $X= (x^1, x^2, \cdots, x^n)$.

In this mixed situation, the expected payoff of $p_i$ is defined as follows:

$$u_i(X) = \sum_{j_1=1}^{m_1} \sum_{j_2=1}^{m_2} \cdots \sum_{j_n=1}^{m_n} P_i(s^1_{j_1}, s^2_{j_2}, \ldots, s^n_{j_n}) \bullet x^1_{j_1} \bullet x^2_{j_2} \bullet \ldots \bullet x^n_{j_n} \quad (1)$$

Where $P_i$ $(s^1_{j1}, s^2_{j2}, \cdots, s^n_{jn})$ denotes the gain of player $p_i$ when $p_1$ select strategy $s^1_{j1}$, player $p_2$ select strategy $s^2_{j2}$, $\cdots$, and player $p_n$ select strategy $s^n_{jn}$.

**Definition 1.** If the mixed situation $X^*$ meets $u_i(X^* || x^i) \leq u_i(X^*)$, the mixed situation $X^*$ is the mixed Nash Equilibrium of an $n$-person non-cooperative game where $X^* || x^i$ denotes that only $p_i$ change its strategy.

**Property 1.** The mixed situation $X^*$ is the mixed Nash equilibrium of an $n$-person non-cooperative game if and only if the pure strategy $s^i_j$ meets $u_i(X^* || s^i_j) \leq u_i(X^*)$.

**Proof:** Suppose that $X^*$ is the mixed Nash equilibrium. If $u_i(X^* || s^i_j) \geq u_i(X^*)$, the player $p_i$ will obtain a better gain when it select strategy $s^i_j$. According to the idea of game theory, Nash equilibrium is the best select of each player, so $X^*$ will not be mixed Nash equilibrium.

### 2.3 Task Allocation

A wireless sensor network consisting of n heterogeneous wireless sensor nodes distributed in a certain range, and 10% of the node elected as the leader node. The number of Coalition is l, and we define the set of coalitions as $C= (c_1, c_2, \ldots, cl)$, where $l=n*10\%$. A set of independent tasks $T= (t_1, t2, \cdots, t_m)$ arrive at sink node at the same time.

An n-dimensional vector $REQ= (req_1, req_2, \cdots, req_n)$ denotes requirements of tasks, where $req_i$ denotes requirement of task $t_i$. Through the dynamic topology and routing control, sink node can obtain energy of node and ability of task of node.

In this paper, a matrix $B_k= (b_{ij})_{l\times m}$ is used to record the capacity of different coalition on different tasks, and we defined the execution time as:

$$Time_{ij} = \frac{req_i}{b_{ij}} \tag{2}$$

Where $b_{ij}$ denotes the capacity that $i$-th coalition executes $j$-th task, $Time_{ij}$ denotes the time required where $j$-th task run in $i$-th coalition.

The energy consumption of wireless sensor networks includes three parts: transmission energy consumption, processing power consumption and access to energy consumption. As the energy of transferring 1 bit data is far greater than the energy of processing 1 bit data, we usually ignore the processing energy consumption and the access to energy consumption. The discussion focused on communication energy consumption in this paper. The minimum transmission energy consumption is $P_{0,trans}$ when the standard distance is $d_0$ i.e., the distance $d_{ij}$ between $i$-th node and $j$-th node determines the energy consumption [13]:

$$P_{i,trans} = \frac{d_{ij}^2}{d_0^2} \times \frac{(4\pi)^2 \beta}{G_t G_r \lambda^2} \times P_{o,trans} \tag{3}$$

Where, $G_t$ denotes emission coefficient, $G_r$ denotes receive coefficient, $\lambda$ denotes Wireless communication wavelength, $\beta$ denotes Factor of the energy consumption of the system. As $(4\pi)^2\beta/G_tG_r\lambda^2 \times P_{0,trans}$ is a constant, $(d_{ij}/d_0)^2$ is the evaluation index of unit data of transmission energy. To simplify the data, a matrix $COST= (cost_{ij})_{m\times l}$ is used to record transmission energy consumption, $cost_{ij}$ denotes the energy consumption when $j$-th task transfer data to $i$-th coalition.

This paper use an n-dimensional vector E to denotes residual energy of coalition. $e_i$ denotes residual energy of $i$-th coalition. $P(e_i)$ denotes the proportion of residual energy of $i$-th coalition in the sum of residual energy of entire network.

$$P(e_i) = e_i \Big/ \sum_{i=1}^{l} e_i \tag{4}$$

In order to prolong the network lifetime, during the process of allocation, we should balance the residual energy of each coalition. The network residual energy average degree is defined as:

$$H = -\sum_{i=1}^{l} P(e_i) \log^{P(e_i)} \tag{5}$$

Where H denotes the energy entropy of networks. The larger the value of entropy, the more average residual energy distribution, and the longer network lifetime.

# 3 Our Algorithm

This paper assumes that a coalition is constituted by a number of sensor nodes, and these nodes are mutually closer in distance. Tasks are scheduled on the coalitions, rather than directly on the sensor nodes. Algorithm assigns tasks according to the current situation of networks. With development of energy consumption, the algorithm adaptively adjusts the allocation plan. The condition that the Nash equilibrium scheduling algorithm directly work on coalitions can be established is: a coalition is constituted by several nodes, therefore, a coalition can be considered to be a virtual node which has stronger ability and higher energy. Meanwhile, as mentioned above, both of multi-tasks allocation and solution of Nash equilibrium belong to NP-hard problem, take such an approach can reduce the scale of problem to obtain the solution of the problem quickly and reduce the difficult of experimental simulation. Specific implementation approach of our algorithm is given below.

**Definition 2.** Three components of game theory in our algorithm:

(1) players of game is s set of non-cooperative tasks, $T=(t_1, t2, ..., t_m)$;

(2) The pure strategy set of players consist of n coalition, coalitions are heterogeneous, and coalitions have own corresponding task ability, transmission consumption and residual energy; The corresponding mixed strategy set of players is $X=(x^1, x^2, \ldots, x^n)$, where $x^i$ is called mixed strategy of $i$-th player;

(3) In game theory, the utility function is an important indicator to measure the gain of players, it defined herein is:

$$u_j^i = w_1 \times nt_j + w_2 \times \cos t_{ij} + w_3 \times e_j \tag{6}$$

Where $u_j^i$ represents utility function which is used to transform multi-target to single target, and denotes the gain that $i$-th task obtain from $j$-th coalition. The smaller the value of utility function, the better; $nt_j$ is the sum of $busy_j$ and $Time_{ji}$, $busy_j$ denotes the busy time of $j$-th coalition; $cost_{ij}$ denotes transmission energy consumption of the $i$-th player in the $j$-th coalition; $e_j$ denotes the residual energy of $j$-th coalition; $w_1$, $w_2$ and $w_3$ denote weight value.

## 3.1 Nash Equilibrium PSO

In this paper, according to Definition 2, we use PSO to find the point of Nash Equilibrium. And our algorithm is called NEPSO.

We use the floating number matrix to represent the task allocation plan. The utility function is defined to optimize task execution time, energy consumption and energy entropy of network. Then we use utility function to further define the fitness function of PSO.

We use a matrix $x_{m \times l}$ to code the position of a particle:

$$X = (x^1, x^2, \cdots, x^m)^T = \begin{bmatrix} x_1^1 & \cdots & x_l^1 \\ \vdots & \ddots & \vdots \\ x_1^m & \cdots & x_l^m \end{bmatrix} \tag{7}$$

Where $x_j^i$ denotes the probability that $i$-th task select the $j$-th coalition, and $x_1^i + x_2^i + \cdots + x_l^i = 1$ .

For solving the Nash equilibrium of mixed strategies, each task $t_i$ is allocated to some coalitions according to its mixed strategy $x^i = (x_1^i, x_2^i, \cdots, x_l^i)$, In such a case, we need to change the utility function of pure strategies, and the expected utility function is defined as:

$$u_i = (u_1^i, u_2^i, \cdots, u_l^i) \bullet \begin{bmatrix} x_1^i \\ x_2^i \\ \vdots \\ x_l^i \end{bmatrix} = \sum_j^l u_j^i \bullet x_j^i \tag{8}$$

And we also need to update status of coalition after assigned a task:

$$busy_j = busy_j + x_j^i * Time_{ji} \tag{9}$$

$$e_j = e_j - x_j^i * \cos t_{ij} \tag{10}$$

The fitness function of PSO is defined as follows:

$$f(X) = \sum_i \max\{\max\{u_i(X_{i,-i}) - u_i(X^*)\}, 0\} \tag{11}$$

This fitness function is based on the fact: from the point of view of each player, if it change its strategy, the gain that take pure strategy is less than the gain that take mixed strategy, and this player will not want to change its strategy. As shown in equation (10), the value of fitness function of X is zero when X is the best solution $X^*$. The smaller the value of fitness, the better.

In each time of iteration, the particles update themselves by tracking the two extreme values. One is the optimal solution of each particle, which is called the local optimal solution, denoted by $X^i_{lBest}$, where $N_p$ denotes the number of particles. The other extreme is the global optimal solution of entire population which is currently found, denoted by $X_{gBest}$. During the iteration of PSO, the $i$-th particle velocity and position update equation:

$$\begin{aligned} V_k^i(t+1) = w * V_k^i(t) + c_1 * r_1 * (X_{lBest}^i - X_k^i(t)) \\ + c_2 * r_2 * (X_{gBest} - X_k^i(t)) \end{aligned} \tag{12}$$

$$X_k^i(t+1) = V_k^i(t+1) + X_k^i(t) \tag{13}$$

Where $V_k^i(t)$ denotes the speed of the $i$-th particle during the $k$-th iteration, $X_k^i(t)$denotes the position of the $i$-th particle during the $k$-th iteration, $X^i_{lBest}$ denotes the current local optimal solution of $i$-th particle, $X_{gBest}$ denotes the current global optimal solution of entire population. $r_1$ and $r_2$ denote the random number between 0-1, $c_1$ and

$c_2$ denotes learning factor. $w$ denotes Inertia weight, and it is linearly decreasing weight, and decrease from $w_{max}$ to $w_{min}$, as shown in equation (13):

$$w = w_{max} - ite \times \frac{w_{max} - w_{\min}}{ite_{max}} \tag{14}$$

Where $ite_{max}$ denotes maximum number of iterations.

**Definition 3.** if mixed Nash equilibrium solution X meets $\forall i, j$ , $x_j^i \geq 0$ and $\sum_j x_j^i = 1$ , it is called standardized solution.

If the solution of particles during the iteration of PSO is not the standardized solution, we should deal it with the method shown in equation (14) and (15):

$$\begin{cases} 0, & x_j^i < 0 \\ 1, & x_j^i > 0 \\ x_j^i & 0 \leq x_j^i \leq 1 \end{cases} \tag{15}$$

$$x_j^i = x_j^i \Big/ \sum_j x_j^i \tag{16}$$

### 3.2 PSO Algorithm Process

Input:

(1) The size of population K, the maximum number $ite_{max}$;
(2) Inertia weight $w$, maximum weight values $w_{max}$, minimum weight value $w_{min}$;
(3) Learning factor $c_1$ and $c_2$, the value is 2 in our experiments;
(4) Initialize set of tasks $T= (t_1, t2, \cdots, t_m)$, set of tasks requirements $REQ= (req_1, req_2, \cdots, req_n)$ , an ability matrix $B = (b_{ij})_{l \times m}$ , and the energy consumption matrix $COST= (cost_{ij})_{m \times l}$.

Output:

(1) the best mixed strategy $X^*$;
(2) Residual energy of each coalition $RE=(re_1, re_2, \ldots, re_l)$ ;
(3) Busy time of coalitions $BUSY= (busy_1, busy2, \cdots, busy_l)$.

**Step1:** Initialize the population. Initialize each particle X, each component of the vector $x^i$ is random number between 0-1, then handle $x^i$ according to equation (14) and (15);

**Step2:** compute $V^i(t+1)$ of $i$-th particle according to equation (11), then update $X^i(t+1)$ according to equation (12);

**Step3:** handle $V^i(t+1)$ according to equation (14) and (15);

**Step4:** compute fitness value of $X^i(t+1)$;

**Step4.1:** input mixed strategy matrix $X$, busy time and energy of each coalition, and set of tasks;

**Step4.2:** for task $t_i$, compute its executing time and transmission energy consumption in the coalitions;

**Step4.3:** according to equation (5), compute gain of pure strategy of task $t_i$ in the coalitions.

**Step4.4:** according to equation (7) and mixed strategy $x^i$, compute expected gain of task $t_i$.

**Step4.5:** update busy time and energy of each coalition according to equation (8) and equation (9);

**Step4.6:** compare expected gain of task $t_i$ and all pure gain, then update the value of fitness according to equation (10);

**Step4.7:** if $t_i$ is the last task, then end; else $i$ plus 1 and go to **step4.2**.

**Step5:** determine whether need to update the local optimal solution or the global optimal solution;

**Step6:** The number of iterations plus 1;

**Step7:** Judge whether the number of iterations reaches the upper limit $ite_{max}$. If $ite=ite_{max}$, then return $X_{gBest}$, else go to **Step2.**

During the process of computing, we need to handle the three parameters of the utility function (execute time, transmission energy consumption and residual energy). In this paper, the value mapped to the interval [0, 0.5] by using sigmoid function, as shown in equation (16) and equation (17):

$$f(x) = -\frac{1}{1+e^{-x}} + 1 \tag{17}$$

$$f(x) = \frac{1}{1+e^{-x}} - 0.5 \tag{18}$$

$$nt_i = -\frac{1}{1+e^{-\frac{nt_i - nt_{\min}}{nt_{\max} - nt_{\min}}}} + 1 \tag{19}$$

$$\cos t_{ij} = -\frac{1}{1+e^{-\frac{\cos t_{ij} - \cos t_{\min}}{\cos t_{\max} - \cos t_{\min}}}} + 1 \tag{20}$$

$$e_i = -\frac{1}{1+e^{-\frac{e_i - e_{\min}}{e_{\max} - e_{\min}}}} + 1 \tag{21}$$

## 4 Simulation and Results

Our simulation study is conducted for a WSN of n nodes that are placed uniformly in a rectangular region of 200 by 200 meters, and 10% of the nodes are elected as the leader. The requirements of the subtask are distributed in the range of the interval (2, 6]. In the same situation, the greater the value is, the longer the time of executing this task is. This value also reflects the difficulty of the task processing. The ability of executing task is distributed in the range of the interval (15, 25], the greater the value is, the stronger the ability is. The energy consumption is distributed in the range of the interval (3, 7], the greater the value is, the greater the consumption is. The energy of each node is distributed in the range of the interval (45000, 55000] mj.

Through several experiments, in order to obtain a high-quality solution rapidly in a short period of time, the parameters of PSO are set as follows: maximum number of iterations $ite_{max}$ is 100, the size of population $K$ is 50, $w_{max}$ is 0.9, $w_{min}$ is 0.5, $c_1$ and $c_2$ is 2, $w_1$ is 1, $w_2$ is 1, $w_3$ is 3.

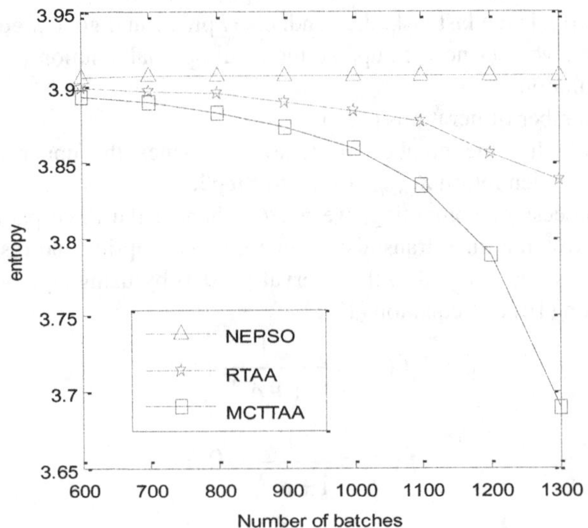


**Fig. 1.** The entropy of different numbers of batches

As shown in Figure 1, here are a set of experiments to observe the performance of wireless sensor networks under different task batch. In the respect of balancing networks energy to improve networks lifecycle, compare to MCTTAA and RTAA, NEPSO shows good results. The Energy Entropy is keeping at about 3.9. From this figure, we can know that three algorithm can let the network has a good entropy when the batches of task is small, especially at the interval [600, 900]. However, with the increasing of the batches of task, entropy of MCTTAA declining much faster than the others. Similarly, although the RTAA let network energy entropy still maintaining at a good level, but compared to the NEPSO algorithm, it is more poor.

Figure 2 and Figure 3 are the compare of execution time. Due to MCTTAA is based on the shortest completion time, whether the average execution time or minimum execution time, it shows a very good performance. RTAA and NEPSO is worse. As shown in Figure 8, the average execution time of NEPSO and RTAA is almost the same, and their corresponding curves are almost overlapping. And on the minimum execution time, as shown in Figure 9, NEPSO after MCTTAA is superior to RTAA.

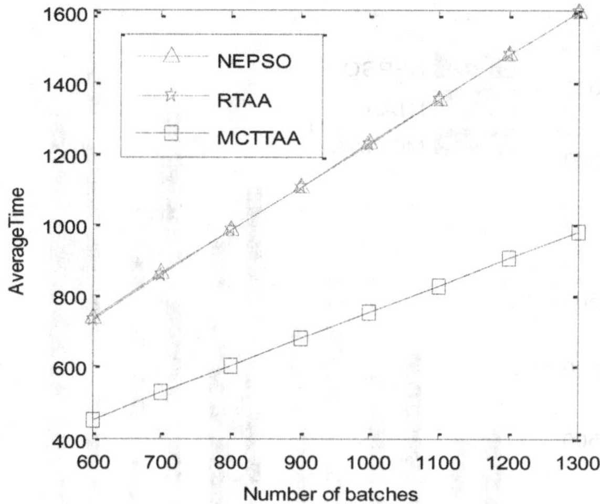


**Fig. 2.** The average of execution time of different numbers of batches

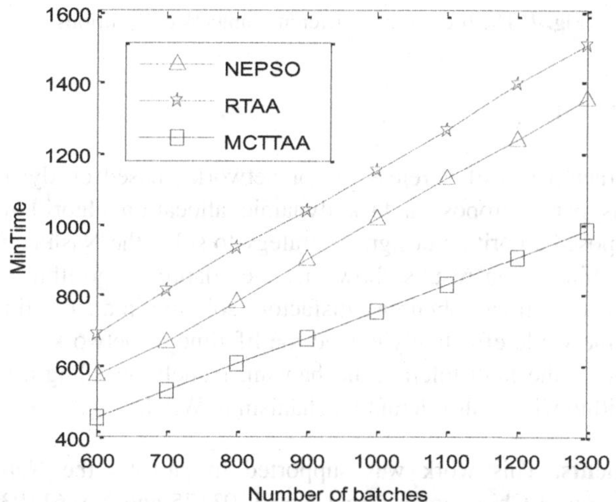


**Fig. 3.** The minimum of execution time of different numbers of batches

In this experiment, the maximum residual energy in coalition is set to be 55000*mj*.When an coalition's residual energy is less than 5% of the maximum residual energy, namely residual energy is less than 2750*mj*, the network will be failure. As shown in Fig.4, under different numbers of alliance, the batches of task executed by NEPSO are the most. When the number of coalition is small, the disparity among the three algorithms is not obvious, but with the increase of coalitions, it can obviously see that performance of NEPSO in improving the network life cycle is excellent, RTAA and MCTTAA are much poor, especially MCTTAA.

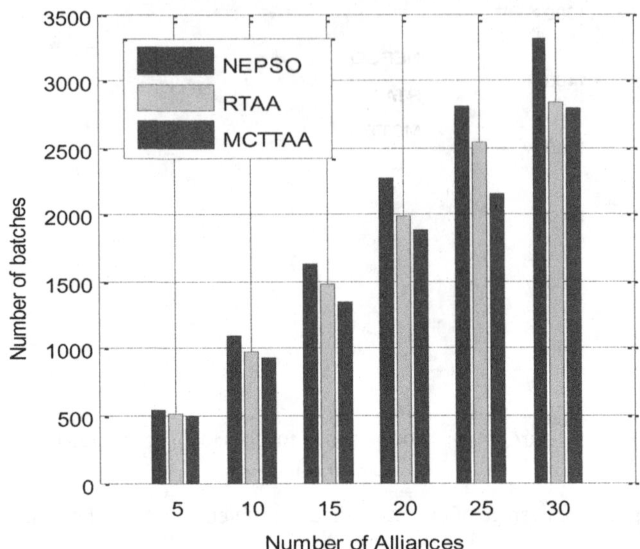


**Fig. 4.** The life cycle of different numbers of coalitions

# 5 Conclusion

For certain characteristics of wireless sensor networks, based on dynamic coalition mechanism, this paper propose a task dynamic allocation algorithm using game theory. The proposed algorithm designs a strategy to solve the Nash equilibrium with PSO algorithm. Simulation results show that the adaptive algorithm constructed in this paper is effective. It can obtain a satisfactory solution in a short time and ensure the execution time while effectively extend the lifetime of network. Further research work will focus on the fault-tolerant mechanism, namely, building a tasks adaptive allocation algorithm with fault-tolerant mechanism in WSN.

**Acknowledgements.** This work was supported in part by the National Natural Science Foundation of China under Grant No.61103175 and No. 61103194, the Key Project of Chinese Ministry of Education under Grant No.212086, the Technology Innovation Platform Project of Fujian Province under Grant No.2009J1007, the Key Project Development Foundation of Education Committee of Fujian province under Grand No. JA11011, and the Fujian Province High School Science Fund for Distinguished Young Scholars under Grand No.JA12016.

# References

1. Akyildiz, I.F., Su, W., Sankarasubramaniam, Y., et al.: Wireless sensor networks: a survey. Computer Networks 38, 393–422 (2002)
2. Yu, Y., Viktor, K.P.: Energy-balanced task allocation for collaborative processing in wireless sensor networks. Mobile Networks and Applications 10(12), 115–131 (2005)

3. Liu, M., Li, H.H., Shen, Y.: Research on task allocation technique for aerial target tracking based on wireless sensor network. Journal of Astronautics 28(4), 960–965 (2007)
4. Chen, G.L., Guo, W.Z., Chen, Y.Z.: Research on dynamic alliance of task allocation and its algorithm in wireless sensor network. Journal on Communication 30(11), 48–55 (2009)
5. Guo, W.Z., Xiong, N.X., Chao, H.C., et al.: Design and Analysis of Self-Adapted Task Scheduling Strategies in Wireless Sensor Networks. Sensors 11(7), 6533–6554 (2011)
6. Maynard, S.J.: Evolution and the Theory of Games. Cambridge University Press, Cambridge (1982)
7. Thomas, R.: Genetic Algorithm Learning and Evolutionary Games. Journal of Economic Dynamics & Control 25, 1019–1037 (2001)
8. Chen, S.J., Sun, Y.G., Wu, Z.G.: A Genetic Algorithm to Acquire the Nash Equilibrium. System Engineering 19(5), 67–70 (2001)
9. Daskalakis, C., Goldberg, P.W., Papadimitriou, C.H.: The complexity of computing Nash equilibrium. In: STOC 2006, pp. 71–78. ACM press, Seattle (2005)
10. Thomas, R.: Genetic algorithm learning and evolutionary games. Journal of Economic Dynamics & Control 25(6), 1019–1037 (2001)
11. Kan, Y., Wang, R.C.: Nash Equilibrium Based Task Scheduling Algorithm of Multi-schedulers in Grid Computing. Acta Electronica Sinica 37(2), 329–333 (2009)
12. Zhang, G.F., Jiang, J.G., Xia, N., Su, Z.P.: Solutions of complicated coalition generation based on discrete particle swarm optimization. Acta Electronica Sinica 35(2), 323–327 (2007)
13. Wu, Q., Rao, N.S., Barhen, J.: On computing mobile agent routes for data fusion in distributed sensor networks. IEEE Trans. on Knowledge and Data Engineering 16(6), 740–753 (2004)
14. Garey, M.R., Johnson, D.S.: "Strong" NP-Completeness Results: Motivation, Examples, and Implications. Journal of the Association for Computing Machinery 25(3), 499–508 (1978)
15. Mezura-Montes, E., Coello, C.A.C.: A simple multi-membered evolution strategy to save constrained optimization problems. IEEE Transactions on Evolutionary Computation 9(1), 1–17 (2005)

# An Efficient Lookup Service in DHT Based Communication System

Kai Shuang, Peng Zhang, and Sen Su

State Key Laboratory of Networking & Switching Technology
Beijing University of Posts & Telecommunications (BUPT)
Beijing, China
{shuangk,susen}@bupt.edu.cn, zhangppmmeer@163.com

**Abstract.** Telecom systems utilize the Distributed Hash Tables (DHTs) approach to build the network infrastructure for advantages of even distribution of workload, high scalability and cost-effectiveness. Although DHT is undoubtedly applicative in such architectures, some practical distinctions still should be considered to meet the performance requirements of telecom infrastructures. This paper focuses in two features of the distributed telecom system, so-called the real-time response and geographic partition, proposes a hierarchical DHT lookup service named Comb. Comb's overlay is organized as a two-layered architecture, workload is distributed evenly among nodes and most queries can be routed in no more than two hops. Comb performs effectively with low bandwidth consumption and satisfactory fault tolerance even in a continuously changing environment. Both theoretical analysis and experimental result demonstrate that the two-layered architecture of Comb is feasible and efficient. Comb improves the performances on routing delay and lookup failure rates with high scalability and availability.

**Keywords:** Distributed Communication System, Peer-to-Peer, Comb, DHT, Two-Hop.

## 1 Introduction

Distributed Hash Table (DHT) are widely applied in building large-scale self-organizing overlay networks [1], such as file-sharing, search engines and content distribution. Currently, both distributed IP Multimedia Subsystem and P2PSIP are proposed to adopt the structured P2P overlay in communication systems. A fundamental problem for a DHT lookup service is resources locating and routing. Overlay topology, routing path latency and maintenance cost are three elements that impact the efficiency of a DHT algorithm [1]. Designs of DHT algorithms vary largely, so far as we know, most proposed DHT algorithms vary routing tables' size from $O(\log N)$ to $O(N)$, with routing hops ranged from $O(\log N)$ to $O(1)$ [2]. Large routing tables are expensive in maintenance and hard to scale to large systems while long routing hops lead a long time routing delay. Trade-off should be made between routing table's size and routing hops in selection of a DHT algorithm.

J. Su et al. (Eds.): ICoC 2013, CCIS 401, pp. 74–84, 2013.

A communication system is used for real-time intercommunication, path latency will directly impact the quality of connections [3]. For this reason, real-time response is required for a distributed communication system and minimizing routing delay is a primary objective. Additionally, communication systems are deployed in accordance with the geographic session distribution pattern, the whole network shall be organized as a multilayer architecture with several regions. Therefore, a hierarchical overlay is necessary for the distributed communication system. Previous work proposes hierarchical P2P algorithms [4] where each hierarchy consists of super-nodes for upper hierarchy. Super-nodes take more responsibility acting as centralized index, makes it impractical for load-balance. The Comb protocol proposed in this article is purely peer-to-peer and protocols on each node are completely the same. The whole overlay is organized as a two-layered architecture, a Comb node maintains information about $O(\sqrt{N})$ other nodes for routing, resolves a lookup in no more than two hops. Mainly two features distinguish our design from many other P2P lookup protocols.

1. Comb is purely distributed. The Comb overlay is divided into several domains, two-layered architecture satisfies the requirement of geographic distribution pattern. Meanwhile, Comb abandons super-node, nodes in Comb overlay have no distinctions. This makes Comb a load-balanced network, avoids single point of failure and performance bottleneck. On the other hand, a purely peer-to-peer network is much better for scalability.

2. Comb is simple and stable. A Comb node requires about $O(\sqrt{N})$ size routing table for lookups resolve, but routing performance degrades gently when routing information is out of date. Comb guarantees correct routing (though slow) of lookups as long as one piece in routing table is correct. This is important for a distributed system to keep steady.

The rest of this paper is organized as follow: Section 2 compares Comb to relevant DHTs. Section 3 presents the system model. Section 4 is the base Comb protocol, and Section 5 evaluates Comb's performance through simulation and experiments. Finally, we summarize our contributions in Section 6.

## 2 Related Work

The first generation of DHT algorithms adopt a completely flat structure, the whole overlay is organized as a ring or other plain topology. Consistent hashing [5] is utilized to assign keys to nodes and resources. Generally, a DHT overlay consists of N nodes which share R resources (N << R), the key space is partitioned randomly by participating nodes, and each node is in charge of the resources belongs to its key space section. Designs of flat DHTs include Chord[6], CAN[7], Kademlia[8], Pastry[9] and Tapestry[10].

Flat DHTs have certain advantages, such as structural stability and workload balancing. On the other hand, they are incapable of achieving latency guarantees for queries and offering a hierarchical overlay network. That makes flat DHTs improper in to utilize in a distributed communication system. Hierarchical DHTs (HDHTs) [11] are the last generation of DHT designs, HDHT nodes are distributed into hierarchies;

each next hierarchy consists of super-nodes for upper hierarchy, leading a tree-like architecture. Distinguished from flat DHTs, Hierarchical DHT algorithms are able to guarantee path latency, for the last decade, a group of HDHT designs have been proposed: OneHop [12,13],Sandstone [14], D1HT [15], 1h-Calot, 2h-Calot[16].

However, two virtual nodes in different slices don't take geographic distribution and network connectivity into consideration. For large system deployed over the countrywide, it is difficult to keep nodes in system connected with all the nodes in two different slices at the same time, especially when the two slices have a long geographical distance. Moreover, two virtual nodes may bring twice as much as bandwidth consumption in joining, leaving procedures and routing table maintenance.

## 3 System Model

Comb is designed for the distributed communication system with two special features affect the design. Geographic Distribution Pattern: The structure of a communication system should be in accordance with the geographic pattern in practice, and interactions and network connectivity between host pairs are also related to this pattern. As a survey on MIIT[17], nearly 80% call sessions are between intra-province host pairs, while 20% call sessions between inter-province host pairs. Therefore, a hierarchical P2P lookup service with regionalism is essential. Real-time Response: Minimizing message delay is an important performance objective for a communication system, it is assumed that 20~50 milliseconds delay between any inter-province and less than 10 milliseconds delay between any intra-province host pairs for an IP based network [14], so less routing hops is critical for the system.

Figure 1 gives a software structure for Comb, it is consisted of four main components: Communication, Topology Routing, Data Storage and Application Layer. Intercommunication between hosts is implemented by the bottom layer communication

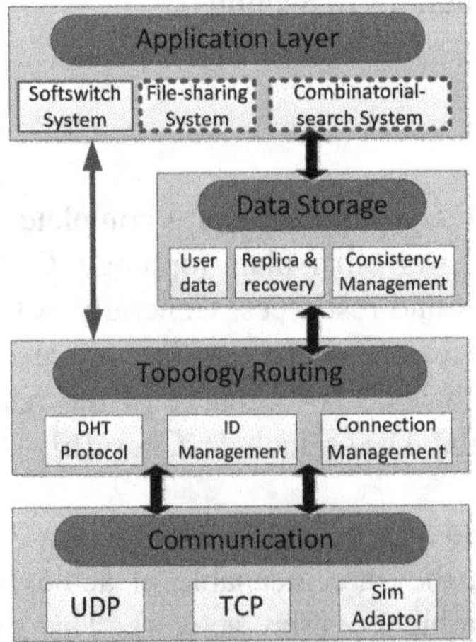


**Fig. 1.** Structure of an example comb-based distributed system

module, applications choose the transport layer protocol according to the scenarios. The topology routing module provides lookup service, finds the best suitable host for a given key, and also includes ID management and topology maintenance. Subscriber data such as storage, consistency verification are taken charge of by the data storage module. Application layer takes topology routing module and data storage module as substruction, specifies logical function of the system despite the underlying details. Modularized designs simplifies the system implementation.

In addition, a mathematical model is presented for system verification. Previous work parameterized the workload of a P2P system by a tuple $< n, f, l >$ [16], which means n nodes in the system with an average node lifetime l, each node process f lookups per second on average. Corresponding to Comb's topology, our work splits f to fl and fg representing the average lookup times of intra-domain and inter-domain per second. Suppose the whole overlay is divided into $k$ domains, then each domain has n/k nodes, in a system with a node lifetime l, on average n/(kl) nodes join and leave each second in one domain. When a node joins or leaves, at least one message will be sent to all its neighbors for informing, Comb maintenances all nodes within the domain as its neighbors, i.e., at least n/k messages are sent during the joining or leaving procedure. Assuming that all messages get unit size s and each request is acknowledged by a response, then the traffic for nodes arrivals and departures B1 in one domain is:

$$B_1 = (1+1)s \bullet (\frac{n}{k} \times \frac{n}{kl} + \frac{n}{k} \times \frac{n}{kl}) \tag{1}$$

Each node process $f_l$ intra-domain lookups with one hop and $f_g$ inter-domain lookups with two hops per second, resulting in traffic for lookups with one domain $B_2$ is:

$$B_2 = (1+1)s \bullet (\frac{n}{k} f_l + 2\frac{n}{k} f_g) \tag{2}$$

As a result, without regard to the inter-domain maintenance and keep-alive traffic, the minimum traffic demand in Comb $B_3$ is:

$$B_{\min} = (B_1 + B_2) \bullet k = (\frac{4sn^2}{k^2 l} + \frac{2snf_l}{k} + \frac{4snf_g}{k}) \bullet k = \frac{4sn^2}{kl} + 2snf_l + 4snf_g \tag{3}$$

## 4 The Base Protocol

Comb provides protocol for key based resources location, how nodes join and leave the system and how to recover from the failures. This section gives a simplified version of description of the Comb protocol.

### 4.1 Overview

As in Figure 2, Comb organizes all the nodes in a circular ring like Chord [6].

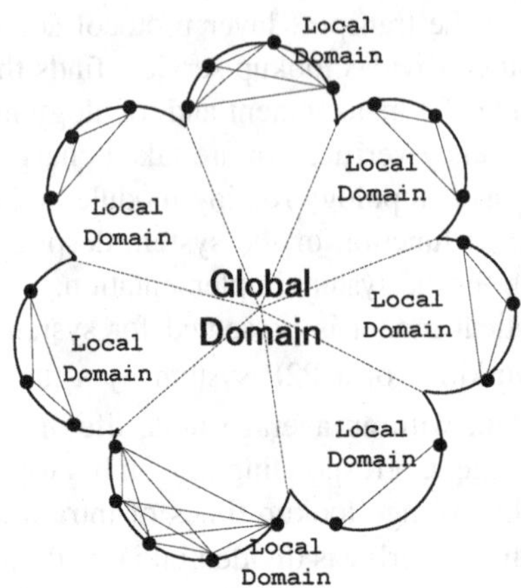


**Fig. 2.** Comb overlay consists of two domains: global domain and local domain

We refer to a node's counter-clockwise neighboring node as its predecessor and clockwise node as successor. Comb divide the whole overlay into several regions named Domain, and runs a one-hop DHT protocol inside each Domain. Correspondingly, overlay of Comb is deployed as a two-layered structure: global layer (correspond to countrywide) map the whole ring and local layer (correspond to a province or a city) map the domain. Table 1 gives an example of the routing tables: a Local Table contains complete information of nodes within domain and a Global Table maintains at least one node's information for each outer domain. To route a message between two different domains, an origin tries to find a node N in destination domain from global table and forwards the message, N looks up its local table and sends the message to the destination node.

**Table 1.** an example of local table and global table

| Node ID | URI | IP Address |
|---|---|---|
| 00100001 | alice@comb.com | xx.xx.xx.xx |
| 00001010 | bob@comb.com | xx.xx.xx.xx |
| 00001000 | tom@comb.com | xx.xx.xx.xx |

Local Table

| Domain | Node ID | URI | IP Address |
|---|---|---|---|
| 01 | 01000011 | a@comb.com | xx.xx.xx.xx |
| 10 | 10000100 | b@comb.com | xx.xx.xx.xx |
| 11 | 11000101 | c@comb.com | xx.xx.xx.xx |

Global Table

### 4.2 Identifier

In Comb, the whole overlay is divided into several domains, organized as a two-layered architecture. Accordingly, the identifier space is separated into two parts: domain ID and host ID as depicted in Figure 3.

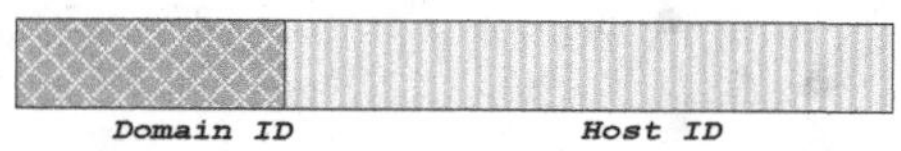


**Fig. 3.** Comb identifier consists of two parts: domain id and host id

When a node joins into the Comb system, it chooses the nearest domain and takes the domain ID as the identifier prefix, then applies consistent hashing to its IP address or URI as the identifier postfix. This assignment also makes it possible to determine the geographic domain of any nodes by its ID.

### 4.3 Node Joins and Leaves

Assume that a new joined node named $JP$ (Joined Peer) knows about at least one node named $BP$ (Bootstrap Peer) already in the system through some out-of-band methods [2], $BP$ is in the nearest domain from $JP$. $JP$ copies $BP$'s local table and global table in order to build routing tables itself. For the local table, a copy from $BP$ is enough, but for the global table, ID Transformation is necessary, though it will function well with a complete copy from $BP$ logically.

**ID Transformation:**

Suppose $BP$ get its identifier $ID_{BP} = ID_{domain}^{BP} + ID_{host}^{AP}$, and $JP$'s identifier $ID_{JP} = ID_{domain}^{JP} + ID_{host}^{JP}$, $ID_{domain}^{BP} = ID_{domain}^{JP}$. define $offset(BP, JP) = ID_{host}^{BP} - ID_{host}^{JP}$, for each node item in $BP$'s global Table $ID_N$, $JP$ builds a new item $ID_M = ID_{domain}^{N} + |ID_{host}^{N} - offset(BP, JP)|$, whose address is fetched through $AP$.

ID transformation makes global table varies from node to node within a domain, requests from domain A to domain B are forwarded by different nodes in domain B, resulting in a network with load balance and scalability. For user information security and system robust, communication operators always choose nodes only when they are deployed as $BP$ instead of all nodes in overlay.

Once $JP$ built its routing tables, it need inform other nodes in domain of its arrival. A multicast tree [15] rooted at $JP$ for disseminating membership changes can be applied: For a N nodes domain, update messages are propagated to the $2^{TTL}$th ($\mathrm{TTL} = 0, \ldots, \log_2 N$) successors of $JP$, each message consists of $JP$'s identifier and value of TTL. Notified successors continue with message propagating to their $2^i$th ($\mathrm{i} = 0, \ldots, \mathrm{TTL}-1$) successors and minus TTL by 1 until TTL = 0. An example of a 8 nodes domain is shown in Figure 4.

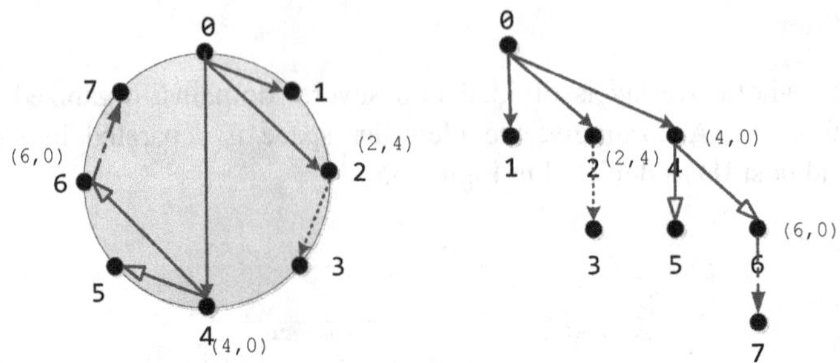


**Fig. 4.** An example of the multicast tree for disseminating membership changes

The multicast tree disseminates messages all over the domain in collaboration, workload are distributed to nodes. However, the workload in disseminating of each node varies greatly, nodes closer to the tree root get more messages to cast [16], sometimes exceeds nodes' bandwidth capacity. We propose another multicast tree for disseminating called the binary-multicast tree for the structure is a binary tree.

A binary-multicast tree is also rooted at $JP$ , among N nodes in its local table, $JP$ selects its immediate successor and the $2^K th$($\mathrm{K} = \log_2 N/2$ )successor as its children (define as $C_1$ and $C_2$) in the tree, and asks them to cover the range $(2, 2^K - 1)$ and $(2^K + 1, N)$, respectively. Node $C_1$ and $C_2$ use a similar process to expand the tree by adding their immediate successor and the $2^{K-1}th$ successor as children, and so forth. The process stops when there is no node in the range. Figure 5 gives a brief example of binary-multicast tree, Node 0 acts as the root of the tree and selects 1 and 4 as its children, each child of node 0 is responsible for a covering range, and they also build their own tree to expand the binary-multicast tree.

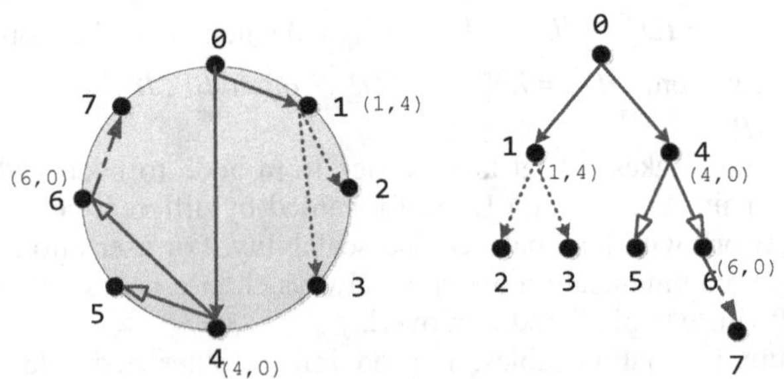


**Fig. 5.** Binary-multicast tree for disseminating membership changes

The binary-multicast tree disseminates messages with more reasonable and balanced bandwidth demands, nodes in a binary-multicast tree propagate update messages to only 2 other nodes at most (see figure 5), the tree is implicitly embedded in the overlay, there is no message to construct the trees before use and no message to tear down the trees after use. However, inaccurate routing tables are acceptable in messages dissemination, suppose node N that should be selected as a child of Node P had not been selected, in the worst case, N will receive the notification from its predecessor as the range narrows. We can prove that binary-multicast tree disseminate messages in the same time complexity with a multicast tree of $O(\log_2 N)$.

When a node leaves, it notifies its predecessor and successor, they (or one of them) propagates this change to all nodes over the domain using a process similar to a node's arrival.

### 4.4 Routing Tables Maintenance

Only nodes in local table are notified when a node leaves, in a purely distributed overlay of Comb, this node is probably also in global tables of other nodes from outer domains. To this end, a heartbeat with nodes in global table to keep alive is necessary. Every $t_g$ seconds afterwards, a heartbeat message is sent to each node item in global table to keep-alive, if a heartbeat is not acknowledged until time fires, we treat it as a departed node, and do ID transformation to find a new substitute item through BP or any other nodes as in node join.

For each node K with an ID of $ID_k$ in Node N's global table, heartbeats can carry the destination identifier of $ID_{dest} = ID^k_{host} + ID^N_{domain}$, when node K receives the heartbeats and find it isn't responsible for $ID_{dest}$, a redirection should be sent back to node K with the new substitute node responsible for $ID_{dest}$.

The period $t_g$ is chosen such that 80% nodes lives longer than $t_g$ seconds, assume node lifetime $t$ follows an exponential distribution $f(t) = \lambda e^{-\lambda t} (t > 0)$, then:

$$\int_{t_g}^{+\infty} f(t)dt = 0.8 \;\Rightarrow\; t_g = -\frac{\ln(0.8)}{\lambda} \tag{4}$$

The expectation of $t$ is:

$$E[t] = \frac{1}{\lambda} = l \text{ ,so we have } \; t_g \approx 0.2l \tag{5}$$

Another situation need to be taken into account is that not all nodes leave the system normally; some nodes may fail without any notifications. Hence, a mechanism to handle failed nodes is needed. Periodically, a node sends an announcement to its immediate predecessor to state its existence, a node also sets timer for its successor's announcement.

If an announcement is received from node N which is already in local table by node P , P would reset the timer for the next announcement. If node $N$ is not in the local table of P or P's timer for N is fired, then P adds/deletes N to/from local table, and broadcast the membership change to all the nodes in domain through a binary-multicast tree.

# 5 Simulation and Experimental Results

In order to evaluate the function and performance of Comb, we implemented a simulator in C++. The simulator can simulate Comb system with up to 8,000 nodes.

**Table 2.** Parameters and Settings of the simulation

| | Parameter | Value |
|---|---|---|
| N | Total number of peers in the network | 1000, 2000, 4000, 8000 |
| D | Total number of Domains | 20, 40, 80 |
| L | Node's lifetime | 90s, 120s, 180s |
| F | Frequency of lookup | 1, 2, 3 |

The simulation is configured by parameters N, D, L and F. When simulator starts up, the Comb system contains N nodes with settled routing tables distributed in D domains averagely, nodes join and leave the system with the lifetime L, and send out lookup messages by every F seconds. The simulator stops when 10N nodes joined in the system accumulatively. Parameters are configured as the table 2.

We evaluate Comb's routing efficiency by figuring out the average routing hops and failed rate per lookup. Figure 6 plots the average number of routing hops per lookup when varying the system size and numbers of domains. The Figure shows that the average routing hops are always below 2 in Comb, and the number increases alone with both the system size and domains number.

Failed lookups should also be considered for routing efficiency. In Comb simulator, messages record every hop it routed through, a lookup (and also other messages) was regarded as a failed message when it is forwarded by more than 10 peers, and would be discarded by the simulator. Figure 7 reports the failed rate of lookups in a variety of conditions, we see that Comb system has a satisfied failed rate, in the experiment environment, failed rates are below 0.5% in all conditions.

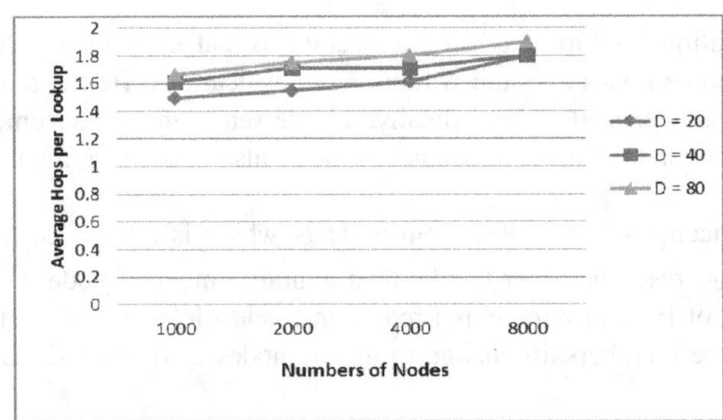


**Fig. 6.** Routing hops per lookup varying nodes' number and domains' number

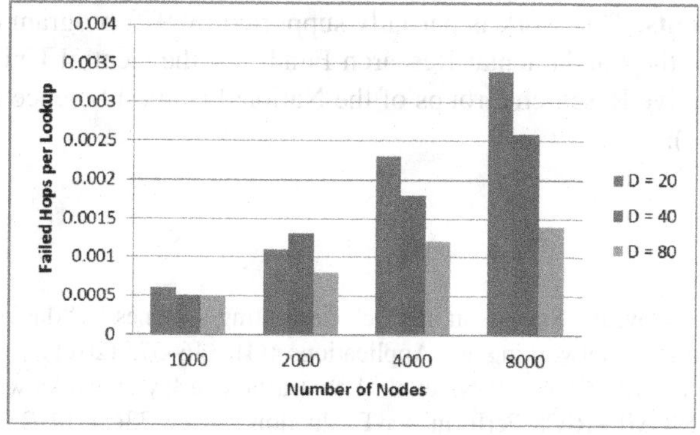


**Fig. 7.** Failed rates per lookup varying nodes' number and domains' number

As well as average routing hops, failed lookup rate increased along with the system size, this is also because more nodes leaving and joining brings about more time delay to keep routing tables up to date, inaccurate routing tables increase the failed probability of failure. On the other hand, small domains number also results in a high failed rate, this is due to few domains generates a big domain size, Comb runs a one-hop protocol within the domain, failed rate increased along with the domain size because of the time delay for routing tables up to date as mentioned before. Therefore, tradeoffs should be made between average routing hops and failed lookup rate on the selection of domains number, generally, the optimal number for minimum traffic we calculated in section 4 is a good choice. Figure 6 and Figure 7 demonstrate that Comb has an excellent performance in routing efficiency.

## 6 Conclusions

This paper presents Comb, a two-hop DHT lookup algorithm for P2P overlay and evaluates Comb by analysis and experiments. Comb algorithm aims at the features of the distributed communication system: real-time response and geographic partition, constructs the whole overlay a two-layered architecture. Nodes in Comb system maintain two routing tables: local table and global table, messages are routed intra-domain and inter-domains.

Compared with other DHT lookup algorithms, the main contributions of Comb are: a non-hierarchical two-layer DHT architecture that avoids unbalanced workload and bottlenecks; a two-hop routing mechanism that routes most lookups in no more than two hops to satisfy the real-time response requirement; a domain-partition mechanism that adapts the geographic distribution pattern of distributed communication system; an improved message dissemination mechanism--binary-multicast tree that balances the workload in disseminating of each node and an abstract model for network traffic calculation.

**Acknowledgements.** This work is partially supported by 973 program of China (No. 2009CB320504), the Fundamental Research Funds for the Central Universities(2013 RC1102), Innovative Research Groups of the National Natural Science Foundation of China (61121061).

## References

1. Korzun, D., Gurtov, A.: Survey on hierarchical routing schemes in "flat" distributed hash tables. Peer-to-Peer Networking and Applications 4(4), 346–375 (2011)
2. Tang, C., Buco, M.J., Chang, R.N., et al.: Low traffic overlay networks with large routing tables. ACM SIGMETRICS Performance Evaluation Review 33(1), 14–25 (2005)
3. Lindman, P., Thorsell, L.: Applying distributed power modules in telecom systems. IEEE Transactions on Power Electronics 11(2), 365–373 (1996)
4. Garces-Erice, L., Biersack, E.W., Ross, K.W., et al.: Hierarchical peer-to-peer systems. Parallel Processing Letters 13(4), 643–657 (2003)
5. Karger, D., Lehman, E., Leighton, T., et al.: Consistent hashing and random trees: Distributed caching protocols for relieving hot spots on the World Wide Web. In: Proceedings of the Twenty-Ninth Annual ACM Symposium on Theory of Computing, pp. 654–663. ACM (1997)
6. Stoica, I., Morris, R., Karger, D., et al.: Chord: A scalable peer-to-peer lookup service for internet applications. ACM SIGCOMM Computer Communication Review 31(4), 149–160 (2001)
7. Ratnasamy, S., Francis, P., Handley, M., et al.: A Scalable Content-Addressable Network (2001)
8. Maymounkov, P., Mazières, D.: Kademlia: A peer-to-peer information system based on the xor metric. In: Druschel, P., Kaashoek, F., Rowstron, A. (eds.) IPTPS 2002. LNCS, vol. 2429, pp. 53–65. Springer, Heidelberg (2002)
9. Rowstron, A., Druschel, P.: Pastry: Scalable, decentralized object location, and routing for large-scale peer-to-peer systems. In: Guerraoui, R. (ed.) Middleware 2001. LNCS, vol. 2218, pp. 329–350. Springer, Heidelberg (2001)
10. Zhao, B.Y., Huang, L., Stribling, J., et al.: Tapestry: A resilient global-scale overlay for service deployment. IEEE Journal on Selected Areas in Communications 22(1), 41–53 (2004)
11. Korzun, D., Gurtov, A.: Hierarchical architectures in structured peer-to-peer overlay networks. Peer-to-Peer Networking and Applications, 1–37 (2013)
12. Fonseca, P., Rodrigues, R., Gupta, A., et al.: Full-information lookups for peer-to-peer overlays. IEEE Transactions on Parallel and Distributed Systems 20(9), 1339–1351 (2009)
13. Gupta, A., Liskov, B., Rodrigues, R.: Efficient routing for peer-to-peer overlays. In: First Symp. on Networked Systems Design and Implementation (NSDI), pp. 113–126 (2004)
14. Shi, G., Chen, J., Gong, H., et al.: Sandstone: A dht based carrier grade distributed storage system. In: IEEE International Conference on Parallel Processing, ICPP 2009, pp. 420–428 (2009)
15. Monnerat, L.R., Amorim, C.L.: D1HT: a distributed one hop hash table. In: IEEE 20th International Parallel and Distributed Processing Symposium, IPDPS 2006, p. 10 (2006)
16. Tang, C., Buco, M.J., Chang, R.N., et al.: Low traffic overlay networks with large routing tables. ACM SIGMETRICS Performance Evaluation Review 33(1), 14–25 (2005)
17. MIIT 2012, http://www.miit.gov.cn

# An Improved Cooperative Model of P2P and ISP

Ying Liu[1,3], Shenglin Zhang[1,3], and Hongying Liu[2]

[1] Institute for Network Sciences and Cyberspace
Tsinghua University, Beijing 100084, China
[2] School of Mathematics and Systems Science
Beihang University, Beijing 100191, China
[3] Tsinghua National Laboratory for Information Science and Technology
Tsinghua University, Beijing 100084, China
liuying@cernet.edu.cn, slzhangsd@gmail.com, liuhongying@buaa.edu.cn

**Abstract.** P4P (Provider Portal for Applications) is a model aiming to incorporate P2P with ISP and improve the performance of both the ISP and the P2P applications. In this study, we analyze the relationship between the link traffic and the P-distance, which is the core interface of P4P, and illustrate the disadvantage of P4P in dealing with network topology with bottleneck links. Further, with *link utility function* as the optimization objective, we propose an improved model–*Improved-P4P*, making the traffic produced by P2P applications more homogeneous, which can reduce the peak link utilization and protect bottleneck links, and then improve both the network efficiency and the P2P performance. We have built a simulation platform based on BitTorrent and conducted extensive simulations. These simulations demonstrate that *Improved-P4P* achieves a lower cost for ISPs and a better performance for P2P applications than native P2P. Moreover, compared with P4P, *Improved-P4P* reduces traffic on bottleneck links without compromising on the performance of the P2P applications. We believe that relieving of pressure on bottleneck links hold great significance especially in extreme settings. *Improved-P4P* performs steadily in different swarm sizes, proving that it is scalable and easy to deploy.

**Keywords:** Subgradient Method, P2P, Traffic Engineering, Cooperative Model, Dual Function.

## 1 Introduction

### 1.1 Background

The P2P (peer-to-peer) concept has fundamental advantages over the traditional C/S (Client/Server) model and the fixed infrastructure content distribution networks because of its excellent robustness and scalability, and plays an important role in modern networks. Some researches have found that more than 50% of the network traffic is introduced by P2P [1,2], and the massive traffic generated by

J. Su et al. (Eds.): ICoC 2013, CCIS 401, pp. 85–96, 2013.

P2P brings significant challenges in traffic engineering for ISP (Internet Service Provider)[3].

Because P2P applications are ignorant of the underlying network topology, most P2P applications apply application-level routing that is based only on the overlay network metrics [5]. Moreover, some P2P applications select the source of their downloading randomly, which may lead a P2P user in New York City to download from a user in Los Angeles, while this kind of data is available in New York City or in Washington DC. This kind of long-distance downloading may decrease the network efficiency and the performance of the P2P applications concurrently. P2P applications can avoid this by selecting neighbors with a lower delay or less router hops, but purely selecting neighbors with a low delay or less router hops may cause a Comcast user to select an AT&T user as its neighbor. This cross-ISP neighboring will generate unnecessary interdomain traffic, thereby significantly increasing the operational costs of ISPs. In conclusion, current P2P applications have the following problems:

(1) A P2P system may cause the dispersion of network traffic and make the traffic to unnecessarily flow through multiple intra-domain links. By conducting practical tests, [6] found that every bit of P2P traffic in Verizon needs 5.5 hops when passing through 1000 miles on average, and this average number of hops can be reduced to 0.89 without compromising the P2P application's performance.

(2) A P2P system may generate massive inter-domain traffic or cause massive traffic that when produced by multiple ISPs pass through a specific network [9]. In [8], Karagiannis studied the BitTorrent performance in a college network. He found that this low-efficiency inter-domain traffic may cause significant financial losses for ISPs. Even in the case of the top-level ISP (tier-1 ISPs who do not pay other ISPs), the inter-domain traffic caused by a P2P system can cause the traffic between these tier-1 ISPs to lose balance and then violate the P2P protocol.

However, a one-sided strategy of P2P and ISP is not ideal. As a result, a cooperative model of P2P and ISP should be built, making both sides exchange information and control the P2P traffic cooperatively, and thereby improving the network efficiency and the P2P performance simultaneously.

### 1.2 Related Works

[4] studied the advantages and disadvantages of P2P, and proposed a middle server called "*oracle*", by which ISPs can provide a neighbor selection policy for P2P users. After a peer sends its list of potential neighbors to "*oracle*", "*oracle*" will sort all the possible neighbors according to certain criteria, such as the nearest principle and the link bandwidth. The sorted neighbor list will guide peers to select neighbors and improve the P2P performance. At the same time, the ISPs can effectively manage massive the P2P traffic with this mechanism, assuring that the traffic does not pass across them and that it is led to the right path. With the abovementioned mechanism, ISPs can provide a better network service for their users.

[7] developed a cooperative model of CP (" *Content Provider*") and ISP, which aimed at co-optimization by sharing control between the ISP and the CP. This study analyzed the optimality of this model by using the game theory and compared this model with the traditional model by means of simulations. The simulation results showed the advantages of the sharing model under circumstances with different congestion levels, and pointed that under some conditions, if the complete network information is shared without any co-optimization control, the co-benefits of the CP and the ISP may be lower than before the sharing of the complete network information.

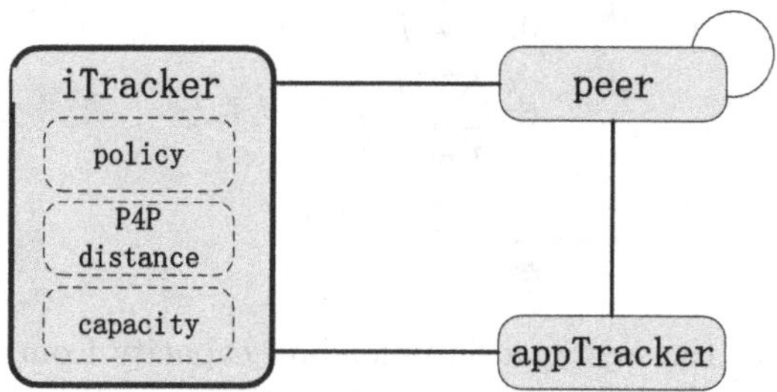


**Fig. 1.** The interactive between iTracker and P2P

## 2 Improved Cooperative Model and Theoretical Analysis

### 2.1 P4P

In the P4P model, each ISP maintains an iTracker for its network, and the iTracker has multiple interfaces for ISPs to communicate with P2P applications with respect to the following: (a) static network policy, (b) P-distance mirroring network policy and status, and (c) network capacity. The main interfaces are shown in Figure 1, where the P-distance interface is the core of P4P. Through the P-distance, an ISP can communicate to the P2P applications the current cost of its intradomain and inter-domain links. The P-distance reflects a network's preference and status with respect to the application's cost. The main algorithm of P-distance is the min-max link utilization with a distributed algorithm as follows:

$$\min_{\forall k: t^k \in T^k} \max_{e \in E} \left(b_e + \sum_k \sum_i \sum_j t_{ij}^k I_e(i,j)\right)/c_e, \tag{1}$$

where $b_e$is the background traffic (i.e. traffic that P4P can't control), $c_e$ is the capacity of link $e$, $I_e(i,j)$ is the indicator link $e$ on the route from PID$-i$ to PID$-j$, and $T^k$ denotes the set of all feasible traffic solutions on the basis of the demand and the property of the P2P applications session $k$. $t^k = (t_{ij}^k)$, where $t_{ij}^k$ denotes the traffic from PID$-i$ to PID$-j$ in the P2P session $k$.

The above mentioned PID (opaque ID) is a virtual network point. There are many types of PIDs, one of which is an aggregation point, i.e. a PID represents a set of points. In fact, a PID can also represent PoP, or a set of points with the same congestion state. In this study, each PID represents an aggregation point.

In particular, $T^k$ is made up of $t^k$ that satisfy the constraint condition as follows,

$$\sum_{j:j\neq i} t_{ij}^k \leq u_i^k, \forall i, \tag{2a}$$

$$\sum_{j:j\neq i} t_{ji}^k \leq d_i^k, \forall i, \tag{2b}$$

$$t_{ij}^k \geq 0, \forall i \neq j, \tag{2c}$$

$$t_{ij}^k \geq \underline{\rho}_{ij}^k \sum_{j'\neq i} t_{ij'}^k, \forall i, \quad j \neq i, \tag{2d}$$

$$\sum_i \sum_{j\neq i} t_{ij}^k \geq \beta * OPT, \tag{2e}$$

where $u_i^k$ denotes the aggregation uploading capacity from PID$-i$ to other PIDs in session $k$, and $d_i^k$ denotes the aggregation downloading capacity from other PIDs to PID$-i$ in session $k$. $\underline{\rho}_{ij}^k$ is the lower bound on the percentage of traffic from PID$-i$ to PID$-j$ among all the traffic from PID$-i$ to other PIDs. Note that $0 < \underline{\rho}_{ij}^k < 1$ and $\sum_{j\neq i} \underline{\rho}_{ij}^k < 1, \forall i$. $\beta$ is the efficient factor that can be configured particularly to P2P applications in engineering. The $OPT$ in (2e) is the lower bound of P2P applications performance. Because the cooperation of the ISP and the P2P application aims at improving the performance of both sides, the cooperation should not compromise the performance of P2P applications. Hence, in general, $OPT$ can be set as the optimal value in the independent optimization of P2P applications . Typically, it can be set as follows:

$$OPT = \mathbf{maximize}_{t^k \in T^k} \sum_i \sum_{j\neq i} t_{ij}^k, \tag{3}$$

i.e. P2P aims at matching downloading and uploading.

Suppose that $t_e^k = \sum_i \sum_j t_{ij}^k I_e(i,j)$, i.e. the total traffic produced by P2P in link $e$, then (1) equals to:

$$\mathbf{minimize}_{\alpha, t^k \in T^k, \forall k} \qquad \alpha \tag{4a}$$

$$\mathbf{subject\ \ to} \qquad b_e + \sum_k t_e^k \leq \alpha c_e, \forall e \in E, \tag{4b}$$

The Lagrange dual function of (4a) is as follows:

$$D(p) = \min_{\alpha, \forall t^k \in T^k, k} \sum_e p_e(b_e + \sum_k t_e^k) + (\sum_e p_e c_e - 1)\alpha.$$

To make $D(p)$ finite, the coefficient of $\alpha$ should be zero. i.e.

$$\sum_e p_e c_e = 1.$$

Then

$$D(p) = \sum_e p_e b_e + \sum_k \min_{t^k \in T^k} \sum_e p_e t_e^k. \tag{5}$$

Its dual problem is

$$\mathbf{maximize}_{p \geq 0} \ D(p) \quad \text{subject to} \sum_e p_e c_e = 1. \tag{6}$$

This dual problem can be resolved into independent sub-problems on different sessions of applications with a distributed algorithm,

$$\mathbf{minimize}_{t^k \in T^k} \qquad \sum_i \sum_{j \neq i} p_{ij} t_{ij}^k, \tag{7}$$

The aforementioned solution is the interactive optimization algorithm between ISP and a P2P application, i.e. the P2P application solves the subproblem (7) independently and delivers the optimal result $\bar{t}^k$ to iTracker, after which iTracker solves the main problem (6) to update $p_e$.

**Assumption A**In the following analysis, we suppose that there exists $\tilde{t}^k \in \tilde{T}^k$ that makes $b_e + \sum_k \tilde{t}_e^k < c_e, \forall e \in E$, i.e. there exists feasible flow solution $\tilde{t}^k$ that makes the restraint on the link capacity strictly feasible.

### 2.2 Properties of P-Distance in P4P

**Theorem 1.** *Suppose that $\{\tilde{t}_e^k\}$ is the solution to* (4)*, and $\{\tilde{p}_e\}$ is the solution to* (6)*. Then there exists at least one link e whose link utilization is maximal and its corresponding $\tilde{p}_e > 0$. The $\tilde{p}_e$ whose corresponding links utilization doesn't achieve maximum is 0.*

**Proof:** (4) is an instance of convex programming, and according to assumption A, we know that the Slater constraint specification is true; hence, the strong dual theory is true. As a result, the solution of (4) and of its dual problem (6) satisfy the following:

$$b_e + \sum_k \tilde{t}_e^k \leq \tilde{\alpha} c_e, \forall e \in E \tag{8a}$$

$$1 - \sum_e \tilde{p}_e c_e = 0 \tag{8b}$$

$$\tilde{p}_e \geq 0, \forall e \in E \tag{8c}$$

$$\tilde{p}_e (b_e + \sum_k \tilde{t}_e^k - \tilde{\alpha} c_e) = 0, \forall e \in E \tag{8d}$$

where (8a) is the original feasible condition, (8b) and (8c) are the dual feasible conditions, and (8d) is the complementarity condition. Further, because of the optimization of (4)

$$\tilde{\alpha} = \max_{e \in E}(b_e + \sum_k \tilde{t_e^k})/c_e,$$

where $\tilde{t_e^k}$ is the solution of (3). Based on (8d), we know that all $\tilde{p}_e$s whose corresponding links do not achieve the maximum utilization equal to 0, and $\tilde{p}_e$s whose corresponding links achieve the maximum are equal to or greater than 0. Moreover, by (8b), we know that there exists at least one $\tilde{p}_e$ that doesn't equal to 0. ■

As we see in the above theorems, all link prices of links that do not achieve the most congested state are equal to 0, i.e., for a flow, the link price of each non-most-congested link is equal to that of another such link. This property of the multiplier makes MLU invalid when dealing with networks with bottleneck links.

In Figure 2, suppose that the capacity of each link is 1, the traffic demand between node 1 and node 3 is 1, and the traffic demand between node 3 and node 4 is 0.9. If we set MLU as the optimization objective of the ISP, the traffic on link (1, 3) will be 0.9 and the traffic on link (1, 2) will be 0.1. Now, there are two bottleneck links in the network, i.e. link (1, 3) and link (3, 4), which lead to the situation that of the two links between node 1 and node 3, one is very congested and the other is free.

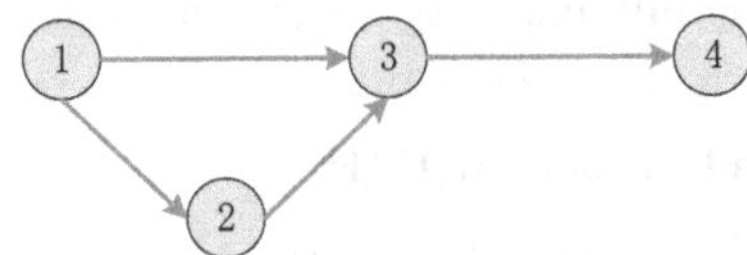


**Fig. 2.** An Example of Network with Bottleneck Links

### 2.3 Improved Cooperation Algorithm

We introduce a *link utility function* as the ISP optimization objective and verify that the new objective can better utilize the network resources by carrying out a theoretical analysis and experimental simulations. In this section, we propose a cooperative algorithm of ISP and P2P with a *link utility function* as the ISP optimization objective, and analyze some issues with this objective.

We follow the methods introduced in congestion control[11], and make the *link utility function* the ISP optimization objective. Consider that

$$\textbf{maximize}_{\{s_e\}, t^k \in T^k, \forall k} \quad \sum_e v_\beta(s_e) \tag{9a}$$

$$\textbf{subject to} \quad s_e \leq c_e - \sum_k t_e^k - b_e, \forall e \in E, \tag{9b}$$

where $s_e$ is the free link capacity of link $e$ and $v_\beta(s_e)$ is an increasing concave function. In this paper, we adopt the form as stated in [11].

$$v_\beta(s_e) = \begin{cases} \log(s_e), & \beta = 1 \\ \frac{s_e^{1-\beta}}{1-\beta}, & \beta \neq 1. \end{cases}$$

The Lagrange dual function of (9) is as follows:

$$\begin{aligned} D(p) = & \max_{\{s_e\},t^k \in T^k, \forall k} \sum_e \Big( v_\beta(s_e) \\ & - \sum_e p_e \Big( s_e - c_e + \sum_k t_e^k + b_e \Big)\Big) \\ = & \max_{s_e} \sum_e (v_\beta(s_e) - p_e s_e) \\ & + \sum_k \min_{t^k \in T^k} \sum_e p_e t_e^k + \sum_e p_e(c_e - b_e). \end{aligned} \tag{10}$$

The dual problem of (9) is as follows:

$$\min_{p \geq 0} D(p). \tag{11}$$

Because $D(p)$ is not differentiable and (11) cannot be solved with the gradient method directly, we solve the problem by using the subgradient method. We can obtain the subgradient of $D(p)$ from [10],

$$\zeta_e = c_e - b_e - \tilde{s}_e - \sum_k \tilde{t}_e^k, \forall e \in E,$$

where $\tilde{s}_e$, $\{\tilde{t}_e^k\}$ is the solution of

$$\textbf{maximize}_{c_e - b_e \geq s_e > 0} \big( v_\beta(s_e) - p_e s_e \big), \forall e \in E \tag{12}$$

and

$$\textbf{minimize}_{t^k \in T^k} \quad \sum_e p_e t_e^k, \forall k. \tag{13}$$

On the basis of the subgradient projection method, $p_e$ can be updated as follows,

$$p_e(\tau + 1) = \begin{cases} p_e(\tau) - \mu(\tau)\zeta_e(\tau), & p_e(\tau) > \mu(\tau)\zeta_e(\tau) \\ 0, & p_e(\tau) \leq \mu(\tau)\zeta_e(\tau) \end{cases}$$

where $\zeta_e$ is the subgradient and $\mu(\tau)$ is the step parameter. Theoretically, the step parameter $\mu(\tau)$ is of vital importance to the convergence of this algorithm. However, practically, owing to the continuous evolving of the network and the P2P applications, we can set the step parameter as a constant value.

After solving (11) by using the subgradient method, we obtain the distributed algorithm for solving (9), which is the interactive optimization algorithm of the

ISP and the P2P application. In other words, P2P applications and ISPs can solve the subproblem (13) and (12) independently at first and then transfer the optimal solution $\tilde{t}^k$ and $\tilde{s}_e$ to iTracker. In the next moment, iTracker will update $p_e$ by solving (11).

With respect to $v_\beta(s_e) = \log(s_e)$, we can express the explicit solution of (12) and the engineering significance of its dual variable as follows:

**Theorem 2.** *When $\beta = 1$, the subproblem (12) has the explicit optimization*

$$\tilde{s}_e = \begin{cases} \frac{1}{p_e}, & p_e \geq \frac{1}{c_e - b_e}, \\ c_e - b_e, & 0 \leq p_e < \frac{1}{c_e - b_e}. \end{cases}$$

**Theorem 3.** *Suppose that $\{\tilde{t}_e^k\}$ is the solution of (9) and $\{\tilde{p}_e\}$ is the solution of the dual problem (11). Then $\forall e \in E$, and when $\tilde{s}_e = c_e - b_e$,*

$$\tilde{p}_e \in [0, \frac{1}{c_e - b_e});$$

*when $\tilde{s}_e < c_e - b_e$,*

$$\tilde{p}_e = \frac{1}{c_e - \sum_k \tilde{t}_e^k - b_e}.$$

As we see from theorem 3, to any link $e$, the larger its free link capacity is, the lower its link price ($\tilde{p}_e$); the smaller its free link capacity is, the higher its link price ($\tilde{p}_e$). This makes the ISPs to control traffic on the non-most-congested links more efficiently when dealing with networks with bottleneck links.

## 3 Simulation Methodology

We have built a discrete-event package for simulation. We have followed the method de-scribed in [12] and performed the simulations by implementing the native BitTorrent protocol. We have also calculated the traffic on every link in order to estimate the link utilization. Our simulation includes keeping statistics of the traffic on bottleneck links, interdomain links, and intradomain links in P2P, P4P, and *Improved-P4P*. Further, we have studied the benefits of P2P applications in P4P and *Improved-P4P* by varying the swarm size.

### 3.1 Assumptions

- We have ignored the propagation delay because the propagation delay relates only to small control packets. We believe that this simplification has very little impact on the conclusion because of the following:
  1. The downloading time depends on the transmission time of the packets.
  2. In practice, the pipelined processing mechanism of BitTorrent reduces most of the propagation delay of the packets.
- We have followed the method proposed in [13] and assumed that all TCP sessions share the link's capacity equally in the stable state.
- After finishing downloading, all peers leave the network immediately.

### 3.2 Detailed Parameters

1. Bandwidth between PIDs: 100MBps (bidirection).
2. Size of block: 256 KB.
3. Number of seeds: 1
4. Upstream access link capacity of a seed: 5 MBps.
5. Upstream access link capacity of peers: uniform distribution between 550 KBps to 1000 KBps.
6. Downstream access link capacity of peers: twice the upstream capacity.

**Table 1.** network topology

| Network | Region | Aggregation level | ♯Nodes | ♯Links |
|---|---|---|---|---|
| Abilene | US | PoP | 11 | 28 |

We use PoP-level topologies of Abilene.Table 1 the detailed parameters of Abilene. Notice that the capacity of each link in Abilene is 10 Gbps on both directions.

### 3.3 Neighbor Selection Policy

P4P and *Improved-P4P* improve the neighbor selection policy with the interaction of the ISP and the P2P application. For a peer,

1. Neighbor selection within PID: appTracker select a certain number of neighbors within peer $i$'s PID; the ratio of this number to the number of peer $i$'s neighbors should be limited below a certain percentage.
2. Neighbor selection between PIDs: Suppose that the link price between PID $i$ and PID $j$ is $p_{ij}$. For each $i \neq j$, if $p_{ij} \neq 0$, $w_{ij} = \frac{1}{p_{ij}}$, else we can set $w_{ij}$ to be a very large value.
$$W_{ij} = \frac{w_{ij}}{\sum_{i \neq j} w_{ij}} \tag{14}$$

For peers in PID $i$, after finishing neighbor selection within PID, they will select a certain percentage of neighbors from other PIDs according to $W_{ij}$. For robustness, concave function $f(x)$ can be introduced to enlarge the relative weight of $W_{ij}$. In this paper, we apply $f(x) = \sqrt[6]{x}$.

### 3.4 Performance Metrics

We consider the following performance metrics:

1. Completion time: It includes statistics of time that all peers need to finish downloading and the time that each single peer needs to finish downloading.
2. P2P bottleneck traffic: It is the total P2P traffic on a link that achieves the maximum link utilization.
3. Interdomain traffic: It is the totalP2P traffic on links between ASes; this metric is used only in interdomain settings.

## 4 Simulation Results

We have detected bottleneck link traffic and traffic on links between PoPs in Abilene, and kept a record of the peers' completion time for different swarm sizes in different topologies. Further, we have obtained the statistics of traffic on links between ASes in interdomain settings.

In this section, we considers a case in which all peers share a 250-MB file, and discuss the performance of P2P, P4P, and *Improved-P4P* for different swarm sizes and network topologies within AS .

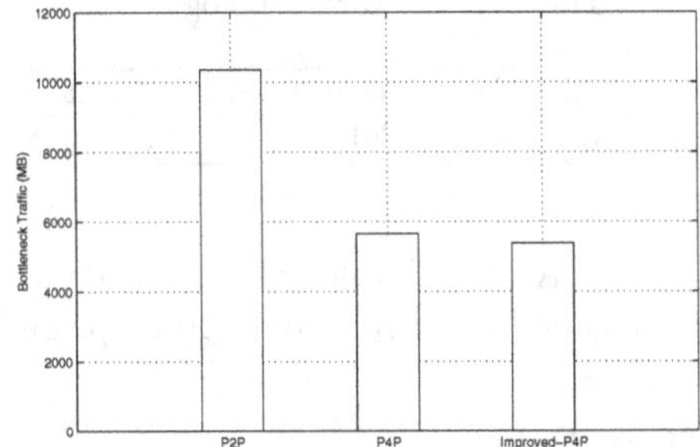


**Fig. 3.** Variance of Traffic (Swarm Size = 600)

Figure 3 shows that when the swarm size is 600, compared with the native Bit-Torrent that is based on P2P, BitTorrent integrated with *Improved-P4P* can reduce the bottleneck traffic substantially. Moreover, to some degree, the *Improved-P4P* can reduce the P4P's bottleneck. In particular, in the case of Abilene, the bottleneck traffic produced by the native BitTorrent is 1.93 times that produced by the BitTorrent integrated with *Improved-P4P*, and BitTorrent integrated with *Improved-P4P* can reduce the bottleneck traffic of BitTorrent integrated with P4P by 4.74%.

We can conclude from the above result that compared with P2P and P4P, *Improved-P4P* can considerably reduce the bottleneck traffic and better protect the bottleneck.

In conclusion, *Improved-P4P* can reduce bottleneck link utilization and the duration of high-level bottleneck traffic. Undoubtedly, *Improved-P4P* can relieve the pressure on bottleneck links.

We can observe from the result that compared with P2P and P4P, *Improved-P4P* makes the traffic on every link more even, which then reduces the traffic on the bottleneck links.

Figure 4 shows how the normalized completion time varies with the swarm size. The normalized completion time refers to the normalized value based on the maximum average downloading time of the peers in the native BitTorrent system. In particular, in the case of Abilene, the BitTorrent integrated with *Improved-P4P* and that integrated with P4P has almost the same average completion

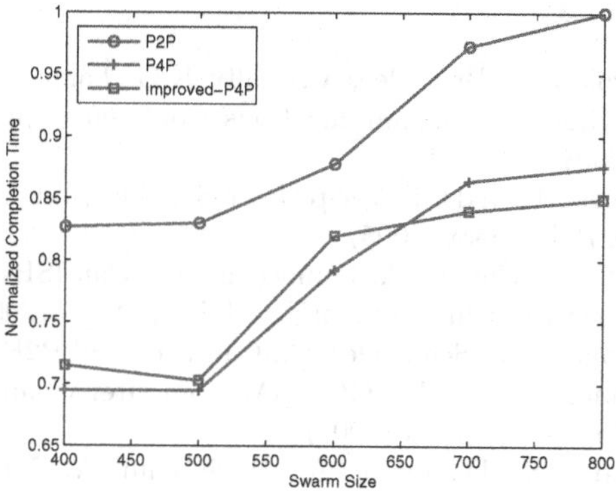


**Fig. 4.** Average Completion Time

time, and they all reduce the average completion time by approximately 20% compared with the native BitTorrent.

In other words, in intradomain settings, *Improved-P4P* can reduce the bottleneck link utilization and therefore relieve the pressure on networks with bottlenecks without degrading the performance of the P2P applications.

## 5 Conclusion

We analyzed the P-distance in a P4P cooperative model theoretically and showed the relationship between the P-distance and the link traffic. We concluded that for a network topology with bottlenecks, the application of MLU as the optimization objective of the P4P cooperative model does not achieve good performance. Therefore, we proposed an improved model, *Improved-P4P*, which introduced a *link utility function* as its objective. We analyzed the relationship between the link price and the traffic in this model, and demonstrated that *Improved-P4P* could make the traffic in a network more homogeneous. We carried out a considerable number of simulations on P2P, P4P, and *Improved-P4P* in order to verify that the *Improved-P4P* could implement the inter-active control of ISP and P2P with respect to the network traffic and that it could benefit ISPs with a reduction of the bottleneck traffic without compromising the performance of the P2P applications. Further, *Improved-P4P* performed stably for various swarm sizes, proving its feasibility, scalability, and effectiveness. In conclusion, *Improved-P4P* could solve the cooperation problem of P2P and ISP efficiently.

**Acknowledgement.** This research is supported by the National Natural Science Foundation of China (No.60873253 ), and National Key Basic Research Program ("973" Program) of China (No.2009CB320500 and 2009CB320501).

## References


1. Karagiannis, T., Broido, A., Brownlee, A., Claffy, K.C., Faloutsos, M.: Is P2P dying or just hiding. In: Global Telecommunications Conference, pp. 1532–1538. IEEE Press, New York (2004)
2. Steinmetz, R., Wehrle, K. (eds.): Peer-to-Peer Systems and Applications. LNCS, vol. 3485. Springer, Heidelberg (2005)
3. Keralapura, R., Taft, N., Chuah, C., Iannaccone, G.: Can ISPs take the heat from overlay networks. In: Proceedings of HotNets III, pp. 8–15 (2004)
4. Aggarwal, V., Feldmann, A., Scheideler, C.: Can ISPs and P2P users cooperate for improved performance. In: ACM SIGCOMM Computer Communication Review, pp. 31–40. ACM Press, New York (2007)
5. Aggarwal, V., Bender, S., Feldmann, A., Wichmann, A.: Methodology for estimating network distances of gnutella neighbors. In: Proceedings of the Workshop on Algorithms and Protocols for Efficient Peer-to-Peer Applications, pp. 219–223 (2004)
6. Xie, H., Yang, Y.R., Krishnamurthy, A., Liu, Y.G.: P4P: Provider portal for applications. In: Proceedings of the ACM SIGCOMM 2008 Conference on Data Communication, pp. 351–362. ACM Press, New York (2008)
7. Jiang, W., Zhang, R., Rexford, J., Chiang, M.: Cooperative content distribution and traffic engineering in an ISP network. In: Proceedings of the Eleventh International Joint Conference on Measurement and Modeling of Computer Systems, pp. 239–250. ACM Press, New York (2009)
8. Karagiannis, T., Rodriguez, P., Papagiannaki, K.: Should internet service providers fear peer-assisted content distribution. In: Proceedings of the 5th ACM SIGCOMM Conference on Internet Measurement, pp. 63–76. ACM Press, New York (2005)
9. Seetharaman, S., Ammar, M.: Characterizing and mitigating inter-domain policy violations in overlay routes. In: Proceedings of the 2006 14th IEEE International Conference, pp. 259–268. IEEE Press, New York (2006)
10. Palomar, D.P., Chiang, M.: Alternative distributed algorithms for network utility maximization: Framework and applications. IEEE Transactions on Automatic Control 52(12), 2254–2269 (2007)
11. Mo, J., Walrand, J.: Fair end-to-end window-based congestion control. IEEE/ACM Transactions on Networking 8, 556–567 (2000)
12. Bharambe, A.R., Herley, C., Padmanabhan, V.: Analyzing and improving a BitTorrent network's performance mechanisms. In: Proceedings of 25th IEEE International Conference on Computer Communications, pp. 1–12. IEEE Press, New York (2006)
13. Bindal, R., Cao, P., Chan, W., Medval, J., Suwala, G., Bates, T., Zhang, A.: Improving traffic locality in BitTorrent via biased neighbor selection. In: 26th IEEE International Conference on Distributed Computing Systems. IEEE Press, New York (2006)
14. PlanetLab, `http://www.planet-lab.org/`

# Assessing Survivability of Inter-domain Routing System under Cascading Failures

Yujing Liu[1], Wei Peng[1], Jinshu Su[1], and Zhilin Wang[2]

[1] College of Computer, National University of Defense Technology
Changsha, China
{liuyujing,wpeng,sjs}@nudt.edu.cn

[2] Education Department, National University of Defense Technology
Changsha, China
wangzhilin@nudt.edu.cn

**Abstract.** The Internet is designed to bypass failures by rerouting around connectivity outages. Consequently, dynamical redistribution of loads may result in congestion in other networks. Due to the co-location of data plane and control plane traffic of Border Gateway Protocol (BGP), the survivability of inter-domain routing system is sensitive to severe congestion. Therefore, an initial outage may lead to a cascade of failures in the Internet. In this paper, we characterize the survivability of inter-domain routing system by reachability and number of rerouting messages, and propose a model for studying the relationship between the survivability and the capacity of AS links under intentional attacks and random breakdowns. Through simulations on an empirical topology of the Internet, we find that the cascading failures bring a great deal of added burden to almost all the core ASes. When the tolerance parameter of AS links is less than 0.1, the cascading effect tends to be amplified globally. Moreover, the effect triggered by intentional attack is greater than that triggered by random breakdown. But the difference between them is not as prominent as previous research due to the unique automatic-restoration process in inter-domain routing system.

**Keywords:** the Internet, inter-domain routing, survivability, cascading failure.

## 1 Introduction

The Internet is composed of tens of thousands of Autonomous Systems (ASes), which exchange routing messages with each other by the de-facto inter-domain routing protocol - BGP. The reliability of BGP is very important to achieve stable communications in the Internet. Currently, the routing control packets of BGP share resources such as bandwidth and buffer space with normal data traffic in Internet packet forwarding. This co-location of control plane and data plane makes BGP sensitive to severe network congestion.

In the Internet, traffic is rerouted to bypass malfunctioning segments, probably leading to overloads on some of other healthy networks, resulting in congestion there. Loss of routing messages due to the congestion can cause BGP

J. Su et al. (Eds.): ICoC 2013, CCIS 401, pp. 97–108, 2013.

session failures between ASes, leading to another round of rerouting. Similarly, the dynamical redistribution of traffic loads may disconnect other pairs of BGP sessions. Meanwhile, the previous 'failed' sessions may re-establish since the links are no longer congested after all the traffic were rerouted around them. A single fault in routers or links can trigger a sequence of route changes on a global scale. This process is what we call cascading failures in inter-domain routing system.

Previous works about robustness of BGP in congested networks study the relationship between traffic overload factors (i.e. queueing delays, packet sizes, TCP retransmission parameters and so on) and lifetime of a BGP session [1], [2]. This is a micro-view of survivability of BGP, focusing on single component in the system. However, inter-domain routing system is a complex network, whose behaviour is better characterized by the dynamics induced by interactions of BGP routers in the whole Internet. On the other hand, studies on cascading failures in complex networks have shown that networks with highly heterogeneous distribution of loads such as the Internet and electrical power grids are particularly vulnerable to attacks in that a large-scale cascade may be triggered by disabling a single key node [3], [4]. But in these models, overloaded nodes are either removed or avoided. They are not suitable to describe the unique 'virtual cut' and 'automatic restoration' characteristics of BGP links under dynamical congested state. Recently, a CXPST attack is presented utilizing this property of BGP to create control plane instability by using only data plane traffic [5]. Besides this specific attacking technique, it's also important to further analyse factors that affect the instability scope and the difference between random breakdowns and intentional attacks.

In this paper, we try to answer questions that: Considering the distinct property of inter-domain routing system, under what conditions can a global cascade take place? And who will be affected worst? Our contributions with respect to previous works are summarized as follows.

(1) We propose a model for studying the inter-domain routing process under a cascade of congested and resumed link states. In this model, the overloaded links are not removed from the network. They have chances to be restored in the future. Moreover, we apply *customer-prefer* and *valley-free* policy to routing process instead of simply using shortest path algorithm, in order to better comply with the actual situation.

(2) We characterize the survivability of inter-domain routing system by *reachability* and *number of rerouting messages*. The most critical ability of routing system is making routing decisions. Reachability can evaluate how the incomplete topology will affect the capability; and number of rerouting messages can evaluate the effect of instability of the routing system. Because a surge of BGP updates generated by large-scale reroutings may exceed the computational capacity of affected routers, causing a degradation of such capability.

(3) In our model, the survivability depends on congested state of AS links, which are decided by the comparison of their loads and capacities. Therefore, we study the relationship between survivability of inter-domain routing system and capacity of AS links. This examination reveals that when the tolerance

parameter of links is less than 0.1, a global cascading failure of the Internet will emerge.

(4) An initial failure is the trigger that causes consequent cascades. Here we focus on failure of a single AS link. We divide the initial failure as intentional attack and random breakdown, and further analyse the survivability under these two kinds of initial failures. We find that intentional attack causes greater effect than random breakdown. But the effect is weakened by the automatic-restoration process in inter-domain routing system.

## 2 Model for Cascading Failures in Inter-domain Routing System

We demonstrate the cascading process in inter-domain routing system by a simple example as shown in Fig. 1. In this simple topology of ASes, the initial path from $S$ to $D$ is $S \to A \to B \to D$. After an initial failure happens on the link between $A$ and $B$, routers compute new routes to bypass the faulty link. Path 1, i.e., $S \to A \to C \to B \to D$ is chosen to carry the rerouted traffic from the initial path. However, the redistribution of traffic load surpasses the capacity of link $A-C$. Unlike the electrical power grids, the overload in the Internet will not lead to breakdown of the link, but cause a congestion between $A$ and $C$. Furthermore, large amount of packets are lost. Unfortunately, the routing message in control plane and the data traffic in data plane share limited resources in BGP routers. So sever congestion will drop the *KEEPALIVE* messages spoken by BGP routers at two ends of link, and make them 'think' that the session between them is disconnected. Hence routers start to compute other new but less preferred route from $S$ to $D$. It turns out to be path 2, i.e., $S \to A \to E \to F \to B \to D$. At this time, traffic is rerouted away from link $A - C$. The link is no longer congested. Routers in $A$ and $C$ resume their BGP session automatically. And the more preferred route - path 1 is available again. Traffic is rerouted to path 1, then another round of congestion happens.

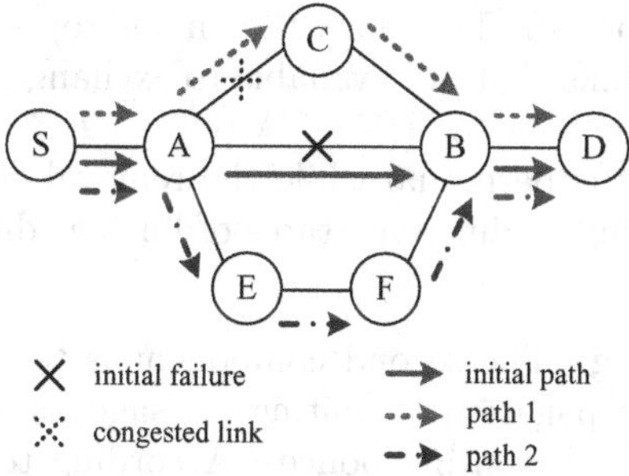


**Fig. 1.** An example of cascading failures in inter-domain routing system

If the topology of the network is as complex as the Internet, the dynamics of rerouting will be more complicated. A single initial failure may lead to lots of 'virtually cut' and 'automatically restored' links, causing a cascade of instabilities. To better understand the process and the effect of this type of failure, we propose a model to study it. As shown in Fig. 2, our model for cascading failures in inter-domain routing system consists of three interconnected components, and iterates along with time. One iteration indicates a step in the cascades.

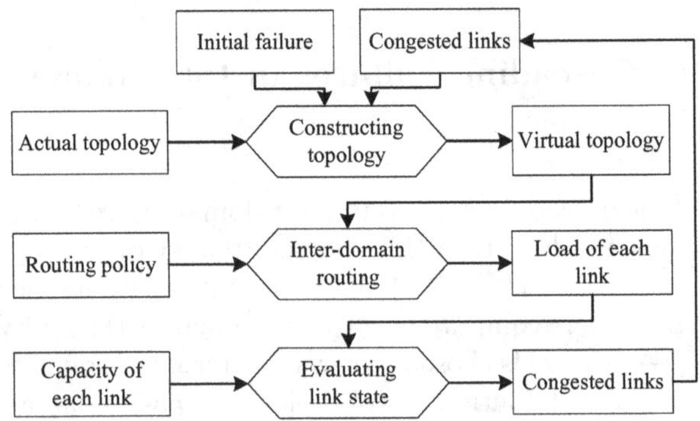


**Fig. 2.** Model for cascading failures in inter-domain routing system

**Constructing Topology.** The first component is to construct a virtual topology from the actual topology, initial failure and congested links. We present the actual topology as an annotated undirected graph $G = (V, E)$, where $V$ is the set of all ASes in the inter-domain routing system, and $E$ is the set of AS links annotated with their relationships, which include provider-customer, customer-provider and peer-peer. Since BGP is a policy-based routing protocol and AS relationship is the essential factor to set routing policy, it is important to take this information into account. The initial failure is the disconnection of an AS link $e^{ini} \in E$ at the first place that triggers follow-up instabilities. Congested links, denoted as $E^{con}(t) \subseteq E$, are AS links disconnected by the overload of traffic on them at a certain time $t$. Therefore, the virtual topology $G'(t) = (V, E'(t))$ is the set of ASes and links that are available to exchange routing messages under those failures at time $t$, i.e., $E'(t) = E \setminus \{e^{ini}\} \setminus E^{con}(t)$. It is worth noting that the removal of $e^{ini}$ is perpetual while the removal of $E^{con}(t)$ is temporal. $E^{con}(t)$ changes according to different states of links at different time.

**Inter-domain Routing.** The second component is to simulate inter-domain routing process. The propagation of routing messages is constrained by virtual topology and controlled by routing polices. According to economic considerations of ASes, there are some common points of routing polices summarized by previous research [6]. For import polices, if a BGP router receives routes to the same destination from different neighbours, it prefers route from customer over those from peer then from provider. Metrics such as path length and other BGP attributes are used in route selection if the preference is the same for different routes. This policy is known as *customer-prefer*. For export polices, an AS does not transmit traffic between any of its providers or peers, which is called *valley-free* property. Under these circumstances, connectivity does not mean reachability in the inter-domain routing system. In our model, we assume that all ASes follow customer-prefer and valley-free polices, and simulate route selections from any source to any destination. Since the inter-domain traffic from source to destination follows the AS path in BGP route, the more AS paths an AS link participates in, the more traffic load the link will transmit. Moreover, the size of source and destination AS should be taken into account. Because large AS usually generates more traffic load. In this paper, we use the number of IPs that an AS announces to assess the size of the AS. Therefore, the load on an AS link is formulated as

$$L_e = \frac{\sum_{u,w \in V} \sigma_{uw}(e) \cdot \varphi(u) \cdot \varphi(w)}{\sum_{u,w \in V} \sigma_{uw} \cdot \varphi(u) \cdot \varphi(w)} \tag{1}$$

The summation is over all ASes in $V$. $\sigma_{uw}(e)$ denotes the total number of AS paths between $u$ and $w$ that pass through AS link $e$. $\sigma_{uw}$ denotes the total number of AS paths between $u$ and $w$. $\varphi(u)$ and $\varphi(w)$ denote the number of IPs that $u$ and $w$ have. The value of load is normalized into [0, 1]. Accordingly, we could calculate the load on any AS link at any time, denoted as $L_{e_i}(t)$.

**Evaluating Link State.** The next is to evaluate whether an AS link is congested. The capacity of a link is the maximum load it can handle. We assume that the capacity $C_e$ of link $e$ is proportional to its initial load $L_e(0)$, i.e.,

$$C_e = (1 + \alpha) \cdot L_e(0) \tag{2}$$

where $\alpha \geq 0$ is the tolerance parameter of the network [1]. If the load on an AS link increases and becomes larger than its capacity, the link is congested. The *KEEPALIVE* messages spoken by BGP routers at two ends of link will be dropped along with data packets. As a result, those BGP routers assume that the link is disconnected and end the BGP session between them. Hence we treat congested links as 'virtual cuts' of the network. Meanwhile, if the load on previous congested link decreases below its capacity, the link will 'automatically restore' and be capable of exchanging routing messages again. The current comparison of load and capacity determines congested state of AS link at the next time step in cascades, i.e., $\forall e_i \in E^{con}(t+1), L_{e_i}(t) > C_{e_i}$.

## 3 Assessing Survivability under the Model

To assess survivability of inter-domain routing system under this cascading model, the first step is to characterize the survivability quantitatively. In this paper, we propose two different metrics to measure the survivability from different perspectives.

**Reachability.** The virtually cut links entailed by overload could be plentiful at a certain time. On this incomplete topology regarding to the actual one, we wonder if the routing system is still able to find paths for any pair of source and destination. Hence, as shown in Eqn. (3), we define a metric *reachability*, denoted as $R$ to measure this capability of the inter-domain routing system.

$$R(t) = \frac{\sum_{u,w \in V} \chi_{uw}(t)}{N \cdot (N-1)} \tag{3}$$

where $\chi_{uw}(t)$ is equal to 1 if there exist a path from $u$ to $w$ at time $t$. Otherwise, it is equal to 0. $N$ is the total number of ASes in the Internet, i.e., $N = |V|$. Higher reachability indicates higher survivability of the routing system.

**Rerouting Messages.** The most essential task for a routing system of networks is to make routing decisions. However, if large amounts of paths need to be rerouted around faulty links, large amounts of BGP messages will be generated, sent and processed. In this case, the computational load on a router's CPU increases dramatically, possibly exceeding the capacity of processors, then weakening the system's ability of routing. So we propose the number of *rerouting messages* that received by *core ASes* at a given time to measure how the cascading failures affect every critical ASes in the Internet. We identify the core ASes by sorting the amount of traffic load that every transit AS transmits for other ASes, then selecting the top one percent ASes to form the core AS set $V_c$. In the Internet, most ASes are stub ASes rather than transit ASes. They are not our targets for this study. The number of rerouting messages received by $u$ ($u \in V_c$) is defined as

$$RM_u(t) = \sum_{w \in V} \delta_{uw}(t-1,t) \cdot \rho(w) \tag{4}$$

where $\delta_{uw}(t-1,t)$ is the number of paths from $u$ to $w$ that are different at $t-1$ and $t$. In our model, paths are rerouted only due to changes of virtual topology. $\rho(w)$ is the number of IP prefixes in $w$. Since in BGP, the routing messages are generated regarding to every IP prefix. The more prefixes an AS has, the more routing messages it will generate when paths targeted to it need to be rerouted. The distribution of $RM$ wrt. every AS in core AS set reveals different effects of the failure on different AS. Generally speaking, more rerouting messages indicates lower survivability of the inter-domain routing system.

In our model, many factors could affect the survivability of the inter-domain routing system. In this paper, we focus on analysing the tolerance parameter $\alpha$ and the initial failure of link $e^{ini}$. First of all, we examine the relationship between survivability and capacity of AS links to evaluate under what condition a global instability of the Internet will emerge. Secondly, we divide the initial failure as intentional attack and random breakdown, and further analyse the difference of survivability of inter-domain routing system under these two kinds of initial failures.

## 4 Simulation Results

We build a simulator to simulate the routing dynamics under our model. The topology of the Internet and the AS relationships are inferred from CAIDA's data set [7]. Although the inferred topology doesn't completely agree with the actual Internet, this data set is the most complete and accurate one that is used by present research. The number of IPs and prefixes in every AS are calculated from the BGP routing tables collected by Route Views [8] and RIPE RIS [9]. Many ASes monitored by these two projects distribute in the core of the Internet, so their routing tables cover almost all the routed IP prefixes in the world. More precisely, we construct a connected network with 41204 ASes and 121310 AS links. The tolerance parameter $\alpha$ is set to be $0.1, 0.3, 0.5, 0.7$ and $0.9$, representing five levels of capacity of links. However, in fact, the capacities of links are various. We simplify the situation in our simulator at first. Then we plan to differentiate each link according to its position in the routing hierarchy in our future work.

The distributions of transmitted load of transit ASes and load of AS links are shown in Fig. 3 and Fig. 4. As we can see, the Internet controlled by inter-domain routing system exhibits a highly heterogeneous distribution of load. We choose 79 candidates from the top 1% of transit ASes to construct core AS set, and examine the rerouting dynamics in 20 time steps, denoted as $T$. We cut the AS link with highest load, denoted as $e_A$, to simulate the intentional attack, whereas cut the link $e_B$ at random to simulate the random breakdown. Then we run policy-based BGP among ASes and measure its survivability under different conditions. Next are some results.

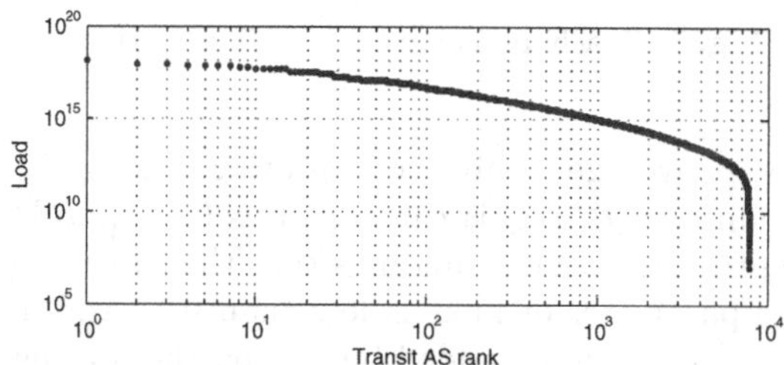


**Fig. 3.** Load of transit ASes

Fig. 5 and Fig. 6 are reachability on links with different capacities under different initial failures. The first time step of every curve is the reachability under the initial failure. Then it is followed by 20 time steps of consequent reroutings. From the results we can see that no matter what kind of initial failure is, the cascading effect on reachability of inter-domain routing system is amplified when the tolerance parameter $\alpha$ is equivalent to 0.1. It's rational to infer that the effect is also amplified when $\alpha$ is less than 0.1. Meanwhile it is constrained into a very limited scope when $\alpha$ is equal to and greater than

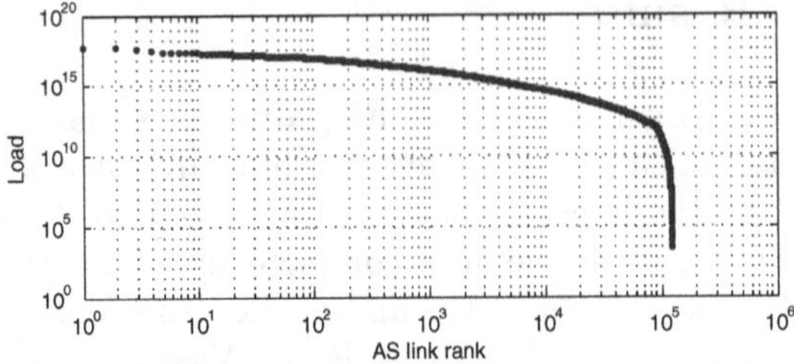


**Fig. 4.** Load of AS links

0.3. Moreover, as anticipated, with the same tolerance parameter, the cascading effect under intentional attack is greater than that under random breakdown. However, due to the automatically restoration of some faulty links, the difference between these two cases is deflated comparing with previous research [3].

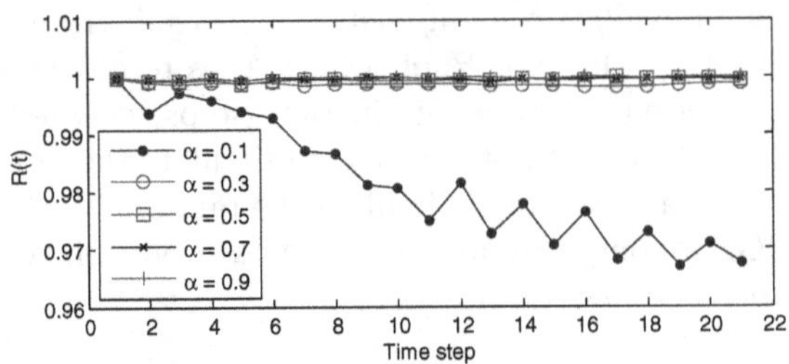


**Fig. 5.** Reachability under intentional attack

Fig. 7 and Fig. 8 are average numbers of rerouting messages in every time step under different conditions. $RM(t)$ is calculated as $(\sum_{v \in V_c} RM_v(t))/|V_c|$. From this metric we confirm our previous findings that the cascading failures emerge when the tolerance parameter of links is less than 0.1. And a failed link with higher traffic load can cause more added burden on the routing system.

Fig. 9 and Fig. 10 show distributions of rerouting messages associated with every core AS under different conditions. In these cases, we put emphasis on comparing the rerouting messages generated by initial failure and by cascading failures. So we just consider conditions that $\alpha$ is 0.1, 0.5 and 0.9, represented as low, median and high tolerant AS links. In the case of initial failure, $RM_v$ is the number of rerouting messages in the initial time, i.e., the first time step. In the case of cascading failures, $RM_v$ is calculated as $(\sum_{t \in T} RM_v(t))/|T|$, i.e., the average number of rerouting messages during the following 20 time steps. From the distributions we can see that most of core ASes encounter dramatically increased routing messages due to the cascading effect on the routing system. Especially when $\alpha$ is 0.1, the failures tend to affect all the core ASes, causing a global effect. Table 1 shows the number of rerouting messages that the 95th

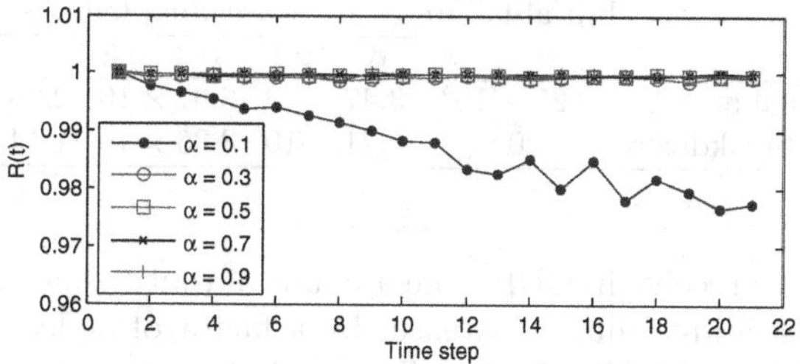


**Fig. 6.** Reachability under random breakdown

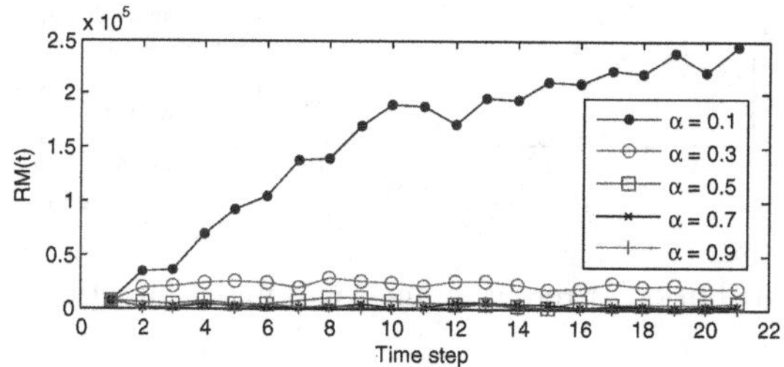


**Fig. 7.** Average number of rerouting messages under intentional attack

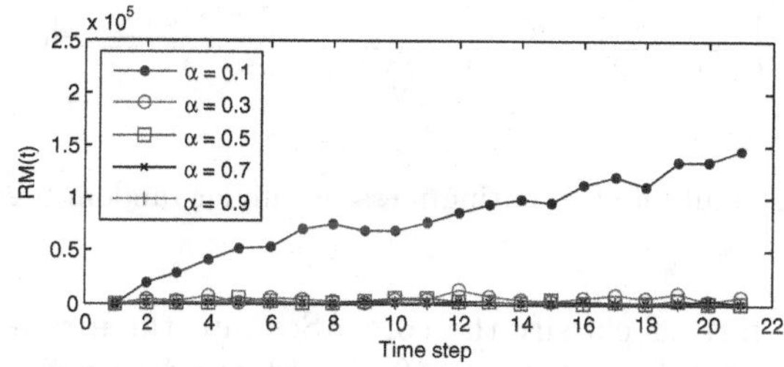


**Fig. 8.** Average number of rerouting messages under random breakdown

**Table 1.** Number of rerouting messages received by the 95th percentile core ASes in CDF

| | Initial failure | Cascading failures | | |
|---|---|---|---|---|
| | | $\alpha = 0.1$ | $\alpha = 0.5$ | $\alpha = 0.9$ |
| Intentional attack | $0.25 \times 10^3$ | $3.47 \times 10^5$ | $6.01 \times 10^3$ | $2.36 \times 10^3$ |
| Random breakdown | 0 | $1.21 \times 10^5$ | $3.36 \times 10^3$ | $1.14 \times 10^3$ |

percentile core ASes receive in CDF. The amount of routing messages generated by consequent cascading failures increases by a factor of at least 10 than that only generated by the initial link failure. These additional overloads bring a great deal of added burden to almost all the core ASes, crippling their routers' ability to make routing decisions.

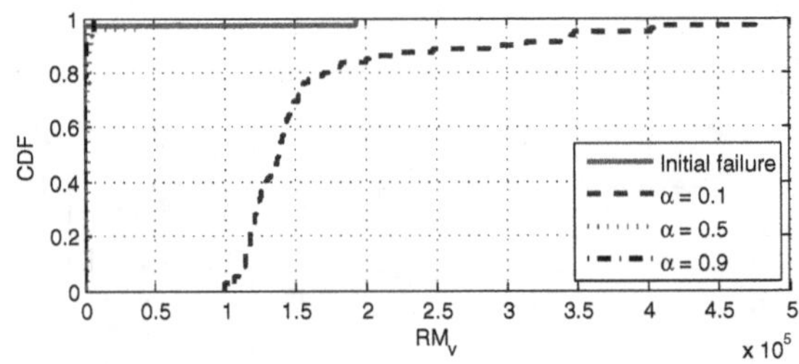


**Fig. 9.** Distribution of rerouting messages under intentional attack

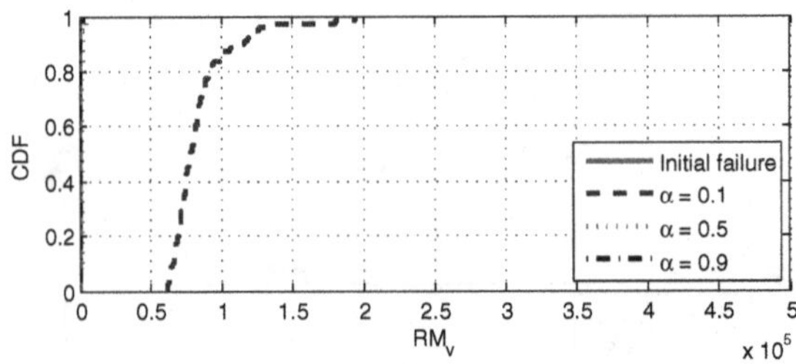


**Fig. 10.** Distribution of rerouting messages under random breakdown

Moreover, if we further classify the core ASes into three ranks according to the load they transmit for others, we find that the heaviest laden ASes are sorted into median or low ranks. It's rational to infer that the ranked ASes have matching capability to process routing messages. So the large amount of additional overloads on median- and low-rank ASes will have worse effect than that on high-rank ASes.

## 5 Conclusion and Future Work

In this paper, we present a model for cascading failures in inter-domain routing system, which is proposed for the first time to the best of our knowledge. Then we propose two metrics for measuring the survivability of the inter-domain routing system, and assess the survivability under different conditions based on empirical topology and property of the AS-level Internet.

From the simulation results, we get the following insights. First of all, due to the co-location of data plane and control plane in BGP, the inter-domain routing system is affected by the cascading effect triggered by link failures. This cascading effect brings a great deal of added burden to almost all the core ASes, crippling their ability to make routing decisions. Secondly, the cascading effect is amplified when the tolerance parameter of AS links is less than 0.1. Moreover, the effect triggered by intentional attack is greater than that triggered by random breakdown. But the difference between them is not as prominent as previous research due to the unique automatic-restoration process in inter-domain routing system.

In future work, we will examine the affecting scope of cascading failures topologically, to see whether it spreads over the global Internet or just causes impact to a local area. In addition, we are going to differentiate the capability of each link according to its position in the routing hierarchy. Moreover, it's also important to study the relationship between the initial failed portions of the Internet and its survivability, because the intentional attacks or the random breakdowns may take place to several links or ASes.

**Acknowledgement.** This research is supported by Program for Changjiang Scholars and Innovative Research Team in University (No. IRT1012); Program for Science and Technology Innovative Research Team in Higher Educational Institutions of Hunan Province (Network Technology, NUDT); Hunan Province Natural Science Foundation of China (11JJ7003); the National Natural Science Foundation of China (Grant Nos. 61070199, 61003303); and the National High Technology Research and Development Program of China (Grant No. 2011AA01A103).

## References

1. Shaikh, A., Varma, A., Kalampoukas, L., Dube, R.: Routing Stability in Congested Networks: Experimentation and Analysis. In: SIGCOMM 2000, pp. 163–174. ACM, New York (2000)
2. Xiao, L., He, G., Nahrstedt, K.: Understanding BGP Session Robustness in Bandwidth Saturation Regime. Technical Report, UIUCDCS-R-2004-2483, http://hdl.handle.net/2142/10918
3. Motter, A., Lai, Y.: Cascade-based Attacks on Complex Networks. Phys. Rev. E 66, 065102 (2002)

4. Crucitti, P., Latora, V., Marchiori, M.: Model for Cascading Failures in Complex Networks. Phys. Rev. E 69, 045104 (2004)
5. Schuchard, M., Mohaisen, A., Kune, D., Hopper, N., Kim, Y., Vasserman, E.: Losing Control of the Internet: Using the Data Plane to Attack the Control Plane. In: CCS 2010, pp. 726–728. ACM, New York (2010)
6. Gao, L.: On Inferring Autonomous System Relationships in the Internet. IEEE/ACM Transactions on Networking (ToN) 9(6), 733–745 (2001)
7. CAIDA - The Cooperative Association for Internet Data Analysis, http://www.caida.org
8. University of Oregon Route Views Project, http://www.routeviews.org
9. RIPE Routing Information Service (RIS), http://www.ripe.net/ris

# The Adaptive Multicast Data Origin Authentication Protocol

Liehuang Zhu*, Hao Yang, and Zhenghe Yang

Beijing Engineering Research Center of Massive Language Information Processing and Cloud Computing Application, School of Computer Science and Technology, Beijing Institute of Technology, China, Beijing
{liehuangz,haoy0320,zhenghey}@bit.edu.cn

**Abstract.** Most multicast data origin authentication schemes work under the fixed parameters without taking the problem of changeable network environment into account. However, the network conditions will obviously influence the efficiency of a protocol such as the time delay and the overhead. So adjusting the parameters adaptively to achieve the ideal state with the dynamic network is necessary. To achieve a high authentication rate and adapt to the changeable and unstable network environment, we proposed a multicast data origin authentication protocol which is adaptive depending on the packet error rates as well as the time delay, and is robust against the packet loss and injection. Our model can estimate a more appropriate packet error rate and make the time delay lower according to the feedback values got from the receivers using the Markov chain so that it can be adaptive. This strategy is especially efficient in terms of not only the adaptation of dynamic network but also the shortcut of overhead and delay.

**Keywords:** Authentication, adaptive, estimate, packet error rate, time delay, Markov chain.

## 1 Introduction

With the rapid development of broadcasting technology, it's applied to a lot of network applications for group communication. The constantly abundance and development of such applications makes the security and non-repudiation of group communication attract more and more attention. At the same time, the efficiency is also very important especially considering the low storage capacity nodes in the channel such as the mobile phone users as well as the dynamic network conditions.

In the group communication channel, it's probable that the data packets on the way be attacked by malicious participants or the adversary. So it's very necessary to guarantee the privacy as well as the non-repudiation. The digital signature can make sure

* This paper is supported by National Natural Science Foundation of China No.61272512 and Beijing Municipal Natural Science Foundation No.4121001.

J. Su et al. (Eds.): ICoC 2013, CCIS 401, pp. 109–121, 2013.

the non-repudiation of the scheme. However, the traditional way to sign every packet would make the computation and communication overhead very high. So the erasure code is included in to increase the authentication rate and decrease the overhead. Currently, most of the secure data origin authentication model is simply built on the hybrid model of the digital signature and the erasure code such as the SAIDA [1]. In the SAIDA scheme, the lost packets can be recovered in the range of $m$ / $n$ ($m$ < $n$). What's more, the time delay is proportional to the parameter $n$ and the overhead also increases with 1 / $m$. It is obvious that do not adjust the parameters with the change of network will decrease the efficiency and may increase the pressure of low storage capacity nodes. So the service provider could adjust itself to the network environment dynamically to achieve the best effect becomes necessary.

However, most of the authentication schemes have no idea about adapting themselves to the variable network environment. The parameters in the schemes are always set at the beginning and never changed.

In this paper, we proposed an effective scheme to solve this problem. The Markov model is included in to make the system adaptive. The Markov chain can estimate the next state based on the states came before according to the state transition matrix, but it needs a lot of prior experience data to determine the matrix. According to a mass of time delay values and packet error rates before from the receiving nodes, the estimated ones can be given. So we combined the IDA, the Merkle HASH tree, as well as the Markov algorithm to achieve the adaptive and secure data origin authentication model. It can achieve the followed abilities:

- Resist the packet loss and injection. The IDA and Merkle HASH tree are combined to achieve the perfect non-reputation and can resist all kinds of packet attack from the network.
- Be adaptive to reduce the time delay. According to the feedback values, the parameter $n$ will be adjusted to adapt the network environment and make the delay lower.
- Be adaptive to balance the overhead. The key parameter $m$ / $n$ can be estimated using Markov model to adapt the following network condition so that the communication and computation overhead is balanced.

## 2 Related Works

The TESLA scheme [2] proposed by Perrig realized the group data origin authentication by postponing sending the key of the MAC. This scheme has advantages of fast computation speed, less overhead and so on. However, TESLA needs the synchronous clock between the sender and the receivers, and it's difficult to be guaranteed under the open network environment.

Park proposed the SAIDA protocol [1] which can disperse the hash values and the digital signatures of all packets of one block according to the Information Disperse Algorithm (IDA). The receivers could recover the hash value and the digital signature messages as soon as received parts of the packets, and in this way the loss of signature packets is solved. Lysyanskaya proposed the LLT protocol [3] which firstly solved the forged packets injection problem using the Reed-Solomon error correcting code, but it needs more computation overhead.

An authentication scheme based on the Reed-Solomon erasure code and the one-way hash function was proposed by Anna Lysyanskaya et al. in 2010 [4]. Similarly, it calculates the signature of the whole group and disperses it using the RS erasure code. This protocol adds only one signature on one group and decreases the computation and communication cost, but it needs $O(n^2)$ time delay between the participants.

In 2010, an optimized scheme based on Merkle tree as well as TESLA was presented by Yang Li [5]. It uses the Merkle tree to authenticate and use delayed disclosure of keys in TESLA algorithm to ensure authenticity of message. This scheme not only obviously decreased the storage cost, but also could be compatible with complex network environment and treat burst loss well. But it needs high computation overhead especially for the receivers.

Then Seyed Ali Ahmadzadeh gave a scheme based on the geometrical model named GMAC [6]. It maps the hash values of data packets in one group to a vector space with n degrees to filter the illegal packets. The cost of this protocol is far less than PRABS and can resist the packet loss and injection, but it has a high computation complexity due to the use of geometrical model.

In 2012, Yongsheng Liu et al. [7] proposed a kind of signature dispersal authentication scheme based on the PKC. It calculates only one ECC digital signature for one group and then disperses it into all the packets in one group. It costs little communication and computation cost whereas the time delay cannot be avoided.

Kannan Balasubramanian et al. proposed the HTSS scheme [8] in 2012. It generates the keys by the hash tree and after signing the messages, it divides the signature to the packets in its period with the SDA. This protocol decreases the overhead added to every packet and can resist the packet loss well. However, it has nothing to do with the packet injection or forgery.

Hong Tang et al. proposed a kind of broadcasting data origin authentication protocol called EPJRSA [9] based on the Merkle HASH tree in 2008. This protocol combines the erasure coed as well as the Merkle HASH tree, and by adding all the brother nodes' hash values in the tree to one packet, it can resist the packet injection as well as the packet loss. This guarantees the reliability of the authentication. But it also increases the communication cost and the time delay.

Gaolei Fei and Guangmin Hu proposed the unicast network loss tomography based on $k$-th order Markov chain in 2011 [10]. This protocol introduces the $k$-th order Markov chain ($k$-MC) to describe the link packet loss process, and then uses the pseudo maximum likelihood protocol to estimate the state transition probabilities of the $k$-th order Markov chain. When the $k$ is large enough, this protocol can be capable of obtaining an accurate loss probability estimate of each packet based on unicast end-to-end measurements. However, this protocol can only be used in the unicast network and the computation overhead is high.

# 3 Our Adaptive System Model

## 3.1 The Robust Data Origin Authentication Model

Our protocol combined the IDA and the Merkle HASH tree to construct a kind of trusted data origin authentication model [11] that can resist both the packet loss and the pack injection within the threshold values.

The IDA [12] is constructed with two important parameters *n* and *m*. The file to be encoded can be segmented into *n* pieces. And only *m* pieces of File are given, we can reconstruct File according to the steps of IDA.

In our method, firstly two important encode parameters have to be set: *n* and *m*. Then we use the Merkle HASH tree as the base framework, dividing a block of data into *n* packets and then construct the Merkle HASH tree as Fig. 1.

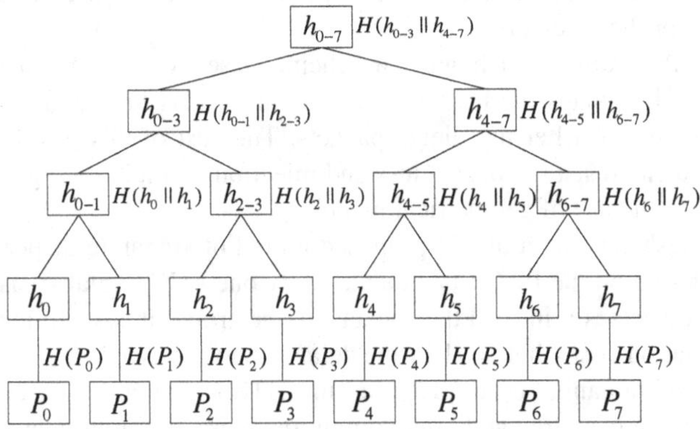


**Fig. 1.** The Merkle HASH tree of 8 nodes

Secondly we get the concatenation value $F = H(P_0) \| H(P_1) \| \ldots \| H(P_{n-1})$ and the signature of the group $\sigma(K_{public}, H(F))$. Next using IDA, we can encode and disperse both the concatenation value and the signature into n pieces as $\{F_0, F_1, \ldots, F_{n-1}\}$ and $\{\sigma_0, \sigma_1, \ldots, \sigma_{n-1}\}$. So a complete packet *i* includes three parts as Fig. 2, the data block $P_i$ itself, the hash and signature segments $F_i$ and $\sigma_i$, and all the related hash values of the brother nodes from it to the root in the Merkle HASH tree, such as $\{h_0, h_{2\text{-}3}, h_{4\text{-}7}\}$ to packet $P_1$ in Fig. 1.

| $P_i$ | $F_i, \sigma_i$ | $\{h_a, h_b, \ldots, h_z\}$ |
|---|---|---|
| Message data | Authentication message | HASH values |

**Fig. 2.** Three parts of one packet

According to the IDA, as long as *m* in the *n* pieces of $F_i$ or $\sigma_i$ received, the intact hash value or signature can be recovered, and then the data can be authenticated. So it can tolerate the packet error in the range of *m*. Then for the packet injection or forgery, the Merkle HASH tree can guarantee that the forged packets are recognized based on the third part of one packet. Every packet received can recompute the hash value of the root using the third part, so the different group with fewer ones will be discarded.

## 3.2 The Estimate Model Using the Markov Chain

We apply the Markov chain to estimate the incoming packet error rate based on the previous ones. As we all know, the Markov chain describes a kind of state sequence that every state in the sequence depends on the previous finite ones according to the state transition matrix constituted by the transition probabilities. So what we want to get is the transition matrix of the data packet error rate. At the same time, we adjust the time delay based on the feedback values.

**The Adjustment of Block Size Parameter**

We can know from the IDA that the more packets included in one block, the smaller overhead each packet will take. On the other hand, the time delay will increase with $n$. So the balance between these factors is necessary.

Here we define a threshold value of the time delay as $t$, as well as a threshold limit time $t_0$. Only if the average time delay in one period exceeds the threshold value $t$, the size $n$ will be decreased. And if the time delay keeps under the threshold value for $t_0$ time, then we will increase the size $n$.

Then we also need to consider the overhead with the value $n$. It should be controlled so that the overhead per packet would not be too big. In our experiments, the $n$ should be no more than 128 considering the limit of the experiment environment.

**The Estimate of Packet Error Rate**

First of all, we define $k$ states which present the default values of packet error rate as $O_1, O_2,\dots, O_k$ ($0 \le O_i < 1$ and $1 \le i \le k$). And the $k$ values are set as the coordinates of the transition matrix, in which the $a_{ij}$ ($1 \le i, j \le k$) presents the probability count of transition between the rates as (1). For example, $a_{2k}$ means the situation that the previous packet error rate is $O_2$ and the next one is $O_k$ appears $a_{2k}$ times in this period.

$$\begin{array}{c} \\ O_1 \\ O_2 \\ \\ O_k \end{array} \begin{array}{c} \quad O_1 \quad O_2 \qquad O_k \\ \begin{bmatrix} a_{11}, a_{12}, \dots, a_{1k} \\ a_{21}, a_{22}, \dots, a_{2k} \\ \vdots \\ a_{k1}, a_{k2}, \dots, a_{kk} \end{bmatrix} \end{array} \tag{1}$$

What should be noticed is that $k$ must be an integer in the range of $(0, n]$. The bigger the $k$ is, the more accurate the matrix is but the estimate may be inaccurate with too many $a_{ij} = 0$ in the matrix. The smaller the $k$ is, the more accurate the estimate is. However, the estimate may be limit within several values. So the $k$ is better fixed in the range of $[8, 32]$ to get a good result in the following experiments. And the values of $O_i$ $(1 \le i \le k)$ should be chosen evenly in [0, 1), so that all rates can be assorted to one nearest state $O_i$. Then we get a state transition matrix whose scale is $k \times k$.

An example is given. Suppose we have $n$ = 128 packets in one block, then the data packet sequence can be donated as $P_0P_1...P_{127}$. And at the clients, the correctly received ones are signed as 1 and the others are signed as 0. Then the packet error rates $Q_j$s ($Q_j = N_0 / n$, $N_0$ presents the number of $P_{0\sim n\text{-}1} = 0$ in the $j$-th sequence) can be given. Here we set the scale $k$ = 8 and the $O_i$s of the transition matrix are 0, 1/8,..., 7/8 (chosen evenly in [0, 1)). If the adjacent two packet error rates $Q$ and $Q'$ got from the feedback strings are 75/128 and 23/128, they will be respectively assorted to the nearest states $O_6$ = 5/8 and $O_2$ = 1/8. Then the count $a_{62}$ in the matrix should plus 1. So we fill the transition matrix as (2) after all the rates are assorted to the nearest $O_i$ in one experiment. After that, it will search the matrix according to the following rate $Q_A$, assumed to be assorted to state $O_7$, to find out the maximum probability $a_{7Max} = a_{74}$ to reach the next state $O_4 = Q_B$. Then $Q_B$ is the estimate the Markov chain model made.

$$\begin{array}{c|cccccccc|} & 0 & 1/8 & 2/8 & 3/8 & 4/8 & 5/8 & 6/8 & 7/8 \\ \hline 0 & 7 & 1 & 1 & 8 & 53 & 38 & 9 & 1 \\ 1/8 & 8 & 1 & 0 & 1 & 1 & 35 & 34 & 2 \\ 2/8 & 19 & 2 & 1 & 1 & 0 & 1 & 1 & 27 \\ 3/8 & 55 & 5 & 2 & 2 & 0 & 1 & 1 & 1 \\ 4/8 & 24 & 41 & 6 & 2 & 1 & 0 & 0 & 1 \\ 5/8 & 4 & 31 & 41 & 4 & 2 & 0 & 0 & 0 \\ 6/8 & 0 & 0 & 23 & 32 & 8 & 3 & 4 & 0 \\ 7/8 & 1 & 0 & 0 & 17 & 10 & 4 & 0 & 0 \end{array} \quad (2)$$

So in this way, we can estimate the incoming possible packet error rate according to the feedback values. All the probability values $a_{ij}$ $(1 \le i, j \le k)$ in the state transition matrix should be got from a mass of feedback values in one period and are believable.

### 3.3 The Adaptive Multicast Data Origin Authentication Model

In our model, we set three kinds of end as the server, the adversary and the clients. The network model is set as Fig. 3. The server broadcasts messages to the heterogeneous clients and then the chosen clients will respond the bit strings which represent whether the packets received correctly or not as well as the time delay messages. The adversary could control parts of the network and attack the data packets on the way.

At the server, firstly some initial parameters are determined: the encoding parameters $n$ ($n = 2^p$, $p$ is a positive integer) and $m$ ($m < n$), a set of $k$ values of packet error rate $O_i$ $(0 \le O_i < 1, 1 \le i \le n)$ as the coordinates of the transition matrix, and then three threshold values, the time delay threshold value $t$, the limit time $t_0$ and the packet error rate threshold value $\beta$ $(0 < \beta < 1)$. The same parameters are shared at the clients too.

Secondly, the server starts to broadcast the message packets and the authentication messages encoded by the IDA and the Merkle HASH tree as Fig. 2 with the initial parameters $n$ and $m$. The clients would send feedback messages of the time delay and packet error rate to the server.

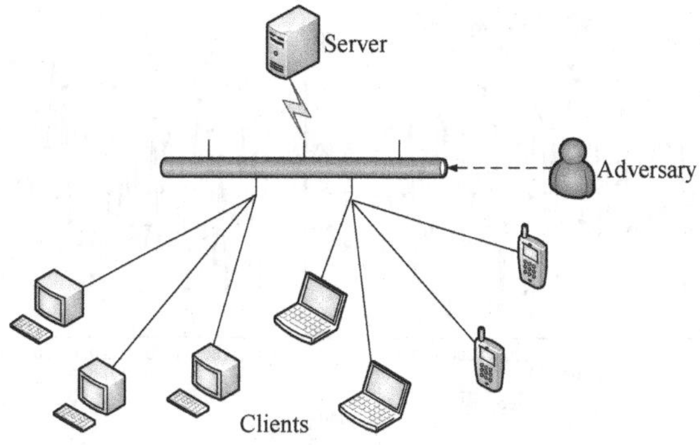


**Fig. 3.** The multicast framework model

If the average decoding time in one period is beyond the threshold value $t$, the representative clients will send the server a timeout label, and then the server will decrease the value of $n$ as $n = n / 2$. On the other hand, if the average time delay keeps under the threshold value $t$ for $t_0$ time, then the server recovers the size $n$ as $n = n \times 2$.

And if the packet error rate is beyond the threshold value $\beta$, for example, the lost packets and the forged packets from the adversary are altogether $\omega$ in a block of $n$ packets, and $\omega / n > \beta$, then the representative clients will send the server the packet sequence bit strings $P_1P_2...P_n$. And the state transition matrix can be filled up using our protocol as (1).

Next the server will estimate the incoming packet error rate according to the state transition matrix. It will get a maximum probability to reach the next state $O$ with the last received rate, and the rate $Q = O$ is the result estimated by the Markov chain. At the same time, after the messages of one block received, the clients do the decoding operation to the packets and authenticate the messages.

At last, a new encoding rate $m / n$ is determined by the server according to the estimated packet error rate $Q$ ($m / n = 1 - Q$). With the block size parameter $n$ adjusted by the timeout threshold value, a pair of new values of $n$ and $m$ will be used.

# 4 Experiments and Results

We do our experiments under the local area network environment, and control the network as three kinds of packet error model: random, stable and burst. One end broadcasts the messages as the server, one end simulates the adversary to attack the channel randomly, and other ends receive as the clients.

In our experiments, the server firstly sets $n = 128$, $m / n = 1/2$, and the transition matrix scale as $k = 8$ ($O_i = 0, 1/8, \dots, 7/8$). Then it broadcasts a message, and the adversary randomly attacks. The clients will receive the attacked packets and authenticate them. During this period, the chosen nodes will send the feedback to the server (here we ignore the error threshold and send every packet error rate back). The server needs to gather the feedback values and then do the Markov estimation every 10 minutes. Also the time delay values are calculated and sent back in the same way.

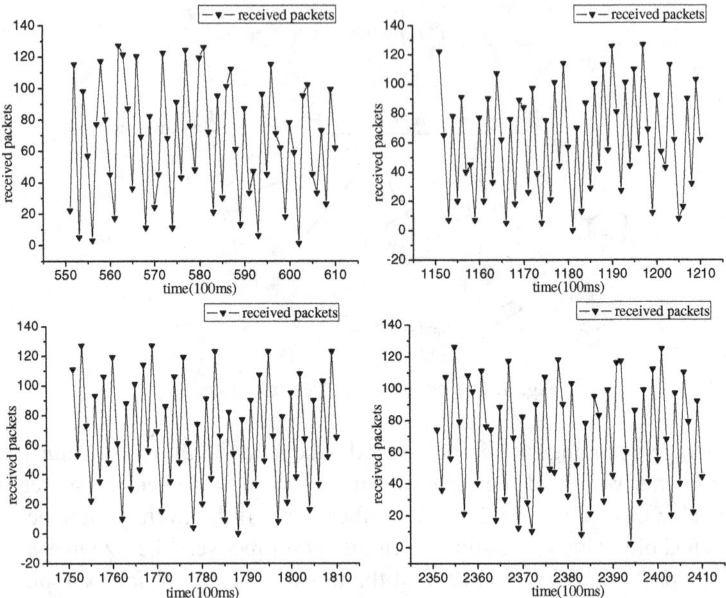


**Fig. 4.** The error rates under random condition

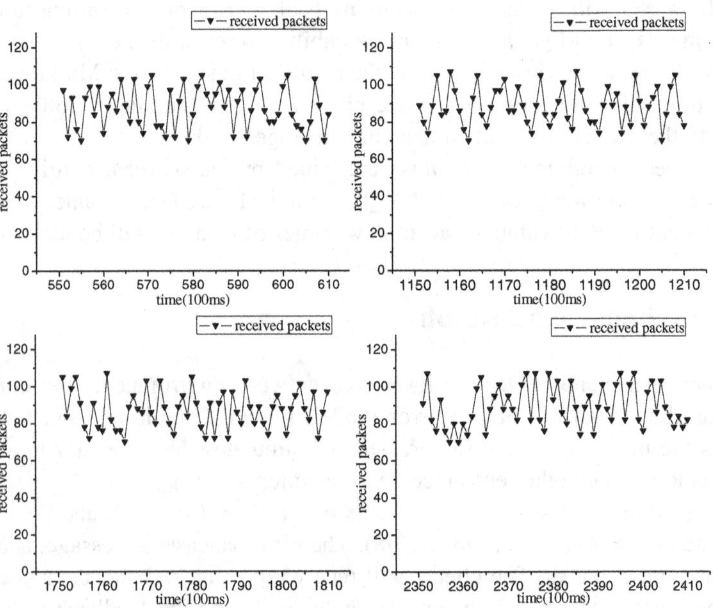


**Fig. 5.** The error rates under stable condition

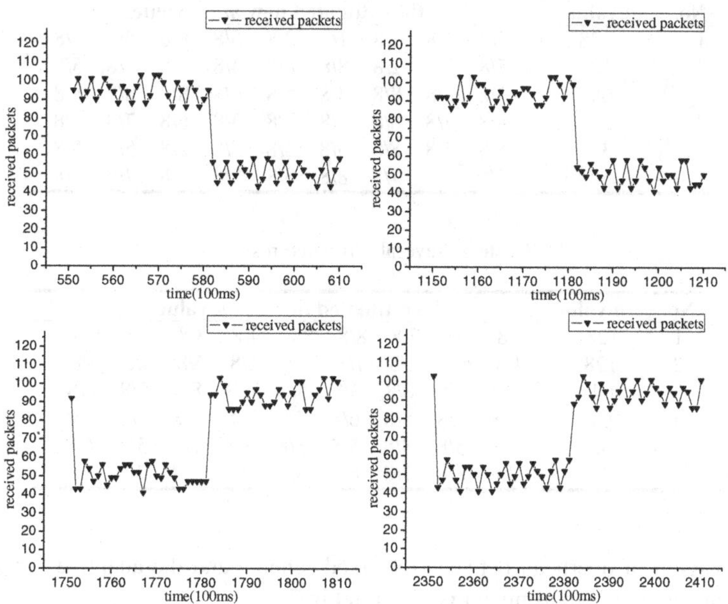


**Fig. 6.** The error rates under burst condition

In the random error model, we can see from Fig. 4 that the error rates vary with time randomly. So we estimate every 10 minutes. And the following $m / n = 1 - Q_e$ values can be given.

Also we can see from Fig. 5 and Fig. 6 that our scheme works well under the stable as well as the burst error conditions. The network is relatively stable in the stable model which means that the error rate keeps within a permissible range. In the burst error model, the error rate may vary suddenly at any time for the changeable network.

Under the stable network environment, the $m / n$ parameter is also relatively stable as Table 1. On the other hand, if the network condition changes suddenly, the rate may be varied obviously and frequently as Table 2.

And our scheme can work very well with different $n$ values. We can get this conclusion from Table 3 (the initial $m / n$ rates are all 1/2).

**Table 1.** The estimated error rates under stable network environment

| **the values of $n$** | **the estimated new $m / n$ values** | | | | | | | | |
|---|---|---|---|---|---|---|---|---|---|
| 128 | 4/8 | 4/8 | 3/8 | 3/8 | 4/8 | 3/8 | 4/8 | 4/8 | 3/8 |

**Table 2.** The estimated error rates under unstable network environment

| No. | *n* value | the estimated new *m* / *n* values | | | | | | | | |
|---|---|---|---|---|---|---|---|---|---|---|
| 1 | 128 | 8/8 | 7/8 | 7/8 | 1/8 | 2/8 | 6/8 | 8/8 | 5/8 | 8/8 |
| 2 | 128 | 7/8 | 2/8 | 2/8 | 8/8 | 8/8 | 4/8 | 8/8 | 7/8 | 5/8 |
| 3 | 64 | 3/8 | 8/8 | 8/8 | 3/8 | 5/8 | 6/8 | 8/8 | 8/8 | 8/8 |
| 4 | 64 | 8/8 | 7/8 | 8/8 | 6/8 | 7/8 | 3/8 | 6/8 | 7/8 | 3/8 |
| 5 | 32 | 5/8 | 5/8 | 8/8 | 5/8 | 3/8 | 8/8 | 2/8 | 5/8 | 5/8 |
| 6 | 32 | 2/8 | 8/8 | 7/8 | 8/8 | 8/8 | 2/8 | 5/8 | 7/8 | 8/8 |

**Table 3.** Several estimated results

| No. | *n* value | the estimated new *m* / *n* values | | | | | | | | |
|---|---|---|---|---|---|---|---|---|---|---|
| 1 | 128 | 7/8 | 2/8 | 2/8 | 8/8 | 8/8 | 4/8 | 8/8 | 7/8 | 5/8 |
| 2 | 128 | 4/8 | 6/8 | 2/8 | 7/8 | 8/8 | 2/8 | 6/8 | 4/8 | 3/8 |
| 3 | 64 | 3/8 | 8/8 | 8/8 | 3/8 | 5/8 | 6/8 | 8/8 | 8/8 | 8/8 |
| 4 | 64 | 8/8 | 7/8 | 8/8 | 6/8 | 7/8 | 3/8 | 6/8 | 7/8 | 3/8 |
| 5 | 32 | 5/8 | 5/8 | 8/8 | 5/8 | 3/8 | 8/8 | 2/8 | 5/8 | 5/8 |
| 6 | 32 | 2/8 | 8/8 | 7/8 | 8/8 | 8/8 | 2/8 | 5/8 | 7/8 | 8/8 |

The comparison of overhead between the fixed scheme and the adaptive scheme under the same network environment is given in Fig.7.

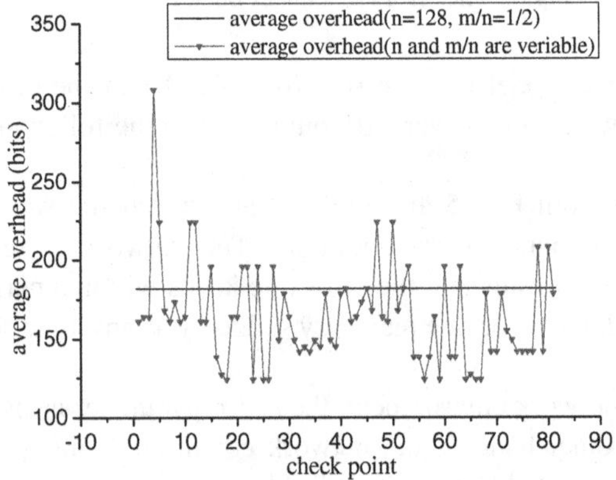


**Fig. 7.** The overhead comparison

We can see from it that most overhead of the check points in the adaptive scheme in which the parameters vary with the network environment is much lower than the fixed parameters scheme ($n$ = 128 and $m$ / $n$ = 1/2). And the average overhead of the whole check points is 164.205, which is less than 182 of the original scheme.

Also, the superiority of the verification rate of the adaptive scheme is obvious too as Fig. 8. With the changeable packet error rate which varies randomly between 0 and 1 and the fixed initial parameters *m* / *n*, the verification rate of the system is not as expected. On the other hand, the adaptive scheme can achieve an ideal verification rate in any condition.

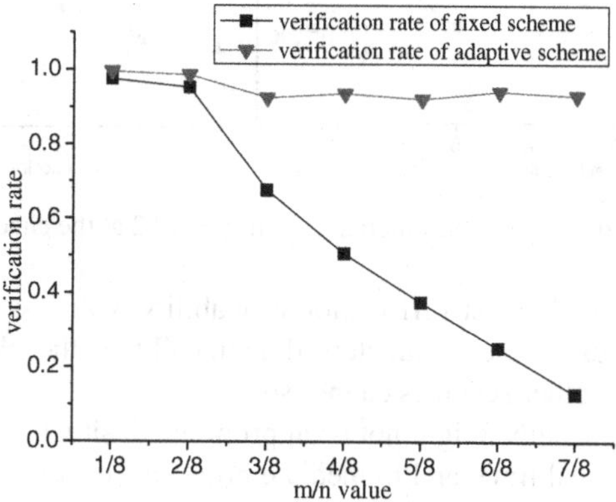


**Fig. 8.** Verification rate under unstable environment

At the same time, the chosen nodes will count the decoding time of every block and compared to the threshold value *t*. Here we set $t$ = 250ms and $t_0$ = 103ms, so we can get the Table 4 as followed (the bold italic column presents the time $t_0$).

**Table 4.** The time delay values changing table

| No. | *n* value | the time delay near the critical point (ms) | | | | | |
|---|---|---|---|---|---|---|---|
| 1 | 128 | 276.4 | 313.7 | 263.2 | ***290.1*** | 203.3 | 236.1 |
| 2 | 128 | 234.7 | 229.2 | 227.8 | ***231.6*** | 303.4 | 343.7 |
| 3 | 64 | 225.9 | 198.3 | 246.1 | ***209.3*** | 258.0 | 269.4 |
| 4 | 64 | 257.3 | 254.9 | 273.4 | ***289.0*** | 226.1 | 231.8 |
| 5 | 32 | 193.2 | 197.7 | 215.2 | ***220.4*** | 267.9 | 258.5 |
| 6 | 32 | 265.9 | 282.3 | 280.7 | ***274.1*** | 238.4 | 240.2 |

We can get from the Table 4 that when the time delay values exceed the threshold value *t* for $t_0$ time, then the value of *n* would be decreased to reduce the time delay (the 1st, 4th and 6th rows). Otherwise the delay values keep under the threshold value *t* for $t_0$ time, the value of *n* would be increased (the 2nd, 3rd and 5th rows) as Fig. 9.

## 5 Conclusion

We can see from the experiment results that our protocol is efficient in adapting itself in all kinds of network environment especially when the network changes frequently.

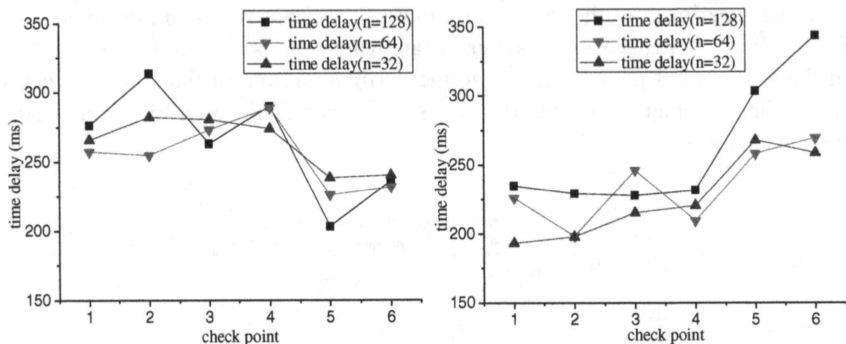


**Fig. 9.** Time delay decreases/increases with $n = n / 2$ at the check point 4

Our scheme achieved the highest verification probability with less overhead within a certain range and adjusted the parameters dynamically in the changeable network environment which the other schemes cannot solve.

And obviously, our scheme might not be appropriate in situations where the data to be sent is generated in real time, and immediate broadcast of it is crucial. Our scheme will be most useful in situations where it needs high authentication rate and efficiency with less overhead but the network varies frequently and irregularly.

## References

1. Park, J.M., Chong, E.K.P., Siegel, H.J.: Efficient multicast packet authentication using signature amortization. In: Proc. IEEE Symposium on Security and Privacy, pp. 227–240 (2002)
2. Perrig, A., Canetti, R., Tygar, J.D., Song, D.X.: Efficient authentication and signing of multicast streams over lossy channels. In: Proc. IEEE Symposium on Security and Privacy, pp. 56–73 (2000)
3. Lysyanskaya, A., Tamassia, R., Triandopoulos, N.: Multicast authentication in fully adversarial networks. In: Proc. IEEE Symposium on Security and Privacy, p. 241 (2004)
4. Lysyanskaya, A., Tamassia, R., Triandopoulos, N.: Authenticated error-correcting codes with applications to multicast authentication. In: Proc. ACM Trans. Inf. Syst. Secur. (2010)
5. Li, Y., Zhang, M., Guo, Y., Xu, G.: Optimized source authentication scheme for multicast based on Merkle Tree and TESLA. In: Proc. Information Theory and Information Security (ICITIS), pp. 195–198 (2010)
6. Ahmadzadeh, S.A., Agnew, G.B.: Poster: a geometric approach for multicast authentication in adversarial channels. In: Proc. ACM Conference on Computer and Communications Security, pp. 729–732 (2011)
7. Liu, Y., Li, J., Guizani, M.: PKC Based Broadcast Authentication using Signature Amortization for WSNs. In: Proc. IEEE Transactions on Wireless Communications, pp. 2106–2115 (2012)
8. Balasubramanian, K., Roopa, R.: HTSS: Hash Tree Signature Scheme for Multicast Authentication. In: Proc. International Conference on Recent Trends in Computational Methods, Communication and Controls (ICON3C 2012), pp. 28–32 (2012)

9. Tang, H., Zhu, L.: Efficient packet-injection resistant data source authentication protocol for group communication. Proc. Journal on Communications 11A, 96–100 (2008)
10. Fei, G., Hu, G.: Unicast network loss tomography based on k-th order Markov chain. Proc. Journal of Electronics & Information Technology 33(9), 2278–2282 (2011)
11. Yang, H., Zhu, L.: The application of data origin authentication to video multicast communication. In: Proc. International Conference on Multimedia Technology (ICMT), July 26-28, pp. 5129–5132 (2011)
12. Rabin, M.O.: Efficient dispersal of information for security, load balancing, and fault tolerance. Proc. J. ACM, 335–348 (1989)

# A Computer Network Defense Policy Refinement Method

Zhao Wei[1], Yanli Lv[2], Chunhe Xia[1], Yang Luo[1], and Qing Wei[1]

[1] Key Laboratory of Beijing Network Technology
School of Computer Science and Engineering, Beihang University, Beijing, China
[2] Information Center of Ministry of Science and Technology, The Ministry of Science and Technology of the People's Republic of China, Beijing, China
wz@cse.buaa.edu.cn, lvyl@most.cn, xch@buaa.edu.cn,
veotax@sae.buaa.edu.cn, wq2012_buaa@163.com

**Abstract.** The existing methods of policy refinement in computer network defense (CND) can only support the refinement of access control policy, but not the policies of protection, detection, response, and recovery. To solve this problem, we constructed a computer network defense policy refinement model and its formalism specification. An algorithm of defense policy refinement is designed. At last, the effectiveness of our methods was verified through one experiment cases of the composition policies with intrusion detection, vulnerabilities detection, and access control.

**Keywords:** computer network defense, formalism specifications, policy refinement, semantic consistency.

## 1 Introduction

The growing network information system and the emergence of new technology such as cloud computing and big data have brought up a huge challenge to the efficiency and accuracy of the network management. It is time-consuming and easy to make mistakes for the traditional manual network security management in the large- scale network system. In order to solve these problems, researchers have proposed policy-based architecture [1], policy-driven management methods [2] to simplify the management for the complicated and distributed network system, such as cloud framework [3]. Administrator may specify the targets and constraints only in the form of policy. A policy can be defined as a set of rules. These rules are used to express how to reach a desired behavior. Policy refinement can complete this process. Policy refinement is a process of transforming high-level abstract policy to low-level concrete ones[4].

Because of the complicated policy refinement process and manual operation for some refinement process, some researchers have proposed automatic policy refinement methods in different fields, such as policy refinement in usage control policies [5]. Reference [6-7] discussed policy refinement methods in the network security management. However, these policy refinement methods only support the refinement of access control policies instead of defense policy, such as detection, recovery policy, et al.

J. Su et al. (Eds.): ICoC 2013, CCIS 401, pp. 122–133, 2013.

Computer network defenses are actions through the use of computer networks to protect, monitor, analyze, detect and respond to unauthorized activities within Department of Defense information systems and computer networks [8].

It remains unclear about how to expand the policy refinement methods to computer network defense field in order to support the refinement of defense policy including protection, detection, response, and recovery. Based on this problem, we have proposed a computer network defense policy refinement method. A formalism model of policy refinement is provided. This model supports the refinement of four types of defense policies including protection, detection, response, and recovery policies. At last, we designed an algorithm of defense policy refinement and the effectiveness of the methods we proposed is verified through two experiments.

The rest of this paper is organized as follows. Section 2 gives related works of policy refinement. CND policy refinement model and its formalism specification are provided in Section 3. A CND policy refinement algorithm is designed in Section 4 Section 5 gives the experiment analysis and verification for CND policy refinement. Finally, Section 6 concludes the paper.

## 2 Related Works

Automatic policy refinement methods simplify security service management in complex network environment. Previous researchers have proposed various policy refinement methods for the network security management. These methods are shown as follows:

Reference [9] proposed a policy refinement method that can get action sequence to achieve high-level goal based on event-calculation and abductive reasoning.

Reference [10] proposed a policy refinement method based on MBM model. Reference [11] proposed a model-based refinement of security policy method in the collaborative virtual organization. This model-to-model transformation technique can transform XACML-based VO policy to the resource level. Reference [12] shows a security policy refinement framework in the network environment. This framework includes a three-level model. The top level of RBAC model is used to express security goals. The middle level of the network security tactics model is used to express the constraints of data stream. The bottom of the model is an abstract view oriented towards the technical capacity. At last, the implementation of this model is realized within the framework of CIM/WBEM. Reference [13] proposed a policy refinement method based on event-B. The policy has four levels including user-service level, process-terminal service level, host-port level, and interface-port level. Reference [14] extended OrBAC model and proposed a policy refinement method transforming a high-level security policy into low-level security mechanism. An example is provided to verify the effectiveness of the method.

In conclusion, most of the policy refinement methods [12-14] only support the refinement of access control policy instead of defense policies such as protection and detection policies, et al. Reference [9] can support policy refinement of network management. However, they cannot support defense policy refinement from the perspective of computer network defense.

Based on the existing policy refinement methods and the characteristics of computer network defense, we proposed a computer network defense policy refinement method. A formalism policy refinement model is provided. Compared with other policy refinement methods, our method not only supports the refinement of access control policy, but also the defense policy.

## 3 Computer Network Defense Policy Refinement Model

Computer network defense policy refinement is a process transforming goal-level (high-level) defense policy goals to operational-level (low-level) defense policies.

Defense policy refinement model has two levels: Goals level and Operational level. The elements of operational level are refined by goal level. So it forms a hierarchical structure form high-level to low-level. The policies of goal level express the high-level security requirements and defense goals. The policies of operational level express the operational actions related to concrete network environment.

**Definition** Defense Policy Refinement Model: The defense policy refinement model consists of elements at both goal level and operation level as well as defense policy goals, operational-level defense policies and refinement relations among elements at these two levels. We can conclude that the elements of operational-level are refined by goal-level. So it forms a hierarchical structure form high-level to low-level. The formalism of this model is shown as follows:

$$\begin{cases} M ::= (G,O,R), \\ G = \{Domain, Role, Target, Activity, Means, ContextType, MeansConstraints\} \\ O = \begin{Bmatrix} SNode, User, TNode, Resource, Action, DefenseAction, \\ DefenseEntity, Context, PolicyRelation \end{Bmatrix} \\ R \subseteq G \times O; HPR \subseteq G \times G; LPR \subseteq O \times O; \\ HPGOAL ::= (G, HPR); LPOPERATION ::= (O, LPR); \end{cases}$$

Wherein, G denotes the set of elements of the goal level, O the set of the operational level, R the set of the refinement relations between the elements of goal level and operational level. HPGOAL the set of the policy goals which consists of goal-level elements and theirs relations, LPOPERATION the set of the operational-level policy which consists of operational-level elements and theirs relations

The meaning of the elements of the goal level are explained as follow:

Domain: It denotes a scope or area. Domain can be divided depending on the environment of network such as organization structure, geographical boundary, security level, and management responsibility. It is shown as a hierarchical structure.

Role: It is a set of users who share common characteristics.

Target: It is a set of resources with common characteristics. Target is divided into four classes such as data, operation system, application programs, and services.

Activity: It is a set of actions with common characteristics. It is divided two classes including activities of local process with configuring, acquiring and operating and activities of interact process with accessing and transferring.

Means: Means is a set of defense activities. According to the model of PDRR, means are divided into four classes such as protection ( including the permission access control and the denying access control, user authentication, encryption communication, backup), detection (including intrusion detection, vulnerabilities detection), response (including access control, system rebooting and system shutdown), and recovery (including rebuild and making patch).

MeansConstraints: Meansconstraints means time series and logic relations between defense means including sequence and, sequence or, parallel and, parallel or. They are shown as follow:

$$R_{means} = \left\{ r_{seq\_and}, r_{seq\_or}, r_{concu\_and}, r_{concu\_or}, r_{xor} \right\}$$

In brief, we assume that there are only two means in one composition policy goal. $Means = \{mean_1, mean_2\}$ . Each relation is explained separately as follows:

$r_{seq\_and}$ : If $seq\_and(mean_1, mean_2)$, it denotes that the $mean_1$ is executed first. If the executing effect of $mean_1$ is true, the $mean_2$ is executed. Only if both means are successfully completed can we say the policy goal is completed successfully.

$r_{seq\_or}$ : If $seq\_or(mean_1, mean_2)$, it denotes that the $mean_1$ is executed first. If the executing effect of $mean_1$ is true, the $mean_2$ does not need to be executed. If the executing effect of $mean_1$ is false, the $mean_2$ must be executed. Whether the policy goal is completed successfully or not depends on the success of $mean_1$ or $mean_2$ .

$r_{concu\_and}$ : If $concu\_and(mean_1, mean_2)$, it denotes that both $mean_1$ and $mean_2$ are executed at the same time. If the effects of $mean_1$ and $mean_2$ are true, we can say that the policy goal is successfully accomplished.

$r_{\text{concu}\_or}$ : If $concu\_or(mean_1, mean_2)$, it denotes that both $mean_1$ and $mean_2$ are executed at the same time. Only if there is a true executed effect between $mean_1$ and $mean_2$ , can we say that the policy goal is successfully accomplished.

$r_{xor}$ : If $xor(mean_1, mean_2)$, it denotes that there exists one executing means between $mean_1$ and $mean_2$ . Whether the policy goal is completed successfully depends on the true effect of $mean_1$ or $mean_2$ .

ContextType: It is a set of contexts with common characteristics. It is divided into two classes including vulnerability $ct_{vul}$ and event $ct_{event}$.

The meaning of the elements at the operational level are explained as follow:

SNode: It denotes a host node in which a user initiates an operation to resource.

TNode: It denotes a host node in which the resource exists.

User: It denotes people who can initiate an operation.

Resource: It denotes an entity that needs protection, such as the instance of the data, operation system, service, application program, and data.

Action: It denotes a change that cannot be subdivided, such as the actions of adding, deleting, and changing corresponding to operating activity; the actions of sending, receiving, requesting and replying corresponding to transferring activity.

DefenseEntity: It means security device that can executed as defense action. It denotes in device number. Defense entity includes firewall $de_{firewall}$, IPsec VPN $de_{ip\sec\_vpn}$, backup server $de_{backup\_server}$, system management server $de_{sysmanage\_server}$, IDS $de_{\text{int}rude\det ect}$, vulnerabilities scan server $de_{vul\_server}$.

DefenseAction: It is an atomic defense action leading to state change. Defense actions include permit action $da_{permit}$ and deny action $da_{deny}$ of firewall, the permission Encryption action $da_{permit\_crypt}$ of IPsec VPN, backup action $da_{backup}$ and rebuild action $da_{rebuild}$ of backup server, user authentication action $da^{authenticate}$, making patch action $da_{makepatch}$ and rebooting and shutdown action of system management server, alerting action $da_{alert}$ of IDS, scan action $da_{vulscan}$ of vulnerability scan server.

PolicyRelation: It denotes time series and logic relations among operational-level policies including sequence and, sequence or, parallel and, parallel or. It is equivalent to the means relation.

Context: It means a concrete environment in which we can deploy some means in domain, such as a concrete vulnerability (its vulnerability number is CVE-2002-0073), intruding event (DoS attacking).

The refinement relations of elements between goal-level and operational-level are defined as follows:

$R = \{RS, RU, RT, RR, RA, RDD, RC, RP\}$

$RS \subseteq Role \times Domain \times SNode$, representing refinement from role that belongs to a domain of source node;

$RU \subseteq Role \times User$, representing refinement from the role of user;

$RT \subseteq Target \times Domain \times TNode$, representing refinement from target that belongs to a domain of target node;

$RR \subseteq Target \times Resource$, representing refinement from target to resource;

$RA \subseteq Activity \times Action$, representing refinement from activity to action;

$RDD \subseteq Means \times DefenseAction \times DefenseEntity$, representing refinement from defense means to defense action and defense entity;

$RC \subseteq ContextType \times Context$, representing refinement from context type to context ;

$RP \subseteq MeansConstraints \times PolicyRelation$ ,representing refinement from MeansConstraints to PolicyRelation; In this paper, PolicyRelation is equivalent to MeansConstraints.

## 4 The Algorithm of Computer Network Defense Policy Refinement

Based on our computer network defense policy refinement model, we first constructed a defense policy refinement repository that includes network situation information and refinement rules. Then, we designed a CND policy refinement algorithm combined with defense policy refinement repository.

1. Repository of CND policy refinement. The repository includes network situation information and policy refinement rules. They are created with MySQL database.

Network situation information includes domain information that divides organization and forms a hierarchy structure; it also includes nodes information that describes the name, ID of nodes, user, and resources; linking relations among nodes that is constructed with adjacent matrix; roles information that describes the name, ID of roles and the domain of role; targets information that describes the name, ID of targets and the domain of target; defense entities information that describes the name, ID of defense entities, defense action; defense means that describes the name, ID of defense means; means relations among means; context type that describes the vulnerabilities and events.

Refinement rules describe the refinement relations between the elements of goal-level and operational-level. Refinement rules include the role-user rules that specify the refinement relations between role and user; the domain-node rules that specify the refinement relations between domain and node; the activity-action rules that specify the refinement relations between activity and action; context rules that specify the refinement relations between context type and context; means-defense entity rules that specify the refinement relations between means and defense entity.

2. The process of CND policy refinement algorithm.

We have designed a description language CNDIDL [15] for the CND policy goal. A scanning method was devised based on the lexical and syntax rules to decompose the defense policy goal described by CNDIDL and stored into the memory data structure. After the decomposition, we can transform a CND policy goal to one or more operational-level defense policies through policy refinement repository.

The process of transformation algorithm is shown as follow:

(1)At first, we used each defense means in the list of defense to estimate which type of defense policy goal it is. Based on the goals of protection (access control, user authentication, encryption communication, backup, patch making), detection (intrusion detection and vulnerabilities detection), response (rebooting, shutdown and the adding of access control rules) and recovery (rebuild), we completed the CND policy refinement with corresponding refinement algorithm. Now, we take the policy goal refinement of access control for example.

(2)According to defense means, we derived a type of defense entity-firewall through looking into the table of means-defense entity. In addition, in order to get the instance of defense entity to execute operational-level access control policy, we would first find a set of simple paths from source node to destination node. Simple path is a node sequence in which there is not a same node. For the permission policy, we would choose all firewalls in these paths. For the denial policy, we would choose the nearest firewalls from the source node in these paths. The pseudocode of algorithm of getting simple path set between source node and target node is shown as follow:

```
Algorithm GETSimplePathSet
INPUT : InitialNode : u, TargetNode : v, d = −1
OUTPUT : The set of simple path between node of u and v : PathSet
Procedure GetSimplePathSet(u, v, d)
d+1 ← d;
visited[u] = true;
path[d] = u;
IF(u == v) THEN
  FOR (i = 0) TO (d+1) DO
  PATH ← path[i]; // put all nodes into set PATH between u and v
  REPEAT
PathSet ← PathSet ∪ PATH; // get the set of all simple paths
```

```
ELSE THEN
    N = getAdjVetxSet(u); // get adjacent node set of u
    WHILE(n = GetFirstNode(N))
        IF(!visited[n]) THEN
        GetSimplePath(n,v,d);
            END IF
        n ← GetNextNode(N);
    END WHILE
ENDIF
END GetSimplePathSet
```

In this algorithm, we used an undirected graph to express the connecting relation between nodes for network topology and used an adjacency list to store an undirected graph. The time complexity of the algorithm is $O(n+e)$ .wherein, n denotes the number of vertex in undirected graph, e denotes the number of edge in undirected graph.

In choosing instance of other defense entity (such as IDS, system management server…et..al ), we would choose the nearest defense entity for the protection resource.

(3)According to the role, we can derive a set of users by looking into the table of role-user. Then we can get the set A of nodes by looking into table of node information. According to the domain, we can derive a set B of nodes by looking into the table of domain-node. At last, we can get the set C of node by operation of $A \cap B$ and get the corresponding IP address for these nodes by looking into the table of node information. In the same way, according to the target, we can derive a set of resources by looking into the table of target-resource. Then we can get the set A of nodes by looking into table of node information. According to the domain, we can derive a set B of nodes by looking into the table of domain-node. At last, we can get the set C of node by operation of $A \cap B$ and get the corresponding IP address and port number for these nodes by looking into the table of node information.

(4)According to the activity, we can derive a set of actions by looking into the table of activity-action.

(5)We can get an operational-level policy for firewall through the composition of the source IP address, the target IP address, port number, the set of actions and defense action.

(6)If more than two defense means exist in the list of defense means, we would get the next defense means and repeat the operation of (3)~(6) until all the means were processed. Then we get the means constraints and transform them to the relations of operational-level policies.

The pseudocode of transformation algorithm is shown as follows:

```
Algorithm CNDPolicyTransformation
INPUT : CNDPolicyGoal : G = {g_1, g_2, ...g_n}; RefinementRule : R
OUTPUT : CND Opreational Policy and Policy relations Set : O
Procedure PolicyTransform(G,R)
 // find the set of means g_i in a policy goal G and
  assign all elements of the g_i to the set M //
  M = findelement(G,Means,g_i) ;
```

*// find the set of means constraints* $g_t$ *in a policy goal G and*
*assign all elements of the* $g_t$ *to the set MC //*
$MC = findelement(G, MeansConstraints, g_t);$
$G = G - g_i - g_t;$
$1 \leftarrow x;$
$WHILE(m_x \in M)$
$FOR\ (j=1)\ TO\ (n-2)\ DO$
*// Base on R, get the elements of operational level corresponding*
*to the elements of goal level //*
$O^x_j \leftarrow g_j$
$REPEAT$
$O^x = \sum_{j}^{1} \cup O^x_j$ *// the corresponding operational level policy for the xth means //*
$x \leftarrow x+1;$
$REPEAT$
*// refinement from means constraints "MC" to operational level policy relation "PR" //*
$PR \leftarrow MC$
$O = \sum_{k=1}^{|M|} \cup O^k \cup PR$
*END PolicyRefine*

The time complexity of the algorithm is $O(s \bullet m)$ .wherein, n denotes the number of means in one policy goal, m denotes the number of elements in one policy goal.

# 5 The Experiment

In this section, we provide some examples to illustrate the effectiveness of policy refinement through our experiments.

## 5.1 Experimental Environment

Experiment goal: In order to test the validity of our refinement methods, we use CNDIDL[15] to describe one or more high-level defense policy goals. These high-level defense policy goals can be transformed to operational-level defense policies automatically with ours policy refinement method and the generated operational-level policies would be simulated in simulation platform GTNeTs in which the defense effect can be observed.

Network topology environment is shown in Fig. 1. The whole network is divided into three main parts: external network, DMZ, and internal network. DMZ includes Web server, DNS server, FTP server, and SMTP server (Corresponding IP addresses are 192.168.1.4/24, 192.168.1.5/24, 192.168.1.3/24, and 192.168.1.2/24.). The internal network is partitioned into two segments by switcher, i.e. Net 1 and Net 2. There are three hosts and one system management server (IP:192.168.2.2/24)in Net 1; one host and one Database Server (IP :192.168.3.2/24) in Net 2. There exist vulnerabilities in hosts and servers of DMZ and internal network (They are shown in Table 2). By exploiting these vulnerabilities, the attacker gains root access and brings about DoS attack.

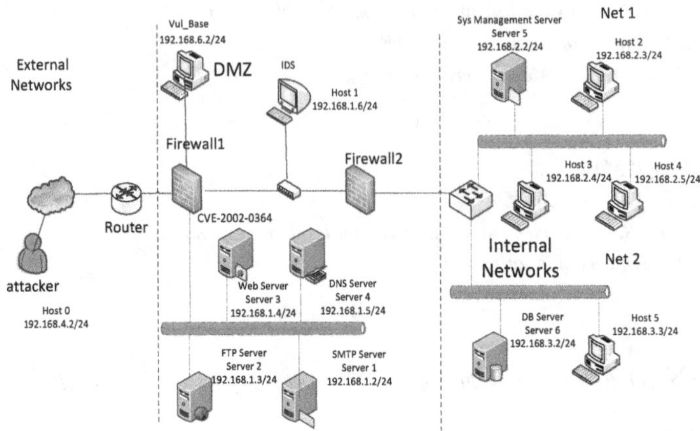


**Fig. 1.** Network topology

### 5.2 Experiment Verification and Analysis

The refinement of composition policies including intrusion detection, vulnerabilities detection, and access control.

Scenario: It was assumed that the attacker Host0 (IP Address 192.168.4.2) can access FTP server in DMZ, and bypass the Firewall2 and access DB server6 to conduct a DoS attack according to the configuration vulnerability of firewall. We deployed IDS, Vulnerability scan and Firewall1 to protect database server that provides services, when Dos attack was detected. The high-level policy goals are described by CNDIDL as follow:

$$PolicyGoal1\{Extranet, Unauthorized(user), \{DMZ, Net2\}, \{FTPservice, DBservice\},$$
$$TCP\ access, \{intrusion\_detect, vul\_scan, \neg access\_control\},$$
$$\{seq\_and(intrusion\_detect, vul\_scan), seq\_and(vul\_scan, \neg access\_control)\}\}$$

The description text for high-level policy goals includes a composition policy goal that describes intrusion detection and access control for FTP server2 and DB server6. Our policy refinement methods were used to transform high-level defense policy goals to operational-level defense policies. The operational-level defense policies are shown as follow:

$$PolicyOperation1\{$$
$$IDS1(alert\ TCP\ 192.168.4.2/24\ 192.168.1.0/24\ 21, "bufferoverflow";$$
$$alert\ TCP\ 192.168.4.2/24\ \ 192.168.3.0/24\ 1521, "dos";)\},$$
$$PolicyOperation2\{Vul\_Base(scan\ 192.168.1.0/24; scan\ 192.168.3.0/24;)\},$$
$$PolicyOperation3\{firewall\ 1$$
$$(deny\ TCP\ 192.168.4.2/24\ 192.168.1.3/24\ 21;$$
$$deny\ TCP\ 192.168.4.2/24\ \ 192.168.3.2/24\ 1521;)inpara:\{interface:4\}\},$$
$$policy\_relations: seq\_and(1,2); seq\_and(2,3)$$

The description text for operational-level policy includes three operational policies and relation of “sequence and”. These operational policies specify the availability requirements that guarantee that the server can provide services under the attacks of "bufferflow" and "dos". Wherein, when IDS1 detects the attacks including "bufferflow" and "dos", IDS1 sends information to the vulnerability server where the distributed vulnerabilities detection software is installed. The vulnerability server is informed of vulnerability CVE-2002-0509 and CVE-2002-0037 and it sends alert information subsequently. Then, the firewall interface of IP 192.168.1.5 will add a denying rule. The running effectiveness in simulation platform GTNetS is shown in the Fig.2. The yellow packet in the circle denotes enquiring packet from IDS to vulnerability library.

The vulnerability server queries the database and affirms this attack. Then it sends affirmed information to IDS. In Fig. 3, the gray packet in the circle denotes affirmed packet from vulnerability library to IDS.

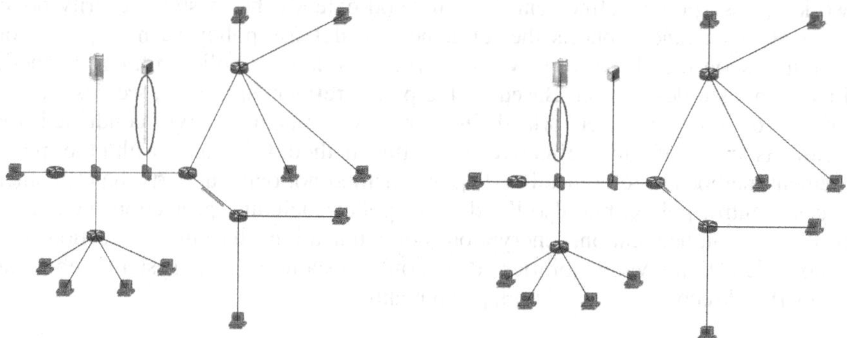

**Fig. 2.** Inquiring message **Fig. 3.** Affirming message

In Fig. 4, the red packet in the circle denotes that IDS informs the firewall1 to forbid the unlawful access after receiving the vulnerability affirmed information.

In this way, the packet of attacker cannot bypass the firewall1. It is shown in Fig. 5. The control platform results of the packet denying from attacker are shown in Fig. 6.

Based on this experiment, we find that IDS, Firewall, and vulnerability server execute policy correctly. When there is some vulnerability in the network, the linkage of security equipment can complete network defense effectively. And there is no need for human interference.

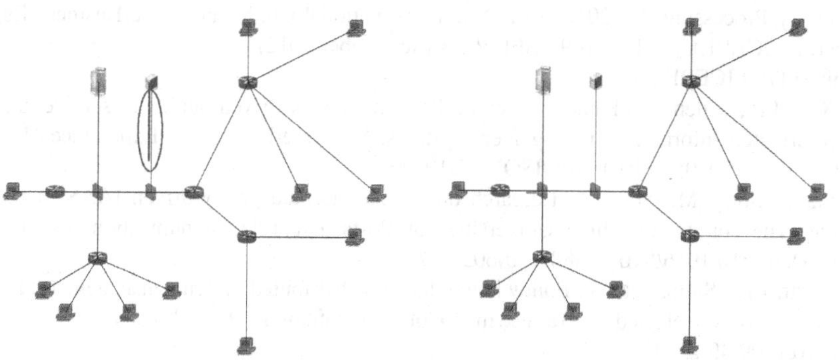

**Fig. 4.** Denying packet message **Fig. 5.** The packet denied from attacker

```
IP access list 4
the packet from 192.168.4.2 has been blocked
```

**Fig. 6.** The control platform results of the packet denying from attacker

## 6 Conclusions

The existing security policy refinement methods and model are not constructed on the grounds of computer network defense. Thus they can only support the refinement of access control policy, but not the refinement of defense policy, such as the policies of IDS, backup, and recovery. For this reason, we proposed a method for computer network defense policy refinement. This method extends the existing security policy refinement model and supports the refinement of defense policy such as protection, detection, response and recovery. We constructed a defense policy refinement model and its formalism description. Based on the policy refinement model, we designed an algorithm of computer network defense policy refinement. We conducted two experiments and verified the effectiveness of this method. Compared with other policy refinement methods in reference [12-14], our method not only supports the refinement of access control policy, but also the defense policy including protection (i.e., access control, user authentication, encryption communication, backup), detection (i.e., intrusion detection, vulnerabilities detection), response (i.e., system rebooting, shutdown) and recovery (i.e., rebuild, patch making).

**Acknowledgment.** This work is supported by the following funding sources: the National Nature Science Foundation of China under Grant No. 61170295, the Project of National ministry under Grant No.A2120110006, the Co-Funding Project of Beijing Municipal education Commission under Grant No.JD100060630 and the Project of BUAA Basal Research Fund under Grant No.YWF-11-03-Q-001.

## References

1. Zeng, H., Ma, D.F., Li, Z.Q., Zhao, Y.W.: A Policy-Based Architecture for Web Services Security Processing. In: 2012 IEEE Ninth International Conference on e-Business Engineering (ICEBE), pp. 163–169. IEEE Press (September 2012), doi:10.1109/ICEBE.2012.35
2. Loyall, J.P., Gillen, M., Paulos, A., et al.: Dynamic policy-driven quality of service in service-oriented information management systems. Software-Practice & Experience 41(12), 1459–1489 (2010), doi:10.1109/ISORC.2010.13
3. Luo, X., Song, M., Song, J.: Research on service-oriented policy-driven IAAS management. The Journal of China Universities of Posts and Telecommunications 18, 64–70 (2011), doi:10.1016/S1005-8885(10)60208-7
4. Moffett, J.D., Sloman, M.S.: Policy hierarchies for distributed systems management. IEEE Journal on Selected Areas in Communications 11(9), 1404–1414 (1993), doi:10.1109/49.257932

5. Kumari, P., Pretschner, A.: Deriving implementation-level policies for usage control enforcement. In: Proceedings of the Second ACM Conference on Data and Application Security and Privacy, pp. 83–94. ACM Press (2012), doi:10.1145/2133601.2133612
6. Basile, C., Lioy, A., Vallini, M.: Towards a Network-Independent Policy Specification. In: 2010 18th Euromicro International Conference on Parallel, Distributed and Network-Based Processing (PDP 2010), pp. 649–653. IEEE Press (February 2010), doi:10.1109/PDP.2010.45
7. Maity, S., Ghosh, S.K.: Enforcement of access control policy for mobile ad hoc networks. In: Proceedings of the Fifth International Conference on Security of Information and Networks (SIN 2012), pp. 47–52. ACM Press (2012), doi:10.1145/2388576.2388582
8. Department of Defense. JP3-13: Information Operations. US Government printing, Washington, DC (February 2006)
9. Bandara, A.K., Lupu, E.C., Moffett, J., Russo, A.: A goal-based approach to policy refinement. In: Fifth IEEE International Workshop on Policies for Distributed Systems and Networks, pp. 229–239. IEEE Press (June 2004), doi:10.1109/POLICY.2004.1309175
10. de Albuquerque, J.P., Krumm, H., de Geus, P.L., Jeruschkat, R.: Scalable model-based configuration management of security services in complex enterprise networks. Software: Practice and Experience 41(3), 307–338 (2011), doi:10.1002/spe.1014
11. Bryans, J.W., Fitzgerald, J.S., McCutcheon, T.: Refinement-Based Techniques in the Analysis of Information Flow Policies for Dynamic Virtual Organisations. In: Camarinha-Matos, L.M., Pereira-Klen, A., Afsarmanesh, H. (eds.) PRO-VE 2011. IFIP AICT, vol. 362, pp. 314–321. Springer, Heidelberg (2011)
12. Laborde, R., Kamel, M., Barrere, F., Benzekri, A.: Implementation of a formal security policy refinement process in WBEM architecture. Journal of Network and Systems Management 15(2), 241–266 (2007), doi:10.1007/s10922-007-9063-z
13. Stouls, N., Potet, M.-L.: Security policy enforcement through refinement process. In: Julliand, J., Kouchnarenko, O. (eds.) B 2007. LNCS, vol. 4355, pp. 216–231. Springer, Heidelberg (2006)
14. Hassan, A.A., Bahgat, W.M.: A Framework for Translating a High Level Security Policy into Low Level Security Mechanisms. In: 2009 IEEE/ACS International Conference on Computer Systems and Applications, pp. 504–511. IEEE Press (2009), doi:10.1109/AICCSA.2009.5069371
15. Wei, Q., Lü, L.S., Wei, Z., Wu, W.K., Xia, C.H.: CNDIDL:A CND Intention Description Language for CND Decision. In: 2012 World Congress on Information and Communication Technologies (WICT 2012), pp. 1142–1147. IEEE Press (November 2012), doi:10.1109/WICT.2012.6409246

# An Efficient Update Mechanism for GPU-Based IP Lookup Engine Using Threaded Segment Tree

Yanbiao Li[1], Dafang Zhang[1], Gaogang Xie[2], Jintao Zheng[1], and Wei Zhao[1]

[1] College of Information Science and Engineering, Hunan University, Changsha, 410082, China
[2] Institute of Computing Technology, Chinese Academy of Sciences, Beijing, 100190, China

**Abstract.** Recently, the Graphics Processing Unit (GPU) has been used to deploy high-speed software routers. On this platform, designing an efficient IP lookup engine is still a challenging task, especially when taking into account the comprehensive performance under frequent updates. Existing solutions either fail in dealing with update overhead, or can not provide stable throughput. In this paper, we first propose the Threaded Segment Tree, a novel tree-like structure. On this basis, we then present a fast IP lookup engine with an efficient parallel update mechanism. According to our experiment results on real-world data, the proposed mechanism reduces the memory accesses on the GPU and the overall update overhead by at least 82.5% and 89.6% respectively. Moreover, it also ensures the lookup engine provides stable throughput under highly frequent updates, which only decreases by less than 1% even though update frequency increases to 100, 000 *updates/s*.

**Keywords:** GPU, IP lookup, parallel update, segment tree.

## 1 Introduction

IP address lookup, as a key function of modern routers for packets forwarding and classifying, aims to determine a proper next hop for each incoming packet, through comparing its destination address against all prefixes stored in the Forwarding Information Base (FIB). It is always modeled as a Longest Prefix Matching (LPM) problem.

### 1.1 Summarize of Prior Arts

Classic solutions to LPM fall into two major categories. Hardware-based solutions always provide very fast lookup [1, 2], but their low flexibilities and high consumptions on power and cost make them unadaptable to large tables, or to growing requirements on scalability. By contrast, software-based solutions are proved more flexible due to some tree-like data structures [3–5]. But processing LPM on them requires multiple memory accesses for one lookup. Though optimized by many techniques [6, 7], their performance are still difficult to meet today's link speed.

J. Su et al. (Eds.): ICoC 2013, CCIS 401, pp. 134–144, 2013.

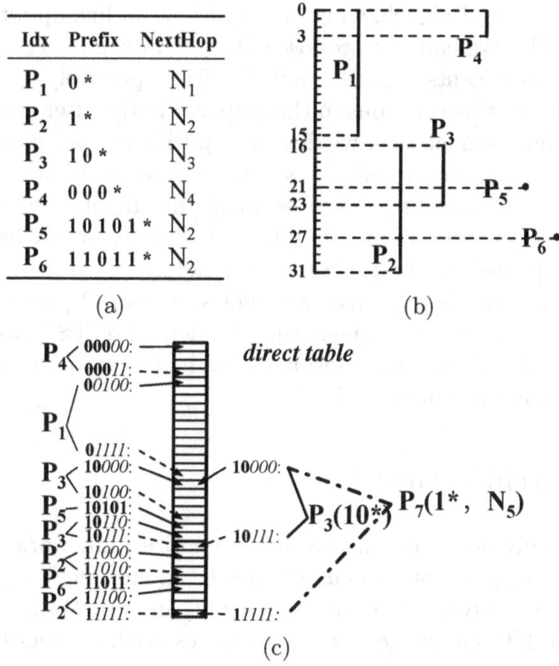

| Idx | Prefix | NextHop |
|---|---|---|
| $P_1$ | 0* | $N_1$ |
| $P_2$ | 1* | $N_2$ |
| $P_3$ | 10* | $N_3$ |
| $P_4$ | 000* | $N_4$ |
| $P_5$ | 10101* | $N_2$ |
| $P_6$ | 11011* | $N_2$ |



**Fig. 1.** (a) FIB. (b) A sample of GALE's direct table. Deleting $P_3(10*)$ from it and then inserting $P_7(1*, N_5)$ into it must be processed in order. (c) Transforming prefixes into segments. To simplify examples, we suppose the focused maximum prefix length is 5 (which is 24 in practice).

Fortunately, some GPU-based software routers [8–10] have been proposed to provide both high throughput and high scalability. However, with major focus on the entire framework design, they all treat the routing table as static and thus fail in dealing with update overhead. In view of this, J. Zhao et al. [11] presented a GPU-Accelerated Lookup Engine (GALE), which provides both fast lookup and the solution to route updates. Due to its update mechanism, a update request, after being used to update a trie, is mapped into a range of unit modifications toward a direct table stored on the GPU. However, different updates may be mapped to the same unit. So, even with a careful length checking, breaking their order may also lead to incorrect updates (as shown in Fig. 1(c)). Accordingly, in GALE, not all updates can be processed in parallel, which obstructs it to benefit enough from GPU's parallelism.

### 1.2 Our Approach and Key Contributions

In this paper, we first implement the TBL24 of DIR-24-8 scheme [12] on the GPU, just like GALE, to enable O(1) lookup. Then, instead of using a trie, we present a novel tree-like structure, Threaded Segment Tree (TST), to process off-line updates on the CPU, achieving more efficient on-line updates toward the TBL24 on the GPU. We call the proposed IP lookup engine TSTT, for its two most important components are TST and TBL24 respectively.

We make three key contributions in this paper. Firstly, after transforming the FIB into a compact segment tree, we design a special leaf-pushing technique, to divide all prefixes into several non-intersecting segments. Besides, we present a series of algorithms to thread necessary segments during off-line updates, ensuring threaded segments cover all update information without any intersecting. As a result, on-line updates can be processed completely in parallel.

The rest of this paper is organized as follows. Section 2 presents the system architecture of our proposed scheme. And the details of TST are proposed in Sect. 3. Section 4 discusses the performance evaluation experiments. At last, a short conclusion are given in Sect. 5.

## 2 System Architecture

Since there are many novel designs toward the entire framework of GPU-based software routers [8, 9], we only focus on the IP lookup engine, which can be deployed into such routers as an additional plug-in [11]. With the help of an optimized packet I/O engine [8], which manages packet queues and extracts pending packets' destination addresses for lookup, we pay our major attention to the GPU-based accelerator for table lookup and update.

As shown in Fig. 2, our system architecture is based on Compute Unified Device Architecture (CUDA), in which, all program codes are divided into two cooperative parts, the *Host* and the *Device*, executed respectively on the CPU and the GPU. In the *Device*, the TBL24, which stores all prefixes no longer than 24 (the rest are stored in a small TCAM, which is not shown in Fig.2), provides O(1) lookup. In the *Host*, as managed by a control thread, a group of working threads process lookup and update requests, by utilizing the computing resources of both the CPU and the GPU.

Processing route updates on TBL24 always needs help from additional structures [11]. In TSTT, TST plays such a role. Actually, in our case, all prefixes no longer than 24 are transformed into segments, each of which corresponds to a range of units of the TBL24. Then, a TST is constructed on bidis of these segments, which is stored in the host memory (on the CPU) for off-line updates. When a route update arrives, it is first used to update this TST, producing several unit modifications toward the TBL24. During such off-line updates on the CPU, all produced unit modifications are collected, and are then processed on the GPU to update the TBL24 for on-line updates.

As the GPU works in Single Instructions with Multiple Threads (SIMT), batch processing is required for improving performance. As long as all unit modifications produced during off-line updates are kept independently with each other, all of them can be processed in parallel on the GPU. In this case, we can

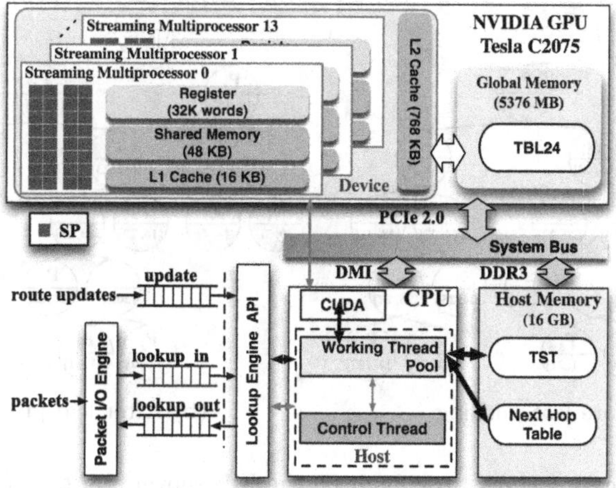


**Fig. 2.** TSTT's architecture based on CUDA

collect all produced unit modifications in batchs, and send them to the GPU batch by batch, by utilizing multiple streams[1].

Besides, to avoid storing complicated next hop information (such as multi-next-hop [13]) on the GPU, we store their index in the TST and the TBL24 instead, with entire next hop information stored in a separated Next Hop Table on the CPU.

## 3 Threaded Segment Tree (TST)

### 3.1 Segment Tree and Prefix Transforming

Segment Tree is a special binary search tree that supports dynamic lookup and update. Some of its extensions have been already used in IP lookup [14] and packet classifying [15]. They all transform prefixes into segments in a straight-forward way. As shown in Fig. 1(b), the maximum prefix length is supposed to be $max$, if the length and value[2] for a prefix are denoted as $len$ and $pre$ respectively, then, its corresponding segment can be calculated as $[pre \times 2^{max-len}, pre \times 2^{max-len} + 2^{max-len} - 1]$.

### 3.2 Building Leaf-pushed Segment Tree

After transforming all prefixes into segments (as shown in Fig. 1(b)), a segment tree can be easily constructed. But in our case, the segment tree is only used to produce segments that represents unit modifications toward TBL24 during

[1] In CUDA, a steam is a sequence of operations executed in order.

[2] For a prefix formatted as $a.b.c.d/len$, its prefix length is $len$ and its prefix value is $(a \times 2^{24} + b \times 2^{16} + c \times 2^{8} + d) >> (32 - len)$.

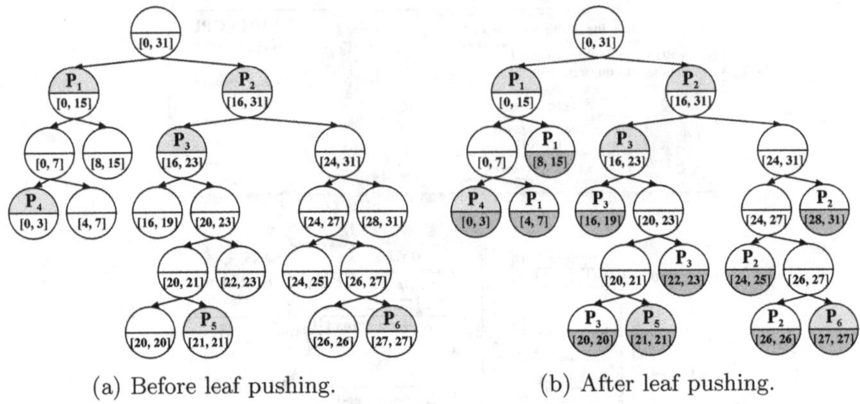


**Fig. 3.** Segment tree built on the FIB shown in Fig. 1(a)

**Algorithm 1.** Leaf Pushing

```
Input: curNode, nextHop
if curNode = NULL or curNode.isPrefixSeg then
 | return;
end
LeafPushing (curNode.leftChild, nextHop);
if curNode.isLeaf then
 | ModifyNode (curNode, nextHop);
end
LeafPushing (curNode.rightChild, nextHop);
```

off-line updates. In order to generate as less segments as possible, we build a compact segment tree (as shown in Fig. 3), in which a segment should not be broken unless necessary. Originally, a prefix corresponds to only one segment (let's call it *prefix segment*), whose value is set as the entry index of this prefix. So, each update request needs only modify just one prefix segment, enabling update process be simple and efficient.

However, since two prefix segments may intersect with each other, on-line updates produced by them may toward the same unit, making it unavailable to process them in parallel. To address this issue, we introduce a special leaf pushing technique[3] to push all prefix segments' values into leaf segments (shown in Fig. 3(b)). Unlike the traditional leaf-pushing algorithm [6], there are two important special rules for ours: **1)** All prefix segments still reserve their own values after leaf pushing. **2)** Each value is pushed from some prefix segment down to all possible leaf segments, until reaching another prefix segment. This algorithm is described in Algorithm 1.

[3] Leaf Pushing is a widely used technique for Trie-based IP lookup.

After leaf pushing, each leaf segment contains an index number that corresponds to a route entry, so as all prefix segments. On the other hand, a segment can be represented by several leaf segments. In another word, instead of producing unit modifications by all prefix segments, we can use a group of leaf segments to do the same thing. Since any two leaf segments will not intersect with each other, all produced unit modifications in this way can be processed in parallel now.

### 3.3 Threading Leaf Segments during Off-line Updates

Based on the leaf-pushed segment tree, several leaf segments can be used to produce unit modifications without intersecting. The next problem is to determine which segments are required. In this section, we present a series of algorithms to solve this problem, by threading all necessary leaf segments during off-line updates. Since modifying an existing prefix can be treated as inserting a new prefix, we only discuss how to delete/insert a prefix.

**Prefix Deletion.** To delete a prefix, we begin with looking up its corresponding segment. If no one matches, nothing needs to do. Otherwise, the value of the matched segment should be modified to the value of the nearest segment along the path from it to the tree root (if no one found, use the default). Then, its new value should be pushed down.

For example, as shown in Fig .4(a), to delete $P_3(10*)$, its corresponding prefix segment $[16, 23 : P_3]$ should be modified to $P_2$ (the nearest segment along the path from it to the root is $16, 31 : P_2$), which is then pushed down to three leaf segments: $[16, 19]$, $[20, 20]$ and $[22, 23]$. While for deleting $P_1(0*)$, the value of its corresponding segment $0, 15 : P_1$ is modified to the default (e.g. 0). And the default is then pushed down to two leaf segments: $[4, 17]$ and $[8, 15]$. During the deleting process, we use a doubly linked list to thread all leaf segments modified. This algorithm is described in Algorithm 2.

**Prefix Insertion.** Inserting a prefix is namely inserting a segment. If this segment is already exist, its value should be set as the inserting prefix's entry index. Then, this new value should be pushed down. During this process, all leaf segments modified should be threaded in the double linked list. If the inserting prefix segment is not exist, a series of leaf segments should be broken into new segments until the inserting segment has been produced. During this process, all generated leaf segments should be threaded. On the other hand, if a threaded segment has been broken, it must be removed from the list.

For example, as shown in Fig. 4(b), to insert $P_7(1*, N_5)$, since its prefix segment $[16, 31]$ is already exist, the value of this segment is set as $P_7$, which is then pushed down. While for inserting $P_8(0001*)$, $[0, 3 : P_4]$ is broken into $[0, 1 : P_4]$ and $[2, 3 : P_8]$, which should be threaded in turn. This algorithm is described in Algorithm 3.

**Algorithm 2.** Delete Segment

```
Input: curNode, delSeg, nextHop
if curNode.seg = delSeg and nextHop ≠ DEFAULT then
    curNode.seg.value = DEFAULT; curNode.isPrefixSeg = FALSE;
    LeafPushing (curNode, nextHop);
end
else
    if curNode.isLeaf then
        return;
    end
    if curNode.isPrefixSeg then
        nextHop = curNode.seg.value;
    end
    mid = (curNode.seg.low + curNode.seg.high)/2;
    if mid < delSeg.low then
        DeleteSegment (curNode.rightChild, delSeg, nextHop);
    end
    if mid ≥ delSeg.high then
        DeleteSegment (curNode.leftChild, delSeg, nextHop);
    end
end
```

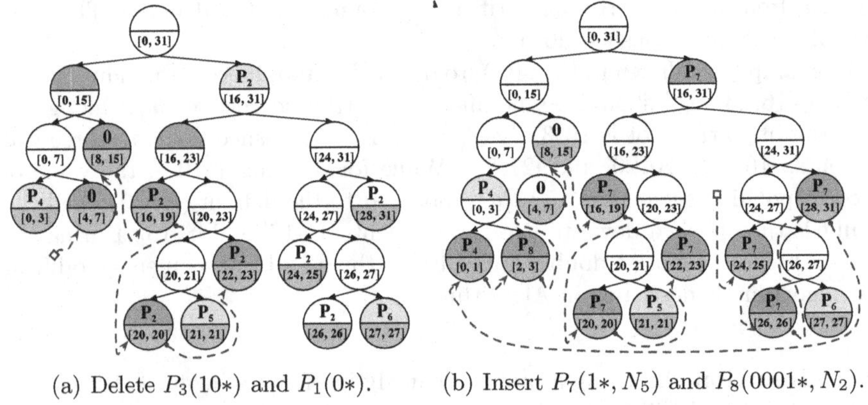


(a) Delete $P_3(10*)$ and $P_1(0*)$. (b) Insert $P_7(1*, N_5)$ and $P_8(0001*, N_2)$.

**Fig. 4.** Threading leaf segments during off-line updates. Only one direction's connection of the double linked list is shown.

## 4 Experimental Evaluation

In this section, based on four real-world routing data sets collected from the RIPE RIS Project [16] (shown in Table.1), we conduct a group of experiments to evaluate TSTT's performance, and demonstrate its superiorities in comparison with GALE. The experimental system is set up on a server with an Intel CPU (Xeon E5-2630, 2.30GHz, 6Cores) and an NVIDIA GPU (Tesla C2075, 1.15 GHz,

**Algorithm 3.** Insert Segment

```
Input: curNode, insSeg
if curNode.seg = insSeg then
    curNode.seg.value = DEFAULT; curNode.isPrefixSeg = FALSE;
    LeafPushing (curNode, nextHop);
end
else
    if curNode.isLeaf then
        BreakSegment (curNode);
    end
    mid = (curNode.seg.low + curNode.seg.high)/2;
    if mid < insSeg.low then
        InsertSegment (curNode.rightChild, insSeg);
    end
    if mid ≥ insSeg.high then
        InsertSegment (curNode.leftChild, insSeg);
    end
end
```

448 Cores) on the basis of CUDA 5.0. We measure all concerned metrics through the *NVIDIA Visual Profiler* [17].

**Table 1.** Routing Data Sets (Collected at Jan. 1, 2013)

| Data Set | Location | Total Prefixes | Total Updates |
|---|---|---|---|
| rrc11 | New York (NY), USA | 442,176 | 1,177,425 |
| rrc12 | Frankfurt, Germany | 450,752 | 4,049,260 |
| rrc13 | Moscow, Russia | 456,580 | 2,025,239 |
| rrc14 | Palo Alto, USA | 446,160 | 1,388,217 |

### 4.1 Memory Accesses Required for On-line Updates

To evaluate the performance of route update, we replay a week's update traces of *rrc*12 and a whole day's update traces for all tables. After processing off-line updates in TST, we get a list of threaded segments, each of which represents several memory writes toward a range of units of the TBL24 on the GPU. While for GALE, due to the length map checking, it requires both memory reads and writes on the GPU to finish on-line updates. We evaluate the performance of on-line updates by measuring the average produced global memory accesses per update on the GPU.

As depicted in Fig. 5(a), the average produced memory accesses in TSTT are far less than that in GALE in all cases. In fact, TSTT achieves a reduction by 92.5% $\sim$ 98.1%, which is still 82.5% $\sim$ 97.3% even ignoring memory reads in

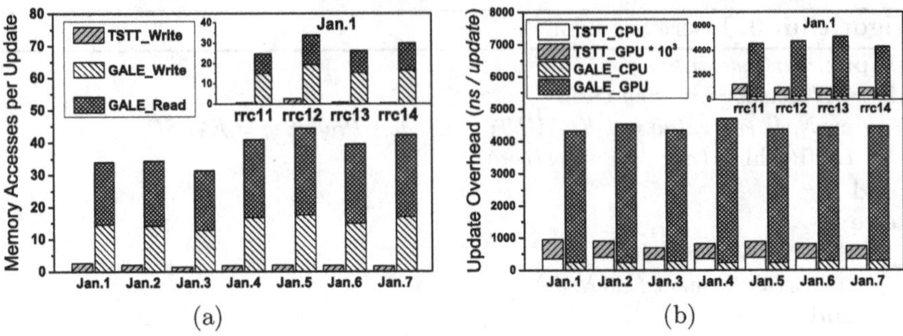


**Fig. 5.** (a) average memory accesses produced per update on the GPU. (b) overall update overhead on both the CPU and the GPU per update.

GALE. Such a significant improvement benefits from our mechanism essentially. Actually, in TSTT, all produced unit modifications cover all update information without any redundancy. So, excluding any of them must lose some update information. In another word, the number of memory modifications for on-line updates are minimized by TSTT.

### 4.2 Overall Update Overhead

Then, we take into account the overall update overhead (in time cost) for both off-line updates (on the CPU) and on-line updates (on the GPU). Since TSTT's on-line update overhead are too small, we **times it by** $10^3$.

As shown in Fig. 5(b), the average update overhead per update of TSTT's on-line updates is only 0.72 *ns* in the worst case, achieving a speedup than GALE by a factor over 5000. Such a fast speed benefits from that the number of produced unit modifications in TSTT are minimized, and all of them can be processed in parallel on the GPU.

However, processing off-line updates in TSTT costs more time than that in GALE by a factor of $2.3 \sim 3.4$. That's because some additional operations are required in TSTT, such as leaf pushing and list management. Even though, in comparison with GALE, TSTT's overall update overhead is still reduced by $89.6\% \sim 93.5\%$, which demonstrates clearly that TSTT's update mechanism is more efficient.

### 4.3 Comprehensive Performance

In order to evaluate the comprehensive performance, we process a $16M$ generated lookup requests in TSTT and GALE respectively, with update frequency increasing to $100,000$ *updates/s*. Then, we measure the throughputs with Million Lookups Per Second (MLPS) in all cases.

As presented in Fig. 6, without any updates, TSTT provides the same throughput (539 *MLPS*) as GALE. That's because their lookup approaches are

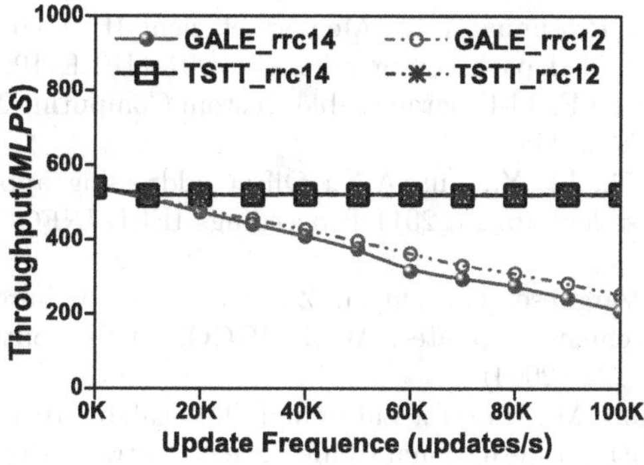


**Fig. 6.** Comprehensive performance on rrc12 and rrc14

all based on the DIR-24-8 scheme. However, as update frequency is increasing, TSTT's superiority becomes more and more significant. Actually, in GALE, the throughput decreases by 53.4% and 61.4% on *rrc*12 and *rrc*14 respectively. But such descents in TSTT are even below 0.4%. In another word, with the help of an efficient update mechanism, TSTT enables more stable throughput under frequent updates than GALE.

## 5 Conclusion

In this paper, we have proposed an efficient update mechanism for a GPU-accelerated IP lookup engine. By deploying the TBL24 of DIR-24-8 onto GPU's global memory, our proposed engine, TSTT, enables O(1) lookup. Moreover, we presented an novel tree-like structure, Threaded Segment Tree (TST), to help update the TBL24 on the GPU. Actually, by threading necessary leaf segments during off-line updates, the number of unit modifications for on-line updates are minimized, and all of them can be processed completely in parallel. According to the experiment results, using our mechanism, the average required memory accesses for on-line updates and the overall update overhead on both the CPU and the GPU in average are reduced by at least 82.5% and 89.6% respectively. What's more, due to the proposed update mechanism, the throughput in TSTT has been proved more stable. Actually, it only decreased by at most 0.9% even if update frequency increases to $100,000/s$.

**Acknowledgment.** This work is supported by the National Basic Research Program of China (973) under Grant 2012CB315805, and the National Science Foundation of China under Grant 61173167.

## References

1. Jiang, W., Wang, Q., Prasanna, V.K.: Beyond TCAMs: An SRAM-based parallel multi-pipeline architecture for terabit ip lookup. In: IEEE INFOCOM 2008 The 27th Conference on Computer Communications, pp. 1786–1794. IEEE (2008)

2. Le, H., Jiang, W., Prasanna, V.K.: Memory-efficient IPv4/v6 lookup on FPGAs using distance-bounded path compression. In: 2011 IEEE 19th Annual International Symposium on Field-Programmable Custom Computing Machines (FCCM), pp. 242–249. IEEE (2011)
3. Huang, K., Xie, G., Li, Y., Liu, A.X.: Offset addressing approach to memory-efficient IP address lookup. In: 2011 Proceedings IEEE INFOCOM, pp. 306–310. IEEE (2011)
4. Eatherton, W., Varghese, G., Dittia, Z.: Tree bitmap: hardware/software IP lookups with incremental updates. ACM SIGCOMM Computer Communication Review 34(2), 97–122 (2004)
5. Song, H., Kodialam, M., Hao, F., Lakshman, T.: Scalable IP lookups using shape graphs. In: 17th IEEE International Conference on Network Protocols, ICNP 2009, pp. 73–82. IEEE (2009)
6. Srinivasan, V., Varghese, G.: Fast IP address lookups using controlled prefix expansion. ACM Transactions on Computer Systems (TOCS) 17(1), 1–40 (1999)
7. Bando, M., Chao, H.J.: Flashtrie: hash-based prefix-compressed trie for ip route lookup beyond 100gbps. In: 2010 Proceedings IEEE INFOCOM, pp. 1–9. IEEE (2010)
8. Han, S., Jang, K., Park, K., Moon, S.: Packetshader: A GPU-accelerated software router. ACM SIGCOMM Computer Communication Review 40(4), 195–206 (2010)
9. Zhu, Y., Deng, Y., Chen, Y.: Hermes: an integrated CPU/GPU microarchitecture for IP routing. In: Proceedings of the 48th Design Automation Conference, pp. 1044–1049. ACM (2011)
10. Mu, S., Zhang, X., Zhang, N., Lu, J., Deng, Y.S., Zhang, S.: IP routing processing with graphic processors. In: Proceedings of the Conference on Design, Automation and Test in Europe, European Design and Automation Association, pp. 93–98 (2010)
11. Zhao, J., Zhang, X., Wang, X., Deng, Y., Fu, X.: Exploiting graphics processors for high-performance IP lookup in software routers. In: 2011 Proceedings IEEE INFOCOM, pp. 301–305. IEEE (2011)
12. Gupta, P., Lin, S., McKeown, N.: Routing lookups in hardware at memory access speeds. In: Proceedings of the INFOCOM 1998, Seventeenth Annual Joint Conference of the IEEE Computer and Communications Societies, vol. 3, pp. 1240–1247. IEEE (1998)
13. Wenping, C., Xingming, Z., Jianhui, Z., Bin, W.: Research on multi next hop rip. In: International Forum on Information Technology and Applications, IFITA 2009, vol. 1, pp. 16–19. IEEE (2009)
14. Chang, Y.K., Lin, Y.C., Su, C.C.: Dynamic multiway segment tree for ip lookups and the fast pipelined search engine. IEEE Transactions on Computers 59(4), 492–506 (2010)
15. Su, C.F.: High-speed packet classification using segment tree. In: IEEE Global Telecommunications Conference, GLOBECOM 2000, pp. 582–586. IEEE (2000)
16. RIPE network coordination centre, `http://www.ripe.net`
17. NVIDIA Corporation: NVIDIA CUDA Profiler User Guide, Version 5.0 (October 2012)

# Research on Resource Management in PaaS Based on IaaS Environment

Peng Xu, Rui Hu, and Sen Su

State Key Lab of Networking and Switching Technology
Beijing University of Posts and Telecommunications
Beijing, China
xupeng@bupt.edu.cn

**Abstract.** As one of the three service models of cloud computing, PaaS (Platform as a Service) has gained more and more popularity for its capabilities in optimizing development productivity and business agility. However, the traditional PaaS uses the dedicated infrastructure, which generally leads to the low infrastructure utilization rate. To solve the above problem, PaaS based on IaaS (PoI) emerged, in which IaaS (Infrastructure as a Service) is involved to provide PaaS the infrastructure, to decrease the response time of the infrastructure scale and to increase the utilization of the infrastructure. Because PoI has many characteristics, resource management mechanisms used in the traditional PaaS or IaaS could no longer adopted in PoI. In this paper, an adaptive resource management framework and the corresponding scale-up, scale-down algorithms are brought forward to guarantee the QoS of applications deployed in PaaS platform as well as to decrease the rental cost of VMs from IaaS providers. Experimental results show that the resource management mechanisms proposed in this paper can not only guarantee QoS of all applications, but also improve the utilization rate of the infrastructure, thus to make PoI possess the advantages of both PaaS and IaaS.

**Keywords:** cloud computing, paas, iaas, resource management.

## 1 Introduction

Cloud computing has gained unprecedented popularity since its inception and becomes a great solution to provide a flexible, on-demand and dynamically scalable computing infrastructure for enterprises. Its *Pay-As-You-Go* pricing model is essentially similar to other public utilities (e.g., electricity, gas and water). Therefore, cloud computing is also called "On-Demand Computing". Cloud computing supports three service models: Infrastructure as a Service (IaaS), Platform as a Service (PaaS) and Software as a Service (SaaS).

IaaS, as the basic cloud service model, enables users to rent the infrastructure (server, storage and network etc.) dynamically as needed. Since the increasing requirements to improve the cost-efficiency of Internet Data Centers (IDCs), IaaS has been widely adopted by more and more enterprises to improve the utilization rate of

J. Su et al. (Eds.): ICoC 2013, CCIS 401, pp. 145–157, 2013.

the infrastructure. At the same time, enterprises, especially IT companies, tend to set up PaaS platforms to provide Application Execution Environment (AEE) for their applications and reuse a variety of application components. Because PaaS also has to rely on the infrastructure such as servers and storage, IaaS becomes a candidate to provide PaaS the infrastructure. That is the PaaS based on IaaS (PoI). PoI could provide the features of both PaaS and IaaS: i) to provide AEE for applications and application components as PaaS; ii) to increase the utilization rate of the infrastructure as IaaS.

Resource management is one of the most important issues of cloud computing which decides the efficiency of the platform. In PoI, resource management also plays a very important role as well. It has many characteristics: i) the traffic model and QoS requirements of different applications on PoI are different and changing fast. ii) PaaS could dynamically use the resource of IaaS according to the requirements of applications.

In this paper, a QoS guaranteed and cost-efficient resource management mechanism in PoI is presented. The rest of the paper is organized as follows. The related works are introduced in Section 2. Then the architecture of PoI is illustrated in Section 3. In section 4, the problems which have to be faced by PoI are stated and the resource management framework of PoI is brought forward in detail. In the end, the experimental results are presented in Section 5 followed by the conclusions and future works in section 6.

## 2 Related Works

Recent research on dynamic resource provisioning in virtualized environments includes [1]. These research attempted to achieve application performance goals with dynamic resource provisioning in virtualized environments. Most recently, people extended the idea into the cloud environment [2]. [3] investigated task scheduling with deadline and budget constraints in the heterogeneous environment. Some research investigated cost-efficiency in the cloud environment. On the cloud providers' point of view, [4][5] discussed the resource allocation and instance consolidation strategies for cloud data centers. The goal is to maximize the profits of cloud providers while maintaining Service Level Agreement (SLAs). [6] discussed power management in cloud environment. On the cloud users' point of view, the hot topic is to build strategies to deploy applications among multiple cloud providers to enhance availability with minimum cost [7].

Because PaaS platform is essentially a distributed system, it faces similar resource management problems like other distributed systems. Computing resources (e.g., CPU, memory, disk I/O and network bandwidth) are limited in distributed systems; therefore how to manage these resources with high efficiency is critical. PaaS platform is asynchronous soft real-time system [8]. On one hand, PaaS platform is asynchronous because requests of applications on PaaS are unpredictable and nondeterministic, and the distribution of the requests cannot be precisely described by mathematical models. On the other hand, it is a soft real-time system because there are some constraints on the response time, but the failure of timeliness will only lead to some small losses rather than disastrous consequences. The workload PaaS platform confronted fluctuates within a wide range. Over-provisioning system resources to accommodate the potential peak will lead to the waste of the resource. As a consequence, it is important for PaaS platform to maintain efficient resource utilization under a wide workload conditions without increasing the possibility of failure of timeliness. [9] proposed a new algorithm called FC-LRU which integrates feedback control with LRU algorithm to perform adaptive resource management in PaaS platform. However, the idea of FC-LRU algorithm is based on the assumption that the PaaS platform is using its dedicated infrastructure. Therefore, the resource management mechanism in traditional PaaS platform is no longer practical in PoI. New mechanism for PoI should be adopted.

## 3 Architecture of PaaS Based on IaaS

Some enterprises adopt PaaS to provide AEE for their applications and application components, because PaaS is famous for optimizing development productivity and business agility. However, the benefits of the traditional PaaS are limited, because the cost of the infrastructure scale-down and scale-up is high and with low efficiency in the typical PaaS. At the same time, IaaS has many advantages in optimizing infrastructure utilization. In order to maximize business agility and development productivity, enterprises are trying to set up PaaS on IaaS, namely PoI. PoI provides application development, testing, execution and provision environment which enables both PaaS' ease of application deployment and IaaS' efficient infrastructure management.

In the traditional PaaS, the infrastructure is dedicated for its usage. In the idle hours, some infrastructure is idle and lead to great waste; while in the busy hours, the infrastructure is inadequate, and QoS of applications could not be guaranteed. In PoI, when it is the idle hours, the infrastructure of PaaS could scale down by using the capability of the underlying IaaS; when it is the busy hours, the infrastructure of PaaS could scale up. This mechanism could greatly increase the Cost Efficiency of the platform.

The architecture of PoI is shown in Figure 2. It can be divided into two layers: PaaS Layer and IaaS Layer. The PaaS Layer dynamically rents VMs from the IaaS according to the workload.

- *App Execution Engine* hosts users' applications. It provides multiple AEEs and supports applications written by several programming languages (e.g., Java, PHP). As one application is scaled up, the App Execute Engine will launch more instances of this particular application.
- *Front End* is the entry to the platform: it accepts all requests from users and forwards them to the appropriate App Execution Engine. In essence, *Front End* is a load balancer that knows the correspondence between requests and applications.
- *Service Pool* manages a set of services including data storage and many other capabilities that can be used by developers via APIs.

- *Platform Master* is the key component of PoI. It is responsible for application scheduling, application resource allocation and interfacing with *VM Management* to acquire or release infrastructure resource from/to IaaS.
- *VM Management* is the key component of IaaS to perform the infrastructure resource scheduling and providing corresponding APIs.

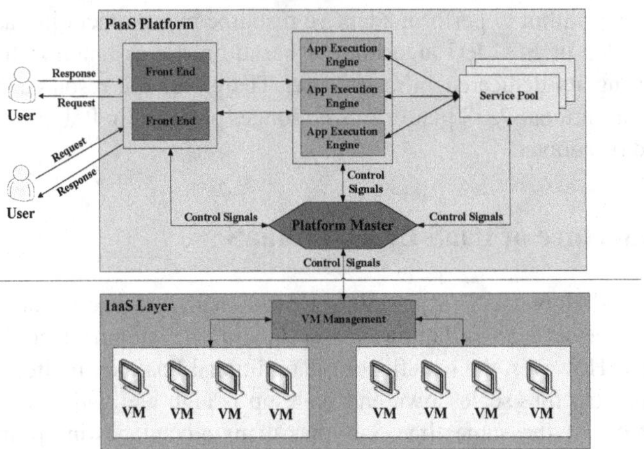


**Fig. 1.** Architecture of POI

In the architecture illustrated above, App Execution Engine and Front End are allowed to have more than one instance running simultaneously. Users' applications are deployed in App Execution Engine. All components of PaaS, including App Execution Engine, are deployed in the VMs provided by IaaS. This architecture ensures the scalability that all applications can easily be accommodated through scale-up and scale-down. When one application's workload increases and the requirements for computing resources increases accordingly, Platform Master can increase application's instances, either based on current set of VMs or acquires more of them from IaaS Layer to guarantee QoS of the applications. When one application's workload decreases, over-provisioning instances will lead to the waste of computing resources; thus Platform Master can decrease its instances and decide whether to return over-provisioning VMs to IaaS Layer in order to save VM rental cost.

# 4 Resource Management of PaaS Base on IaaS

## 4.1 Problem Statement

In this paper, a resource management framework of PoI is brought forward. On one hand, PoI is an asynchronous soft real-time system. Its requests are unpredictable and nondeterministic, and their distribution cannot be precisely described by the mathematical models. On the other hand, it is a soft real-time system because there are some constraints on the response time, but the failure of timeliness will lead to some small losses rather than disastrous consequences. In addition, computing resources that PaaS needs are provided by IaaS Layer as a set of VMs. For those enterprises willing to adopt PoI, it is important to minimize the usage of VMs in order to minimize the rental cost as well as guarantee QoS of their applications.

QoS of the application is measured based on the number of requests missed their deadlines. Missed Deadline Ratio (denoted as MissRatio) is defined as the percentage of requests that missed their deadlines; the formula used to calculate this value is given by (1):

$$\text{MissRatio} = \frac{\text{number of requests missing their deadlines}}{\text{number of total requests}} \tag{1}$$

In terms of resource utilization, CPU utilization is involved in this paper because CPU is the scarcest computing resource. It is important for PoI to maintain CPU utilization at a high level. Different instances of an application may have different CPU utilization, the CPU utilization of the application (denoted as $U_{cpu}$) is defined as the average of CPU utilization of all instances; the formula used to calculate this value is given by (2):

$$U^{j}_{CPUi} = \frac{\sum_{i=0}^{n} U_{cpu_i}}{nM} \tag{2}$$

Where n is the number of instances. M is the maximum CPU utilization that each instance is allowed to use (CPU utilization of one application's instance can be limited by cgroup in recently released Linux version). M means that CPU utilization of an instance should be limited below the M (e.g., 20%). $U^{j}_{CPUi}$ is used to represent the CPU utilization of $i_{th}$ instance of application j. The overall CPU utilization of PaaS can be relatively high if the CPU utilization of each application is high.

Since users' applications are running in VMs provided by IaaS, it is equally important to reduce the usage of VMs in order to lower the rental cost as much as possible. Traditionally IaaS providers charge according to Pay-As-You-Go pricing model. Therefore the rental cost is determined by how long and how many VMs are used. The Usage of VM is defined as the total usage time (denoted as $T_{VM}$); the formula used to calculate this value is given by (3):

$$T_{VM} = \sum_{1}^{n} T_{VM_i} \tag{3}$$

Where $T_{VM_i}$ represents the usage time of $i_{th}$ VM and n represents the number of rented VMs.

In PoI, the resource management framework is designed following three objectives:

- Guaranteed QoS of the application, described by *Missed Deadline Ratio*.
- High resource utilization rate, described by *CPU Utilization*.
- Less VM usage, described by *Time Usage* of VMs.

### 4.2 Resource Management Framework

In [9], the resource management framework is mentioned and resource management problems are simplified into feedback control problems. The first two objectives mentioned above can be achieved by feedback control. PID (Proportional-Integral-Derivative) feedback control is adopted to maintain high CPU utilization. Besides, VM scheduling algorithm is designed to manage VMs in order to achieve cost efficiency as well as QoS guaranteed applications.

With its three-term functionality covering treatments to both transient and steady-state responses, PID control offers the simplest and yet most efficient solutions on many real-world control problems [10]. The reasons why PID control is employed in this paper include: i) PoI is essentially a dynamic system and PID control technique is widely accepted technique in dynamic systems; ii) precise mathematical model of the system is not required in PID control technique. Instead, PID control technique can achieve satisfactory performance based on an approximate model. The complexity of PoI makes it difficult to be described precisely by mathematical model, which makes PID control technique a great candidate for underlying resource management.

A classic feedback control system is composed of a controller, a plant (the object to be controlled no matter what it is) and sensors (the object to measure the output of the plant) [11]. Controlled Variables are the variables to be controlled. Set Points represent the correct and expected values of the Controlled Variables. The difference between the current value and the Set Point is the Errors. The whole feedback and control loop is aimed to reduce the Errors.

- The sensor periodically monitors and compares the *Controlled Variables* to the *Set Points* to determine the *Errors*.
- The controller generates control signals through control function based on the *Errors*.
- The actuator takes actions to control the plant based on the signal generated by the controller, which is aimed to reduce the *Errors*.

Since Platform Master communicates with all components and collect information (distribution of applications' instance, workload of each application's instance, resource utilization rate of each VM etc.) of the whole PoI and perform application scheduling, application resource allocation and VM management (by interfacing with VM Management of IaaS), Platform Master could be reconstructed to support the feedback-control loop, thus the resource management framework is mainly implemented in Platform Master, shown in figure 3.

In the framework shown in figure 3, Missed Deadline Ratio and average CPU Utilization are adopted as the Controlled Variables. Because Controlled Variables are application-independent, a small, non-zero value is used as the Set Point of Missed Deadline Ratio for each application. The Set Point of Missed Deadline Ratio of application j is denoted as $\mathrm{MissRatio}_s^j$. Similarly, an expected percentage is used as the Set Point of CPU Utilization for each application. The Set Point of CPU Utilization of application j is denoted as $\mathrm{U}_{\mathrm{cpu}_s}^j$. Note that the workload of each application in PaaS is unpredictable, it is impossible to achieve 100% CPU utilization and 0% missed deadline ratio. Therefore, a tradeoff between these two metrics is inevitable.

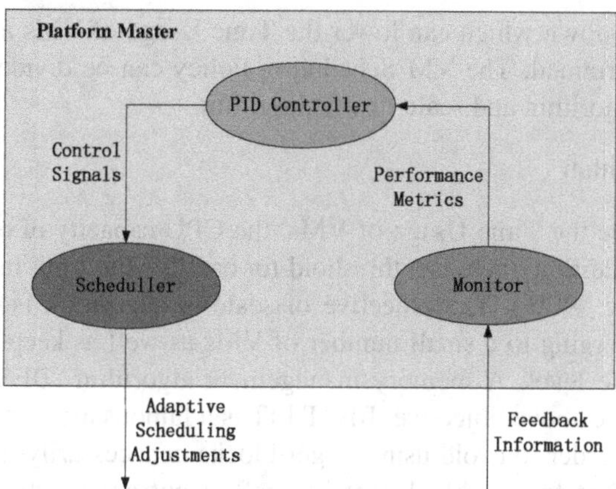


**Fig. 2.** Resource Management Framework

The sampling time is defined to be the end of each period of the arrival of the feedback data. Resource management decisions are made at the beginning of each period based on the feedback data collected previously. Then $\mathrm{error}_k^j$ for application j could be calculated with the following formula (4):

$$\mathrm{error}_k^j = w_1 \times \left(\mathrm{MissRatio}_k^j - \mathrm{MissRatio}_s^j\right) + w_2 \times \left(U_{cpu_i}^j - U_{cpu_s}^j\right) \quad (4)$$

Where k is the sampling instant and $\mathrm{MissRatio}_k^j$ is the Missed Deadline Ratio in the $k_{th}$sampling instant and Coefficients $w_1$ and $w_2$ are tunable. Based on$\mathrm{error}_k^j$, the number of instances of application j to be changed can be calculated in the current period with the following PID control formula (5):

$$\Delta\mathrm{Instance}^j = C_p \times \mathrm{error}_k^j + C_I \times \sum\nolimits_{IW} \mathrm{error}_k^j + C_D \times \frac{\mathrm{error}_k^j - \mathrm{error}_{k-DW}^j}{DW} \quad (5)$$

Where $C_p$, $C_I$, $C_D$, IW and DW are tunable coefficients. The number of instances of application j can be changed according to $\Delta\mathrm{Instance}^j$. $\Delta\mathrm{Instance}^j > 0$ means that the application should scale up (i.e., the number of instances of application j should be increased), and $\Delta\mathrm{Instance}^j < 0$ means that the application should scale down (i.e., the number of instances of application j should be decreased), and $\Delta\mathrm{Instance}^j = 0$ means that current number of instances of application j is appropriate and does not need change.

### 4.3 VM Scheduling Policy

How to set up a feedback control system in PoI and how to determine the number of instances of each application in order to guarantee the QoS of each application are stated above, then the policy to schedule the rented VMs will be illustrated. The decisions on when to scale up and scale down are made on the objective: Low Time Usage of VMs. Specifically, as the ΔInstance has been computed, strategies of scale-up and scale-down which can lower the Time Usage of VMs as much as possible should be determined. The VM Scheduling Policy can be divided into two algorithms: scale-up algorithm and scale-down algorithm.

1. Scale-Up Algorithm

In order to decrease the Time Usage of VMs, the CPU capacity of every VM should be monitored. In addition, there is a threshold for each VM to limit its CPU utilization in a safe level (e.g., 90%). The objective of scale-up algorithm is to make sure all instances are converging to a small number of VMs as well as keep each VM's CPU utilization in a safe level. A memory management algorithm "BEST FIT" is introduced to achieve the above objective. BEST FIT is a famous algorithm for OS memory management in order to avoid using larger blocks unnecessarily. In BEST FIT, the block list is searched for the block that is smallest but greater than or equal to the request size [12].

The suitable VM, into which new instances of the particular application to be expanded are deployed, is chosen based on BEST FIT. Next this algorithm will be further illustrated with an example. Assuming the utilization of all VMs is as figure 4:

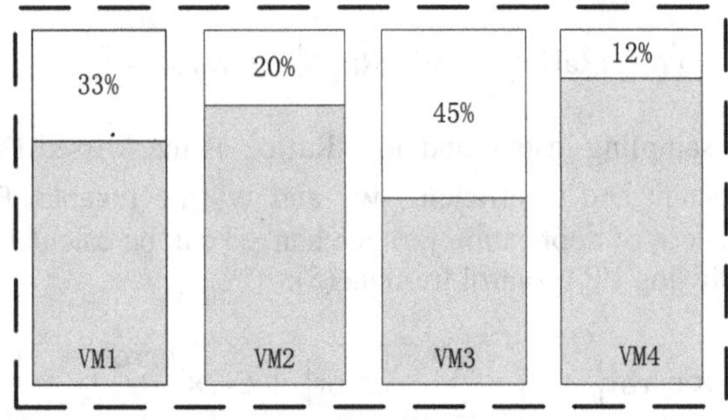


**Fig. 3.** CPU Utilization of VMs

In figure 4, there are 4 VMs. White box represents the percentage of CPU unused. In this example, an instance of application j need to be created and this instance will occupy 10% CPU utilization of a single VM. The safe threshold of VMs is 90%. Therefore, the actual percentages of CPU which could be used are 23%, 10%, 35% and 2% respectively. According to the BEST FIT algorithm, VM2 is chosen as the target to bear application j's instance. If there is more than one instance to be scaled up, the above procedures should be performed iteratively based on BEST FIT algorithm. By using BEST FIT algorithm, the CPU of every rented VMs will be fully exploited over the time. Scale-Down Algorithm

The scale-down algorithm is designed following the same objective as the scale-up algorithm. Differing from scale-up algorithm, the scale-down algorithm tries to determine which instance to be removed in order to acquire as many idle VMs as possible and return them to IaaS Layer.

$k_{th}$ VM is denoted as $VM_k$\{Application Sequence\}, where Application Sequence is the sequence of applications ID whose instances are running in $VM_k$. For example, if 1 instance of application 1, 1 instance of application 2 and 1 instance of application 3 are running in $k_{th}$ VM, this VM can be denoted as $VM_k\{1,2,3\}$. Application Sequence probably has duplicate application ID since there could be more than one instances of one application running simultaneously on the same VM. The above objective is achieved by introducing the heuristic algorithm and removed the instances of the VM which has the least number of running instances and its instances are the subset of the instances to be removed. Assuming there are 4 VMs: $VM_1\{1,2\}$, $VM_2\{1\}$, $VM_3\{2,2,3\}$, $VM_4\{3,4,5\}$, and the instances to be shrunk is $\{1,1,2,2,2,3\}$. Based on our scale-down algorithm, the instances should be removed according to the following sequence: $VM_2\{1\}$, $VM_1\{1,2\}$ and $VM_3\{2,2,3\}$. VM 1, 2 and 3 are set idle after the scale-down and can be returned to IaaS Layer.

### 4.4 Resource Management Process

In summary, the resource management process in PoI is essentially a feedback-control loop. At the beginning of every period, Platform Master collects all feedback data from other components of the platform and makes resource management decisions according to the feedback data. Every feedback-control loop can be divided into 4 phases.

- To collect performance metrics including Missed Deadline Ratio and CPU Utilization of every application deployed on the platform.
- To compute ΔInstance for every application based on PID control function mentioned above.
- To deploy or remove application instances based on scale-up or scale-down algorithms. Rent VMs from IaaS Layer if needed.
- To return all idle VMs to IaaS Layer in order to save rental cost.

## 5 Experiments

In this chapter, the comprehensive evaluation of the resource management framework of PoI is presented. In Section 5.1, the details of the experimental setup are specified. In Section 5.2, the proposed framework under different experimental parameters is illustrated, then the analysis of the experimental results is given.

### 5.1 Experimental Setup

For the evaluation of the proposed resource management framework in PoI, workloads of different patterns as the workloads of the platform are prepared. The different workloads are provided by The Grid Workloads Archive, which could provide anonymous workload traces from grid environments to researchers and to practitioners alike [13]. 3 workloads of different patterns within 24 hours are chosen as shown in Figure 5.

Each workload pattern above represents a typical scenario. For example, workloads of Application 1 and Application 3 slightly differ from each other but show a very common pattern that fluctuates consistently and reaches peaks in the middle of the day. In addition, workload of Application 2 shows a very steady pattern with several wiggles.

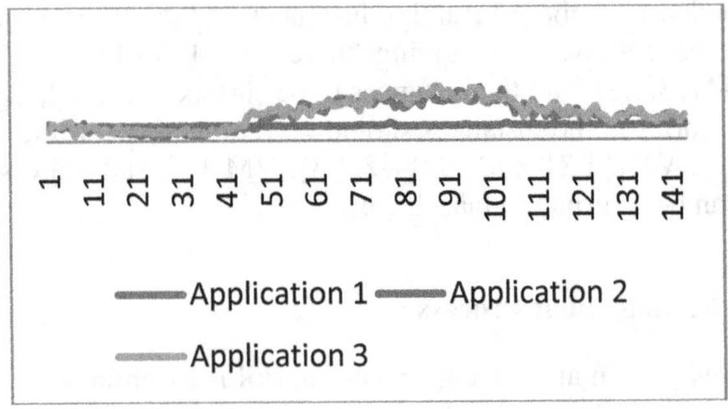


**Fig. 4.** Workload Patterns of Application 1, 2 and 3

The fixed parameters of the experiment are shown in Table 1. Each workload is split into 144 intervals with 10 minutes per interval. Each application is initialized and deployed with 1 instance. Coefficients shown in Table 1 are obtained based on experiences. The values of these coefficients could be determined by using PID tuning techniques [14].

**Table 1.** Fixed Experimental Parameters

| | |
|---|---|
| **Number of Applications** | 3 |
| **Minutes per Interval** | 10 |
| **Number of Intervals** | 144 |
| **Initial Instances of each Application** | 1 |
| **Coefficient $w_1$** | 2 |
| **Coefficient $w_2$** | 1.5 |
| **Coefficient $C_p$** | 1 |
| **Coefficient $C_i$** | 0.5 |
| **Coefficient $C_d$** | 1 |

## 5.2 Evaluation of Resource Management Framework

Besides the fixed experimental parameters shown in Table 1, there are also three kinds of tunable experimental parameters including Set Point of Missed Deadline Ratio for each application (denoted as MissRatio_s), Set Point of CPU Utilization for each application (denoted as U_(cpu_s )) and VM Safe Threshold. For the clarification and simplicity of the following analysis, MissRatio_s and U_(cpu_s) for all applications are set together. The proposed resource management framework is evaluated under different settings of tunable experimental parameters.

Figure 6 shows the Missed Deadline Ratio and CPU Utilization of different applications in the platform with the tunable parameters settings in above table. The proposed resource management framework keeps both the Missed Deadline Ratio and CPU Utilization of all applications around the expected values in response to the workloads of different patterns. The proposed framework also has the predictive capability to the changing workload. Take Application 1 as an example, as its workload increases suddenly and keeps the increasing trend for periods, its Missed Deadline Ratio only increases for a short time and returns to the expected value. The proposed framework gains this predictive capability through PID control function based on which it scales up Application 1 to deal with the future workload increase, with the cost of the temporary fall of CPU Utilization.

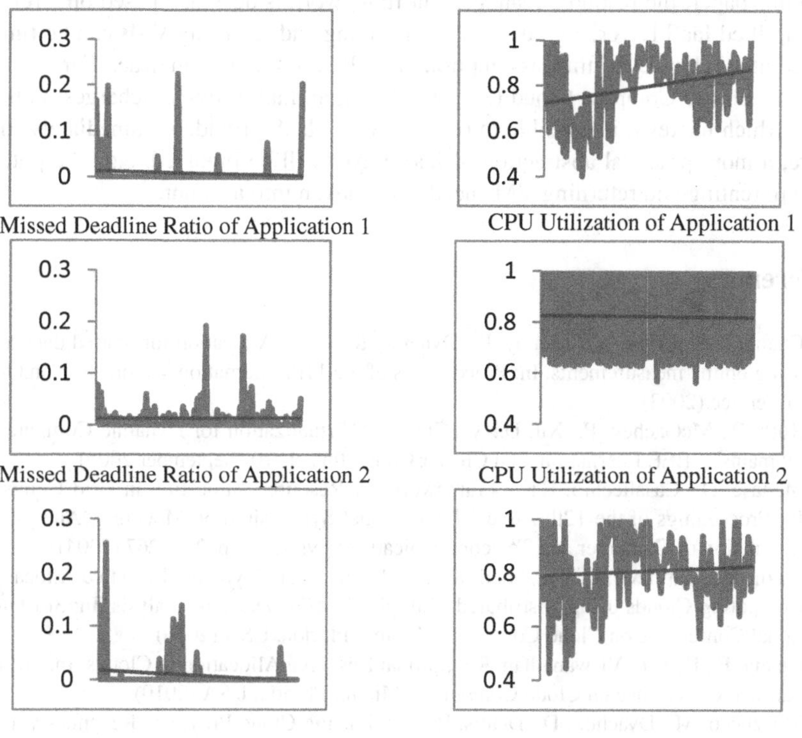


| Set Point of Missed Deadline Ratio | 0.05 |
|---|---|
| Set Point of CPU Utilization | 0.8 |
| VM Safe Threshold | 0.9 |

**Fig. 5.** Missed Deadline Ratio and CPU Utilization of Application 1, 2 and 3

## 6 Conclusion and Future Works

It's becoming a trend for enterprises to adopt PoI. In summary, PoI has many advantages on the flexibility, reliability and cost-efficiency. In this paper, a QoS guaranteed and cost-efficient resource management framework in PoI is proposed. The framework is composed of a feedback control system and two scaling algorithms. Experimental results show that the resource management framework can not only maintain Missed Deadline Ratio of all applications at an expected value, but also improve the CPU Utilization of all applications around an expected value. According to experimental results, it can be found that Time Usage of VMs has negative correlation with the Set Point of Missed Deadline Ratio, the Set Point of CPU Utilization and VM Safe Threshold.

In this paper, the resource management framework is designed based on a relatively simplified IaaS Layer, e.g., the action of renting and returning VMs can be finished immediately. However this assumption usually does not hold true. For example, Amazon Elastic Compute Cloud (Amazon EC2), an IaaS provider, charges on hourly basis, which makes it impossible to return VMs to IaaS providers immediately. In the future, a more practical abstraction of IaaS Layer will be involved, e.g., the potential delay in renting and returning VMs needs to be taken into account.

## References

1. Chandra, A., Gong, W., Shenoy, P.: Dynamic Resource Allocation for Shared data centers using online measurements. In: Proceedings of the 11th International Workshop on Quality of Service (2003)
2. Ruth, P., McGachey, P., Xu, D.: VioCluster, "Virtualization for Dynamic Computational Domains". IEEE International on Cluster Computing, 1–10 (September 2005)
3. Menasc, D., Casalicchio, E.: A Framework for Resource Allocation in Grid Computing. In: Proceedings of the 12th Annual International Symposium on Modeling, Analysis, and Simulation of Computer and Telecommunications Systems, pp. 259–267 (2004)
4. Yazir, Y., Matthews, C., Farahbod, R., Neville, S., et al.: Dynamic Resource Allocation in Computing Clouds using Distributed Multiple Criteria Decision Analysis. In: 3rd International Conference on Cloud Computing, Miami, Florida, USA (2010)
5. Chang, F., Ren, J., Viswanathan, R.: Optimal Resource Allocation in Clouds. In: 3rd International Conference on Cloud Computing, Miami, Florida, USA (2010)
6. Mazzucco, M., Dyachuk, D., Deters, R.: Maximizing Cloud Providers Revenues via Energy Aware Allocation Policies. In: 3rd International Conference on Cloud Computing, Miami, Florida, USA (2010)
7. Bossche, R., Vanmechelen, K., Broeckhove, J.: Cost-Optimal Scheduling in Hybrid IaaS Clouds for Deadline Constrained Workloads. In: 3rd International Conference on Cloud Computing, Miami, Florida, USA (2010)
8. Cristian, F., Fetzer, C.: The Timed Asynchronous Distributed System Model. IEEE Transactions on Parallel and Distributed Systems (June 1999)
9. Hu, R., Li, Y., Zhang, Y.: Adaptive Resource Management in PaaS Platform Using Feedback Control LRU Algorithm. In: 2011 International Conference on Cloud and Service Computing (2011)

10. Ang, K.H., Chong, G., Li, Y.: PID Control System Analysis, Design and Technology. IEEE Transactions on Contr. Syst. Tech. 13(4), 559–576 (2005)
11. Astrom, K.J.: PID Controllers: Theory, Design, and Tuning. Instrument Soc. Amer. Research Triangle Park (1995)
12. Best Fit Allocation Algorithm, http://www.cs.rit.edu/~ark/lectures/gc/03_03_03.html (access on January 2013)
13. The Grid Workloads Archive, http://gwa.ewi.tudelft.nl/pmwiki/pmwiki.php?n=Home.GWA (access on January 2013)
14. Wang, Q.G., Lee, T.H., Fung, H.W., Bi, Q., Zhang, Y.: PID Tuning for Improved Performance. IEEE Trans. Contr. Syst. Tech. 7, 3984–3989 (1999)

# A Conflict-Related Rules Detection Tool for Access Control Policy

Xiaoyan Liang, Liangshuang Lv, Chunhe Xia, Yang Luo, and Yazhuo Li

Key Laboratory of Beijing Network Technology
School of Computer Science and Engineering, Beihang University, Beijing, China
lxy@cse.buaa.edu.cn, {lls,xch}@buaa.edu.cn,
veotax@sae.buaa.edu.cn, lyzalexandra@126.com

**Abstract.** Conflict detection is an important issue of the Access Control Policy. Most conflict detection tools mainly focus on the two rules that have contrary actions, but there are also other rules which are necessary to the conflict situation, which is not considered in these tools. This paper defines all these rules related to the conflict situation as the concept "conflict-related rules", and gives a conflict-related rules detection tool for Access Control Policy which can report the conflict situation more comprehensively. By giving the semantics model of the access control policy and the definition of conflict, we prove the necessary and sufficient condition of conflict, and then give the concept of "conflict-related rules" and deduce its extension. We implement conflict-related rules detection tool based on the description logic, and the experiment results validate the tool's correctness and effectiveness. The results of the correctness experiment showed that instead of detecting the two rules with opposite actions only, it detected all the conflict-related rules for access control policy; the results of the effectiveness experiment showed that our tool's response performance is better than VPN based tools.

**Keywords:** Access control policy, conflict detect, conflict-related rules, description logic.

## 1 Introduction

Policy based access control is an important part of network information security [1,12]. An access control policy is a list of access control rules. The rules may conflict when they declared opposite access control behaviors. Conflicts in a policy can cause hole in security or block legal access. Conflict detection is an important issue for access control policy. Tools for conflict detection give many conflict detection algorithms under various scenarios, and they can report the two rules which have opposite actions.

However, reporting the two rules only can't help security administrator fully understand the situation of conflict. Take the AC (access control) policy of an enterprise information management system as an example, the enterprise has two kinds of users: server and marketer, and three kinds of accessible resources: user-information, contact-information and privacy-information.

J. Su et al. (Eds.): ICoC 2013, CCIS 401, pp. 158–169, 2013.

Security administrator configures following access control rules: r0: server inherit marketer; r1: permit marketer read user-information; r2: permit marketer delete contact-information; r3 deny server read privacy-information; r4 user-information contain contact-information; r5 user-information contain privacy-information.

Rule 1 and rule 3 have semantic conflict: rule 1 indicates that server inherits the authority of marketer and has the permission to access user-information which includes privacy-information; while rule 3 forbids server to access privacy-information.

Security administrator expects to understand not only rule 1 and rule 3 which have opposite actions, but also all rules related to the situation of "conflict". Rule 0 and rule 5 from the example above are also the causes of "conflict" and conflict cannot happen without these rules. We name these rules, which can cause conflict indirectly, as "Conflict-related Rules".

The contributions of this paper are:

1) We abstract all the rules in the conflict situation, not only the two rules that have contrary actions, as the concept of the "conflict-related rules", and we deduce this concept's extension.

2) Based on description logic, we implement the conflict detection tool based to detect the "conflict-related rules".

This paper is organized as follows: Section 2 describes the related work and discussion. Based on the semantic formal representation of access control policy, we give the necessary and sufficient condition of "conflict" and deduce the extension of "conflict-related rules", which makes the range of "conflict-related rules" explicit in section 3. Based on description logic, section 4 Figure and Table shows the implement of the conflict-related rules detection tool. Experiments in section 5 validate the correctness and effectiveness of the tool and Section 6 presents the conclusion.

## 2 Related Work

There are several researches on conflict detection of AC policy at present. Lupu and Sloman proposed a conflict detection tool focusing on authorization policy and obligation policy [3], they suggested that the rule of conflict is two rules which have opposite actions. He lili presented a conflict detection tool which is based upon OWL and RBAC negative authorization [4], which just concerns rules have opposite actions. Jianfeng Lu etc. studied two kinds of conflict of access control policy in the multi-domain environment [5]. Chang-Joo Moon did research on conflict among permission assignment constraints (PAC) in RBAC [6]. Basit Shafiq studied conflict between RBAC policies of each domain in multi-domain environment for collaborative work of multiple organizations [7]. Feng Huang etc. presented a description logic based conflict detection tool for access control policy. After the management of XACML access control policy, reference [8,9] converts the detection problem of XACML policy conflict into the consistency of knowledge base for description logic. Apurva Mohan etc. proposed a terminology based conflict detection method of authorization policy, which uses ontology reasoning to detect the conflict, and the detected "conflict" is defined by existing concept [10]. Mansor et al. give the dynamic conflict detection algorithm for policy-based management [11].

Therefore, we discover that researches on conflict detection tool for access control policy at present are mainly focusing on two rules which have opposite actions, but ignoring other "conflict-related rules". It is necessary to research the extension of "conflict-related rules" and the detection tools.

# 3 Semantic Model for AC Policy

The grammar representation of access control policy is given first, and then we analyze its semantics, giving its semantic formal representation. For convenience of expression, we use "policy" instead of "access control policy" and "rule" instead of "access control rule".

## 3.1 Grammatical Formal Model for Access Control Policy

**Definition 1: Access Control Policy (grammatical definition):** Grammatically, policy is the set of rule statements, and a rule statement comprised of components complying with grammar rules.

Grammatically, the formal representation of access control policy is as follows:

$$\left\{\begin{array}{l} \text{P-STATE}=\left\{ r\!-\!state \mid \begin{array}{l} r\!-\!state=\langle sub\!-\!state, sub\!-\!state\rangle, \\ r\!-\!state=\langle obj\!-\!state, obj\!-\!state\rangle, \\ r\!-\!state=\left\langle \begin{array}{l} sub\!-\!state, obj\!-\!state, act\!-\!state \\ , perm\!-\!state \end{array}\right\rangle \end{array}\right\}; \\ sub\!-\!state, obj\!-\!state, act\!-\!state, perm\!-\!state \in \{ exp \mid grammer(exp)\}; \end{array}\right. \tag{1}$$

Where, P-STATE is the set of rule clarifications, namely policy; $r\!-\!state$ is a rule clarification in policy; $sub\!-\!state$ is the subject expression; $obj-state$ is the object expression; $act\!-\!state$ is the action expression; $perm\!-\!state$ is the permission expression. $grammer(exp)$ is a predicate, indicating that the expression correspond with the specification of grammar.

## 3.2 Semantic Formal Model for Access Control Policy

According to grammar of access control policy presented in part A, we first analyze the implication of expressions, and then analyze the semantics of rule statement of the three types, which will finally deduce the semantics of policy.

**Definition 2: Semantics Expressed by "Subject Expression" and "Object Expression":** Semantics are specific entities. Semantics of subject expression is users or characters affected by policy. Semantics of object expression is resources protected by policy. The formal representation of set is as follows:

$$\begin{cases} \mathrm{SUBJECT}=\{sub \mid \mathrm{U}(sub)\}; \\ \mathrm{OBJECT}=\{source \mid \mathrm{R}(source)\}; \end{cases} \tag{2}$$

Where, SUBJECT is the set, representing the set of semantics for subject expression $sub-state$; $\mathrm{U}(sub)$ is the predicate, representing $sub$ is a user or character; $\mathrm{R}(source)$ is the predicate, representing $source$ is the resource protected by policy.

**Definition 3: Semantics of Statements Comprised of "Subject Expression" and "Subject Expression":** Rules of this type are inheritance relationship in essence, so rule semantics are expressed by using the relationship between semantics of subject expression. The representation is as follows:

$$\xi_{inherit} \in \mathrm{SUBJECT} \times \mathrm{SUBJECT}; \tag{3}$$

Where, $\xi_{inherit}$ represents the semantics of rule on subject. The definition of SUBJECT is as formula (2).

**Definition 4: Semantics of Statements Comprised of "Object Expression" and "Object Expression":** its semantics represents inclusion relation between objects (namely, protected resources), which is expressed as:

$$\xi_{contain} \in \mathrm{OBJECT} \times \mathrm{OBJECT}; \tag{4}$$

Where, $\xi_{contain}$ represents the semantics of object relation rule. The definition of OBJECT is as formula (2).

**Definition 5: Semantics of Statements Comprised of "Object Expression", "Object Expression", "Action Expression" and "Permission Expression":**

Semantics of subject expression is subject (a user or a character); Semantics of object expression is object (protected resources); Semantics of action expression enable actions that subject can do to object (namely, operations like read, write, etc.), and it has different extensions according to different systems. Semantics of permission expression is "permit" and "deny". Therefore, semantics of this kind of rule is the actions taken by subject on object to "permit" or "deny" some kind of operation. So this kind of operation can be expressed as the relationship. The direction of the relationship represents "permit" or "deny". The "permit" is expressed as a directed two-tuple of "from subject to object" and the "deny" is expressed as a directed two-tuple of "from object to subject". Various "actions" are usually declared in access control. Each action and its "permission" will be represented by a directed relationship. There are k kinds of actions. Its formal representation is as follows:

$$\xi_{\mathrm{ACTION}\,k} \subseteq \mathrm{SUBJECT} \times \mathrm{OBJECT} \cup \mathrm{OBJECT} \times \mathrm{SUBJECT}; k=1,2,\ldots\ldots,n; n \in N; \tag{5}$$

**Definition 6: Access Control Policy (Semantic Definition):**
Semantics of access control policy consists of semantics of access control rules. So the semantic formal representation of access control policy is as follows:

$$\begin{cases} \mathrm{POLICY} = \begin{pmatrix} \xi_{\mathrm{INHERIT}}, \xi_{\mathrm{CONTAIN}}, \xi_{\mathrm{ACTION}1}, \\ \xi_{\mathrm{ACTION}2}, \dots, \xi_{\mathrm{ACTION}n} \end{pmatrix}; \\ \xi_{\mathrm{INHERIT}} \subseteq \mathrm{SUBJECT} \times \mathrm{SUBJECT}; \\ \xi_{\mathrm{CONTAIN}} \subseteq \mathrm{OBJECT} \times \mathrm{OBJECT}; \\ \xi_{\mathrm{ACTION}k} \subseteq \mathrm{SUBJECT} \times \mathrm{OBJECT} \cup \mathrm{OBJECT} \times \mathrm{SUBJECT}; \\ 1 \le k \le n; n \ge 1; \end{cases} \tag{6}$$

Where, POLICY represents the semantic of access control policy, which includes the inheritance relationship of subject $\xi_{\mathrm{INHERIT}}$, the relationship between objects $\xi_{\mathrm{CONTAIN}}$ and the relationship between subject and object $\xi_{\mathrm{ACTION}1}$, $\xi_{\mathrm{ACTION}2}$,…, $\xi_{\mathrm{ACTION}n}$.

The semantics between rules of access control policy is implicit, since there are inheritance relationship and inclusion relationship between the rules. The implicit semantics of access control policy between subjects having inheritance relationship is expressed as axiom 1, 2 and 3.

**Axiom 1: Relationship of $\xi_{\mathrm{INHERIT}}$, $\xi_{\mathrm{CONTAIN}}$ is reflexive and transitive.**

**Axiom 2: Semantics implied by the inheritance relationship between subjects is:**

For any $subject_i$, $subject_j$, $object_k$:

(1) if $\langle subject_i, subject_j \rangle \in \xi_{\mathrm{INHERIT}}$ and $\langle subject_j, object_k \rangle \in \xi_{\mathrm{ACTION}k}$, then: $\langle subject_i, object_k \rangle \in \xi_{\mathrm{ACTION}k}$

(2) if $\langle subject_i, subject_j \rangle \in \xi_{\mathrm{INHERIT}}$ and $\langle object_k, subject_j \rangle \in \xi_{\mathrm{ACTION}k}$, then: $\langle object_k, subject_i \rangle \in \xi_{\mathrm{ACTION}k}$

**Axiom 3: Semantics implied by the inclusion relationship between objects is**:

For any $subject_l$, $object_m$, $object_n$:

if $\langle object_m, object_n \rangle \in \xi_{\mathrm{CONTAIN}}$ and $\langle subject_l, object_m \rangle \in \xi_{\mathrm{ACTION}k}$, then: $\langle subject_l, object_n \rangle \in \xi_{\mathrm{ACTION}k}$

(2) if $\langle object_m, object_n \rangle \in \xi_{\mathrm{CONTAIN}}$ and $\langle object_m, subject_l \rangle \in \xi_{\mathrm{ACTION}k}$, then: $\langle object_n, subject_l \rangle \in \xi_{\mathrm{ACTION}k}$

### 3.3 Conflict-Related Rules

**Conflict.**

**Definition 7 Conflict in Access Control Policy:** The conflict discussed in AC policy is that two rules with the same subjects and objects but have opposite actions.

From the characteristic "with the same subjects and objects have opposite actions" in Definition 7, we know that two access control rules of conflict are all statements consisting of "subject expression", "object expression", "action expression" and "permission expression", and in the semantics they expressed, the actions are from the same type but opposite.

**Theorem 1 The Necessary and Sufficient Condition of Conflict in Access Control Policy:**

For $\xi_1 = \langle subj_1, obje_1 \rangle$, $\xi_2 = \langle obje_2, subj_2 \rangle$, the necessary and sufficient condition for conflict of $\xi_1$ and $\xi_2$ is:

(1) condition 1 $\exists x \in$ SUBJECT that:

$$\langle x, subj_1 \rangle \in (\xi_{\text{INHERIT}})^m \wedge \langle x, subj_2 \rangle \in (\xi_{\text{INHERIT}})^n \;; m,n \geq 0; m,n \in N;$$

(2) condition 2 $\exists y \in$ OBJECT that:

$$\langle obje_1, y \rangle \in (\xi_{\text{CONTAIN}})^j \wedge \langle obje_2, y \rangle \in (\xi_{\text{CONTAIN}})^k \;; j,k \geq 0; j,k \in N;$$

Proof:

- the Proof of Sufficient Condition

$$\frac{\langle x, subj_1 \rangle \in (\xi_{\text{INHERIT}})^m, \text{axiom 1}}{\langle x, subj_1 \rangle \in \xi'_{\text{INHERIT}}}, \frac{\langle x, subj_1 \rangle \in \xi'_{\text{INHERIT}}, \xi_1 = \langle subj_1, obje_1 \rangle \text{ axiom 2}}{\langle x, obje_1 \rangle}$$

$$\frac{\langle x, obje_1 \rangle, \langle obje_1, y \rangle \in (\xi_{\text{CONTAIN}})^k, \text{axiom 3}}{\langle x, y \rangle}$$

Thus, $\langle x, y \rangle$ was deduced .

$$\frac{\langle x, subj_2 \rangle \in (\xi_{\text{INHERIT}})^m, \text{axiom1}}{\langle x, subj_2 \rangle \in \xi'_{\text{INHERIT}}}, \frac{\langle x, subj_2 \rangle \in \xi'_{\text{INHERIT}}, \xi_2 = \langle obje_2, subj_2 \rangle \text{ axiom2}}{\langle obje_2, x \rangle}$$

$$\frac{\langle obje_2, x \rangle, \langle obje_2, y \rangle \in (\xi_{\text{CONTAIN}})^k, \text{axiom3}}{\langle y, x \rangle}$$

Thus, $\langle y, x \rangle$ was deduced.

Therefore, for x and y, conflict happens since $\langle x, y \rangle$ and $\langle y, x \rangle$ can both be deduced at the same time, so the sufficient condition is proved.

- the Proof of Necessary Condition

For any $\xi_1 = \langle subj_1, obje_1 \rangle$, $\xi_2 = \langle obje_2, subj_2 \rangle$, if there is conflict between $\xi_1$ and $\xi_2$.

Such there are no $x \in$ SUBJECT that:

$$\left(\langle x, subj_1 \rangle \in (\xi_{\text{INHERIT}})^m\right) \wedge \left(\langle x, subj_2 \rangle \in (\xi_{\text{INHERIT}})^n\right); m, n \geq 0; m, n \in N;$$

There are no interacting subjects between $subj_1$ and $subj_2$, so two rules are not conflicting.

Similarly, such there are no $y \in$ OBJECT that:

$$\left(\langle obje_1, y \rangle \in (\xi_{\text{CONTAIN}})^j\right) \wedge \left(\langle obje_2, y \rangle \in (\xi_{\text{CONTAIN}})^k\right); j, k \geq 0; j, k \in N;$$

Two rules are not conflicting.

Therefore, if two rules conflicted, the two conditions should be satisfied at the same time.

The necessary condition is proved.

**Conflict-Related Rules.**

**Definition 8 conflict-related rules** is rules that cause conflict in access control policy, written as $\Phi_{related}$. Conflict-Related Rules is a set of rules:

$$\text{CONFLICTRULES} = \left\{ rule_1, rule_2, \ldots\ldots, rule_n \mid rule_i \in \text{POLICY}, 1 < i < n \right\} \tag{7}$$

The rules of conflict-related rules satisfy the two conditions as follows:

(1) There is conflict in CONFLICTRULES ;

(2)There would be no conflict, if one rule from CONFLICTRULES were erased.

From Theorem 1, we conclude that the rules cause conflict situation include three kinds of rules:

**Definition 9.** The two rules that have opposite actions, $\xi_1 = \langle subj_1, obje_1 \rangle$, $\xi_2 = \langle obje_2, subj_2 \rangle$, we denote as **rules have opposite actions, written as** $\Phi_{opposite}$.

**Definition 10.** The rules that can deduce subjects between rules having opposite actions $\xi_1$ and $\xi_2$ have inheritance relationship, we denote as **Subject overlap rules, written as** $\Phi_{subjects}$.

**Definition 11.** The rules that can deduce objects between rules having opposite actions $\xi_1$ and $\xi_2$ have contain relationship, we denote as **Object overlap rules, written as** $\Phi_{objects}$.

**Theorem 2** $\Phi_{opposite}$, $\Phi_{subjects}$, $\Phi_{objects}$ **is a complete division of Conflict-related Rules (** $\Phi_{related}$ **).**

Proof:

$$\frac{r\in\Phi_{related},\quad definition8}{\Phi_{related}\Rightarrow conflict}\quad \frac{\Phi_{related}\Rightarrow conflict,\quad theorem1}{\Phi_{related}=\{\xi_1,\xi_2\}\cup\Phi^1_{rules}\cup\Phi^2_{rules}}$$

$$which\quad \Phi^1_{rules}\Rightarrow condition1, \Phi^2_{rules}\Rightarrow condition2$$

$$\frac{\{\xi_1,\xi_2\}, definition9}{\{\xi_1,\xi_2\}=\Phi_{opposite}}\quad \frac{\Phi^1_{rules}, definition10}{\Phi^1_{rules}=\Phi_{subjects}}\quad \frac{\Phi^2_{rules}, definition11}{\Phi^2_{rules}=\Phi_{objects}}$$

$\Phi_{related}=\Phi_{opposite}\cup\Phi_{subjects}\cup\Phi_{objects}$ is proved.

## 4 A Conflict-Related Rules Conflict Detection Tool for AC Policy

This session implements a conflict-related rules conflict detection tool for AC policy, which could do detections of "conflict-related rules" when one access control rule is added by security administrator.

The tool is implemented basing on description logic.

Description logic is a kind of language represents that knowledge has grammar and semantics. Description logic is building on concept and relation (Relation, Role). Concept means the set of objects and relation means the binary relation between objects [2]. Description logic system consists of four basic parts: description logic language, description logic knowledge base, reasoning mechanism and query language supported by description logic system. Description logic language specifies the language of description logic. Description logic knowledge base is comprised of TBox (Terminological Box) and ABox (Assertion Box). TBox means terminology and terminology is the rules used for reasoning. ABox means assertion and assertion is the facts used for reasoning. Reasoning mechanism automatically does reasoning according to knowledge base. Query language supported by description logic system can query facts conforming to conditions.

Therefore, according to the grammar of TBox, axiom can be described as semantic model of access control policy and conditions for conflict-related rules are in session III. The axiom will be used for reasoning and put into TBox. With the semantic model in TBox, the specified access control policy can be converted into instances in ABox and used as the facts of reasoning. Describing the "conditions for conflict-related rule" as axiom, by using the query language which is supported by the description logic system, "conflict-related rule" can be queried to complete the process of detection through reasoning.

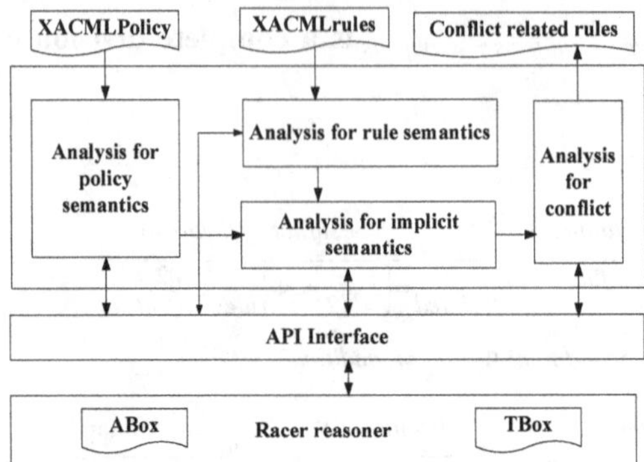


**Fig. 1.** The module structure of the conflict related rules detect tool for AC policy

The module structure of tool is presented as Fig.1.

The tool consists of four modules:

Analysis for policy semantics: read access control policy declaration described by XACML language, analyze its semantics, and put semantics in ABox through API interface.

Analysis for rule semantics: analyze rule semantics according to the input XACML rule, and then add the result in access control policy which is already put into ABox.

Analysis for implicit semantics: analyze implicit semantics in ABox according to the predefined SWRL rule, and then store it in the ABox.

Analysis for conflict: output conflict and conflict-related rules according to conflict reasoning rules which are described by predefined SWRL rule.

Implementation layer includes Racer reasoning machine and API interface. Racer reasoning machine is realized by adopting Racer 1.9.5 reasoning machine which includes ABox and TBox. TBox stores abstract model of access control rules and SWRL reasoning rules. ABox stores instances of access control rules. Through structures of nROL query language offered by JRacer, reports of "conflict-related rules" will query "conflict-related rules" that meet the conditions. The specific implementation of TBox construction, compiling of SWRL rule and "conflict-related rule" report are as follows.

The rules of reasoning the "conflict-related rules" described by SWRL (Semantic Web Rule Language) in the form of TBox axiom is as follows:

---

1) Subject(?sA)→has_Subject_Overlap(?sA, ?sA)
2) Resource(?rA)→has_ Resource_Overlap(?rA, ?rA)
3) Action(?aA)→has_ Action_Overlap(?aA, ?aA)
4) has_subSubject(?sA,?sB)Λhas_subSubject(?sB,?sC)→ has_sub Subject (?sA, ?sC)
5) has_subSubject(?sA,?sB)→has_Subject_Overlap(?sA, ?sB)
6) has_Subject_Overlap(?sA,?sB)→has_Subject_Overlap(?sB, ?s A)
7) has_subResource(?rA, ?rB)Λhas_subResource(?rB, ?rC) → has _subResource(?rA, ?rC)
8) has_subResource(?rA, ?rB)→ has_Subject_Overlap(?rA, ?rB)
9) has_Subject_Overlap(?rA,?rB)→has_Subject_Overlap(?rB, ?rA)
10) has_Subject(?pA, ?sA) Λhas_Subject(?pB, ?sB)Λ has_Subject _Overlap(?sA, ?sB) Λ has_Resource(?pA, ?rA) Λ has_Resource(? pB, ?rB)Λhas_Resource_Overlap(?rA, ?rB)Λhas_

Action(?p A, ?aA) ∧ has_Action(?pB, ?aB) ∧ has_Action_Overlap(?aA, ?aB) → has_Permission_Overlap (?pA, ?pB)
11) has_PermitA(?poA, ?pA)∧has_DenyB(?poB, ?pB) ∧ has_Per mission_Overlap(?pA, ?pB) →has_Policy_Conflict(?poA, ? poB)
12) has_PermitA(?poA, ?pA)∧has_DenyB(?poB, ?pB)∧ has_P ermission_Overlap(?pA, ?pB) →has_Policy_Conflict(?poB, ? poA)
13) has_PermitB(?poA, ?pA)∧has_DenyA(?poB, ?pB)∧has_Permission_Overlap(?pA, ?pB) → has_Policy_Conflict(?poA, ? poB)
14) has_PermitB(?poA,?pA) ∧ has_DenyA(?poB,?pB) ∧ has_Pe rmission_Overlap(?pA, ?pB) → has_Policy_Conflict(?poB, ?poA)

Where, 1)-6) describe conditions for overlap relationship, which includes subject overlap and object overlap. 1)-3) represent reflexivity of overlap relationship. 4) represents transitivity of overlap relationship. 6) represents symmetry of overlap relationship. 7)-9) represent overlap relationship between subjects, overlap relationship between objects, overlap relationship between actions respectively. 10) represents relations with overlapped subject, object and action. 11) -14) represent conflict.

The detection reports of "conflict-related rule" are input through queries on all instances satisfying "conflict-related rule condition". The queries are implemented by nRQL query language which is used by Racer.

# 5 Experiments

This section, we evaluate the correctness and effectiveness of our conflict-related rules detection tool. We use a policy of an information system to evaluate the correctness, and compare the response times of our tool and CPN based tool to evaluate the effectiveness.

The environment of experiments is: CPU: 2.93GHz, Memory: 4.00GB of RAM, operation system: Windows XP, reasoning engine: RacerPro 1.9.2 beta.

## 5.1 Correctness Analysis

We use the access control policy shown in introduction as input, which are written in XACML language and the output as Table 1 showed.

Using the tool to detect "conflict-related rules" in access control policy, the result is obtained after 1.4 second.

The output is represented as Table 1. As Table 1 shown, the "conflict-related rules" detected by the tool are divided into three types: rules of opposite actions, subject overlap rules, and object overlap rules.

**Table 1.** The result of the tool

| Output type | output content |
|---|---|
| rule of opposite actions | "rule 1 and rule 3 have conflict" |
| subject overlap rule | "subject overlap rule is: rule 0" |
| object overlap rule | "object overlap rule is: rule 5" |

The results of experiment show that: our conflict-related rules detection tool for AC policy is correctness: it detected all the conflict-related rules for access control policy, instead of detect the two rules with opposite actions, and this advantage makes our tool can help security administrator understand the information of the conflict situation more comprehensively.

### 5.2 Effectiveness Evaluation

Colored petri net (CPN) is an important method to represent and analyze the policy semantic [13]. In order to evaluate the efficiency of the proposed tool, we compare the response time of our tool and CPN based conflict detection tool. The test results represents as Fig.2.

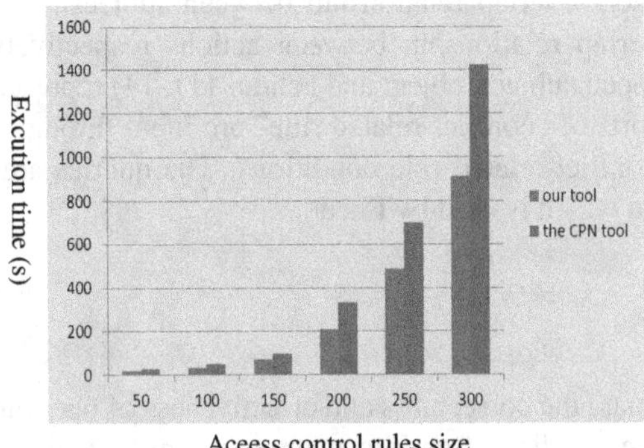


**Fig. 2.** Performance evaluation

The results of Fig.2 show that the response time of conflict-related rules detection tool is under 920s even the rule set size reaches 300, and the performance of our tool is obviously better than CPN based conflict detection tool's, because :

1) The CPN based method represent conflict-related rules and access control rules with place, transition, token and so on, which has many state results to long process time.
2) Our method represents conflict-related rules and access control rules with concepts and relations based on description logic, besides the tableau algorithm of the description logic has been optimized.

## 6 Conclusion

To detect the rules about conflict situation more comprehensively, this paper abstracted all the rules of the conflict situation as the concept of "conflict-related rules" and implemented a conflict detection tool. We analyzed the semantics of access control policy, and formally represented it with set theory; we defined the conflict-related rule for access control policy and deducted its extension. Based on the description logic, we realized the tool to detect conflict-related rules and we validated the correctness and effectiveness of the tool in experiment with a policy of information system. The results of the correctness experiment showed the tool detected all the conflict-related rules for access control policy, which makes our tool can help security administrator understand the information of the conflict situation more comprehensively. And the results of the effectiveness experiment showed that our tool's response performance is better than VPN tools.

Our future work would pay attention to extend this tool to situations may have other types of conflict like SoD to detect the conflict-related rules.

**Acknowledgment.** We would like to express gratitude to associate Mr. Yang Bo, Chao Yuan, Junshun Hu, and Ms. Xue Qiu for many helpful discussions.

## References


1. Sandhu, R., Ferraiolo, D.F., Kuhn, D.R.: The NIST Model for Role Based Access Control: Toward a Unified Standard. In: 5th ACM Workshop on Role Based Access Control, pp. 47–63. ACM Press (2000)
2. Doconta, M.C.: A guide to the future of xml, web services, and knowledge management. China Science and Technology Press, Beijing (2009)
3. Lupu, E.C., Sloman, M.: Conflicts in policy-based distributed systems management. IEEE Transactions on Software Engineering 25(6), 852–869 (1999)
4. Heilili, N., Chen, Y., et al.: An OWL-based approach for RBAC with negative authorization. Knowledge Science, Engineering and Management 4092, 164–175 (2006)
5. Lu, J., Li, R., Varadharajan, V., Lu, Z., Ma, X.: Secure Interoperation in Multi-domain Environments Employing UCON Policies. In: Samarati, P., Yung, M., Martinelli, F., Ardagna, C.A. (eds.) ISC 2009. LNCS, vol. 5735, pp. 395–402. Springer, Heidelberg (2009)
6. Moon, C.-J., Paik, W., Kim, Y.-G., Kwon, J.-H.: The conflict detection between permission assignment constraints in role-based access control. In: Feng, D., Lin, D., Yung, M. (eds.) CISC 2005. LNCS, vol. 3822, pp. 265–278. Springer, Heidelberg (2005)
7. Shafiq, B., Joshi, J.B.D., Bertino, E., Ghafoor, A.: Secure interoperation in a multi-domain environment employing RBAC policies. IEEE Transactions on Knowledge and Data Engineering 17(11), 1557–1577 (2005)
8. Ni, Q.: Privacy-aware role-based access control. ACM Transactions on Information and System Security (TISSEC) 13(3), 1–31 (2010)
9. Huang, F., Huang, Z., Liu, L.: A DL-based method for access control policy conflict detecting. In: Internetware 2009, pp. 1–5. ACM, USA (2009)
10. Mohan, A., Blough, D.M.: Detection of Conflicts and Inconsistencies in Taxonomy-based Authorization Policies. In: 2011 IEEE International Conference on Bioinformatics and Biomedicine, GA, Atlanta, pp. 590–594.
11. Mansor, A.A., et al.: Policy-based approach to detect and resolve policy conflict for static and dynamic architecture. Journal of Theoretical and Applied Information Technology 37(2), 268–278 (2012)
12. Radi, A., et al.: On the three levels security policy comparison between SVM and decision trees. Journal of Theoretical and Applied Information Technology 35(1), 56–68 (2012)
13. Huang, H., Kirchner, H.: Formal specification and verification of modular security policy based on colored petri nets. IEEE Transactions on Dependable and Secure Computing 8(6), 852–865 (2011)

# East-West Bridge for SDN Network Peering

Pingping Lin, Jun Bi, and Yangyang Wang

Institute for Network Sciences and Cyberspace, Department of Computer Science, Tsinghua University
Tsinghua National Laboratory for Information Science and Technology (TNList)
FIT Building, Beijing, 100084, China
linpp@netarchlab.tsinghua.edu.cn, junbi@tsinghua.edu.cn, wyystar@gmail.com

**Abstract.** Large networks are always partitioned into several small networks when deploying software defined networks (SDN), and a dedicated network operating system (NOS) is deployed for each network. Each NOS has the local network view. However, to route data packets in an entire network, a global network is required. Thus, a high performance East-West Bridge with full mesh connection is proposed in this paper for heterogeneous NOSes to exchange network views in enterprise, data center, and intra-domain networks. We implemented the East-West Bridge and analyzed the performance obtained: about 100% of enterprises and data centers, and about 99.5% of autonomous systems can adopt the East-West Bridge solution.

**Keywords:** Software-Defined Networking, Heterogeneous SDN Peers, Network View, East-West Bridge.

## 1 Introduction

When deploying Software defined networking SDN [1] in real networks, large networks are always partitioned into several smaller networks (referred to as sub-networks) due to numerous reasons [19]: scalability, privacy, incremental deployment, network faults isolation, and so on. Each sub-network runs one NOS or controller such as NOX [20], Maestro [21], Beacon [4], Floodlight [18], Trema [10] etc. Each NOS only has a local network view (the network view in this paper refers to topology, reachability, entities, network abilities, network state). However, many network applications (APPs) need a global view of the entire network. Based on such requirements, controllers should be able to construct a global network view and provided it to APPs. In order to do so, multiple NOSes may need to communicate with each other to exchange individual network view information or share a global network view database. Also, there are several distributed NOSes such as Onix [7], HyperFlow [8], DIFANE [17], and so no. However, none of them can coexist with others, because the east-west communication interface is private. The target of this paper is to enable different NOSes from different vendors to work together.

We refer to as an SDN domain a sub-network which runs one NOS and is partitioned from a larger network. In this paper an SDN domain can be a sub-network in a

J. Su et al. (Eds.): ICoC 2013, CCIS 401, pp. 170–181, 2013.

data center (DC) or an enterprise network or an AS (Autonomous System). The main contributions of this paper: (1) we propose that different domains can run heterogeneous NOSes at the same time. (2) We define what network view information can be exchanged among heterogeneous SDN peers. (3) We propose to abstract a physical network into a virtual network for privacy or scalability. (4) We design a high performance network view exchange mechanism. We refer to this mechanism as the East-West Bridge (EWBridge for short).

The rest of the paper is organized as follows: Section 2 presents the related work. Section 3 describes the design of EWBridge among SDN peers. Our work is implemented and evaluated in Section 4. Section 5 concludes the paper.

## 2 Related Work

Currently, there are mainly two kinds of NOSes: (1) Single NOS, (2) Distributed NOS. Single NOS is such as Floodlight [18], NOX [20], Maestro [21], Beacon [4], SNAC [22], and Trema [10]. Distributed NOS is such as Onix [7], HyperFlow [8], and DIFANE [17].

In the SDN centralized control model, all the routes are determined by the NOS, so the first packet of each data flow is sent to the central NOS. Then, the NOS will compute a routing path for each data flow and install the routing path into the related OpenFlow [9] switches according to a global network view. Here, the first packet of each data flow is usually called the "packet-in". To improve the flow initialization requests setting up speed, some NOSes such as Beacon and Maestro are trying to improve the performance of the controller by the multi-thread technology. The NOS software systems are always being deployed on a multicore host or server. However, for large-scale data centers or networks, the request processing capability of a single controller is limited: (1) NOX could process about 30K requests [23] per second; (2) Maestro could process about 600K requests per second.

In fact, large-scale network environments always have vast amounts of data flows: (1) a 1500 server cluster might generate 100K requests per second [24]; (2) a 100 switch data center might generate 10000K requests per second [21]. To achieve a scalable control plane, distributed NOSes are proposed. Then, the scalability in the control plane evolves into a cooperative performance problem of multi-NOSes. Such, the east-west interface and communication has been considered as a very import module in software defined network architecture, such as SDNi [5] and SDN at Google [6].

HyperFlow [8] uses multiple controllers to construct a distributed control plane and each controller takes charge for a small area of network. To learn a global network view, HyperFlow adopts a distributed file system named WheelFS [15] which is designed for the WAN (Wide Area Network) environment. Each HyperFlow controller has the right to deal with network events within a certain local area, and the events which will affect the global network should be announced from time to time. Once other controllers learn the event information, they should replay the event to achieve the synchronization of the global view. This approach can only deal with events which do not occur frequently, such as link status changes. EWBridge proposed in this paper can also work in the HyperFlow architecture and substitute the WheelFS to better synchronize the network view of each domain.

Onix [7] is a distributed controller for large scale production network. It uses the Distributed Hash Table (DHT) to store the network information. Each controller just stores a part of the whole network view. While EWBridge focuses on SDN domains such as sub-networks within intra-domain networks, data centers and enterprise networks. The target of EWBridge is to achieve high performance and high available network view synchronization. We will show later on, that in the above scenarios the performance of EWBridge is better than DHT. Onix is a distributed controller, while EWBridge is a mechanism to support different controllers/ NOSes with different local network view storage systems working together. In such way, EWBridge can encourage third-parties to engage in contributing to the NOS and promote competition and coexistence in the NOS's environment.

Previously, Yin et al. had proposed a message exchange protocol for software defined networks across multiple sub-network domains named SDNi [5]. That proposal only defined several basic messages such as the reachability information and the flow setup/ tear-down/ update processes. But it did not describe how the message should be stored and exchanged in a performance effective manner. In this paper we explore and verify the east-west message exchange protocol.

## 3 East-West Bridge for SDN Peers

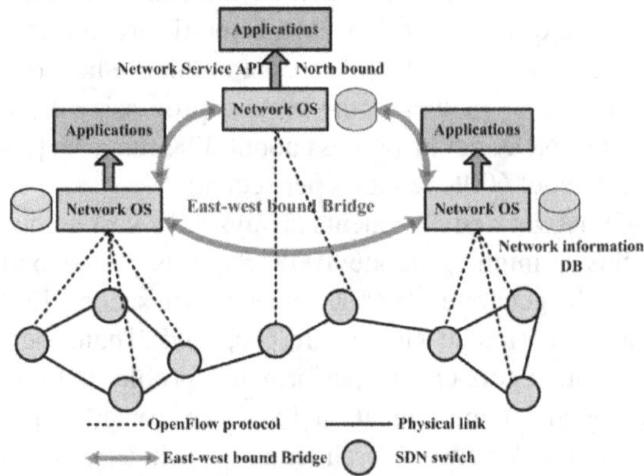


**Fig. 1.** East-west Bridge for heterogeneous NOSes cooperation in SDN

EWBridge is a high performance network view exchange mechanism for multi-domain networks. It is compatible with different third-party controllers/ NOSes and network view information storage systems. We illustrate the EWBridge in Figure 1. The EW-Bridge mechanism mainly includes the controller/ NOS discovery process, definition of network view information in different scenarios, network view information storage and transfer format, and high performance network view exchange mechanism.

## 3.1 Controller Discovery

Before exchanging the network view, the most important problem for controllers is to discover each other. The algorithm for controllers from different sub-networks to find each other can be a distributed controller discovery algorithm or a centralized management system such as a registration center. Since this paper focuses on a same administrative network, a registration server is adopted.

In this paper, all the domains belong to a same intra-domain, enterprise or DC; the network administrator can just establish a central controller list. Each controller can get the information of others from the controller list.

## 3.2 Network View

- **Network View Abstraction and Storage.**

The network view mainly includes two aspects: the network static state information and dynamic state information. The network static aspect includes: (1) Reachability: in carrier network, reachability refers to the IP address prefixes; in DC and enterprise network, it also includes the server/host addresses. (2) Topology: node (e.g., switch, server, host, controller, even firewall, balancer, others), link, link bandwidth, port throughput, link connection; (3) Network service capabilities: such as SLA (Service Level Agreement), GRE (Generic Routing Encapsulation); (4) QoS parameters, such as latency, reliability, packet loss rate, availability, throughput, time delay variation, and cost. The network dynamic aspect mainly includes the network state, such as FlowTable entries information in each switch, real-time bandwidth utilization in the topology, and the all the flow paths in the network.

The network view can be expressed by directed graph with entity (node, virtual node, link, virtual link) attributes. Then, the full network view can be formalized accordingly. EWBridge supports different SDN domains to adopt different network view storage systems and to define the network view differently. As long as the network view messages delivered on the EWBridge have the uniform labels in a specific format which will be showed later. Considering that the network storage should have a higher scalability, availability and data IO speed, EWBridge suggests the "key-value" database [13] plus caching systems, where the key-value storage design is illustrated in Table I. In addition, databases with transactional function should be adopted to guarantee data integrity.

**Table 1.** Key-Value storage design

| Key | Columns | |
|---|---|---|
| Node_ID (physical/virtual) | is_ virtual (first column) | IP_addresses, OF_version, port_numbers, is_edge_node, Vendor_name, MTU Device_type, Device_function |
| Link_ID (physical/virtual) | is_ virtual (first column) | Node_ID_src, Port_ID_src, Node_ID_dst, Port_ID_dst, Bandwidth, is_interdomain_link |

**Table 1.** *(Continued)*

| | | |
|---|---|---|
| Port_ID (physical/virtual) | is_ virtual (first column) | Node_ID, Port_MAC, is_active, is_edge_port, VLAN_ID, throughput |
| Node_capbility | protocol_name, version, port | |
| Reachability | IP_prefixes, length | |
| Node_table_ID (Flow entity) | Columns names are the same as the fields defined in the flowtable in OpenFlow specification | |
| Link_Utilities | Link_ID, Link utilities | |
| Flow_path (Node_ID_src_ Node_ID_dst) | Port_ID (in), Node_ID_src, Port_ID (out), Node Series with ingress and egress ports, Port_ID (in), Node_ID_dst, Port_ID (out) | |

The edge in the table above refers whether this entity is the edge of a domain. Each domain uses the edge information to construct a global network view. The node, link, and port can be a physical entity or a virtual entity.

- **Network View Learning.**

The basic information such as node, node_capbility, port, and link information usually can be learned by the LLDP (Link Layer Discovery Protocol). To learn more network view information such as OpenFlow version and number of the FlowTables on each node, link utilities, and flow entries, we extended the NOS by adding a network view driver module named LLDP extension shown in Figure 2. All the network view information is provided to network applications by Rest API. We can enable EW-bridge in all kinds of NOSes by adding the three modules in the red color shown in Figure 2. Network virtualization and east-west bridge module will be showed later.

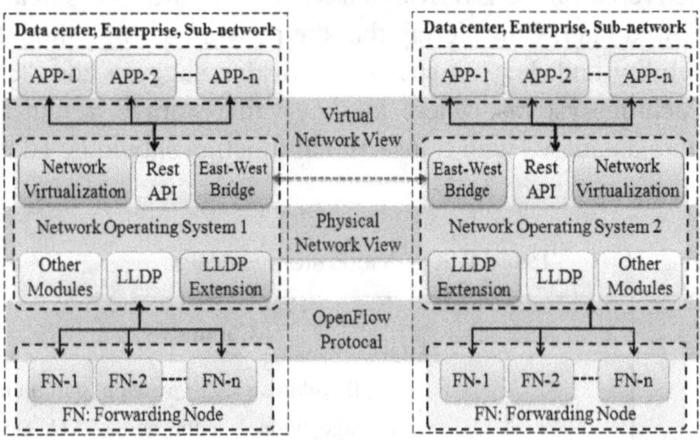


**Fig. 2.** Enable EWBridge in all kinds of NOSes by adding three modules (Network Virtualiztion, East-West Bridge, and LLDP Extension)

By counting the total number of packets related to a certain port in all the FlowTables in forwarding node, the driver can learn the link utilities. By sending certain commands (normally, OpenFlow switches provide those commands) to the OpenFlow switches, LLDP extension module can also learn the OpenFlow version, number of FlowTables, and flow entries in each switch. Furthermore, the LLDP extension can call the OpenFlow switches functions or commands by the SSL (Secure Sockets Layer) control channel between controller and switches.

- **Network View Transfer Format.**

This paper suggests JSON (JavaScript Object Notation) as a basic implementation, and the XML(eXtensible Markup Language), YANG[2], YAML[16] as alternatives. Those languages have the ability to enable EWBridge with the following advantages: (1) They are vendor-independent and application-independent, thus the network view transfer format is independent with the storage systems; (2) They allow explicit definition of the inherent structure according to the requirements; such features make the network view message format flexible and easy to extend; (3) They are files and not a data packet format. The elements are easy to extend.

- **Virtual Network View for Privacy and Scalability.**

Usually the network view is the entire network information. However, some domains may be willing to expose only a part of the network view due to their privacy concerns. EWBridge supports abstracting a physical network to a virtual network for such domains. As showed in Figure 3, routing paths from the ingress port to the egress port of an abstract network can have SLA-level path attributes such as time latency, reliability, bandwidth, packet loss rate like VP 1, VP 2, VP 3. To abstract a network further, EWBridge supports abstracting a network to a virtual node like network 2. The virtual node for network 2 only retains the three physical inter-network links: link2, link3, link4.

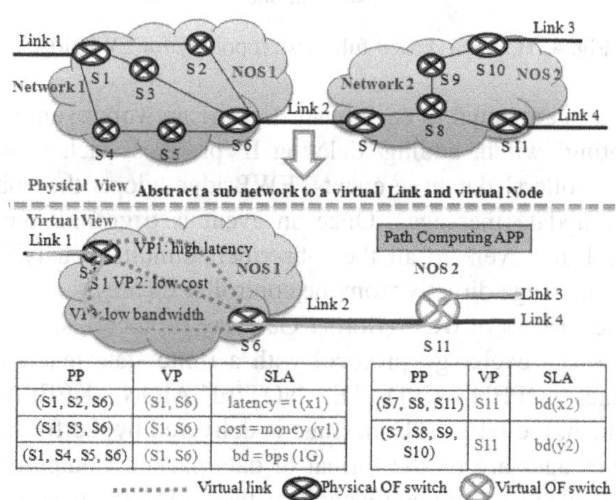


**Fig. 3.** Physical view to virtual view (PP: Physical Path; VP: Virtual Path; OF: OpenFlow; S: Switch; bd: bandwidth; t: time; bps: bits per second)

Each path computing APP on NOS can compute the routing path (just a routing path segment such as VP1 or VP2) within its domain. To compute a complete end to end or global routing path, the NOS should at least know other abstracted virtual network view. The abstracted virtual network view is the minimum information for global network reachability. Then the path computing APP can compute and install a routing path by the restful API provided by NOS into OpenFlow switches.

For the virtual network view, each NOS should store a mapping table between the physical network and the abstracted virtual network views which is showed in the table of Figure 3. To achieve large-scale scalability, each SDN domain can be abstracted to a node with multi-ports and multiple bandwidths like network 2. Other NOSes treat the network domain 2 as an abstract node with 3 ports and 3 links. After exchanging the network views, each NOS can further provide additional specific network view [1] like access network view, edge network view.

### 3.3 High Speed Bridge Exchange Mechanism

After the controller discovery process, each controller learns all the addresses of their peers. Then all the controllers can establish a virtual full mesh topology based on TCP/ SSL shown in Figure 4.

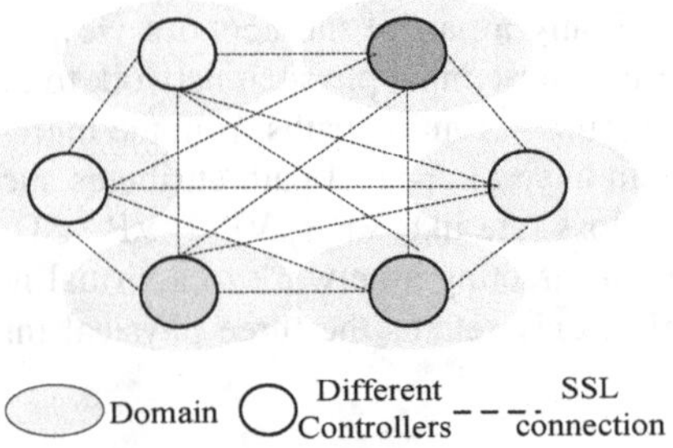


**Fig. 4.** TCP/SSL based full mesh topology for EWBridge

All the SDN peers are equal to each other. For the network event such as link failure, adding/ deleting switch, adding/ deleting IP prefixes, each controller can subscribe to other controllers' database events. EWBridge adopts the publish/ subscribe system to deliver update messages. Once an event is triggered, the corresponding controller will push the event to all the subscribers simultaneously. Each controller can get the update message directly from the controller it cares.

Considering the success of BGP (Border Gateway Protocol), similarly we design a network view message exchange protocol with a finite state machine and define 5 types of messages: OPEN, UPDATE, NOTIFICAION, KEEPALIVE, VIEW-REFRESH. In which, the UPDATE message is delivered by the format of JSON file, and the rest of messages are by the format of data packet. Compared with the BGP protocol, the EWBridge system mainly changes the UPDATE message into JSON file format, and simplifies the finite state machine.

NOS peers use TCP to setup connections. After a TCP connection is established, the first message sent is the OPEN message. Some parameters such as timers should be negotiated in the OPEN message. After the OPEN message is confirmed, NOS will keeps sending out KEEPALIVE message. EWBridge defines a timer for the KEEPALIVE message. If one peer has not been receiving KEEPALIVE packet from a certain NOS, this peer will think the NOS has failed, and will release this connection. All the errors will lead to idle state and NOTIFICAION will be sent to all the peers. NOS also can use the VIEW-REFRESH message to fetch network view information from its certain peers.

In the normal condition each NOS keeps sending out KEEPALIVE messages to its peers in parallel. So it can keep in connection with all its peers. Once network view updates within its domain appear, it can directly send UPDATE file out to its peers in parallel without re-setup TCP connections. Furthermore, each UPDATE file can carry multiple UPDATE messages. In such way, EWBridge can achieve high speed data exchange.

# 4 Implementation and Evaluation

## 4.1 Implementation and Experiment Results

EWBridge has been implemented in two open-source NOSes: Floodlight and NOX. We use Mininet [3] to emulate two data centers. One is located in Beijing, China, and the other is located in California, USA, as shown in Figure 5. The OpenFlow switches in network are Open vSwitches [11].We divide the entire network of Beijing data center into four sub-networks and divide the California data center into three sub-networks. Each sub-network runs one NOS and one database. We run a centralized register center server for EWBridge in sub-network 6 in California. We also run a topology viewer application and a video server process on this server.

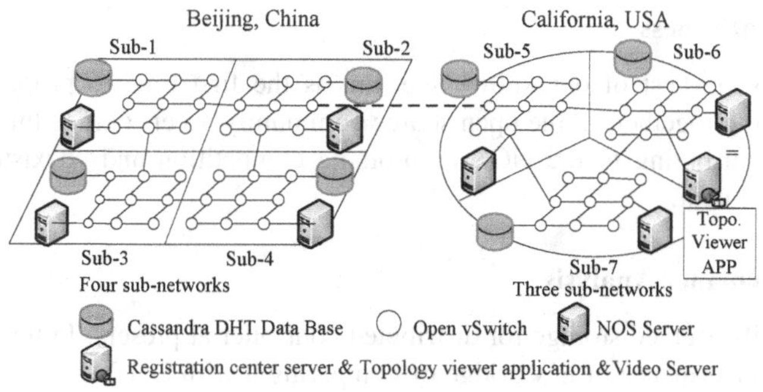


**Fig. 5.** Experiment Topology

In the first experiment, all the NOSes are Floodlight software and all databases are Cassandra [12] DHT databases. We write and run a topology viewer application to fetch the entire topology of all the sub-networks. Then in the second experiment, the controllers in sub-network 1, 3, 5, 7 run Floodlight and the controllers in sub-network 2, 4, 6 run NOX. In addition, we use the Cassandra single PC mode and all the sub networks are connected by EWBridge. We use the topology viewer application to fetch the entire topology of all the sub-networks again. The results are shown in Figure 6.

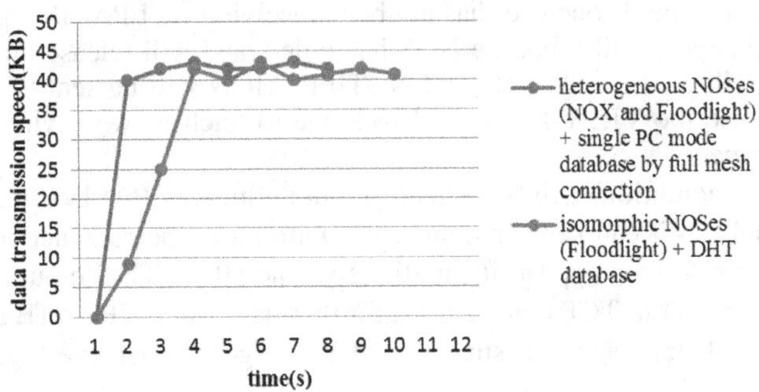


**Fig. 6.** Performance of DHT and EWBridge for data synchronization

As shown in Figure6, the heterogeneous EWBridge system with has two obvious advantages: (1) Low time delay. Once receives the requests from applications, the entire system can respond very quickly. Because in the EWBridge, each database stores the entire network topology locally, while the DHT mode database stores the entire network topology in distributed database located in different places. When a DHT database node receives a data request, it has to fetch other data from different places and then assemble all the data and then return it to the application. (2) For a same size topology, the EWBridge system can finish all the data transmission earlier than the DHT system. That is because the DHT system is a little slower at connection setting up in the very beginning. So it needs longer time to finish transmission. Besides, the EWBridge system can enable different NOSes to cooperate.

### 4.2 Innovativeness

According to the best of our knowledge, this is the first time to propose different NOSes working together, in the open source community, to encourage third-parties to engage in contributing to the NOS to promote competition and coexistence in the NOS's environment.

### 4.3 Performance Analysis

DHT is a well-received storage for distributed controller at present. In this section we analyze the performance of EWBridge by comparing it with DHT.

***Speed of Network view updates.*** EWBridge adopts the subscribe/ publish model. Usually, all the peers are in the established TCP connection state. Once a network view changes in a domain, the controller directly pushes the change to their peers with time $\mathrm{return(t)}$. Each controller stores the global network view. The APPs can directly access the data in local storage. For the DHT storage, entire network view is in distributed locations. The DHT needs to fetch the data. So the time is $\{\mathrm{request(t)} + \mathrm{return(t)}\}$. Thus, EWBridge is $\mathrm{request(t)}$ faster than DHT.

***Network view updates bandwidth cost.*** If we define the update frequency as $f/1\ second$, and the number of NOSes is $n$. Then, in time $1/f$, the amount of link utility change in each domain is $f_{change}(link\ utility)$. EWBridge will transfer $\{n \times f_{change}(link\ utility)\}$ information, while DHT is:

$n \times \{f_{change}(link\ utility) + f_{size}(request\ packet)\}$. Thus, EWBridge is $n \times f_{size}(request\ packet)$ less than DHT.

***Size of network view storage.*** We assume the size of the global SDN network view information is $X$. In DHT, each domain just stores $X/n$. In reality, the controller needs the entire view of all the SDN networks when computing path. It stores the rest size of $(X - X/n)$ outside the DTH table. So the total size storage for each domain is the same. EWBrige can also store the local network view of $X/n$ in high speed database and store the rest in relative lower speed database if there is a limitation in high speed database.

***Data query speed.*** The EWBridge and DHT are both based on the "key-value" storage system, but DHT has routing issues (multi-hop routing), while EWBridge is single-hop routing in more than 99.5% scenarios (will be shown in Section IV.D). Here a hop may really mean multiple physical hops in the underlying network, so EWBridge is faster than DHT in the data query speed.

In summary, EWBridge and Onix are designed for different deployment scenarios. Onix adopts the DHT storage and focuses on large scale network while EWBridge focuses on enterprise/ DC/ intra-domain networks. Onix is more scalable than EWBridge for large scale networks. EWBridge is more efficient than Onix when they are working in enterprise / DC / intra-domain networks.

## 4.4 Scalability

EWBridge supports the network abstraction strategy to improve scalability. As shown in Section III.B, EWBridge supports network view abstraction. A large network can be abstracted into a small virtual network only with the edge switches, or even into a virtual node. To achieve large-scale scalability, each NOS should treat other SDN networks as an abstract node with multi-ports. We use a mathematical model to evaluate the intra-domain level scalability:

**Table 2.** Symbol Definition

| Symbol | Meaning |
|---|---|
| $x$ | Requests a controller can deal in one second |
| $y$ | Requests a computer generates in one second |
| z | Number of computers one person has |
| $N$ | Number of people in an AS/DC/enterprise |

Then there will be about ${}^{Nzy}/_{x}$ domains, and the total number of connections is:

$$ {}^{Nzy}/_{x} \times ({}^{Nzy}/_{x} - 1) $$

Normally, one client uses one computer at the same time and we assume each computer generate 1 $rps$ (request per second). We use the well-known NOX as controller, and NOX could process about 30K $rps$[23]. The number of *online* people or customer on campus are usually less than 100,000, in enterprise is usually less than 500,000, in DC/AS (Autonomous System), it is usually less than 3,000,000 [14].

**Table 3.** Number of domain and connection degree

| | **People/Customer (Online)** | **Domain Number** | **Connection Degree** |
|---|---|---|---|
| **Campus** | ≤100,000 | 4 | 3 |
| **Enterprise** | ≤500,000 | 17 | 16 |
| **DC or AS** | 3,000,000 | 100 | 99 |

The 16bits TCP port can support $2^{16} = 65536$ connections in theory, and it is will very easily to support 3,000,000 (the numbers of online users in 99.5% ASes are less than 3,000,000 [14]) online users with 99 connections. Thus, the estimate of table 3 is feasible.

With the EWBridge, about 99.5% of all the ASes can use the full mesh topology, and about 0.5% Autonomous Systems need to use connection degree less than $({}^{Nzy}/_{x} - 1)$.

## 5 Conclusion and Future Work

This paper designed a high-performance mechanism for heterogeneous NOSes to exchange network view for enterprise, data center, and intra-domain networks. It defined what information should be shared and how it is shared. For network privacy, EWBridge proposed to abstract the physical network to a virtual network view. Enabled by the characteristic of JSON, EWBridge supports NOSes from different vendors. The implementation proved the feasibility of the EWBridge and the evaluation proved that EWBridge is a high performance system. In the future, we are going to deploy it to three SDN networks: SDN networks in CERNET, INTERNET2, and CSTNET.

**Acknowledgment.** Supported by the National High-tech R&D Program ("863" Program) of China (No.2013AA010605), the National Science Foundation of China (No.61073172), and National Key Basic Research Program ("973" Program) of China (No. 2009CB320501).

## References

1. McKeown, N.: Keynote talk: Software-defined networking. In: Proc. of IEEE INFOCOM (April 2009)
2. YANG, https://tools.ietf.org/html/rfc6020
3. Mininet, http://yuba.stanford.edu/foswiki/bin/view/OpenFlow/Mininet
4. Beacon (2012), http://beaconcontroller.net/
5. Yin, H., Xie, H., Tsou, T., Lopez, D., Aranda, P.A., Sidi, R.: SDNi: A message exchange protocol for software defined networks (SDNs) across multiple domains. IRTF Internet-Draft (2012)
6. SDN at Google, http://www.ietf.org/proceedings/84/slides/slides-84-sdnrg-4.pdf
7. Koponen, T., Casado, M., Gude, N., Stribling, J., Poutievski, L., Zhu, M., Ramanathan, R., Iwata, Y., Inoue, H., Hama, T., Shenker, S.: Onix: a distributed control platform for large-scale production networks. In: OSDI (2010)
8. Tootoocian, A., Ganjali, Y.: HyperFlow: A distributed control plane for OpenFlow. In: INM/WREN Workshop (2010)
9. McKeown, N., Anderson, T., Balakrishnan, H., Parulkar, G., Peterson, L., Rexford, J., Shenker, S., Turner, J.: OpenFlow: enabling innovation in campus networks. ACM SIGCOMM Computer Communication Review 38(2) (2008)
10. TREMA, http://trema.github.io/trema/
11. Open vSwitch, http://openvswitch.org/
12. Cassandra, http://cassandra.apache.org/
13. Schütt, T., Schintke, F., Reinefeld, A.: Scalaris: reliable transactional p2p key/value store. In: Proceedings of the 7th ACM SIGPLAN Workshop on ERLANG, Victoria, BC, Canada, September 27 (2008)
14. Caida, http://data.caida.org/datasets/routing/routeviews-prefix2as/
15. Stribling, J., Sovran, Y., Zhang, I., Pretzer, X., Li, J., Kaashoek, M.F., Morris, R.: Flexible, wide-area storage for distributed systems with wheelfs. In: NSDI (April 2009)
16. YAML, http://yaml.org/spec/1.2/spec.html
17. Yu, M., Rexford, J., Freedman, M.J., Wang, J.: Scalable Flow-Based Networking with DIFANE. In: Proc. SIGCOMM (August 2010)
18. Floodlight, http://www.projectfloodlight.org/floodlight/
19. Xie, H., Tsou, T., Lopez, D., Yin, H., Gurbani, V.: Use cases for alto with software defined networks. IETF Internet-Draft (2012)
20. Gude, N., Koponen, T., Pettit, J., Pfa, B., Casado, M., McKeown, N., Shenker, S.: NOX: Towards and operating system for networks. ACM SIGCOMM Computer Communication Review (July 2008)
21. Cai, Z., Cox, A.L., Ng, T.S.E.: Maestro: A System for Scalable OpenFlow Control. Tech. Rep. TR10-08, Rice University (2010)
22. Simple network access control, http://www.openflow.org/wp/snac/
23. Tavakoli, A., Casado, M., Koponen, T., Shenker, S.: Applying nox to the datacenter. In: Proceedings of Workshop on Hot Topics in Networks, HotNets-VIII (2009)
24. Kandula, S., Sengupta, S., Greenberg, A., Patel, P.: The Nature of Datacenter Traffic: Measurements & Analysis. In: Proc. IMC (2009)

# A Connectivity Invariant Dynamic Multichannel Assignment Method for VANET*

Tong Zhao, Shanbo Lu, Wei Yan, and Xiaoming Li

School of Electronics Engineering and Computer Science
Peking University, Beijing, P.R. China, 100871

**Abstract.** Multi-Interface Multi-Channel (MIMC) can be used to reduce the channel interference and improve the network capacity for multi-hop wireless ad-hoc networks, but using multichannel will impact the network connectivity, which is an important QoS factor in VANET. The basic multichannel assignment scheme in our paper can keep the connectivity as good as single channel network. Furthermore, the nodes can periodically monitor the channel usage and dynamically switch the channels to the less busy ones. In order to work in the highly mobile scenarios in VANET, the method works in a fully distributed way with low overhead. Simulations show that our method can notably improve the throughput of VANETs. And the performance keeps steady with various network configurations.

**Keywords:** Multichannel, Connectivity, Channel Usage, VANET.

## 1 Introduction

Vehicular Ad-hoc Network (VANET), as a subset of MANET, is confronted with the same problems of inter-link interference and low capacity [5]. Multichannel technology can alleviate the interference [8]. However, channel diversity and network connectivity are two conflicting factors. Fig. 1 is an example.All the 4 nodes are within direct communication distance. The topology with a single channel is originally a 4-node fully connected graph (Fig. 1(a)). When link (1,4) and (2,3) are working on different channels, the network is partitioned to two parts (Fig. 1(b)). If the nodes can work on two channels concurrently with two interfaces, a topology in Fig. 1(c) can be formed. If the nodes equip as many interfaces as channels, they can freely select the channel to avoid interference while assure connectivity. However, there are 12 orthogonal channels in 802.11a, 3 in 802.11b/g [2] and 7 channels for DSRC [6]. Equipping 3 interfaces on each node seems possible, but mounting 7 or 12 interfaces is a bit too many.

Most existing works have much fewer interfaces than channels, and sacrifice some connectivity for the channel diversity [9,3,7,23,19,4,21,16]. In this condition, an optimal channel assignment method needs to take the routing strategy

* This work is supported in part by 973 Program of the Chinese Ministry of Science and Technology (No. 2009CB320504) and National Natural Science Foundation of China (No. 61073155 and No. 61201245).

J. Su et al. (Eds.): ICoC 2013, CCIS 401, pp. 182–193, 2013.

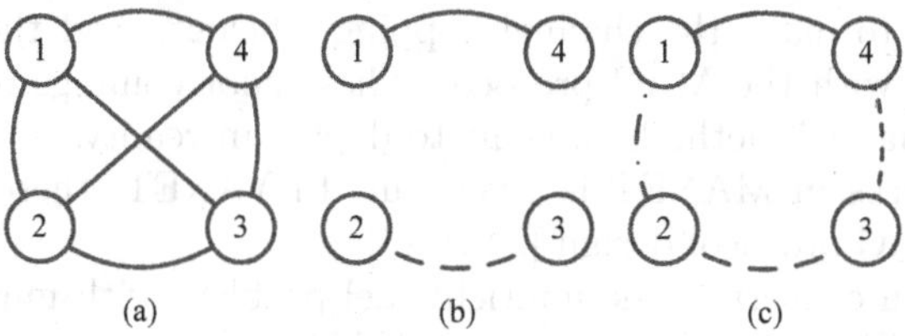


**Fig. 1.** An example of connectivity degradation in multichannel MANET. The configurations are: (a) 1 channel; (b) 2 channels, 1 interface for each node; (c) 4 channels, 2 interfaces for each node.

and network load into consideration. This channel assignment problem is proved to be NP hard [15]. The highly mobile character of VANET makes the problem even harder. In [25], the authors evaluated the QoS indicators of VANET through simulations. They found that delay and jitter are usually within tolerance, but delivery ratio and connection lifetime are difficult to meet the QoS requirements. Thus, sacrificing connectivity for the channel diversity seems not suitable for VANET. On the other hand, vehicles have much fewer energy and hardware constraints than handheld mobile devices. Consequently, we attempt to preserve the VANET connectivity by relax the energy and hardware constraints a bit. A connectivity invariant multichannel assignment protocol can not only benefit the VANET QoS, but also make the other protocol design independent to the multichannel method and preserve the layered network architecture.

In our previous work [24], we proposed a multichannel assignment method based on road topology (MIMC-Road), which can keep the same connectivity as single channel network. In this paper, we first generalize the previous solution by answering how to keep the connectivity while utilizing the multichannel resources using the Pigeon Hole Principle. With the invariant connectivity, we further present a channel usage based dynamic channel assignment method. Each node monitors the channel usages of its own active channels and exchange the channel usage information with the neighbors. With the collected channel usage information, the node can switch from a crowded channel to a channel with sparse nodes, while still keeping the connectivity intact. The method is fully distributed and insensitive to the mobility, which makes it suitable to be used in VANET.

In the rest of the paper, after reviewing the related work in Section 2, we discuss how to keep the network connectivity invariant in Section 3. In Section 4, we describe the details of the channel usage based multichannel assignment method. The evaluations are presented in Section 5 and the conclusion is in the last section.

## 2 Related Work

A lot of papers have studied the Single Interface Multi-Channel protocols (SIMC) using channel hopping methods. A fast switching and time synchronization are usually required to make the channel hopping efficient. And the protocols are tightly bounded with the MAC protocol. These shortcomings make the single interface multichannel methods difficult to deploy in reality. In [13], a comparison of these works in MANET is given out. In VANET, there are also some multichannel MAC protocol design [22,10,11].

Here, our main concern is the multichannel problem with multi-interface architecture (MIMC), which is independent of MAC protocols, and more efficient than single interface architecture [8]. The MIMC algorithms can be divided into the following categories.

### 2.1 Fixed Multichannel Assignment

The algorithms of fixed multichannel assignment will not change the assignment within a quite long period after an assignment is determined. These algorithms is suitable for networks with static topologies and known traffic profiles. In [18], the authors proposed a centralized channel assignment algorithm for mesh networks. The algorithm assumes that the traffic load is known in advance. The channel with few conflicts is assigned to link with high load. This algorithm cannot adapt to dynamic topology and traffic. When some links need re-allocate the channels, they may cause the ripple-effect [18]. In [12], the authors presented a new multichannel assignment algorithm based on a connectivity graph and a conflict graph in mesh network. This algorithm does not cause ripple-effect, but it does not take the traffic load into consideration.

### 2.2 Dynamic Multichannel Assignment

In this sort of algorithms, the interfaces can switch dynamically between available channels to adapt to the dynamic traffic load. In [17] and [16], the authors propose mechanisms to allocate channels dynamically based on the spanning tree in mesh network. the gateway node is treated as the root of the tree. The spanning tree is reconfigured dynamically according to the traffic from and to the gateway.

### 2.3 Mixed Multichannel Assignment

This sort of algorithms combine the above two assignment strategies. some representative algorithms are [9,23]. In [9], each node's interfaces are divided into fixed interfaces and switchable interfaces. The fixed interfaces only receive packets. The switchable interfaces switch to the fixed listening channels of the neighbors to send the packets. The connecitivity is dynamically maintained by exchanging the listening channels of the nodes. In [23], the channels are assigned based on clusters. By selecting the vehicles with the same moving directions, quite steady clusters may be formed. The DSRC channels are then partitioned into intra-cluster and inter-cluster channel sets. Neighboring clusters select channels by observing the busy status of channels.

### 2.4 Optimization Models of MIMC

Besides the above heuristic design, there are also theoretical analysis and optimization models of using multi-interface multi-channel (MIMC) architecture [3,7,21]. These models usually require the topology and traffic to keep steady for the algorithms to converge. This makes them only fit for mesh network with static topology and known traffic pattern. And they will have difficulty in highly dynamic scenarios, such as in VANETs.

In mobile scenarios, channel assignment is usually solved using heuristics (such as [9,23]). Our work is also a heuristic design. But we first find the connectivity invariant condition. The consequent channel usage based multichannel design is simplified and more efficient. The detail analysis and design are given in the following two sections.

## 3 Connectivity Invariant Condition

In our previous work, we have designed a connectivity invariant multichannel assignment method based on road map topology (MIMC-Road)[24]. In MIMC-Road, the road is divided into multiple channel segments in a staggered pattern (as shown in fig 2). This staggered pattern can guarantee that any two vehicles within the communication range will sit in one of the common channel segments. Thus the network connectivity with the multichannel configuration is identical to the single channel network. The vehicles select their active channels according to the position information, and switch the channels when they move to the other channel segments. But this method has the following shortcomings. First, the channel assignment is static according to the position. When the density is high and several vehicles are in the same channel segment, they cannot adapt to the different channels. Second, for those idle vehicles that are not communicating, they also need to switch the channels when they move across the channel segment boundaries. Furthermore, all the interfaces shall have the similar communication ranges to make the multichannel segment division easy and effective.

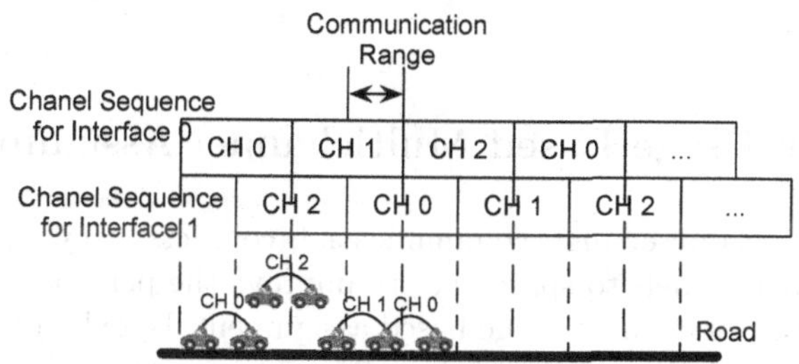


**Fig. 2.** A MIMC-Road example of 3 channels and 2 interfaces of each node

As discussed in the introduction section, connectivity invariant property is valuable to the VANET QoS and layered network protocol design. Here, we want to preserve the connectivity invariant property from MIMC-Road and overcome its shortcomings. Generally, the connectivity invariance can be achieved by insuring that there always exists at least one common channel between any two nodes within the communication range. In MIMC-Road, this is guaranteed by arranging the channels geographically. But more generally, for a network with $C$ available channels, we can insure the common channel between nodes by equipping at lease $\lfloor \frac{C}{2} \rfloor + 1$ interfaces for every node. Letting these interfaces work on different channels and the existence of common channels are insured by the Pigeon Hole Principle. This condition constrains the interface number of the vehicles. Considering that there is fewer hardware and energy limitations on the vehicles than on the conventional mobile devices, the requirement can be satisfied with reasonable costs. Specifically, for 3 channels in 802.11b/g, 7 channels in DSRC and 12 channels in 802.11a, the required number of interfaces are 2, 4 and 7. It is suitable for a vehicle to equip 2 or 4 interfaces. 7 interface per vehicle looks a bit too costly at first glance. But MIMC architecture does not need to modify the MAC, which means the hardware can be obtained off the shelf. And the connectivity invariance simplifies the protocol design and reduces the implementation cost. The total cost may not be as much as one would expect at first glance.

With the above connectivity invariant condition, the topology of multichannel network is identical to that of the single channel network. There's no constraints of using channels geographically as MIMC-Road did, or timely as channel hopping methods did. Idle nodes will not be required to switch the channels to keep the connectivity anymore. For the dense networks, the nodes can freely switch their channels to find unbusy channels. This gives nodes more opportunity to use more channels for a better performance in a small area than MIMC-Road. The channel usage based dynamic multichannel assignment method in Section 4 achieves this. Moreover, only the interfaces on the same node are required to have the same communication ranges. The interfaces of different vehicles are no longer required to be identical. Different vehicles can equip hardwares from different manufacturers with various characters. This also simplifies the VANET deployment.

## 4 Channel Usage Based Multichannel Assignment

When vehicles encounter high communication conflicts, they can switch interfaces from busy channels to spare ones to improve the performance. This is the design philosophy of channel usage based assignment. Based on the connectivity invariant condition in Section 3, we do not need to worry about the connectivity and can concentrate our attention on the channel usage conditions. In the following subsections, we first give out the mathematic expression of channel usage in Section 4.1. Then, the design of the dynamic channel assignment algorithm is described in detail in Section 4.2.

### 4.1 Channel Usage Analysis

Before discuss the channel usage, we make the following assumptions and definitions. There are $C$ available channels in the network. Each node equips $K$ network interfaces that work on $K$ different channels. $K$ satisfies the connectivity invariant condition, which is $K \geq \lfloor \frac{C}{2} \rfloor + 1$. The transmission probability of node $n$ on channel $c$ is $P(n, c)$. The neighbors of node $n$ is defined as $B(n)$.

The node $n$ detects no communication conflicts on channel $c$ only if there is no nodes transmitting or one node transmitting. The probability that only one node is transmitting is

$$\sum_{i \in B(n) \bigcup \{n\}} \left( P(i,c) \times \prod_{j \in B(n) \bigcup \{n\} - \{i\}} (1 - P(j,c)) \right)$$
$$= \prod_{j \in B(n) \bigcup \{n\}} (1 - P(j,c)) \times \sum_{i \in B(n) \bigcup \{n\}} \frac{P(i,c)}{1 - P(i,c)}.$$

And the probability that no node is transmitting is

$$\prod_{i \in B(n) \bigcup \{n\}} (1 - P(i,c)).$$

Then, the conflicting probability is 1 minus the above two parts. Thus:

$$P_{conflict}(n,c) = 1 - \left( \sum_{i \in B(n) \bigcup \{n\}} \frac{P(i,c)}{1 - P(i,c)} + 1 \right) \times \prod_{j \in B(c) \bigcup \{n\}} (1 - P(j,c)). \quad (1)$$

Assume that

$$\sum_{i \in B(n) \bigcup \{n\}} P(i,c) = q \quad \text{and} \quad |B(n) \bigcup \{n\}| = m.$$

$q$ can be considered as the total channel usage. Usually, if all the nodes access the channel based on CSMA/CA and there is no hidden terminal, $q$ will be $\leq 1$. If there are hidden terminals, $q$ can be $> 1$. Because the transmission probability of each node is $\leq 1$, $q$ is always $\leq m$, . We can prove that with $0 \leq q \leq 1$, $P_{conflict}(n, c)$ reaches the maximum when $P(i, c) = \frac{q}{m}$ for all $i$, using Lagrange multiplier method. The maximum of $P_{conflict}(n, c)$ is

$$1 - \left[ \left(1 - \frac{q}{m}\right)^m + q \left(1 - \frac{q}{m}\right)^{m-1} \right].$$

For a fixed $m$, we define function

$$f_m(q) = \left(1 - \frac{q}{m}\right)^m + q \left(1 - \frac{q}{m}\right)^{m-1}.$$

The derivative of $f_m(q)$ is

$$f'_m(q) = -q\frac{m-1}{m}(1-\frac{q}{m})^{m-2}.$$

For $m \geq 1$ and $0 < q \leq m$, we have $f'_m(q) \geq 0$. That means the conflict probability increase with increased transmission probability.

For a given $q$, define function

$$g_q(m) = \left(1-\frac{q}{m}\right)^m + q\left(1-\frac{q}{m}\right)^{m-1} \qquad (m \geq 1).$$

It can be proved that $g_q(m)$ is a monotonically decreasing function when $0 \leq q \leq 1$ and $m \geq 2$. It is proved by showing $g'_q(m) < 0$ under these conditions. So $1 - g_q(m)$ is monotonically increasing with increased $m$ when $0 \leq q \leq 1$. Thus, the conflict probability is increased with increased neighbors when there is no hidden terminals. If hidden terminals exist and $q > 1$. $g_q(m)$ is no longer monotonic. The values of $1 - g_q(m)$ is calculated in Table 1 with $0 < q \leq 2$ and m from 2 to $+\infty$. It is shown in Table 1 that the conflict probability is increasing with increased $q$. It is increasing with increasing $m$ when $q \leq 1$. And it is mostly decreasing with increased $m$ when $q > 1$. The only exception in the table is the bold numbers when $q = 1.1$. With $q > 1$, there are hidden terminals. The impact of hidden terminals is averaged over more nodes when $m$ is larger, which may lead to a lower conflict probability. But with fixed $m$, the monotonicity is always hold with $q$. We will use this property to select the threshold to judge whether a channel is too busy or not in Section 4.2.

**Table 1.** The Maximum Conflict Probability with Various Nodes and Channel Usages

| $q\backslash m$ | 2 | 3 | 4 | 6 | 8 | $+\infty$ |
|---|---|---|---|---|---|---|
| 0.1 | 0.0025 | 0.0032 | 0.0036 | 0.0039 | 0.0041 | 0.0047 |
| 0.3 | 0.0225 | 0.0280 | 0.0304 | 0.0327 | 0.0338 | 0.0369 |
| 0.5 | 0.0625 | 0.0741 | 0.0788 | 0.0831 | 0.0850 | 0.0902 |
| 0.7 | 0.1225 | 0.1379 | 0.1436 | 0.1484 | 0.1505 | 0.1558 |
| 0.8 | 0.1600 | 0.1754 | 0.1808 | 0.1850 | 0.1868 | 0.1912 |
| 0.9 | 0.2025 | 0.2160 | 0.2203 | 0.2235 | 0.2247 | **0.2275** |
| 1.0 | 0.2500 | 0.2592 | 0.2617 | 0.2632 | 0.2636 | 0.2642 |
| 1.1 | **0.3025** | **0.3047** | **0.3045** | 0.3037 | 0.3032 | 0.3009 |
| 1.2 | 0.3600 | 0.3520 | 0.3483 | 0.3446 | 0.3428 | 0.3675 |
| 1.4 | 0.4900 | 0.4501 | 0.4370 | 0.4261 | 0.4212 | 0.4082 |
| 1.6 | 0.6400 | 0.5499 | 0.5248 | 0.5051 | 0.4966 | 0.4750 |
| 1.8 | 0.8100 | 0.6480 | 0.6090 | 0.5798 | 0.5676 | 0.5371 |
| 2.0 | 1.000 | 0.7407 | 0.6875 | 0.6488 | 0.6329 | 0.5940 |

With the above analysis, we can estimate the conflict probability from the transmission probability of a single node. By comparing all the conflict probabilities of the channels, we can select the channels with low conflict probabilities for the vehicles. We discuss the details this dynamic channel selection algorithm in Section 4.2.

### 4.2 Dynamic Channel Assignment Algorithm

The analysis in Section 4.1 is based on the transmission probability. In reality, the transmission probability can be estimated by the channel usage time. By recording the active transmission time $\Delta T$ on channel $c$ in every $T$ period by the node itself, it can estimate its current channel usage level. We still denote it using $P(n, c)$ as

$$P_t(n, c) = \frac{\Delta T}{T} \tag{2}$$

for node $n$ on channel $c$ in time period $t$. In algorithm, the Exponentially Weighted Moving Average (EWMA) of $P_t$ is used to filter out the random fluctuations:

$$\overline{P}_{t+1}(n, c) = \alpha P_{t+1}(n, c) + (1 - \alpha)\overline{P}_t(n, c). \tag{3}$$

$\alpha$ is the EWMA parameter. The initial value of $\overline{P}$ is set to $\overline{P}_0(n, c) = 0$. This channel usage level in Equation (2) and (3) is used to predict the transmission probability in a short period of time. They are exchanged by hello/beacon messages between nodes and substituted into Equation (1) to calculate the conflict probability.

With the estimated conflict probability on every channels, the node can select the channels with lower conflict probability to use in the next time period. Consider that network interfaces have channel switch delays, too frequent switches waste the channel time. Moreover, too frequent switches will cause the thrashing problem. Also, if all the channel usages are low, channel switching is unnecessary. In order to minimize the channel switching cost and make full use of the channels, interface will switch their channel only when the conflict probability of the current channel is larger than a threshold, denoted as $P_{threshold}$. We set $P_{threshold} = 0.2275$. It can be seen in Table 1 that 0.2275 is the value of maximized $P_{conflict}$ at $q = 0.9$ and $m = +\infty$. According to the monotonic property of the conflict probability we analyzed in Section 4.1, the threshold can keep the conflict within tolerance and the summed channel usage $q$ below 1.0.

The algorithm is fully distributed. The communication cost is the channel usage information and the active channel announcements of the nodes exchanged by the hello/beacon messages. 2 bytes are enough to indicate the channels in use (1 bit for each channel). One byte (256 levels) is enough to indicate the usage level of each channel. Since the number of channels is quite small (for example, 12 for 802.11a), the total message overheads in one hello message are within twenty bytes.

The neighbor table is required to store the extra 1-byte channel usage levels and a 4-byte updating timestamp of every channel for every neighbor. For a network with $C$ channels and a node with $M$ neighbors, the total storage cost is $M \times C \times 5Bytes$. For a dense VANET with 256 neighbors and the 802.11a network with 12 channels, the extra storage cost on each node is 15KB, which is a quite small memory requirement compared with the hardware resources of today's mobile devices.

For a node with $M$ neighbors, the number of multiplications/divisions it needs to calculate in Equation (1) is $2M+1$, For a network with $C$ channels, the number of multiplications/divisions the node needs to do is $C \times (2M+1)$. With $C = 12$ and $M = 256$, the calculation time is quite small compared with the seconds long refreshing period for the conflict probabilities.

## 5 Evaluations

We implemented this channel usage based multichannel assignment algorithm for MIMC VANETs (MIMC-Chan-Usage) in NS2 [1]. The parameters used in Section 4 to describe the algorithm are listed in Table 2. We use AODV [14] to evaluate the network performance, and compare MIMC-Chan-Usage with Single Interface Single Channel (SISC), Fix-Switch [9], and MIMC-Road [24]. In order to compare with Fix-Switch, the number of channels is set to a small number of 3, and the interfaces is 2. A channel switch delay of 10ms is also implemented in the simulations. The communication range is set to 150m. The channel segment size is set to about 300m according to the rules in [24].

**Table 2.** The Parameters of the Mutli-Channel Assignment Algorithm

| **Parameters** | **Values** |
|---|---|
| $T$ | varying randomly between 1.25 and 1.75 seconds |
| $T_{switch}$ | varying randomly between 2.5 and 4.5 seconds |
| $\alpha$ | 0.15 |
| $P_{threshold}$ | 0.2275 |

We simulate the network with 100, 200, 300 and 400 moving vehicles on a real road topology shown in Fig. 3 (the black lines). It's the main roads extracted from a $2000 \times 1700m^2$ area in south Beijing. The roads are simulated with several separated lanes. And the vehicles are moving according to the Intelligent Driver Motion (IDM) Model [20].

Fig. 4 is the comparison of the number of all the packets delivered during the simulations on different network sizes. It shows that the channel usage based MIMC outperforms the others. With two interfaces, the channel usage based MIMC can keep the total delivered packets about double of the the SISC's, while Fix-Switch and MIMC-Road can not. This shows the channel usage based MIMC can better utilize the channel resources under different scenarios. The average delays of the packets in Fig. 5 show that the channel usage based MIMC still performs the best in all the configurations.

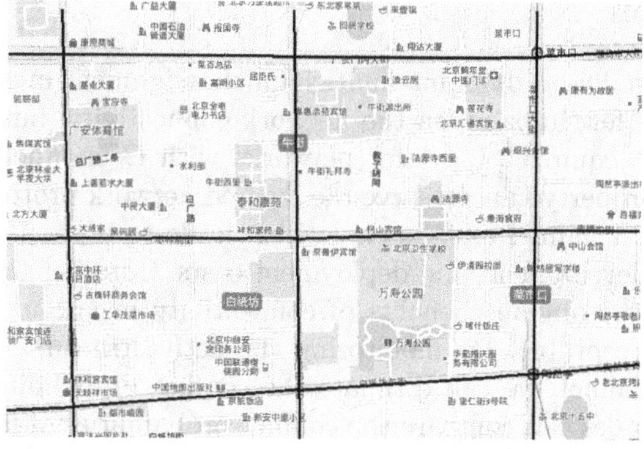


**Fig. 3.** Road topology from the real map of south Beijing

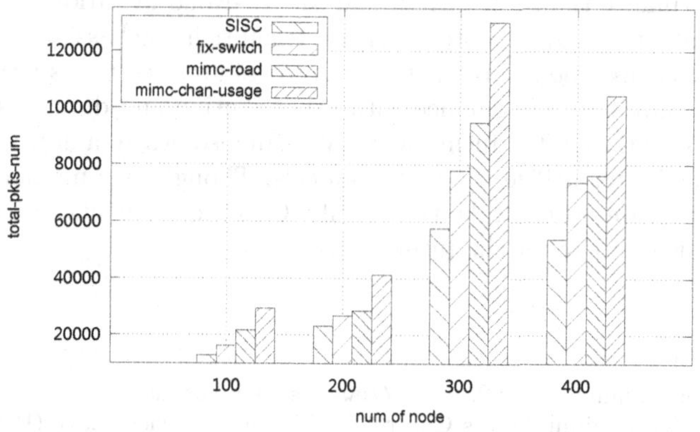


**Fig. 4.** The total delivered packets on different network sizes

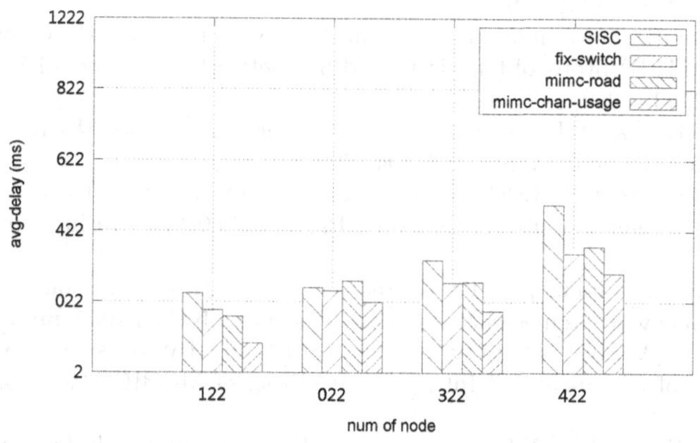


**Fig. 5.** The average delays of the flows indifferent network sizes

## 6 Conclusion

The channel usage based dynamic multichannel assignment method introduced in this paper has few impacts on the network connectivity, but it requires the network nodes to equip $\lfloor \frac{C}{2} \rfloor + 1$ for networks with $C$ channels. This connectivity invariant property can preserve the layered network protocol architecture and ease the multichannel assignment, which leads to a good network performance with low development and deployment costs. Consider the small number of channels and the obvious benefits of connectivity invariance, this hardware requirement is acceptable. By monitoring the active transmission time of the nodes on each channel, we can estimate the conflict probabilities of the channels. Then, the nodes can compare the conflict probabilities of the channels and select the channels with low conflicts. Since we do not need to worry about the connectivity, the dynamic channel selection is kept simple and efficient. Simulations show that this channel usage based multichannel assignment method has a better performance than Fix-Switch and MIMC-Road in various scenarios.

We only evaluated AODV protocol with this multichannel assignment method in this work. Because the layered network protocol architecture is preserved, we can easily evaluate the performance with other routing and data disseminating protocols for VANETs in the future work. We can also design a data disseminating protocol to better utilize the multichannels. Though, our method improves the performance, we do not take the specific QoS requirements into consideration. This is also a topic for the future work.

## References

1. The Network Simulator: NS2, `http://www.isi.edu/nsnam/ns/`
2. Wireless LAN Medium Access Control (MAC) and Physical Laye (PHY) Specifications, `http://standards.ieee.org/getieee802/download/802.11-2007.pdf`
3. Alicherry, M., Bhatia, R., Li, L.E.: Joint channel assignment and routing for throughput optimization in multi-radio wireless mesh networks. In: Proc. of MobiCom 2005, pp. 58–72 (2005)
4. Anguswamy, R., Zawodniok, M., Jagannathan, S.: A multi-interface multi-channel routing (MMCR) protocol for wireless ad hoc networks. In: Proc. of WCNC 2009, pp. 2338–2343 (2009)
5. Gupta, P., Kumar, P.R.: The Capacity of Wireless Networks. IEEE Transactions on Information Theory 46(2), 388–404 (2000)
6. Jiang, D., Delgrossi, L.: IEEE 802.11p: Towards an international standard for wireless access in vehicular environments. In: Proc. of VTC 2008 Spring, pp. 2036–2040 (2008)
7. Kodialam, M., Nandagopal, T.: Characterizing the capacity region in multi-radio multi-channel wireless mesh networks. In: Proc. of MobiCom 2005, pp. 73–87 (2005)
8. Kyasanur, P., Vaidya, N.H.: Capacity of Multi-channel Wireless Networks: Impact of Number of Channels and Interfaces. In: Proc. of MOBICOM 2005, pp. 43–57 (2005)
9. Kyasanur, P., Vaidya, N.H.: Routing and link-layer protocols for multi-channel multi-interface ad hoc wireless networks. Mob. Comput. Commun. Rev. 10(1), 31–43 (2006)

10. Liu, K., Guo, J., Lu, N., Liu, F., Wang, X., Wang, P.: RAMC: A RSU-assisted multi-channel coordination MAC protocol for VANET. IEICE Transactions on Communications 94(1), 203–214 (2011)
11. Lu, N., Ji, Y., Liu, F., Wang, X.: A dedicated multi-channel MAC protocol design for VANET with adaptive broadcasting. In: Proc. of IEEE WCNC 2010, pp. 1–6 (2010)
12. Marina, M.K., Das, S.R.: A topology control approach for utilizing multiple channels in multi-radio wireless mesh networks. In: Proc. of the 2nd International Conference on Broadband Networks, vol. 1, pp. 381–390 (2005)
13. Mo, J., So, H., Walrand, J.: Comparison of multichannel MAC protocols. IEEE Transactions on Mobile Computing 7(1), 50–65 (2008)
14. Perkins, C.E., Royer, E.M.: Ad-hoc On-demand Distance Vector Routing. In: Proc. of the 2nd IEEE Workshop on Mobile Computing Systems and Applications, pp. 90–100 (1999)
15. Raman, B.: Channel Allocation in 802.11-based Mesh Networks. In: Proc. of IEEE Infocom 2006, Barcelona, Spain (2006)
16. Raniwala, A., Chiueh, T.: Architecture and algorithms for an IEEE 802.11-based multi-channel wireless mesh network. In: Proc. of INFOCOM 2005, vol. 3, pp. 2223–2234 (2005)
17. Raniwala, A., Chiueh, T.C.: Evaluation of a wireless enterprise backbone network architecture. In: Proc. of the 12th Annual IEEE Symposium on High Performance Interconnects, pp. 98–104 (2004)
18. Raniwala, A., Gopalan, K., Chiueh, T.C.: Centralized channel assignment and routing algorithms for multi-channel wireless mesh networks. Mobile Computing and Communications Review 8(2), 50–65 (2004)
19. Su, H., Zhang, X.: Clustering-based multichannel MAC protocols for QoS provisionings over vehicular ad hoc networks. IEEE Transactions on Vehicular Technology 56(6), 3309–3323 (2007)
20. Treiber, M., Hennecke, A., Helbing, D.: Congested traffic states in empirical observations and microscopic simulations. Phys. Rev. E 62, 1805–1824 (2000)
21. Wellons, J., Xue, Y.: Towards robust and efficient routing in multi-radio, multi-channel wireless mesh networks. In: Proc. of INFOCOM 2011, pp. 91–95 (2011)
22. Xie, X., Wang, F., Li, K., Zhang, P., Wang, H.: Improvement of multi-channel MAC protocol for dense VANET with directional antennas. In: Proc. of IEEE WCNC 2009, pp. 1–6 (2009)
23. Zhang, X., Su, H., Chen, H.: Cluster-based multi-channel communications protocols in vehicle ad hoc networks. IEEE Wireless Communications 13(5), 44–51 (2006)
24. Zhao, T., Lu, S., Yan, W., Li, X.: A Road Based Multi-Channel Assignment Method for VANET. In: Proc. of IEEE ICNC 2013, San Diego, CA, USA (2013)
25. Zhu, J., Roy, S.: MAC for dedicated short range communications in intelligent transport system. IEEE Communications Magazine 41(12), 60–67 (2003)

# VRBAC: An Extended RBAC Model for Virtualized Environment and Its Conflict Checking Approach

Yang Luo[1,3], Yazhuo Li[1,3], Qing Tang[1,3], Zhao Wei[1,3], and Chunhe Xia[1,2,3]

[1] Beijing Key Laboratory of Network Technology
[2] State Key Laboratory of Virtual Reality Technology and Systems
[3] School of Computer Science and Engineering, Beihang University, Beijing, China

veotax@sae.buaa.edu.cn, lyzalexandra@126.com, tangiqingkd@sina.com, wz@cse.buaa.edu.cn, xch@buaa.edu.cn

**Abstract.** This paper extends RBAC's authorizing ability via adding domain and virtual machine features aiming at applying in the virtualized scenarios. We define a new model named VRBAC in which authorized users can migrate or copy virtual machines from one domain to another without causing a conflict. Subjects can also share permissions of not only resources but also virtual machines with other subjects from the same or different domains. Three types of conflicts in VRBAC policies are discussed and described in form of description logic, which provides extra access to reasoning engines and facilitates the conflict checking procedure. Based on Active Directory and Xen Cloud Platform, VRBAC model visualization and its conflict checking can be enforced within the prototype system. The experimental results indicate that all conflicts can be effectively detected and the literal report generated can provide conflict details such as conflict types, positions and causes as guidance for further conflict resolution.

**Keywords:** virtualization, RBAC, policy conflict, description logic.

## 1 Introduction

As an approach to manage system access to authorized users, RBAC model has been widely used in most practical collaborative environments and also successfully applied in many of the systems such as Microsoft Active Directory, SELinux, FreeBSD and so on[1]. In recent years, virtualization is known as one of the most popular technologies. Most companies intend to transfer their services and data into the virtualized network without abandoning the existing RBAC mechanism, however, due to some intrinsic characteristics of virtualization, the original RBAC model are not applicable any more. Therefore we need a new authorization framework which remains compatible with currently existing RBAC model.

Aiming at the shortage of the authorization mechanism in the virtualized environment, we propose the virtualized RBAC model, abbreviated as VRBAC,

J. Su et al. (Eds.): ICoC 2013, CCIS 401, pp. 194–205, 2013.

to improve the granularity of authorization management in virtualization fields. The contributions of this paper are twofold: (1) extends specification of RBAC by introducing VM (Virtual Machine) and Domain concept, (2) provides a conflict checking framework for VRBAC policies based on ontology and description logic technique.

The most significant features of VRBAC model lie in its two new concepts: VM and Domain. The VM concept is used to indicate a virtual machine which can be accessed as a resource by a virtual machine user or administrator. Binding can be set up between a VM instance and its shared resources via the inheritance relationship. The Domain concept is a property that applied to nearly all RBAC elements like a tag. It helps to determine if a virtual machine is migrated or replicated by monitoring the change of the domain tag. In the conflict checking phase, we convert VRBAC definitions and instances into concepts and assertions in format of description logic, and then construct some deduce rules from underlying factors to conflict assertions which would indicate the occurrence of VRBAC policy conflicts. This paper mainly discussed about how to adapt the existing RBAC model into the virtualized environment by importing VM and Domain concepts, and how to check its policy conflicts using description logic approach. Consequences of experiments show that the well-organized conflict report generated by our prototype system actually does help to administrators in finding out possible policy conflicts and dealing with improper authorization and illegal access.

The rest of the paper is organized as the following. Section 2 investigates related work showing limitations of previous RBAC model and the originality of the issues addressed in this paper. Section 3 formally defines the VRBAC model and shows how it applies in controlling access behaviors of virtualized scenarios. Section 4 establishes our conflict checking framework by means of ontology and description logic. Section 5 explains the implementation of the VRBAC conflict-free access control system based on Active Directory and Xen. Finally section 6 concludes the paper.

## 2 Related Work

Recently, most of the access control enforcement mechanism is based on a Virtual Machine Monitor (VMM)[2]. A VMM is a piece of computer software that creates and runs VMs. An ideal VMM architecture should be able to provide complete isolation and sufficient integrity for the VMs[3]. Meantime, some security-purpose VMM systems have been developed[4-6]. We can implant a specified access control mechanism via inserting security layer without modifying existing guest operating systems. Multi-level security between virtual machines has been studied from the perspective of extended BLP model[7], however, the involvement with the out-of-date mandatory access control (MAC) makes this approach inapplicable in modern systems. The Flexible Authorization Manager Framework (FAM)[8] enables the integration of multiple access control frameworks within a single model. This approach specifies one description language to define and govern access control decisions. This may lead to considerable complexity when dealing with several access control models like MAC, RBAC and so on. A well-designed model should be simple and robust enough for efficient and secure run-time enforcement.

RBAC has been introduced to access control area for above twenty years[9, 10], in fact it's proven to be one of the most promising candidates for access control security in VMM. Conflict checking approaches for RBAC models have been widely studied. In practice, a verifying method between access control constraints and user-role assignment has been proposed[11]. This paper mainly discussed about the fundamental problem about how to verify whether a user-role assignment satisfies all constraints and how to generate an optimal user-role assignment. While experimental results show that the computational complexity of this approach can be NP-hard. The approach based on role mapping mainly concerns about data sharing conflicts between constrains like cyclic inheritance and separations of duties[12, 13]. The prototype system proves to be effective and efficient in conflict resolution. This approach is not appropriate for our analysis because we need a method considering the virtual machines as objects for the virtualized scenario. Also the domain tagging mechanism would lead to some changes in conflict checking procedure.

## 3 A RBAC Model for Virtualization

Unlike the ordinary access control systems, the authorization for virtualized scenario has its own distinctive characteristics. For instance, VM replaces the Role to be the key concept in virtualized environment. Meantime, all elements and relations in RBAC will been tagged with different domain labels for distributed management purpose. All these new requirements have exceeded the expression ability of current RBAC model and therefore VRBAC is proposed in this section with features as following.

Conception model of VRBAC is shown in Fig. 1, in which we could see that VM element is added between Role and Resource to represent the virtual machines in the resource pool. Also UA and PA could have been imbedded in a VM instead of a global context. So a User or Role who's in charge of a VM will implicitly control all the UA and PA instances in a VM.

We use the following notation and definitions to describe VRBAC.

- $USERS$ is a set of users.
- $ROLES$ is a set of roles.
- $VMS$ is a set of virtual machines.
- $OBS$ is a set of resources.
- $OPS$ is a set of operations.
- $PRMS = 2^{(VMS \times OBS \times OPS)}$ is a set of permissions.
- $UAS \subseteq USERS \times ROLES$ is a set of User-Role assignment.
- $PAS \subseteq PRMS \times ROLES$ is a set of Role-Permission assignment.

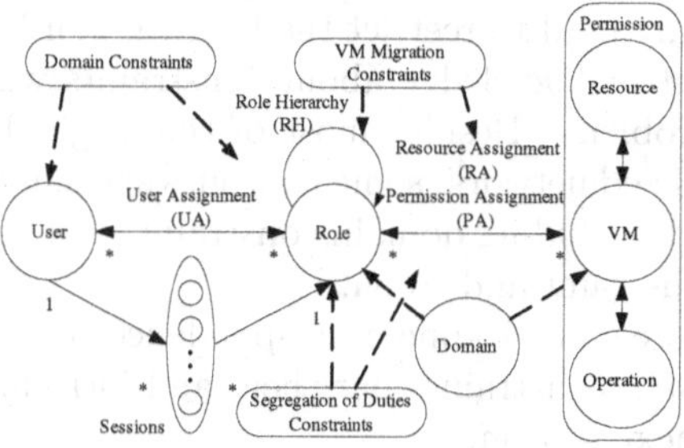


**Fig. 1.** Concept model of VRBAC

### 3.1 New Elements of VRBAC

Considering that most of RBAC implementations have also introduced the domain conception into their systems, so it's significant to integrate domain notion into the RBAC model for multi-level managing purpose.

In virtualized environment, the interoperability between VMs including VM migration, VM template replication, and so on can be very complicated. For this reason, the traditional RBAC model are not applicable any more[2]. In order to accommodate RBAC to the new virtualized situation, some of changes have to been made: (1) supports VM authorizing in RBAC, (2) propose an automatic conflict checking and solving method when a VM motion, replication or resource assignment operation performed.

The VM concept is actually a sub-concept deriving from Resource. It behaves more like a resource container instead of an individual resource. In VBRAC model, VM is regarded as one of the most primary concepts from the perspective of information services and resources sharing in the virtualized environment.

### 3.2 New Relations and Policies of VRBAC

Given the new elements of VRBAC, we will have some discussions about the changes of relevant relations in this section.

The foundations of VRBAC are the UA and PA relations defined between its elements as the form:

- $UA : USERS \times ROLES \rightarrow [0, 1]$
- $PA : ROLES \times PRMS \rightarrow [0, 1]$

A UA relation means a mapping relating users with roles, and a PA means a mapping relating roles with permissions. According to these relations, we can describe relevant policies as below:

- $Policy_{access} = (USERS \cup ROLES) \times PRMS$
- $Policy_{inherit} = (USERS \cup ROLES) \times ROLES$

Constraints are mainly used to restrict the behaviors of VRBAC instances or so-called policies. A better knowledge about constraints will help analyze corresponding conflicts problems. Besides most of the original RBAC constraints which still fit for virtualized network, some new ones specially for virtualized network must be presented, including domain constraint, VM migration constraint, separation of duties constraint and so on.

Considering that there's one-to-one correspondence between constraints and conflicts, we'd like to skip constraints part here and introduce conflicts classification directly in the next section.

## 4 Conflict Checking for VRBAC Policies

As the RBAC-like model is usually represented in form of policies, the violation of the constraints in VRBAC could lead to conflicts in the policy level. In an attempt to tackle these conflicts, a conflict checking model based on description logic and Semantic Web Rule Language (SWRL) is proposed. We will describe it after conflict classification.

### 4.1 Classification of VRBAC Conflicts

According to the VRBAC model we defined, the conflicts of VRBAC policies can be categorized into 3 types: Domain Conflict (Dom-C), VM Migration Conflict (Mig-C) and Separation of Duties Conflict (SoD-C).

Dom-C is a kind of conflict that occurs when a domain resource or virtual machine has been assigned to a role or user from another domain which isn't in friend relationship with the former. Denote it as $DOM-C$ , then we get $DOM-C = \{(r, re)|r \in Roles \cup Users \wedge re \in Resources \cup VMs \wedge has\_permission(r, re) \wedge diff(r.dom, re.dom)\}$ , where $has\_permission$ indicates the PA relationship and the next $diff$ predicate means that $r$ and $re$ belongs to different domains. An example of Dom-C in the context of inter-domain cooperation is depicted in Fig. 2. $r_{A3}$ inherits the permission of $r_{B1}$ which belongs to neither the same domain or a friendly one. These conflicts, if remain undetected and unresolved, would expose the cooperating system to numerous vulnerabilities and risks pertaining to the security and privacy of their data and resources.

Mig-C takes place when a virtual machine is about to be migrated or replicated from one domain to another, which would probably lead to a naming error for resource authentication. So a checking process running in background context is necessary for handling a missing or a second virtual machine in some domain. We denote this conflict as $MIG-C$ , we have $MIG-C = \{(vm_1, vm_2)|vm_1 \in VMs \wedge vm_2 \in VMs \wedge \neg diff(vm_1, vm_2) \wedge diff(vm_1.dom, vm_2.dom)\}$ . The following example in Fig. 3 illustrates the Mig-C conflict. When the migrating operation from $v_{A1}$ to $v_{B1}$ is done, $v_{B1}$ has acquired exactly the same identity with $v_{A1}$ owing to replication enforcing mechanism. Users who own permissions to $v_{A1}$ in Domain A will implicitly gain the access to $v_{B1}$ which obviously belongs to another domain, Domain B. These unwanted sharing between domains would violate the securities of individual domains of the multi-domain system.

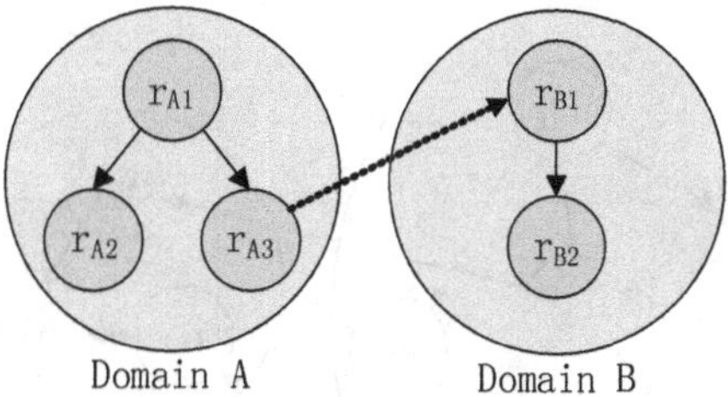


**Fig. 2.** An example of Dom-C in multi-domain systems

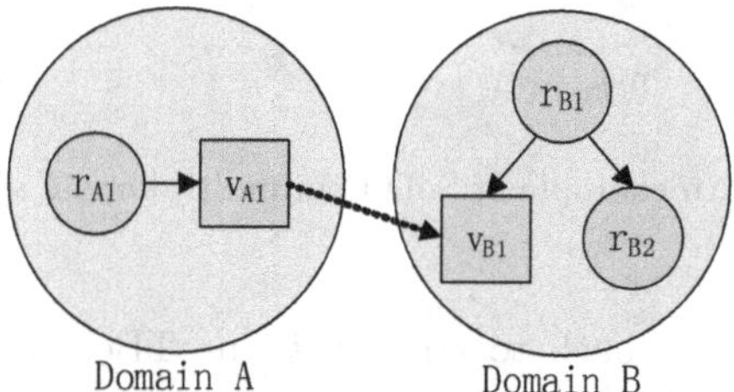


**Fig. 3.** An example of Mig-C in multi-domain systems

SoD-C is one of the most frequently occurred conflict type in VRBAC as well as in other RBAC models. It occurs when one's access has been permitted and denied to a resource simultaneously. This contradiction would lead to unauthorized access and malfunction of cross-domain interoperation. This conflict can be denoted as $SOD-C$ , we get $SOD-C = \{(r_1, r_2)|\exists u \exists res(u \in Users \wedge res \in Resources \wedge u \in assign(r_1) \wedge u \in assign(r_2)) \wedge diff(policy(r1, res).action, policy(r2, res).action))\}$ , where $assign$ means all users assigned with the role. In Fig. 4, we provide an example of an interoperation generated by merging the access control policies of different domains. From the inheritance hierarchy semantics we can see that $r_{A1}$ indirectly inherits $r_{B1}$ by role mappings of $\mathrm{r}_{\mathrm{A1}} \rightarrow \mathrm{r}_{\mathrm{A3}}$ and $\mathrm{r}_{\mathrm{A3}} \rightarrow \mathrm{r}_{\mathrm{B1}}$ , at the same time $r_{A1}$ also inherits $r_{B2}$ via role mappings of $\mathrm{r}_{\mathrm{A1}} \rightarrow \mathrm{r}_{\mathrm{A4}}$ , $\mathrm{r}_{\mathrm{A4}} \rightarrow \mathrm{r}_{\mathrm{A5}}$ and $\mathrm{r}_{\mathrm{A5}} \rightarrow \mathrm{r}_{B2}$ . However, in Domain B, the assignments of $r_{B1}$ and $r_{B2}$ for virtual machine $v_{B1}$ are opposite from each other, like one permitted and another denied. This would lead to uncertain policy enforcement in $r_{A1}$ and could even cause far more serious danger like unauthorized accesses.

### 4.2 Conflict Checking Approach

At the conflict checking phase, We choose OWL-DL, a type of ontology language to describe our model and conflicts, then use Description Logic (DL), one of the most promising reasoning technique to reason them. The knowledge base of DL contains two parts: TBox and ABox. TBox specifies the field terminology knowledge, while ABox offers the assertions about instances of TBox. We'd like

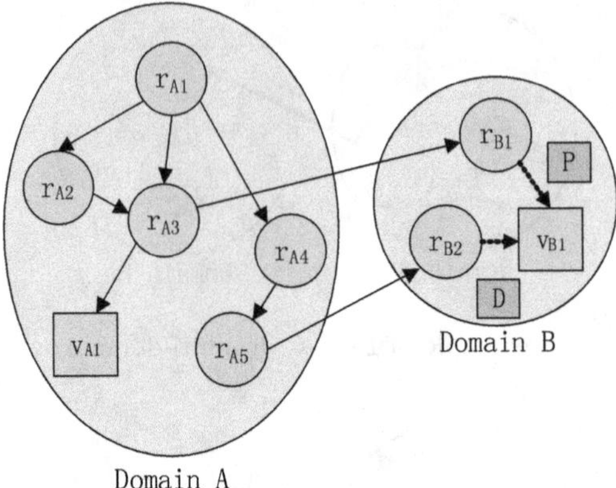


**Fig. 4.** An example of SoD-C in multi-domain systems

to use the following approach to construct our TBox and ABox: Firstly we extract TBox from VRBAC model manually as shown in Fig. 5, in which *dom* represents the definitional domain while *ran* means the range of the predicate, :transitive is optional for relations with transitivity.

From Fig. 2 we can see that, besides the new VM and Domain concepts, some predicate relations have also been declared, including with_Domain for indicating the instance's domain, has_subResource for inheritance relationship between VM and Resource and so on.

Although the vast majority of ABox will be generated automatically, a fracture of them just behaves in a fundamental way like TBox and requires initialization before DL reasoning. Actually, most of the initialized ABox are about the definitions of operation and action:

- (instance *read Operation*)
- (instance *write Operation*)
- (instance *execute Operation*)
- (instance *permit Action*)
- (instance *deny Action*)

The functionality of DL reasoning has been greatly enhanced when using with SWRL. SWRL is a declarative language which specifies the abstract syntax for horn-like rules. If we express every VRBAC constraint in a SWRL rule form, we can establish a one-to-one mapping between VRBAC constrains and SWRL rules. The SWRL rules converted can then be used for deduction of new ABox based on pre-existing assertions.

In our VRBAC model, we have applied 9 SWRL rules, 6 auxiliary ones and 3 primary ones. Among auxiliary ones, two of them are of great importance:

- $has\_subSubject(?s1, ?s2) \wedge has\_subSubject(?s2, ?s3)$
  $\rightarrow has\_subSubject(?s1, ?s3)$

:atomic-concepts (*Subject Resource Operation Action Domain*) :extends (*Top*)
:atomic-concepts (*VM*) :extends(*Resource*)
(*has_Subject* :dom *Policy* :ran *Subject*)
(*has_Resource* :dom *Policy* :ran *Resource*)
(*has_VM* :dom *Policy* :ran *VM*)
(*has_Operation* :dom *Policy* :ran *Operation*)
(*has_Action* :dom *Policy* :ran *Action*)
(*with_Domain* :dom *Subject, Resource* :ran *Domain*)
(*has_subSubject :transitive* :dom *Subject* :ran *Subject*)
(*has_Subject_Overlap* :dom *Subject* :ran *Subject*)
(*has_subResource :transitive* :dom *Resource* :ran *Resource*)
(*has_Resource_Overlap* :dom *Resource* :ran *Resource*)
(*has_Operation_Overlap* :dom *Operation* :ran *Operation*)
(*has_Action_Overlap* :dom *Action* :ran *Action*)
(*has_Domain_Conflict* :dom *Policy* :ran *Policy*)
(*has_Migration_Conflict* :dom *Policy* :ran *Policy*)
(*has_SoD_Conflict* :dom *Policy* :ran *Policy*)

**Fig. 5.** TBox of VRBAC model

- $has\_subResource(?r1, ?r2) \wedge has\_subResource(?r2, ?r3)$
  $\rightarrow has\_subResource(?r1, ?r3)$

The first rule indicates that when ?s1 has ?s2 as its child subject and ?s2 also has ?s3 as its child subject, we can gain that ?s3 is a child subject of ?s1. In another word, these two rules furnish the inheritance assertions of Subject and Resource with transitivity. Then there comes 3 primary rules which map exactly into 3 types of conflicts:

The rule for Dom-C:

- $has\_subject(?p1, ?s1) \wedge has\_subject(?p2, ?s2) \wedge has\_subSubject(?s1, ?s2) \wedge$
  $with\_Domain(?s1, ?d1) \wedge with\_Domain(?s2, ?d2) \wedge \neg has\_Relation$
  $(?d1, ?d2) \rightarrow has\_DomC(?p1, ?p2)$

This rule means that the subject belonging to domain ?d1 cannot hold an inheritance relation with the subject belonging to domain ?d2, if not, the two relevant policies would lead to Dom-C type conflict.

The rule for Mig-C:

- $has\_VM(?p1, ?v1) \wedge has\_VM(?p2, ?v2) \wedge with\_Domain(?v1, ?d1) \wedge$
  $with\_Domain(?v2, ?d2) \wedge \neg same(?d1, ?d2) \wedge same(?v1, ?v2)$
  $\rightarrow has\_MigC(?p1, ?p2)$

This rule indicates that the virtual machine migrated from another domain must modify its identity immediately when the operation finished, or a Mig-C type conflict occurs because there're two resembled virtual machines in different domains which may confuse the VMM and admins.

The rule for SoD-C:

- $has\_Subject(?p1, ?s1) \wedge has\_Resource(?p1, ?r1) \wedge has\_Operation(?p1, ?o1) \wedge has\_Action(?p1, ?a1) \wedge has\_Subject(?p2, ?s2) \wedge has\_VM(?p2, ?v2) \wedge has\_Operation(?p2, ?o2) \wedge has\_Action(?p2, ?a2) \wedge has\_Subject\_Overlap(?s1, ?s2) \wedge has\_subResource(?v2, ?r1) \wedge same(?o1, ?o2) \wedge \neg same(?a1, ?a2) \rightarrow has\_SoDC(?p1, ?p2)$

This rule means that two policies which share overlapped subjects, resources and operations must have consistent actions, or this may cause a conflict of SoD-C type because the policy enforcement mechanism have no idea which policy to follow.

We find out that all these rules actually share similar forms which can be extracted into tuples like Policy (Subject, Resource, Operation, Action) in which Policy is the tuple key which governs other elements. In fact, we can divide a rule into 3 parts: affiliating declarations within respective Policy instance, contradictory declarations between member elements and conflict declaration between policies. Apparently, if one policy's elements are constructed incompatible with another one's, it will contribute to the possible conflicts between their policies.

## 5 Implementaion and Experiments

VRBAC Visualizer and Conflict Checker (VVCC), the prototype system, is implemented in one of the most popular virtualized environments: Microsoft Active Directory and Xen Cloud Platform (XCP). The architecture of our virtualized environment is shown in Fig. 6 in which VVCC lies at the third level. Various APIs are employed to help collect the data of VRBAC policies automatically, including Active Directory Service Interface (ADSI), Windows Management Instrumentation (WMI), Microsoft Remote Procedure Call (MSRPC), and APIs of Xen. Besides XCP, we also give it a try in the VMware platform and feel glad to find it's almost compatible with our VVCC system.

The policy data collected in the previous step will be transformed into ABox style and then delivered to RacerPro engine for reasoning. Via nRQL (new RacerPro Query Language) interface, VRBAC policy conflicts are retrieved and analyzed.

The sketch map for of conflict checking results is shown in Fig. 7. There we can see a SoD-C type conflict occurs between role NRDC1001 AND NSFC0902. It's because filex has denied alice's access via role NRDC1001 from Domain1, however, the data store where the file is actually stored is in the charge of NSFC0902 from Domain2, which alice inherits some of her permissions from. So it's inappropriate to both permit and deny one's access simultaneously in vrbac policies. besides the sketch map, there's also a textual report available for detailed information such as type, position of a conflict and the cause that leads to the conflict, which is shown in Table 1. the number in "No." column indicates

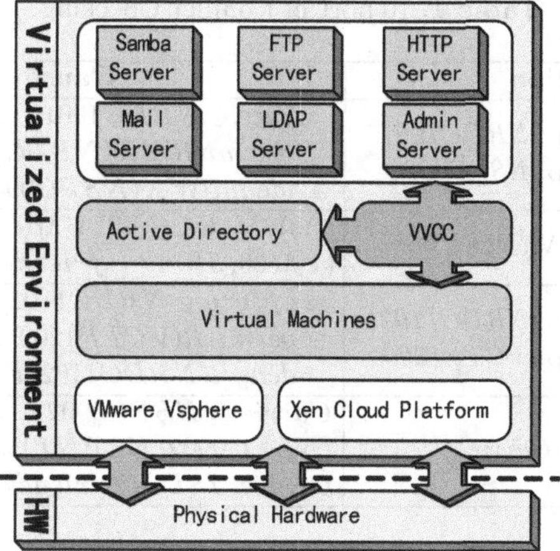


**Fig. 6.** Map of virtualized network Architecture of virtualized environment

the sequence of conflicts, 3 categories of content are "Type", "Position" and "Cause" which depict the details of conflicts. every vrbac entity is braced with a bracket in which entity type lies before the double colons and entity name after them.

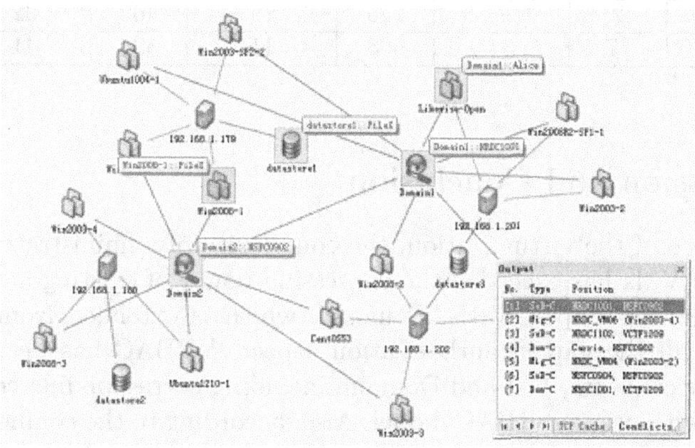


**Fig. 7.** Sketch map of virtualized network

Also a comparison experiment between VVCC and manual checking procedure is conducted, whose result is shown in Table 2. We deploy dozens of virtual machines and hundreds of users and groups for both domains in order to reach the scale of a medium-sized organization. It turns out that for each type of conflict we defined, the recall rate of VVCC method reaches nearly 98%, which is way higher than that of the manual way. also checking time of VVCC can be

**Table 1.** Report of Conflict Checking

| No. | Type | Position | Cause |
|---|---|---|---|
| 1 | SoD | Group::*NRDC1001* Group::*NSFC0902* | $Alice \in NRDC1001 \cap NSFC0902$ $\wedge permitRWX(NRDC1001, FileX)$ $\wedge denyRWX(NSFC0902, FileX)$ |
| 2 | Mig | VM::*NRDC_VM06* | $hasVM(KLBNT, VM06) \wedge withDom$ $(VM06, JSI) \wedge \neg friend(KLBNT, JSI)$ |
| 3 | SoD | Group::*NRDC1102* Group:: *VCTF1209* | $Jeffery \in NRDC1102 \cap VCTF1209$ $\wedge permitR(VCTF1209, FileZ)$ $\wedge denyR(NRDC1102, FileZ)$ |
| 4 | Dom | User::*Carrie* | $Carrie \subseteq NSFC0902 \wedge withDom$ $(NSFC0902, KLBNT) \wedge withDom($ $Carrie, JSI) \wedge \neg friend(KLBNT, JSI)$ |

controlled below 20 seconds with parallel processing enabled. Also the conflict report generated by VVCC also relieves the burden of administrators by reducing the time of conflict resolution for nearly 90%.

**Table 2.** Consequence of Comparative Experiment

| Type | Conflict Number | | Checking time (s) | | Solving Time (s) | |
|---|---|---|---|---|---|---|
| | *Manual* | *VVCC* | *Manual* | *VVCC* | *Manual* | *VVCC* |
| Dom-C | 15 | 24 | 425 | 12 | 320 | 25 |
| Mig-C | 2 | 7 | 236 | 19 | 462 | 32 |
| SoD-C | 17 | 53 | 968 | 11 | 594 | 41 |

## 6 Discussion and Conclusion

In the practice of the virtualization, the complexity of administrative tasks for cross-domain VMs has exceeded the expressing power of existing access control framework. In this paper, VRBAC model, which is extended from RBAC, is proposed to fill the gap in authorization aspect. VRBAC has been enhanced with two new concepts, VM and Domain, including corresponding constrains in comparison with original RBAC model. Also, according to the conflict classification, a conflict checking approach is presented to figure out the type, cause and location of conflicts. Experimental results show that our prototype system actually facilitates the administrators of virtualized network in aspects of alerting unauthorized access danger and helping improve the safety of the access control system.

**Acknowledgments.** This work was supported by the National Natural Science Foundation of China under Grant No. 61170295, the Co-Funding Project of Beijing Municipal Education Commission under Grant No.JD100060630 and the Project of National Ministry under Grant No.A2120110006.

## References

1. Claycomb, W.R., Shin, D.: Detecting insider activity using enhanced directory virtualization. In: Proceedings of the 2010 ACM Workshop on Insider Threats, pp. 29–36. ACM (2010)
2. Hirano, M., Shinagawa, T., Eiraku, H., Hasegawa, S., Omote, K., Tanimoto, K., Horie, T., Kato, K., Okuda, T., Kawai, E.: Introducing role-based access control to a secure virtual machine monitor: security policy enforcement mechanism for distributed computers. In: IEEE Asia-Pacific Services Computing Conference, APSCC 2008, pp. 1225–1230. IEEE (2008)
3. Madnick, S.E., Donovan, J.J.: Application and analysis of the virtual machine approach to information system security and isolation. In: Proceedings of the Workshop on Virtual Computer Systems, pp. 210–224. ACM (1973)
4. Sailer, R., Jaeger, T., Valdez, E., Caceres, R., Perez, R., Berger, S., Griffin, J.L., van Doorn, L.: Building a MAC-based security architecture for the Xen open-source hypervisor. In: 21st Annual Computer Security Applications Conference, pp. 276–285. IEEE (2005)
5. Meushaw, R., Simard, D.: NetTop: Commercial technology in high assurance applications. Tech. Trend Notes: Preview of Tomorrow's Information Technologies 9 (2000)
6. Garfinkel, T., Pfaff, B., Chow, J., Rosenblum, M., Boneh, D.: Terra: A virtual machine-based platform for trusted computing. In: ACM SIGOPS Operating Systems Review, pp. 193–206. ACM (2003)
7. Liu, Q., Wang, G., Weng, C., Luo, Y., Li, M.: A Mandatory Access Control Framework in Virtual Machine System with Respect to Multi-level Security I: Theory. China Communications 7, 137–143 (2010)
8. Jajodia, S., Samarati, P., Subrahmanian, V.S., Bertino, E.: A unified framework for enforcing multiple access control policies. In: ACM Sigmod Record, pp. 474–485. ACM (1997)
9. Ferraiolo, D.F., Kuhn, D.R.: Role-based access controls. arXiv preprint arXiv:0903.2171 (2009)
10. Sandhu, R., Ferraiolo, D., Kuhn, R.: The NIST model for role-based access control: towards a unified standard. In: Symposium on Access Control Models and Technologies: Proceedings of the Fifth ACM Workshop on Role-Based Access Control, pp. 47–63 (2000)
11. Sun, Y., Wang, Q., Li, N., Bertino, E., Atallah, M.J.: On the complexity of authorization in RBAC under qualification and security constraints. IEEE Transactions on Dependable and Secure Computing 8, 883–897 (2011)
12. Wang, X., Gu, T., Guo, Y., Zheng, Y., Zong, J., Gong, B.: An Algorithm for Role Mapping Across Multi-domains Employing RBAC. Chinese Journal of Electronics 18 (2009)
13. Fan, B., Liang, X., Luo, Y., Bo, Y., Xia, C.: Conflict Detection Model of Access Control Policy in Collaborative Environment. In: 2011 International Conference on Computational and Information Sciences (ICCIS), pp. 377–381. IEEE (2011)

# TraSt: A Traffic Statistic Framework for Evaluating 3G Charging System and Smart Phone Applications*

Wenshan Fu, Tong Zhao, Kaigui Bian, and Wei Yan

School of Electronics Engineering and Computer Science
Peking University, Beijing, P.R. China, 100871

**Abstract.** We designed and implemented a traffic analyze framework TraSt (Traffic Statistics) based on tcpdump for Android. This framework can get more detailed traffic usage than any other existing traffic monitor frameworks or applications on smart phones, and help us to explore four aspects of Chinese three major operators' charging system as well as four kinds of popular smart phone applications. Our work helps 3G users and software developers have a clearer understanding of the similarities and differences among the operators' charging services, so as to promote the improvement of software development and operators' services, and our analysis with recommendations to application developers can lead to better system design and network infrastructure support.

**Keywords:** Framework, 3G, Charging, Smart phone, Application.

## 1 Introduction

With the rapid development of 3G technologies and smart phones, millions of mobile applications emerge on the market. Report by the Ministry of Industry and Information Technology [4] shows that by the end of 2012, the number of 3G users in China is over 210 million. And the the usage trend will be accelerated with the explosive growth of smart phones in the coming years. Which makes traffic, revenues and profits continue to grow.

However, behind the flourishing 3G and smart phone market, there are also some issues. For the operators' charging system, because they are not open to public, some unreasonable phenomenon is difficult to get a satisfactory explanation. For example, a user only download 1KB size of file, but the charging result will always larger than 1KB. The user also can't know the smallest units of charging: if he only used a small amount of traffic, such as 50B, will it not be charging or charging for 50B or even 1KB? Furthermore, whether some protocol overhead is not taking into account? Etc. For the smart phone applications the lack of rigorous review mechanism in unofficial app markets makes users not

* This work is supported in part by 973 Program of the Chinese Ministry of Science and Technology (No. 2009CB320504) and National Natural Science Foundation of China (No. 61073155 and No. 61001075).

J. Su et al. (Eds.): ICoC 2013, CCIS 401, pp. 206–217, 2013.

sure whether network flows consumed by these applications are really what they need, and among the same kind of applications, which is more provincial traffic?

Existing researches on 3G network and smart phone applications are always focus on common metrics in the general wireless network. Netdiff [12] is a benchmark used to compare different Internet Service Providers (ISP) performance. M. C. Chan et. al. [11] proposed an algorithm to evaluate 3G networks TCP/IP transmission rate and delay. H. Junxian et. al. [9] compared the performance of different smart phone applications under different operator networks. But there are almost no efforts on the study of operators charging system, neither comparison among same kind of smart phone applications.

### 1.1 Our Contribution

The main contributions of our work are:

1. We have designed and implemented an expandable phone side evaluation framework TraSt (Traffic Statistics). This framework can get more detailed traffic usage than any other existing traffic monitor frameworks or applications on Android. And since it is running on the phone, the result can better reflect users real experience.
2. We have proposed some methods to utilize TraSt to explore four aspects of the Chinese three major operators' charging systems (see section IV.A), and get the following result: a. Operators are charging for the traffic of network layer. b. Some protocol overheads such as ARP and ICMPv6 are not taking into account. c. Different operators have different minimum charging units, B or KB. d. the phone will not receive any packet before it initiate a request. These result will lead 3G users to a clearer understanding of the similarities and differences among different operators' charging services.
3. We also have used TraSt to evaluate four kinds of popular smart phone applications (browser, map, online music player and video call). We made experiments in different scenarios, and accurate comparisons of network traffic between different mobile applications. The results show that even among same kind of applications existing great differences. Our analysis with recommendations to software developers can lead to better system design and network infrastructure support.

The rest of the paper is organized as follows. Section 2 introduces data charging process of 3G networks and smart phone applications. Section 3 presents an overview of TraSt. Section 4 proposes the issues and study methodology. Section 5 shows the result and Section 6 draws the conclusion and further discusses future work. Since Android is the most widely used smart phone operating system [1], the ensuing discussions are all made on the Android.

## 2 Preliminaries

We first give a brief overview of 3G charging architecture for data services in context of UMTS [8]. Then introduce the classification of smart phone applications

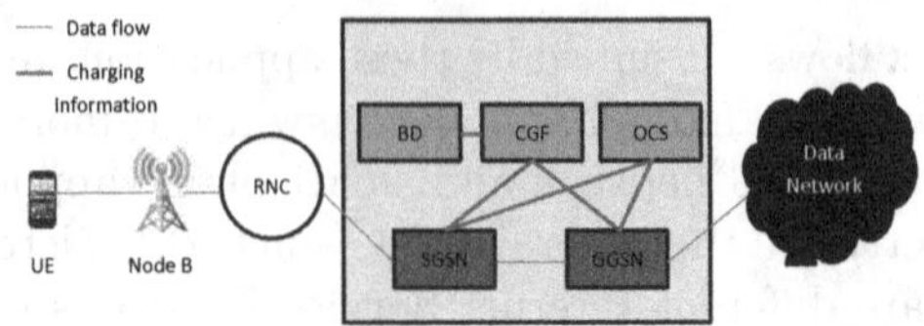


**Fig. 1.** 3G network data charging architecture

and give the definition of content controllable applications and the reason why we chose them to evaluate.

### 2.1 3G Data Charging

The overall 3G charging architecture for data services in context of UMTS is shown in Figure 1. 3G network has two main components—the Core Network (CN) and the Access Network (AN) [10]. The AN includes the User Equipment (UE), the Node B, and the Radio Network Controller (RNC). Its main functions are to control access and exchange data with the Packet-Switch (PS) core network. While the PS core network include the Serving GPRS Support Node (SGSN), Gateway GPRS Support Node (GGSN), Charging Gateway Function (CGF), Billing Domain (BD) and Online Charging System (OCS). Its main functions are to delivery data between UE and the external data networks, perform user authentication and charging functions.

When an application needs to access the Internet, the SGSN will perform the authentication function then the UE can access the network through the AN and establish a bearer. For offline charging, whenever a billing event (such as the use of traffic) occurs, the SGSN and GGSN will collect charging information and transfer it to the BD. And for online charging, the charging information will be directly transferred to the OCS, and the OCS will calculate the fee and deduct it from the users prepaid expenses. For more details, please refer to [7].

### 2.2 Smart Phone Applications

A variety of smart phone applications are now available. According to Google Play, Android applications can be divided into the following categories: 1. Game (Angry Birds); 2. Social(renren); 3. On the go(Google Map); 4. Music and Photos(Duomi Music); 5 Entertainment(Mobile TV); 6. Life(Taobao); 7. Office(Gmail).

For some different applications from a same kind, if we can make the content of traffic basically the same in repeated experiments by certain experimental design and control means, we refer them to *content controllable applications*. For example, we can control the contents of network data of web browser by control its access URL. On the contrary, for some kinds of application such as mail client, different client has different number of messages and information, which we can not control it. We refer them to *content uncontrollable applications*.

For content uncontrollable applications, their data traffic consumptions are largely depend on the actual contents they have accessed, we can not control it, leading the difficulty of comparative experiment control, and making the result unfair. So in this paper, we choose four kinds of content controllable applications including web browsers, maps, online music players and video calls to evaluate.

## 3 Evaluation Framework

We need a framework to help us explore the 3G charging system and evaluate smart phone applications. In order to meet all kinds of requirements including future needs, this framework should be running on smart phone and be able to record every detail information including protocol header of each layer, the content and the time of send/receive for each packet. As far as we know, there is no such framework to accomplish these tasks. However, this framework is very necessary. since compared with laptops and netbooks, the transmission power and signal strength of smart phones is quite different (generally weaker), a framework can accurately reflect the actual experience of the user only when it is running on the phone. It can bring considerable convenience for the test and evaluation process when it can get detail information of each packet. And it can also reduce manual operation thus making the test and evaluation process more efficient.

Next, we will introduce TraSt, a traffic statistics framework that can meets the requirements. It is an open application framework. Which can get detailed information of each packet, and provide interfaces for the test and evaluation process.

### 3.1 Challenges

It is difficult to implement such a framework. Although Android is an open source platform and its kernel is Linux, a lot of tools that can be used on Linux cannot be directly ported to Android because of the difference of system architecture. The statistical result should be displayed on UI, so we should implement the framework at the Application Layer. Application Layer's program can only get the System Permissions (lower than the Root Privileges). But the Root Privileges is needed to capture packets. So the best solution is a combination of the Application Layer and Libraries or Linux Kernel Layer. This also involves the Android NDK development [2], which needs cross compiling.

### 3.2 Framework

The framework of TraSt is depicted in Figure 2. We compiled a Tcpdump [5] which is able to run on Android. And cross compiled the C part of Jnetpcap [3] and libpcap [5] source code with NDK to build a shared library libjnetpcap.so. This shared library will run on Android Libraries Layer. When TraSt starts running, it will call Tcpdump to capture packet and save it to a .pcap file. Then the libjnetpcap.so will read the .pcap file, get the detailed information of each packet and send them to the Application Layer for further processing. The

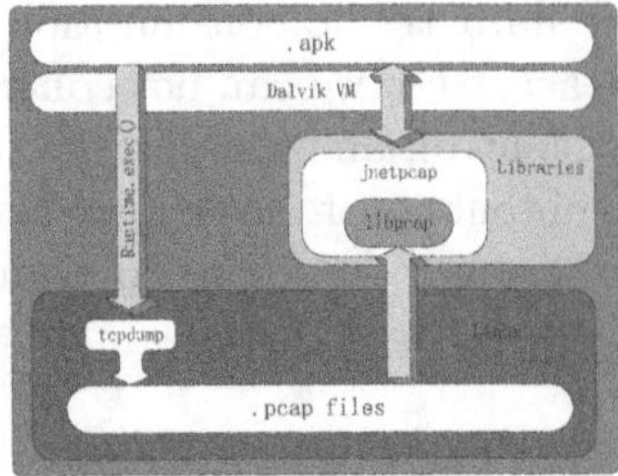


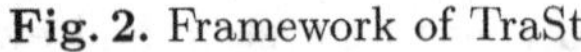
**Fig. 2.** Framework of TraSt

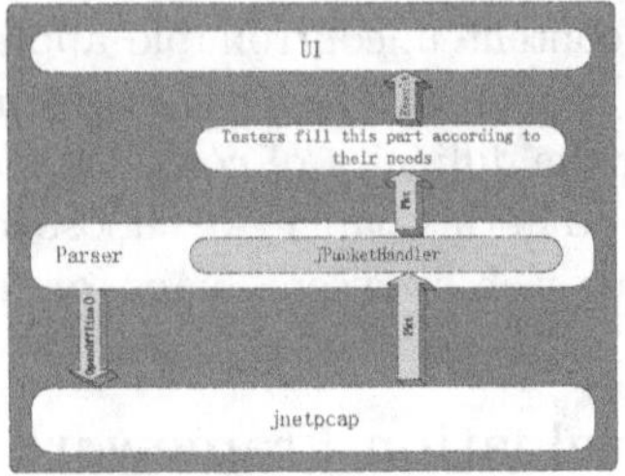


**Fig. 3.** Framework of Application Layer's apk

Tcpdump, libjnetpcap.so and the Application Layers apk will be automatically deployed to the phone at the time of installation.

The Application Layer code is not fixed, but filled by testers according to their needs, such as get the total data traffic, or average handshake time of Tcp, etc. Figure 3 is the framework of the Application Layer's apk. The major components are the Java part of the jnetpcap source code and the Parser class. The Parser class will get every packet from .pcap file through jnetpcap and callback the nextPacket method of JPacketHandler. What testers need to do is just to implement this method, get what they want, and display the result on UI.

### 3.3 Scalability

We would like to emphasize again the scalability of TraSt. TraSt is not an unmodifiable application, but an open framework. It has completed the repeated work that must be done in the process of getting traffic statistics, such as open the device, grab packets, etc. It also provides the interface to obtain the detailed information of each packet for the test or evaluation process. In this way, testers can just focus on how to handle each packet, without having to care about how the packet be obtained. Therefore, TraSt is so powerful that it can be used to measure network performance (such as average TCP handshake time), monitoring the usage of the traffic by each application (according the port of each packet), etc.

## 4 Issues and Methodology

In this section, we clearly describe the issues to address and propose experimental methods.

### 4.1 Issues in 3G Charging

The 3G data charging system is a large and complex "black box". In this paper, we will get some detail information of the "black box" via external measurement. We explore four aspects:

1. Which layer in the protocol stack does each operator charging for?
2. Whether some protocol overhead is not taking into account?
3. What is the smallest units of charging for each operator?
4. Will smart phone receive packets passively without initiate a request? If so, will this part of traffic be charging?

The first two issues concern what to charge, the third concerns whether the charging result is accurate, and the last concerns whether there exist some irrational case in the charging process.

We need to describe in detail the last issue. In general, an application sends a request to the server, the server reply to it. This traffic should be charging of course. But what if the application doesn't send any request, and the server send packets to the device, will it receive the packets and will operators charge for this traffic? Obviously, it is unfair if the operators charging for this traffic. Even more frightening is that if the server is running a malicious program which continue to send packets to a user, will bring huge losses to the user.

### 4.2 Issues in Smart Phone Applications

There are many same types of applications on Android markets. The main problem is:

1. How great the difference is among the same kind applications?
2. What makes the difference?

These issues are what users and developers most concerned separately.

### 4.3 Methodology

We first study the issues in the operators' charging system. We conduct a series of experiments, get the data volume at the end device with TraSt, and compare it with that recorded by operators. We run tests with the three major mobile operators in China, which are China Mobile, China Unicom and China Telecom.

For the first issue, we open the network to run commonly used applications such as browsers and maps and get the data volume of each layer in the protocol stack ($V_{UE}$). Then close the network and get the operators' charging result ($V_{Op}$). Calculate the RE (Relative Error) of each layer:

$$RE = \frac{|V_{UE} - V_{Op}|}{V_{Op}} \times 100\% \tag{1}$$

We repeat the experiment three times, to see which layer's RE is the smallest. This layer's traffic is what the operators charging for. But at this moment, we don't know whether operators are charging for some special traffic, such as the traffic produce by TCP handshake. In order to make the ratio of special traffic as small as possible, we let the applications run enough time (10 minutes) so that they can receive/send enough data.

For the second and the third issue, we need to implement the smart phone application and the server ourselves. At this moment, we know which layer's traffic the operators are charging for, so we can deliberately let the client send specific protocol packets to the server, and observe whether the operators will charge for this traffic, and then we can get the result of the second issue. We can let the client send data as little as possible using the protocol that will be charged, and see how much the data volume recorded by the operators. Thus get the result of the third issue.

To make clear of the fourth issue, we just need to know whether the operators are using the NAT (Network Address Translator) technology, if so, what kind of NAT are they using? Only the Port Restricted Cone and Symmetric NAT have no such loophole [6]. If the address of the device is an internal IP, we know that the operator is using NAT. If so, we deploy two servers with different IPs running same service, let the smart phone application uses a same port to send packets to the two servers. Then the servers can obtain the source port of received packets. If the source ports are the same at the two servers, the operator is using Cone NAT, otherwise Symmetric NAT [6].

There are two methods to obtain data usage logged by operators. The first one is via the SMS from the operators, the second is to login the operators website and inquire data usage. China Mobile and China Telecom support both methods. But for getting finer result, we choose the second method for both of them. China Unicom SIM card used in our experiment only support the first method, the device will receive the billing SMS only when its traffic consumption since last billing SMS is greater than 50 KB.

After exploring the four aspect of the operators' charging system, we can further take evaluation of traffic consumption of smart phone applications. Because users and developers only concern traffic consumption charged by the operators, we could get more accurate comparison if we just taking this part of traffic into account. Table 1 lists the application kinds and corresponding applications to be evaluated. They are all content controllable applications. For the first issue, we take experiment in different scenarios on each type of applications, and use TraSt to get the part of traffic that is generated by the application and will be charged, and then we can compare the result among the applications. For the second issue, we can further analysis the traffic with the specific application, and try to get the root cause. Notice that we are evaluating content controllable applications. For the applications of the same type, we can make the data content basically the same at each network condition repeatedly.

Our mobile devices are HTC Desire and HTC Incredible S, running on Android 2.2 and 2.3.1 respectively.

## 5 Result

In this section, we will show our testing result for the operators' charging system and evaluation results for the four kinds of applications. All the following results are obtained in May 2012.

**Table 1.** Application types and applications

| | |
|---|---|
| Browser | Build-in Webkit 533.1 |
| | Opera Mobile 11.5.2 |
| | UC Browser 7.9.3 |
| | Firefox 10.0 |
| Map | Google Map 6.3.0 |
| | Baidu Map 2.1.0 |
| | Sogou Map 2.1.0 |
| Online Music Player | Xiaomi Music 1.4.3 |
| | Duomi Music 4.0.1.00 |
| | Douban FM 2.1.0 |
| Video Call | Fring 3.9.3.33 |
| | Tango 1.6.8607 |
| | Skype 2.5.0.108 |

### 5.1 Charging System

**Issue 1.** Intuitively, all the three operators should charge for the same layer. We find that only China Mobile take Byte as statistical units. So we start with it. Figure 4 shows the $(1 - RE)$ of each layer by three experiments. It is obvious that the Network Layer's data volume is most close to the operator's charging result. The error is less than 1.5%. Therefore we can conclude that China Mobile is charging for the traffic of network layer. We can get the same result for China Unicom and China TeleCom, just by producing a large traffic (1MB is enough), so that the RE is different at each layer even the units of each element in formula 1 is KB or 10KB.

**Issue 2.** There are two main causees of the difference between TraSt and operators charging result. First, since experiment lasts long time, it is likely to occur packet loss. Second, there may exists some traffic that are not charged by the operators.

To verify the second cause, we use TraSt to count traffic consumption of each Network Layer protocol, including ARP, ICMP, ICMPv6 IPv4, IPv6 and others. Figure 5 shows the result. Since $217 + 160 = 377$, which is exactly the traffic consumption of IPv4. So we can conclude that China Mobile is not charging for ARP and ICMPv6. It is very hard to test for China Unicom and China Telecom because of the larger units in the bill. But we believe the results are the same.

**Issue 3.** For China Mobile we send a UDP packet with 1 Byte payload, its total length is 29 Byte. The charging result is 29 Byte. So the smallest charging units of China Mobile is Byte. For China Telecom, we send a UDP packet with 1 Byte payload two times at a same bearer. The charging result is 1 KB. So the China Telecom will add the packet length in Byte at each bearer and count the part less than 1 KB as 1KB. For China Unicom, it is more complicated since the

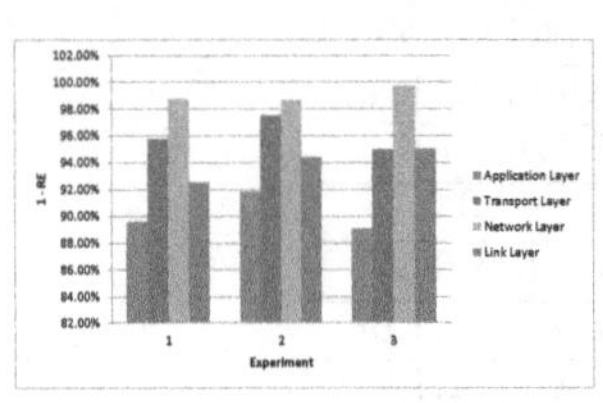


**Fig. 4.** 1 - RE of each layer

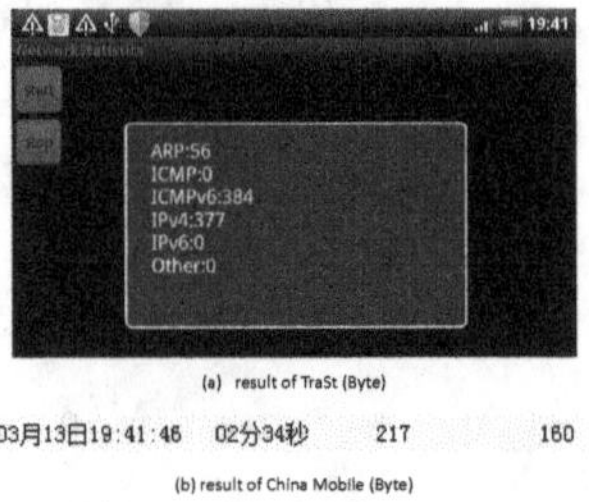


**Fig. 5.** Comparison of the result of TraSt and China Mobile

units on bill is 10 KB, but this does not indicate that China Unicom's charging units is 10 KB.

We let the client establish a TCP connection with the server at each bearer, and repeat it 20 times. The results of TraSt are (APR and ICMPv6 are removed): 184, 184, 360, 180, 273, 273, 180, 460, 630, 180, 180, 180, 180, 180, 180, 630, 327, 1770, 276, 313 (Byte). To make the total traffic consumption larger than 50 KB, we then run a Map application which consumed 255KB traffic. China Unicom's charging result is 0.27 MB. If the charging units is 1 KB, the result should be $1 \times 20 + 0.255 = 0.28$ MB. So the charging units of China Unicom is not KB. We guess it is also Byte like China Mobile.

**Issue 4.** The IP address of UEs are internal network IP (10.0.0.0–10.255.255.255 for China Mobile and China Telecom, 172.16.0.0–172.31.255.255 for China Unicom). So the operators are using NAT technology. We further take experiment mentioned in section IV.C and get the result that the operators are using Symmetric NAT. That means the smart phone won't receive any packet passively without initiate a request.

**Table 2.** Experiment scenarios for browser

| Factors | Setting 1 | Setting 2 |
|---|---|---|
| Image | with image | without image |
| network condition | Wifi | 3G |
| Buffer setting | turn off buffer | turn on buffer |

**Table 3.** Experiment scenarios for map

| Factors | Setting 1 | Setting 2 | Setting 3 |
|---|---|---|---|
| Motion state | static | slow | fast |
| Buffer setting | turn off buffer | turn on buffer | |

**Table 4.** Experiment scenarios for online music player

| Factors | Setting 1 | Setting 2 |
|---|---|---|
| network condition | Wifi | 3G |
| Signal strength | strong | weak |

**Table 5.** Experiment scenarios for video call

| Factors | Setting 1 | Setting 2 | Setting 3 |
|---|---|---|---|
| network condition | Wifi to Wifi | Wifi to 3G | 3G to 3G |

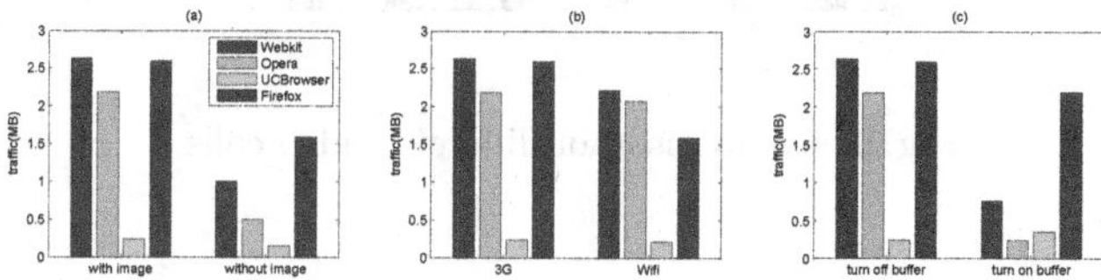


**Fig. 6.** Comparison of different browsers

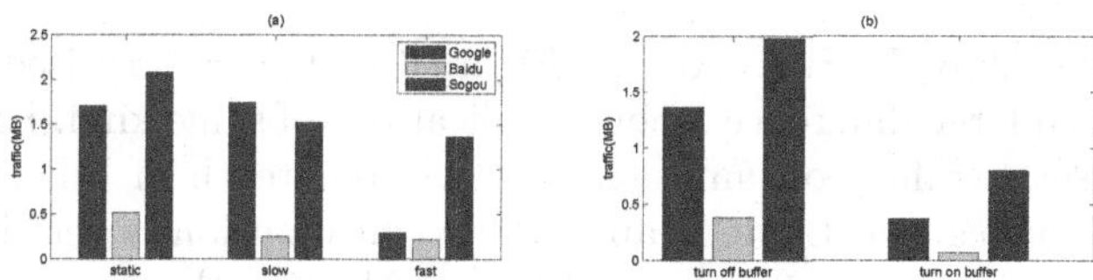


**Fig. 7.** Comparison of different maps

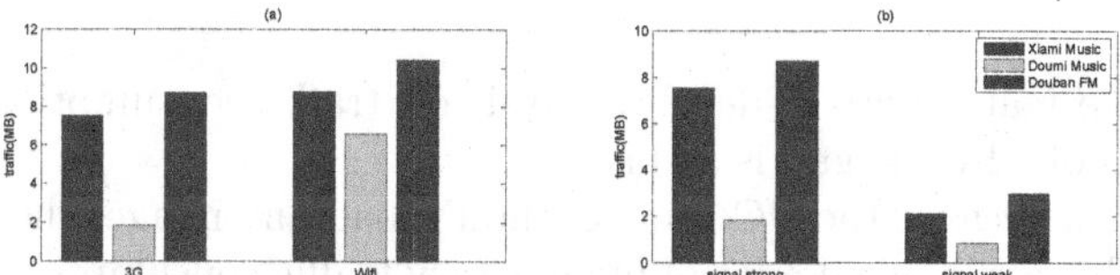


**Fig. 8.** Comparison of different online music players

## 5.2 Smart Phone Applications

We select specific scenario for each kind of applications to make comparative experiments. See in Table 2,3,4,5. For browsers, we let each application visit four website's homepage successively: http://www.youku.com, http://www.qq.com, http://3g.sina.com.cn/?from=www, http://map.baidu.com. For maps, in the static scenario, we search for "Poly Theater", find its location, set it as destination, and set "Peking University" as starting point. Then search for bus route. In the slow movement scenario, we open each map and then walk from the south-west gate of Peking University to the north-east gate. In the fast movement scenario, we open each map and travel from the south-east gate of Peking University to the west gate of Tsinghua University by bus. For online music play-

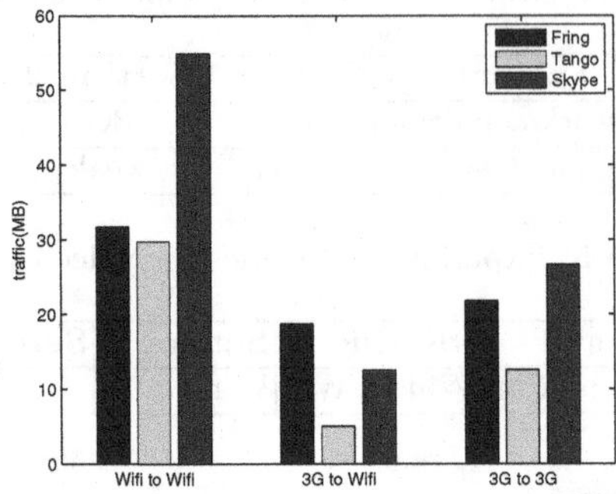


**Fig. 9.** Comparison of different video calls

ers we play music 10 minutes in each scenario for each application. For video calls, we use same application at tow phones to communicate 10 minutes.

**Issue 1.** The result of TraSt is shown in Figure 6 7 8 9. It is surprised to see that there exists such large difference among applications of same kind. For example, the UC browser's traffic consumption is nearly one-tenth of other browsers'! For the map application, Baidu Map's traffic consumption is relatively small, while Sogou Map's is relatively big. And Duomi Music is the most traffic saving among the three online music players. Tango consumed the smallest traffic than the other two video call applications in most scenarios.

**Issue 2.** If we make more in-depth analysis on traffic consumption, we could get the reason of why the gap is so big.

For browsers, because the UC browser didn't load any image when visited qq and youku. This could avoid a lot of unnecessary traffic consumption. Moreover, UC browser has done some optimizations in request mechanism to save uploading traffic.

For maps, different applications have different map source, many location details and information storage means are not the same. Google Map will only show the main building in the fast scenario. Sogou Map will update buffer automatically.

For online music players, Doumi Music will select smooth version in 3G network scenario to save traffic, and high-quality version in Wifi scenario. It also use buffer to save traffic. While the other two application doesn't support these features.

For video calls, although Tango is most traffic saving, the video quality is not good. It is saving traffic on the expense of user experience.

## 6 Conclusion and Future Work

The explosive growth of smart phones and rapid deployment of 3G networks have brought great convenience to people's lives. But there are still a lot of issues to be concerned. In this paper, we present TraSt, a framework that can record every detail information for each packet and help testers to do tests and evaluations on 3G networks and smart phone applications. We also do some experiments to explore four aspect of Chinese three major operators charging system and evaluate four kinds of popular smart phone applications. Our study offers some insight. For the operators' charging system, we could see that in general, the operators' charging results are quite accurate. The reasons why they are different from some traffic statistic applications' results are: first, some protocol overheads such as ARP are not charged by operators but counted by these applications; second, packet loss may lead some packets to be charged by operators but not received by the smart phone or vice versa; third, some services such as MMS (Multimedia Messaging Service), will produce traffic and be counted by these applications, but operators will charge it separately. For the applications of same kind, we could see their traffic consumption are always quite different. The reason is that the degree of optimization and user experience of different application are not the same.

At present, TraSt use file to store packets, when traffic is very large, it can not meet the real-time requirements. So in the future, we will use more efficient way such as interprocess communication to get packets.

## References


1. Analysis Report on China's Smart Phone Market in March 2012, `http://tech.hexun.com/2012-04-16/140429422.html`
2. Android NDK, `http://developer.android.com/sdk/ndk/overview.html`
3. Jnetpcap, `http://jnetpcap.com/`
4. Ministry of Industry and Information Technology. 3G into the Large-scale Development Stage, `http://www.miit.gov.cn`
5. Tcpdump, `http://tcpdump.org/`
6. RFC 3489: STUN — simple traversal of user datagram protocol (UDP) through network address translators, NATs (2003)
7. 3GPP TS32.240: Telecommunication management; Charging management; Charging architecture and principles (2006)
8. G, A.: Global 3G Deployments UMTS HSPA HSPA+ (2010)
9. Huang, J., Xu, Q., Tiwana, B., Mao, Z.M., Zhang, M., Bahl, P.: Anatomizing application performance differences on smartphones. In: MobiSys 2010, pp. 165–178 (2010)
10. Koutsopoulou, M., Kaloxylos, A., Alonistioti, A., Merakos, L.F., Kawamura, K.: Charging, accounting and billing management schemes in mobile telecommunication networks and the internet, pp. 50–58 (2004)
11. Chan, M.C., Ramjee, R.: TCP/IP Performance over 3G Wireless Links with Rate and Delay Variation. In: MobiCom 2002, pp. 71–82 (2002)
12. Mahajan, R., Zhang, M., Poole, L., Pai, V.: Uncovering Performance Differences among Backbone ISPs with Netdiff. In: NSDI 2008, pp. 205–218 (2008)

# A Novel Direct Anonymous Attestation Scheme Using Secure Two-Party Computation

Xiaohan Yue[1] and Fucai Zhou[2]

[1] College of information science and engineering, Shenyang University of Technology Shenyang, China
xhyuer@gmail.com
[2] College of information science and engineering, Northeastern University Shenyang, China
fczhou@mail.neu.edu.cn

**Abstract.** Direct Anonymous Attestation (DAA) is a cryptographic scheme which enables the remote authentication of a trusted platform whilst preserving privacy under the user's control. In term of construction of DAA, due to the limited computational and storage capability of trusted platform module (TPM), in this paper, we propose a novel approach for constructing an efficient DAA scheme: we design a secure two-party computation protocol for the Join/Issue protocol of DAA, and construct the DAA scheme concretely under the $q$-SDH assumption and XDH assumption. Based on the DAA security model, we prove that our DAA scheme meets user-controlled anonymity, user-controlled traceability in the random oracle model. Finally compared with other existing DAA schemes, our DAA scheme has better performance.

**Keywords:** Trusted Computing, direct anonymous attestation, secure two-party computation, security proof.

## 1 Introduction

Trusted Computing [1] is a hardware-based security guarantee mechanism, which allows commodity computers to provide cryptographic assurances about their behavior. The core of this architecture is a device called Trusted Platform Module [2] (TPM). TPM is a hardware chip embedded in platforms that can carry out various cryptographic functions. One important function of TPM is integrity reporting, and the process of reporting the integrity of a platform is known as remote attestation. To achieve the goals of remote attestation and ensure the user privacy, Trusted Computing Group (TCG) has introduced two ways as follows:

One way to preserve user privacy is to employ a trusted third party to manage the relationship between a platform's true unique identity, and one or more pseudonyms that can be employed to generate attestations for different purposes. TCG initially adopted this approach in the TPM specification 1.1[3], dubbing the trusted third party a Privacy CA and associating the pseudonyms with Attestation Identity Keys (AIKs). A TPM's true unique identity is represented by the Endorsement Key (EK) embedded

J. Su et al. (Eds.): ICoC 2013, CCIS 401, pp. 218–235, 2013.

in the TPM. However, the Privacy CA architecture has met with some real-world limitations as described in [4].

To address the limitations of Privacy CA, another way called Direct Anonymous Attestation (DAA) [4] was developed and incorporated into the latest TPM specification 1.2 [2] and the Mobile Trusted Module specification [5]. DAA is a remote authentication mechanism for trusted computing platform, and mainly consists of the Join/Issue protocol and the Sign protocol. The participants in a DAA scheme have three types: the issuer, the signer and the verifier. The issuer is in charge of verifying the legitimating of signers and of issuing a signing key to each signer. The signer, which consists of a TPM and a host where the TPM is attached, can convince a verifier that the DAA signatures generated by the signer are valid. The verifier can verify the membership of the signer from the DAA signatures but it cannot learn the identity of the signer. The DAA scheme is completely decentralized and achieves anonymity by combining research on group signatures and credential systems. Unlike the group signatures, the issuer in DAA is not a privileged group manager, so anonymity can never be revoked, i.e., a DAA signature cannot be opened by anyone including the issuer to reveal the identity of the signer. Instead of full-anonymity and traceability as held in group signatures[6], DAA has user-controlled anonymity and traceability, that means the DAA signer (user) and verifier are able to decide whether the verifier enables to determine if any two signatures have been produced by the same signer.

*Related works.* DAA has drawn a lot of attention from both industry and cryptographic researchers after the concept and a concrete scheme of DAA were first introduced by Brickell, Camenisch, and Chen [4]. Durahim et al.[7] constructed a privacy-preserving mutual authentication and key agreement protocol using DAA scheme for ensuring privacy. Bichsel et al. [8] made use of a variant DAA scheme to build an anonymous credential system on a standard Java card. Bella et al. [9] utilized a DAA scheme to enforce privacy in e-commerce and proposed a self-enforcing privacy protocol. Gummadi et al. [10] developed a NAB ("Not-A-Bot") system which can preserve the current privacy semantics of web and email by extending the DAA service. Many other DAA-based works have been presented in literatures [11, 12, 13].

However the performance of original DAA scheme is inefficient, hence many other DAA schemes were proposed from the view of performance. Recently, researchers have been working on how to create DAA schemes with elliptic curves and pairings, since ECC-based DAA is more efficient in both computation and communication than RSA-based DAA. The first ECC-based DAA scheme was proposed by Brickell et al.[14] This scheme is based on symmetric pairings. Chen et al. [15,16] improved the above scheme [14] and proposed two extended DAA schemes by using asymmetric pairings for the purpose of increasing implementation flexibility and efficiency. To further improve the performance of the scheme [16], Chen et al. [17] modified the scheme, and compared with the original DAA scheme via a concrete implementation. Recently, Chen [18] introduced a more efficient DAA scheme by making use of batch proof and verification technique. But the efficient scheme [18] has some security drawbacks, Brickell et al [31] then fix these drawbacks by proposing a new batch proof and verification protocol. These DAA schemes are based on the LRSW assumption and DDH assumption. Other DAA schemes were proposed by Chen and

Feng[19], Brickell and Li[20], Chen[21], respectively. Security of these schemes is based on the $q$-SDH assumption and DDH assumption. To the best of our knowledge, Brickell's DAA scheme [31] is the most efficient DAA scheme and it requires least amount of TPM resources.

*Our contributions.* In this paper, our contribution is the novel DAA scheme. In the construction of our DAA scheme, we focus on the efficiency of Sign protocol and Verify algorithm rather than that of the Join/Issue protocol, since in practice the Join/Issue protocol is executed much less times than the Sign protocol and Verify algorithm. With the motivation, our works are as follows:

We design a secure two-party computation (2PC) protocol for the Join/Issue protocol to generate the signing key by making use of additive homomorphic encryption[23] and verifiable encryption technique[24].

Under the $q$-SDH assumption [25] and XDH assumption [25], we propose a new DAA scheme. At the performance aspect, in the signing phase our DAA scheme only requires one exponentiation when unlinkability is necessary or two exponentiations when linkability is necessary for TPM, and three exponentiations (unlinkability) or four exponetiations (linkability) for the host to respectively perform.

At last, we give a comparison between our scheme and all the existing ECC-based DAA schemes, the result shows that our DAA scheme has better performance than all the existing schemes.

*Roadmap.* Rest of this paper is organized as follows. We first present the formal definition and the enhanced security model of DAA scheme in Section 2. We then review some cryptography assumptions and tools of which we make use in Section 3. We focus on the design of security two-party computation protocol in Section 4. We construct our new DAA scheme in Section 5 and the corresponding security proofs and performance comparison with the existing DAA schemes in Section 6. We then conclude the paper in Section 7.

## 2 Formal Definition and Security Model of DAA

### 2.1 Formal Definition of DAA

We firstly present the formal definition of DAA. There are four types of players in the DAA scheme: the issuer $\mathcal{I}$, the TPM $\mathcal{M}$, the host $\mathcal{H}$ and the verifier $\mathcal{V}$. $\mathcal{M}$ and $\mathcal{H}$ form a platform in the trusted computing environment and share the role of the DAA signer $\mathcal{S}$. A DAA scheme $\mathcal{DAA}$ = (Setup, Join/Issue, Sign, Verify, Link) consists of the following five polynomial-time algorithms and protocols:

**Setup**: On input of a security parameter $1^\kappa$, this randomized algorithm can produce two pairs (*ipk*, *isk*) where *isk* is the issuer's secret key, and *ipk* is the public key including the global public parameters. Formally, the algorithm can be written as:

$$\text{Setup}(1^\kappa) \rightarrow (ipk, isk)\,.$$

**Join/Issue**: This protocol runs between a signer ($\mathcal{M}$, $\mathcal{H}$) and an issuer $\mathcal{I}$. Each of the algorithms (Join, Issue) takes input a secret value, and output the signer's DAA signing key *sigk* associated with signer's secret key *sk*. Note that the *sigk* is given to

$\mathcal{H}$, but the secret value *sk* is only known to $\mathcal{M}$. Formally, the protocol can be written as:

$$\text{Join/ Issue}(\text{In}_{\mathcal{M}} : (ipk, sk), \text{In}_{\mathcal{I}} : (ipk, isk)) \rightarrow \text{Out}_{\mathcal{M}} : sigk.$$

**Sign:** The protocol consists of two interactive algorithms, $\text{Sign}_{\mathcal{M}}$ and $\text{Sign}_{\mathcal{H}}$, which implement the $\mathcal{M}$'s and $\mathcal{H}$'s sides of interaction respectively. The input of $\text{Sign}_{\mathcal{M}}$ is (*sk*, *ipk*), and that of $\text{Sign}_{\mathcal{H}}$ is a message *m* that includes the date to be signed, a verifier's nonce $n_{\mathcal{V}}$ for freshness, a basename *bsn* (the name string of $\mathcal{V}$ or a special symbol $\perp$) and *ipk*, *sigk*. The final output by $\text{Sign}_{\mathcal{H}}$ is a randomized signature $\sigma$ on *m* under (*sk*, *sigk*) associated with *bsn*. The basename *bsn* is used for controlling the linkability. Formally, the protocol can be written as:

$$\text{Sign}(\text{In}_{\mathcal{H}} : (ipk, sigk, m, n_{\mathcal{V}}, bsn), \text{In}_{\mathcal{M}} : (sk, ipk)) \rightarrow \text{Out}_{\mathcal{H}} : \sigma$$

**Verify:** On input of *m*, *bsn*, a candidate signature $\sigma$ for *m*, and a set of revoked signer's secret keys RL, $\mathcal{V}$ uses this deterministic algorithm to return either 1(accept) or 0 (reject). How to build the rogue list RL is out of the scope of the DAA scheme. Formally, the algorithm can be written as:

$$\text{Verify}(ipk, m, bsn, \text{RL}, \sigma) \rightarrow 1/0.$$

**Link**: On input of two message-signature pairs $(m_0, \sigma_0)$ and $(m_1, \sigma_1)$, $\mathcal{V}$ uses this deterministic algorithm to return 1 (linked), 0 (unlinked) or $\perp$(invalid signatures). Link will output $\perp$ if, by using an empty RL, either Verify($m_0, \sigma_0$) or Verify($m_1, \sigma_1$) holds. Otherwise, Link will output 1 if signatures can be linked or 0 if the signatures cannot be linked. Formally, the algorithm can be written as:

$$\text{Link}(ipk, \sigma_0, m_0, \sigma_1, m_1, bsn) \rightarrow 1/0.$$

## 2.2 Security Model of DAA

We use the game-based model to formalize our security notions of DAA. In our enhanced security model of DAA, a DAA scheme must hold the notions of correctness, user-controlled anonymity and user-controlled traceability.

To define these notions, we need to present a series of oracles that an adversary can access to. All oracles maintain the following global variables, a set HS of honest signers, a set CS of corrupted signers, a set $\text{Ch}_{ID}$ of challenge *ID* and a list $\text{L}_S$ of queries to the Sign queries. All the sets and lists are assumed to be initially empty.

$\mathcal{O}_{\text{AddS}}$: By calling this *add signer* oracle with an identity *ID*, the adversary can create an honest signer *ID*. The oracle adds *ID* to the set HS of honest signers, and generates a signer secret key $sk_{ID}$ for *ID*. Then it executes the Join/Issue protocol on behalf of *ID* and the issuer. Its final state is recorded as the signing key $sigk_{ID}$ for *ID*.

$\mathcal{O}_{\text{SndToI}}$: The adversary can use this *send to issuer* oracle to impersonate signer *ID*∈CS and engage in a Join/Issue protocol with the honest, Issue-executing issuer. The oracle computes a response as per Issue, returns the outgoing message to the adversary.

$\mathcal{O}_{\text{SndToS}}$: The *send to signer* oracle can be used by such an adversary to engage in a Join/Issue protocol with an honest, Join-executing signer, itself playing the role of the issuer. On successful completion of the Join/Issue protocol the oracle adds *ID* to HS and sets the DAA signing key $sigk_{ID}$ of *ID* to Join's final state. Since the internal state of the signer *ID* is exposed, the adversary knows the corresponding $sigk_{ID}$ and can be able to make DAA signatures on behalf of the signer.

$\mathcal{O}_{\text{SIGK}}$: Calling this *signing key* oracle enables the adversary to obtain the DAA signing key of signer *ID*. The signer remains honest.

$\mathcal{O}_{\text{SK}}$: The adversary can call this *signer secret key* oracle to obtain the signer secret keys of signer $ID \in \text{HS}$, and then the oracle moves *ID* from HS to CS.

$\mathcal{O}_{\text{Sig}}$: The signing oracle, enabling the adversary to specify the identity *ID* of a signer, a message *m* and a basename *bsn*, and obtain the DAA signature of *m* under the signing key $sigk_{ID}$ of *ID*, as long as *ID* is an honest signer whose DAA signing key is defined.

$\mathcal{O}_{\text{Ch}}$: The adversary sends a pair of honest identities ($ID_0$, $ID_1$), a message *m* and a basename *bsn* to the challenge oracle and gets back a DAA signature $\sigma$ by the signer $ID_b$, $b \in_R \{0,1\}$.

**Correctness.** The DAA signatures generated by honest signers are accepted by verifiers. In addition, two DAA signatures generated by the same signer with the same basename can be linked. To formalize this, we define $\text{Adv}_{\mathcal{A}}^{corr}(\kappa) = \Pr[\text{Game}_{\mathcal{A}}^{corr}(\kappa) = 1]$ and we say that the DAA scheme is *correct* if $\text{Adv}_{\mathcal{A}}^{corr}(\kappa) = 0$ for all adversaries $\mathcal{A}$ and $\kappa \in \mathbb{N}$. The game $\text{Game}_{\mathcal{A}}^{corr}(\kappa)$ is defined as below:

Attack-Game $\text{Game}_{\mathcal{A}}^{corr}(\kappa)$:

$(ipk, isk) \leftarrow \text{Setup}(1^{\kappa}); \text{HS} \leftarrow \phi; (ID, m_0, m_1, bsn) \leftarrow \mathcal{A}(ipk : \mathcal{O}_{\text{AddS}});$

If $i \notin \text{HS}$ then return 0; If $sigk_{ID} = \perp$ then return 0.

$\sigma_0 \leftarrow \text{Sign}(\mathcal{H} : (ipk, sigk_{ID}, m_0, n_V, bsn), \mathcal{M} : (sk_{ID}, ipk));$

$\sigma_1 \leftarrow \text{Sign}(\mathcal{H} : (ipk, sigk_{ID}, m_1, n_V, bsn), \mathcal{M} : (sk_{ID}, ipk));$

If $\text{Verify}(ipk, m_0, bsn, \text{RL}, \sigma_0) = 0$ then return 1.

If $\text{Verify}(ipk, m_1, bsn, \text{RL}, \sigma_1) = 0$ then return 1.

If $bsn \neq \perp \wedge \text{Link}(ipk, \sigma_0, m_0, \sigma_1, m_1, bsn) = 0$ then return 1.

Return 0.

**User-Controlled Anonymity.** The definition of user-controlled anonymity requires two security properties in the DAA scheme. The first one is *anonymity* that no adversary can reveal the identity of the signer from its signature without the signer's secret key *sk*. The second property is *user-controlled unlinkability* that given two signatures $\sigma_0$ and $\sigma_1$ associated with two different basenames, it is infeasible for an adversary to distinguish whether or not the two signatures are generated by the same signer. We define $\text{Adv}_{\mathcal{A}}^{anon}(\kappa) = |\Pr[\text{Game}_{\mathcal{A}}^{anon-b}(\kappa) = 1] - 1/2|$ and say that the DAA scheme has *user-controlled anonymity* if $\text{Adv}_{\mathcal{A}}^{anon}(\kappa)$ is negligible in $\kappa$ for any polynomial-time adversary $\mathcal{A}$. The game $\text{Game}_{\mathcal{A}}^{anon-b}(\kappa)$ is defined as below:

Attack-Game $\text{Game}_{\mathcal{A}}^{anon-b}(\kappa)$: // $b \in_R \{0,1\}$

$(ipk, isk) \leftarrow \text{Setup}(1^k); \text{CS} \leftarrow \phi; \text{HS} \leftarrow \phi;$

$b' \leftarrow \mathcal{A}(ipk, isk : \mathcal{O}_{\text{SndToS}}, \mathcal{O}_{\text{SigK}}, \mathcal{O}_{\text{SK}}, \mathcal{O}_{\text{Sig}}, \mathcal{O}_{\text{Ch}});$

If $b' = b$ then return 1 else return 0.

**User-Controlled Traceability.** The definition of user-controlled traceability requires two security properties in the DAA scheme. The first one is *unfakeability* that means no adversary can create a valid DAA signature under a faked signing key. The second property is *user-controlled linkability* that means given a single basename it is hard for an adversary to generate two different DAA signatures under the same signer secret key and the same basename, while the output of the algorithm Link is 0 (unlinked). We define $\mathrm{Adv}_{\mathcal{A}}^{trace}(\kappa) = \Pr[\mathrm{Game}_{\mathcal{A}}^{trace}(\kappa) = 1]$ and say that the DAA scheme has *user-controlled traceability* if $\mathrm{Adv}_{\mathcal{A}}^{trace}(\kappa)$ is negligible in $\kappa$ for any polynomial-time adversary $\mathcal{A}$. The game $\mathrm{Game}_{\mathcal{A}}^{trace}(\kappa)$ is defined as below:

Attack-Game $\mathrm{Game}_{\mathcal{A}}^{trace}(\kappa)$:

$(ipk, isk) \leftarrow \mathrm{Setup}(1^k); \mathrm{CS} \leftarrow \phi; \mathrm{HS} \leftarrow \phi$

Case 1://*Unfakeability*.

$(m, \sigma, bsn, ID) \leftarrow \mathcal{A}(ipk : \mathcal{O}_{\mathrm{SndToI}}, \mathcal{O}_{\mathrm{AddS}}, \mathcal{O}_{\mathrm{SK}})$

If $\mathrm{Verify}(ipk, m, \sigma, \mathrm{RL}, bsn) = 1 \wedge ID \notin \mathrm{CS}$ then return 1.

Case 2: //*User - controlled linkability*

$(m_0, \sigma_0, m_1, \sigma_1, bsn, ID) \leftarrow \mathcal{A}(ipk : \mathcal{O}_{\mathrm{SndToI}}, \mathcal{O}_{\mathrm{AddS}}, \mathcal{O}_{\mathrm{SK}})$

If $\mathrm{Link}(ipk, m_0, \sigma_0, m_1, \sigma_1, bsn) = 0 \wedge bsn \neq \perp$ then return 1.

Return 0.

# 3 Preliminaries

## 3.1 Bilnear Groups and Complexity Assumptions

**Bilinear Groups.** Bilinear groups are a set of three groups $\mathbb{G}_1$, $\mathbb{G}_2$ and $\mathbb{G}_T$, of order $p$, along with a bilinear map $e : \mathbb{G}_1 \times \mathbb{G}_2 \rightarrow \mathbb{G}_T$. We write $\mathbb{G}_1 = \langle g_1 \rangle, \mathbb{G}_2 = \langle g_2 \rangle$ for two explicitly given generators $g_1$ and $g_2$, and define $par_{\mathrm{Bilinear}} = (p, \mathbb{G}_1, \mathbb{G}_2, \mathbb{G}_T, e, g_1, g_2)$ to be the set of pairing group parameters. The function e must have the following three properties.

- Bilinearity: $\forall f_1 \in \mathbb{G}_1, \forall f_2 \in \mathbb{G}_2$ and $\forall a, b \in \mathbb{Z}$, we have $e(f_1^a, f_2^b) = e(f_1, f_2)^{ab}$;
- Non-degeneracy: The value $e(g_1, g_2)$ generates $\mathbb{G}_T$;
- Computability: The function e is efficiently computable.

Following [26] there are three distinct types of bilinear groups, in this paper we consider type-3 pairings. Such type is the asymmetric setting in which $\mathbb{G}_1 \neq \mathbb{G}_2$ and there is no known efficiently computable isomorphism between $\mathbb{G}_1$ and $\mathbb{G}_2$. For a security parameter $\kappa$, we let $\mathrm{Setup}_{\mathrm{Bilinear}}(1^\kappa)$ denote an algorithm which produces a pairing group instance $par_{\mathrm{Bilinear}}$ of type-3.

In these groups, we rely on hardness assumptions that are all falsifiable.

**Definition 1** (eXternal Diffie-Hellman (XDH) assumption). The XDH assumption [25] holds in $\mathbb{G}_1$, if the following probability is negligible in the security parameter $\kappa$, for all adversaries $\mathcal{A}$ and all parameter sets $par_{\mathrm{Bilinear}}$ output by $\mathrm{Setup}_{\mathrm{Bilinear}}(1^\kappa)$:

$$\mathrm{Adv}_{\mathcal{A}}^{\mathrm{XDH}}(\kappa)=\Pr[x,y\leftarrow\mathbb{Z}_p;b\leftarrow\{0,1\};h_0=g_1^{xy},h_1\leftarrow\mathbb{G}_1:\mathcal{A}(h_b,g_1^x,g_1^y,par_{\mathrm{Bilinear}})\rightarrow b]$$

**Definition 2** ($q$-Strong Diffie-Hellman ($q$-SDH) assumption). The $q$-SDH assumption [25] holds, if the following probability is negligible in the security parameter $\kappa$, for all adversaries $\mathcal{A}$ and all parameter sets $par_{\mathrm{Bilinear}}$ output by $\mathrm{Setup}_{\mathrm{Bilinear}}(1^\kappa)$:

$$\mathrm{Adv}_{\mathcal{A}}^{q\text{-SDH}}(\kappa)=\Pr[x\leftarrow\mathbb{Z}_p;g_1^x,g_1^{x^2},\ldots,g_1^{x^q}\leftarrow\mathbb{G}_1;g_2^x\leftarrow\mathbb{G}_2:\mathcal{A}(g_1^x,g_1^{x^2},\ldots,g_1^{x^q},g_2^x,par_{\mathrm{Bilinear}})$$
$$\rightarrow(g_1^{1/(x+c)},c\in\mathbb{Z}_p)].$$

### 3.2 Paillier Cryptosystem

Paillier cryptosystem [23] has additive homomorphic and self-blinding properties, and is usually employed to construct various cryptography schemes. The cryptosystem consists of three algorithms as follows:

**P-Setup**($1^\kappa$): On input of the security parameter $\kappa$, the algorithm picks two random primes $(P,Q)$ and computes $N=P\cdot Q$. It also selects a random base $g\in\mathbb{Z}_{N^2}^*$ which meet $\gcd(L(g^{\lambda(N)} \bmod N^2),\ N)=1$ where $L(u)=\ (u-1)/N$ and $\lambda(N)$ = lcm($P$-1, $Q$-1). Then it chooses a random $r\in\mathbb{Z}_{N^2}^*$ and computes $h=r^N \bmod N^2$, explicitly the order of h is $\lambda(N)$. Finally, the algorithm outputs the public key $\mathrm{PK_P}$ = ($N$, $g$, $h$) and the secret key $\mathrm{SK_P}$ = ($P$, $Q$).

**P-Enc**($\mathrm{PK_P}$, $m$): On input of the public key $\mathrm{PK_P}$ and a plaintext $m$, the algorithm chooses a random value $s\in\mathbb{Z}_N^*$ and computes the ciphertext as $C=g^m\cdot h^s \bmod N^2$ as output.

**P-Dec**($\mathrm{SK_P}$, $C$): On input of the secret key $\mathrm{SK_P}$ and a ciphertext $C$, the algorithm retrieves the plaintext as: $m=(L(C^{\lambda(N)} \bmod N^2)/L(g^{\lambda(N)} \bmod N^2)) \bmod N$.

## 4 The 2PC Protocol for the SDH Instance

The framework and security model of our 2PC protocol are based on previous work which has been done in [27]. In this section, based on Paillier cryptosystem and verifiable encryption technique, we give an instantiation of such a protocol which has not been done in [27]. Our 2PC protocol actively involves two parties, an issuer with a secret value $\gamma$ and a user with a secret value $f$, and passively involves one party who is a trusted third party TTP. Notes that TTP does not directly participate in the 2PC protocol, but only provides the public parameters $par_T=(\mathfrak{n},\mathfrak{g},\mathfrak{h})$ where $\mathfrak{n}=\mathfrak{p}\mathfrak{q}$ is a RSA modulus and $(\mathfrak{g},\mathfrak{h})\in\mathbb{Z}_{\mathfrak{n}}^*$, and keeps $\mathfrak{p}$ and $\mathfrak{q}$ secret. In order to generate a SDH instance $(g_1^{1/(f+\gamma)},f)$ within bilinear group parameters $par_{\mathrm{Bilinear}}=(p,\mathbb{G}_1,\mathbb{G}_2,\mathbb{G}_T,e,g_1,g_2)$ for the user, we design the processes of the 2PC protocol as follows:

1) The issuer generates the parameters of Paillier cryptosystem, ($\mathrm{PK_P}$, $\mathrm{SK_P}$):=(($N$, $g$, $h$), ($P$, $Q$)) and publishes the $\mathrm{PK_P}$ to the user. The issuer picks a random $r_1\in_R\mathbb{Z}_N$ and computes a ciphertext $e_1=\text{P-Enc}(\gamma)$ and a commitment $\mathfrak{c}_1=\mathfrak{g}^\gamma\mathfrak{h}^{\mathfrak{r}'} \bmod n$ with a random $\mathfrak{r}'\in_R\mathbb{Z}_{\mathfrak{n}}$. Then the issuer and the user execute the following zero-knowledge proof protocol with each other:

$$PK\{(\gamma,r_1,\mathfrak{r}'):\Omega=g_2^\gamma\wedge e_1=g^\gamma h^{r_1} \bmod N^2\wedge\mathfrak{c}_1=\mathfrak{g}^\gamma\mathfrak{h}^{\mathfrak{r}'} \bmod \mathfrak{n}\wedge\gamma\in\mathbb{Z}_p^*\}.$$

2) The user receives $e_1$ and $\mathfrak{c}_1$, selects two random $r_2 \in_R \mathbb{Z}_p^*$, $r_3 \in_R \mathbb{Z}_N$ and computes $e_2 := (e_1)^{r_2} g^{f \cdot r_2} h^{r_3} = g^{(\gamma+f)\cdot r_2} h^{r_1 r_2 + r_3} \bmod N^2$, a commitment $\mathfrak{c}_2 = \mathfrak{g}^{f} \mathfrak{h}^{r''} \bmod n$ for $r'' \in_R \mathbb{Z}_{n/p}$, the value $\bar{f} := f \cdot r_2$ and $\bar{r} := r_2 \cdot r''$. The user and the issuer run the following zero-knowledge proof protocol with each other:

$PK\{(f, \bar{f}, r_2, r_3, \bar{r}, r''): e_2 := (e_1)^{r_2} g^{\bar{f}} h^{r_3} \bmod N^2 \wedge \mathfrak{c}_2 = \mathfrak{g}^{f} \mathfrak{h}^{r''} \bmod n \wedge 1 = \mathfrak{c}_2^{r_2} / (\mathfrak{g}^{\bar{f}} \mathfrak{h}^{\bar{r}}) \wedge r_2, f \in \mathbb{Z}_p^*\}$

3) The issuer decrypts $e_2$ by computing $m := \text{P-Dec}(e_2) = (\gamma + f) \cdot r_2$, $D' := g_1^{1/m} \in \mathbb{G}_1$ computes and forwards $D'$ to the user.

4) The user computes $D := (D')^{r_2} = g_1^{1/(\gamma+f)}$ and verifies that $e(g_1^{1/(\gamma+f)}, g_2^{f} \cdot \Omega) = e(g_1, g_2)$, if successfully, outputs *accept*.

The security of the above 2PC protocol follows straight forward from known works i.e., [23, 24, 27]. The 2PC protocol ensures that the issuer cannot learn any information about the secret value $f$ of the user since the commitment has perfect hiding property.

**Theorem 1.** *The above 2PC protocol has correctness, and assuming the discrete logarithm problem is hard, it is possible to black-box simulate views of both the user and the issuer.*

*Proof.* It easy to see that correctness follows by direct verification. And since the protocol is implemented by making use of zero-knowledge proof of knowledge protocol, there exists black-box simulators for both the malicious issuer and the adversary user.

We will use this theorem to prove security of our DAA scheme in section 6. In addition, one can use more efficient additive homomorphic encryption schemes or verifiable encryption schemes to construct the above 2PC protocol. In this paper, we just give an example to implement this protocol.

# 5 Our DAA Scheme

## 5.1 The Setup Algorithm

On input of the security parameter $1^{\kappa}$, the setup algorithm executes the following:

1) Run the algorithm $\text{Setup}_{\text{Bilinear}}(1^{\kappa}) \rightarrow (p, \mathbb{G}_1, \mathbb{G}_2, \mathbb{G}_T, e, g_1, g_2)$.

2) Select five hash functions $\text{H}_1 : \{0,1\}^* \rightarrow \mathbb{Z}_p$, $\text{H}_2 : \{0,1\}^* \rightarrow \mathbb{G}_1$, $\text{H}_3 : \{0,1\}^* \rightarrow \mathbb{Z}_p$., $\text{H}_\alpha : \{0,1\}^* \rightarrow \{0,1\}^L$, $\text{H}_\beta : \{0,1\}^* \rightarrow \{0,1\}^L$.

3) Choose a random $\gamma \in_R \mathbb{Z}_p^*$ uniformly as the issuer's private key and compute $\Omega := g_2^{\gamma}$. Output the DAA public key and the issuer's private key:

$(ipk, isk) := ((\mathbb{G}_1, \mathbb{G}_2, \mathbb{G}_T, p, e, g_1, g_2, \text{H}_1, \text{H}_2, \text{H}_3, \text{H}_\alpha, \text{H}_\beta, \Omega), \gamma)$.

Note that, in the actual implementation, we can choose the same hash function for $\text{H}_1$ and $\text{H}_3$, and implement $\text{H}_\alpha$ and $\text{H}_\beta$ by many methods as mentioned in [31]. We use different hash functions in order to prove the security.

## 5.2 The Join/Issue Protocol

This protocol is performed by a TPM $\mathcal{M}$, the corresponding host $\mathcal{H}$ and an issuer $\mathcal{I}$. We assume that $\mathcal{M}$ and $\mathcal{I}$ have already established a one-way secure authentica-ted channel using $\mathcal{M}$'s endorsement key[2]. Let *DAAseed* be $\mathcal{M}$'s internal secret seed. Let *cnt* be a count value. The purpose of using *cnt* can be found in the original DAA scheme[4]. This protocol takes the following steps.

1) $\mathcal{M}$ computes $f := \mathrm{H}_1(DAAseed \,\|\, cnt \,\|\, ipk)$ and sets its signer secret key $sk := f$.

2) $\mathcal{M}$ and $\mathcal{I}$ perform the 2PC protocol described in section 4, i.e., $\mathcal{I}$ and $\mathcal{M}$ take their own secret key as input and play the roles of the issuer and the user in 2PC protocol respectively. If successful, $\mathcal{M}$ obtains $D = g_1^{1/(\gamma+f)} \in \mathbb{G}_1$.

3) $\mathcal{M}$ computes a pair $(A,B) := ((D)^f, D) = (g_1^{f/(\gamma+f)},\ g_1^{1/(\gamma+f)})$ and sends the pair to $\mathcal{H}$.

4) $\mathcal{H}$ receives the pair and verifies that $e(B,\Omega) = e(g_1 / A, g_2)$. If verification fails, then abort. Otherwise, $\mathcal{H}$ stores the pair $(A,B)$ as the DAA signing key *sigk*.

## 5.3 The Sign Protocol

This protocol is performed by the TPM $\mathcal{M}$ and the host $\mathcal{H}$. $\mathcal{M}$ and $\mathcal{H}$ work together to produce a DAA signature on some messages. The signature should prove knowledge of a discrete logarithm *f*, knowledge of a valid DAA signing key which was computed for the same value *f* by a given issuer $\mathcal{I}$. The protocol proceeds as follows.

1) $\mathcal{H}$ selects a random $r \in_R \mathbb{Z}_p$ and computes $T_1 := A^r, T_2 := B^r,\ T_3 := g_1^r$.

2) If $bsn \neq \perp$, $\mathcal{H}$ computes and sends $J := \mathrm{H}_2(bsn) \in \mathbb{G}_1$ to $\mathcal{M}$. $\mathcal{M}$ computes $K := J^f$ and returns $K$ to $\mathcal{H}$. Then $\mathcal{H}$ computes $t_0 = \mathrm{H}_\alpha(J \,\|\, K \,\|\, T_1 \,\|\, T_2)$ and $t_1 = \mathrm{H}_\beta(J \,\|\, K \,\|,\ T_1 \,\|\, T_2)$ and lets $V := T_2^{t_0} \cdot J^{t_1}$ ; Otherwise, $\mathcal{H}$ sets $J := \perp,\ K := \perp$ and $V := T_2$.

3) $\mathcal{H}$ computes $c' := \mathrm{H}_1(T_1 \,\|\, T_2 \,\|\, T_3 \,\|\, n_V \,\|\, bsn)$., and forwards $(V, c', m)$ to $\mathcal{M}$.

4) $\mathcal{M}$ picks a random $r_f \in \mathbb{Z}_p$ and computes $U := V^{r_f}$.

5) $\mathcal{M}$ chooses a random nonce $n_T \leftarrow \{1,0\}^\kappa$ for freshness and computes $c := \mathrm{H}_3(c' \,\|\, K \,\|\, U \,\|\, m \,\|\, n_T)$ and $s_f := r_f + c \cdot f$, then sends $(K, c, s_f)$ to $\mathcal{H}$.

6) $\mathcal{H}$ outputs the DAA signature $\sigma := (T_1, T_2, T_3, K,\ c, s_f)$ to $\mathcal{V}$.

## 5.4 The Verify Algorithm

This algorithm is run by a verifier $\mathcal{V}$. Intuitively the verifier checks that a signature provided proofs of knowledge of a discrete logarithm *f*, checks that it proves knowledge of a valid signing key issued by a given issuer on the same value of *f* and that this value of *f* is not on the list of rogue values. On input of a signature $\sigma$, a message *m*, two nonces $(n_V, n_T)$ a basename *bsn*, the issuer's public key *ipk*, and the rogue list RL (a list of revoked signer secret keys), the algorithm takes the following steps:

1) Verify that $T_1, T_2, T_3, K \in \mathbb{G}_1$ and $s_f \in \mathbb{Z}_p$.

2) For each revoked signer secret key $f' \in \mathrm{RL}$, if $T_1 = T_2^{f'}$ holds, return 0 (reject).

3) Verify that $e(T_2,\Omega)=e(T_3/T_1,g_2)$.

4) If $bsn\neq\perp$, set $J':=\mathrm{H}_2(bsn)$ and compute $t_0=\mathrm{H}_\alpha(J\,||\,K\,||\,T_1\,||\,T_2)$, $t_1=\mathrm{H}_\beta(J\,||\,K\,||\,T_1\,||\,T_2)$, $V':=T_2^{t_0}\cdot J'^{t_1}$ and $W':=T_1^{t_0}\cdot K^{t_1}$; Otherwise set $V':=T_2$ and $W':=T_1$. Computes $U':=V'^{s_f}\cdot W'^{-c}$ and verify that: $c=\mathrm{H}_3(\mathrm{H}_1(T_1\,||\,T_2\,||\,T_3\,||\,n_V\,||\,bsn)\,||\,K\,||\,U'\,||\,m\,||\,n_T)$.

If any of the above verification fails, return 0 (reject), otherwise, return 1(accept).

### 5.5 The Link Algorithm

This algorithm is run by a given verifier $\mathcal{V}$ who has a set of non-null basenames in order to determine if the pair of signatures was produced by the same TPM. Signatures can only be linked if they were produced by the same TPM and the signer wanted them to be able to be linked together. On input a tuple $((m_0,\sigma_0),(m_1,\sigma_1),bsn,ipk)$, the algorithm performs the following steps:

1) For each signature $\sigma_b$ where $b\in\{0,1\}$, run the verification algorithm. If either of two verification returns 0, output $\perp$ (invalid).

2) If $(J,K)\in\sigma_0$ are the same as $(J,K)\in\sigma_1$, output 1 (linked), otherwise output 0 (unlinked).

## 6 Security Proof and Performance

### 6.1 Security Proof

In this subsection, we will state the security results for our DAA scheme under the definitions of security notions in section 2.2. We argue that our DAA scheme is secure, i.e., correct, user-controlled anonymous and user-controlled traceable.

**Theorem 2.** *The DAA scheme specified in section 5 is correct.*

*Proof.* This theorem follows directly from the specification of the scheme.

**Theorem 3.** *Under the XDH assumption, our DAA scheme is user-controlled anonymous. More specifically, if there is an adversary $\mathcal{A}$ that succeeds with a non-negligible probability to break the user-controlled anonymity game, then there is a simulator $\mathcal{S}$ running in polynomial-time that solves the XDH problem with a non-negligible probability.*

*Proof.* In our DAA scheme, since there are two types of signatures depend on the basename is empty or not, we use the following two lemmas to prove this theorem.

**Lemma 1.** *If the basename is empty, our DAA scheme meets anonymity under the XDH assumption.*

*Proof.* Given a XDH problem $(u,v=u^x,w=u^y,z)$ as input where $u\in\mathbb{G}_1$, $x,y\in\mathbb{Z}_p$ and either $z=u^{xy}$ or $z$ is a random element in $\mathbb{G}_1$, $\mathcal{S}$ decides which $z$ was given by interacting with $\mathcal{A}$ as follows.

**Initialization.** $\mathcal{S}$ performs the Setup($1^\kappa$) algorithm to generate the public key and private key of the issuer, i.e., $(ipk, isk) := ((\mathbb{G}_1, \mathbb{G}_2, \mathbb{G}_T, p, e, g_1, g_2, \mathrm{H}_1, \mathrm{H}_2, \mathrm{H}_3, \mathrm{H}_\alpha, \mathrm{H}_\beta, \Omega), \gamma)$ and sends *ipk* and *isk* to $\mathcal{A}$.

To maintain consistency between queries made by $\mathcal{A}$, $\mathcal{S}$ keeps the lists: $\mathrm{L}_j$ and $\mathrm{L}_S$. Each item of $\mathrm{L}_j$ is (*ID*, *sk*, *sigk*), and each item of $\mathrm{L}_s$ is (*ID*, *m*, $\sigma$).

$\mathcal{O}_{\mathrm{Hash}}$: Let $q_h$ be the expected number of hash queries. If the query string has been queried, $\mathcal{S}$ returns the previously queried result to ensure consistency. Otherwise, $\mathcal{S}$ chooses a value uniformly at random from $\mathbb{Z}_p^*$ (the result of $\mathrm{H}_1$, $\mathrm{H}_3$).

$\mathcal{O}_{\mathrm{SndToS}}$: $\mathcal{A}$ requests for creating a new signer with *ID*. Let $q_j$ be the expected number of Join/Issue requests from $\mathcal{A}$. $\mathcal{S}$ chooses a random $i^* \leftarrow \{1, \ldots, q_j\}$. There are two cases for $\mathcal{S}$ to respond:

*Case* 1: If the query $i = i^*$, $\mathcal{S}$ lets $sigk = (v, u)$ and simulates $\mathcal{A}$'s view by using the black-box simulation technique of theorem 1. $\mathcal{S}$ stores $(ID^*, \perp, (u, v))$ in $\mathrm{L}_j$ where $ID^*$ denotes the identity of this signer, and adds $ID^* \rightarrow \mathrm{HS}$.

*Case* 2: If the query $i \neq i^*$, $\mathcal{S}$ chooses a random $f \leftarrow \mathbb{Z}_p^*$, runs the Join/Issue protocol as the signer by interacting with $\mathcal{A}$ as the issuer, and obtains $sigk = (g^{f/(f+\gamma)}, g^{1/(f+\gamma)})$. $\mathcal{S}$ stores $(ID, f, sigk)$ in $\mathrm{L}_j$ and adds $ID \rightarrow \mathrm{HS}$.

$\mathcal{O}_{\mathrm{Sig}}$: Given a signer's identity *ID*, a message *m* to be signed, a nonce $n_V$ from $\mathcal{A}$, $\mathcal{S}$ responds with a DAA signature $\sigma$ as follows:

*Case* 1: If the identity $ID \neq ID^*$, $\mathcal{S}$ finds the corresponding secret key *sk* and signing key *sigk* associated with *ID* in $\mathrm{L}_j$, runs the Sign protocol and outputs $\sigma$ to $\mathcal{A}$. Then $\mathcal{S}$ stores (*ID*, *m*, $\sigma$) to $\mathrm{L}_s$.

*Case* 2: If the identity $ID = ID^*$, $\mathcal{S}$ needs to forge a DAA signature as follows:

1) $\mathcal{S}$ selects a random $r \in \mathbb{Z}_p^*$, computes $T_1 := v^r = u^{x \cdot r}$, $T_2 := u^r$, $T_3 := v^r \cdot u^{\gamma \cdot r} = u^{r(x+\gamma)}$ and sets $V := T_2$, $W := T_1$.

2) $\mathcal{S}$ picks a nonce $n_M \leftarrow (0,1)^\kappa$ and $c$, $s_f \in_{\mathrm{R}} \mathbb{Z}_p$, then computes $U := V^{s_f} \cdot W^{-c}$.

3) $\mathcal{S}$ patches the oracle $\mathrm{H}_3$ by setting $\mathrm{H}_3(\mathrm{H}_1(T_1 \| T_2 \| T_3 \| n_V) \| U \| m \| n_M) = c$. If $\mathrm{H}_3(\mathrm{H}_1(T_1 \| T_2 \| T_3 \| n_V) \| U \| m \| n_M)$ has been queried before, $\mathcal{S}$ aborts and outputs $a' \in_{\mathrm{R}} \{0,1\}$.

4) $\mathcal{S}$ forwards the DAA signature $\sigma := (T_1, T_2, T_3, c, s_f, n_V, n_M)$ to $\mathcal{A}$. Then $\mathcal{S}$ stores ($ID^*$, *m*, $\sigma$) to $\mathrm{L}_S$.

$\mathcal{O}_{\mathrm{SIGK}}$: We assume that $\mathcal{A}$ has already made the $\mathcal{O}_{\mathrm{SndToS}}$ queries with the identity *ID*, then $\mathcal{S}$ responds with the signing key corresponding to *ID* in $\mathrm{L}_j$.

$\mathcal{O}_{\mathrm{SK}}$: If a query is for a signer $ID \neq ID^*$, then $\mathcal{S}$ responds with the signer secret key corresponding to *ID* in $\mathrm{L}_j$, removes *ID* from HS and adds *ID* in CS. Otherwise, $\mathcal{S}$ aborts and outputs $a' \in_{\mathrm{R}} \{0,1\}$.

$\mathcal{O}_{\mathrm{Ch}}$: $\mathcal{A}$ submits a message *m* and two identities $(ID_0, ID_1)$. If $ID^* \notin (ID_0, ID_1)$ or $(ID_0, ID_1) \notin \mathrm{HS}$, then $\mathcal{S}$ aborts and outputs $a' \in_{\mathrm{R}} \{0,1\}$. Otherwise, $\mathcal{S}$ picks $b \in \{0,1\}$ such that $ID_b = ID^*$, and generates a DAA signature $\sigma^*$ for *m* by performing the following steps:

1) $\mathcal{S}$ picks a random $r \in_R \mathbb{Z}_p$, computes $T_1 := z^r$, $T_2 := w^r$, $T_3 := z^r \cdot w^{\gamma \cdot r}$, and sets $V := T_2$, $W := T_1$;

2) The rest of the signing algorithm is the same as the Case 2 in the $\mathcal{O}_{\text{Sig}}$ oracle.

3) $\mathcal{S}$ sends the resulting $\sigma^*$ to $\mathcal{A}$.

**Output.** In the end, $\mathcal{A}$ outputs $b' \in \{0,1\}$ as the guess for $b$. If $b = b'$, then $\mathcal{S}$ outputs 1, which means that $z = u^{xy}$. Otherwise $\mathcal{S}$ outputs 0, which means that $z \in_R \mathbb{G}_1$.

Now, we evaluate the advantage of the guess of $\mathcal{S}$. Let $a \in \{0,1\}$ denote whether the input $z$ is a random element in $\mathbb{G}_1$ $(a=0)$ or $u^{xy}$ $(a=1)$. Let **abort** be the event that $\mathcal{S}$ aborts. Then, we have $\Pr[a = a' \mid \textbf{abort}] = 1/2$. We assume that $\mathcal{S}$ does not abort. If $a=0$, i.e., $z \in_R \mathbb{G}_1$, then the challenged signature has no information on $x$. Thus, $\Pr[a' = 0 \mid \neg\textbf{abort} \wedge a = 0] = 1/2$. If $a=1$, i.e., $z = u^{xy}$, then $\mathcal{S}$ perfectly simulates the real and thus $\mathcal{A}$ guesses correctly with the advantage ε. Therefore, we obtain $\Pr[a' = 1 \mid \neg\textbf{abort} \wedge a = 1] = 1/2 + \varepsilon$. Putting everything together, we obtain the advantage of $\mathcal{S}$'s guess as follows:

$$|\Pr[\mathcal{S}((u, v=u^x, w=u^y, z) \wedge (z = u^{x\cdot y})) = 0] - \Pr[\mathcal{S}((u, v=u^x, w=u^y, z) \wedge (z \in_R \mathbb{G}_1)) = 0]|$$
$$= |\Pr[a' = 0 \mid a = 1] - \Pr[a' = 0 \mid a = 0]|$$
$$= |1 - \Pr[a' = 1 \mid a = 1] - \Pr[a' = 0 \mid a = 0]|$$
$$= |1 - \Pr[\textbf{abort}]\Pr[a' = 1 \mid \textbf{abort} \wedge a = 1] - \Pr[\neg\textbf{abort}]\Pr[a' = 1 \mid \neg\textbf{abort} \wedge a = 1]$$
$$- \Pr[\textbf{abort}]\Pr[a' = 0 \mid \textbf{abort} \wedge a = 0] - \Pr[\neg\textbf{abort}]\Pr[a' = 0 \mid \neg\textbf{abort} \wedge a = 0]|$$
$$= |1 - \Pr[\textbf{abort}](1/2 + 1/2) - \Pr[\neg\textbf{abort}]((1/2 + \varepsilon) + 1/2)|$$
$$= \Pr[\neg\textbf{abort}]\varepsilon$$

$\Pr[\neg\textbf{abort}]$ denotes the probability that $\mathcal{S}$ does not abort. In the signing oracle query, $\mathcal{S}$ aborts only when the backpatch is failure. The probability that a specific signature causes the failure is at most $q_h / p^4$. In $\mathcal{O}_{\text{SK}}$, as $\mathcal{A}$ cannot corrupt all the signers, the probability that $\mathcal{S}$ does not abort is at least $(1 - 1/(q_j - 1))$. In the challenge oracle query, $\mathcal{S}$ does not abort in this case if $\mathcal{A}$ selects $ID^*$. Thus the probability that $\mathcal{S}$ does not abort in this case is $1/q_j$. To sum up, $\Pr[\neg\textbf{abort}] \geq (1 - q_h / p^4) \cdot (1 - 1/(q_j - 1)) \cdot 1/q_j$. Therefore, assuming $\mathcal{S}$ does not abort, it has probability at least $\varepsilon \cdot (1 - q_h / p^4) \cdot (1 - 1/(q_j - 1)) \cdot 1/q_j$ in solving the XDH problem.

**Lemma 2.** *If the basename is non-empty, our DAA scheme meets user-controlled unlinkability under the XDH assumption.*

*Proof.* The processes of the proof are similar to the above lemma 1. Given a XDH problem $(u, v = u^x, w = u^y, z)$ as input where $u \in \mathbb{G}_1$, $x, y \in \mathbb{Z}_p$ and either $z = u^{xy}$ or $z$ is a random element in $\mathbb{G}_1$, $\mathcal{S}$ decides which $z$ was given by interacting with $\mathcal{A}$ as follows.

**Initialization.** The step is the same as that of lemma 1. $\mathcal{S}$ runs the Setup($1^\kappa$) algorithm, sets $L_j$ and $L_S$ empty, and sends *ipk* and *isk* to $\mathcal{A}$.

$\mathcal{O}_{\text{Hash-2}}$: Let $q_h'$ be the expected number of unique $H_2$ queries. $\mathcal{S}$ chooses a random $i^* \leftarrow \{1, \ldots, q_h'\}$. If the basename *bsn* has been queried before, $\mathcal{S}$ returns the previously queried result on *bsn* to ensure consistency. Otherwise, if *bsn* is the $i^*$ unique query on $H_2$, $\mathcal{S}$ chooses a random $r \leftarrow \mathbb{Z}_p^*$ and sets $H_2(bsn) := w^r$. For rest of the queries, $\mathcal{S}$ chooses a random $r \leftarrow \mathbb{Z}_p^*$ and sets $H_2(bsn) := u^r$. We use $bsn^*$ to denote the $i^*$ unique query.

$\mathcal{O}_{\text{Hash}}$: Let $q_h$ be the expected number of hash queries of $H_1$ and $H_3$. If the query string *str* has been queried, $\mathcal{S}$ returns the previously queried result to ensure consistency. Otherwise, $\mathcal{S}$ chooses a random uniformly at random from $\mathbb{Z}_p^*$ (the result of $H_1, H_3$).

$\mathcal{O}_{\text{SndToS}}$: $\mathcal{A}$ requests for creating a new signer with *ID*. Let $q_j$ be the expected number of joining requests from $\mathcal{A}$. There are two cases for $\mathcal{S}$ to respond:

*Case* 1: If the query $i = i^*$, $\mathcal{S}$ lets $sigk = (D^s, D)$ where $D \in_R \mathbb{G}_1, s \in_R \mathbb{Z}_p^*$ and simulates $\mathcal{A}$'s view by using the black-box simulation technique of theorem 1. $\mathcal{S}$ stores $(ID^*, \perp, (D, D^s))$ in $L_j$ where $ID^*$ denotes the identity of this signer, and adds $ID^* \rightarrow \text{HS}$.

*Case* 2: If the query $i \neq i^*$, $\mathcal{S}$ chooses a random $f \leftarrow \mathbb{Z}_p^*$, runs the Join/Issue protocol as the signer by interacting with $\mathcal{A}$ as the issuer, and obtains $sigk = (g^{f/(f+\gamma)}, g^{1/(f+\gamma)})$. $\mathcal{S}$ stores $(ID, f, sigk)$ in $L_j$ and adds $ID \rightarrow \text{HS}$.

$\mathcal{O}_{\text{Sig}}$: Given a signer's identity *ID*, a message *m* to be signed, a nonce $n_V$ from $\mathcal{A}$, a basename *bsn*, $\mathcal{S}$ responds with a DAA signature $\sigma$ as follows:

*Case* 1: If the identity $ID \neq ID^*$, $\mathcal{S}$ finds the corresponding secret key *sk* and signing key *sigk* associated with *ID* in $L_j$, runs the Sign protocol and outputs $\sigma$ to $\mathcal{A}$. Then $\mathcal{S}$ stores (*ID*, *m*, $\sigma$, *bsn*) in $L_S$.

*Case* 2: If the identity $ID = ID^*$, $\mathcal{S}$ needs to forge a DAA signature as follows:

1) If $bsn = bsn^*$, $\mathcal{S}$ aborts and outputs $a' \in_R \{0,1\}$. Otherwise, $\mathcal{S}$ researches the log of $H_2$ queries and retrieves $r$ where $H_2(bsn) := u^r$. $\mathcal{S}$ sets $J := u^r$ and $K := v^r$.

2) $\mathcal{S}$ chooses a random $t \leftarrow \mathbb{Z}_p$, computes $T_1 := (D^s)^t$, $T_2 := D^t$, $T_3 := D^{t(s+\gamma)}$.

3) $\mathcal{S}$ computes $t_0 = H_\alpha(J \| K \| T_1 \| T_2)$ and $t_1 = H_\beta(J \| K \| T_1 \| T_2)$, and sets $V := T_2^{t_0} \cdot J^{t_1}, W := T_1^{t_0} \cdot K^{t_1}$.

4) $\mathcal{S}$ picks a nonce $n_M \leftarrow (0,1)^\kappa$ and $c, s_f \in_R \mathbb{Z}_p$, then computes $U := V^{s_f} \cdot W^{-c}$.

5) $\mathcal{S}$ patches the oracle $H_3$ by setting $H_3(H_1(T_1 \| T_2 \| T_3 \| n_V \| bsn) \| K \| U \| m \| n_M) = c$. If $H_3(H_1(T_1 \| T_2 \| T_3 \| n_V \| bsn) \| K \| U \| m \| n_M)$ has been queried before, $\mathcal{S}$ aborts and outputs $a' \in_R \{0,1\}$.

6) $\mathcal{S}$ forwards the signature $\sigma := (T_1, T_2, T_3, K, c, s_f, n_V, n_M)$ to $\mathcal{A}$. $\mathcal{S}$ stores ($ID^*$, *m*, $\sigma$, *bsn*) in $L_S$.

$\mathcal{O}_{\text{SIGK}}$: We assume that $\mathcal{A}$ has already made the $\mathcal{O}_{\text{SndToS}}$ queries with the identity *ID*, then $\mathcal{S}$ responds with the signing key corresponding to *ID* in $L_j$.

$\mathcal{O}_{\text{SK}}$: If a query is for a signer $ID \neq ID^*$, then $\mathcal{S}$ responds with the signer secret key corresponding to *ID* in $L_j$, removes *ID* from HS and adds *ID* in CS. Otherwise, $\mathcal{S}$ aborts and outputs $a' \in_R \{0,1\}$.

$\mathcal{O}_{\text{Ch}}$: $\mathcal{A}$ outputs a message *m*, a basename *bsn* and two identities $(ID_0, ID_1)$. If $bsn \neq bsn^*$ or $ID^* \notin (ID_0, ID_1)$ or $(ID_0, ID_1) \notin \text{HU}$, then $\mathcal{S}$ aborts and outputs $a' \in_R \{0,1\}$. Otherwise, $\mathcal{S}$ picks $b \in \{0,1\}$ such that $ID_b = ID^*$, and generates a DAA signature $\sigma^*$ for *m* by performing the following steps:

1) $\mathcal{S}$ searches the log of $\mathrm{H}_1$ queries and retrieves $r$ where $\mathrm{H}_2(bsn) := w^r$. $\mathcal{S}$ sets $J := w^r$ and $K := z^r$;

2) The rest of the signing algorithm is the same as the Case 2 in the $\mathcal{O}_{\mathrm{Sig}}$ oracle;

3) $\mathcal{S}$ sends the resulting to $\sigma^*$ $\mathcal{A}$.

**Output.** In the end, $\mathcal{A}$ outputs $b' \in \{0,1\}$ as the guess for *b*. If $b = b'$, then $\mathcal{S}$ outputs 1, which means that $z = u^{xy}$. Otherwise $\mathcal{S}$ outputs 0, which means that $z \in_R \mathbb{G}_1$.

The evaluation of advantage of the guess of $\mathcal{S}$ is the same as that of lemma 1. In the signing oracle query, $\mathcal{S}$ aborts when the backpatch is failure and $bsn = bsn^*$. The probability is at most $q_h / p^6 \cdot q_h'$. In $\mathcal{O}_{\mathrm{SK}}$, as $\mathcal{A}$ cannot corrupt all the signers, the probability that $\mathcal{S}$ does not abort is at least $(1 - 1/(q_j - 1))$. In the challenge oracle query, $\mathcal{S}$ does not abort in this case if $\mathcal{A}$ selects $ID^*$ and $bsn^*$. Thus the probability that $\mathcal{S}$ does not abort in this case is $1/q_j \cdot q_h'$. To sum up, $\Pr[\neg\mathbf{abort}] \geq (1 - q_h / p^6 \cdot q_h') \cdot (1 - 1/(q_j - 1)) \cdot 1/q_j \cdot q_h'$. Therefore, assuming $\mathcal{S}$ does not abort, it has probability at least $\varepsilon \cdot (1 - q_h / p^6 \cdot q_h') \cdot (1 - 1/(q_j - 1)) \cdot 1/q_j \cdot q_h'$ in solving the XDH problem.

**Theorem 4**. *Under the q-SDH assumption, our DAA scheme is user-controlled traceable. More specifically, if there is an adversary $\mathcal{A}$ that succeeds with a non-negligible probability to break the user-controlled traceability game, then there is a simulator $\mathcal{S}$ running in polynomial-time that solves the q-SDH problem with a non-negligible probability.*

*Proof.* In this proof, we show how to construct a simulator $\mathcal{S}$ that solves the $q$-SDH problem by interacting with $\mathcal{A}$ that succeeds with a non-negligible probability to break the user-controlled traceability game. We use a technique from Boneh and Boyen[28] that, given $(g_1^\gamma, g_1^{\gamma^2}, \ldots, g_1^{\gamma^q}, g_2^\gamma, par_{\mathrm{Bilinear}})$, one more SDH instance $(g_1^{1/(\gamma+x^*)},\ x^*)$ can be transformed into a solution to the $q$-SDH problem. We now describe how $\mathcal{S}$ interacts with $\mathcal{A}$ as follows:

**Initialization.** $\mathcal{S}$ is given the above $q$-SDH problem parameters, and generates the issuer public key as follows: Assuming that $\mathcal{A}$ will query the oracle $\mathcal{O}_{\mathrm{SndToI}}$ with $q$-1 distinct values $x_1, \ldots x_{q-1} \in \mathbb{Z}_p^*$, $X = \{x_i\}_{i=1,\ldots,q-1}$. $\mathcal{S}$ chooses $a, b, \theta \leftarrow \mathbb{Z}_p^*$ and computes $g_1' = g_1^{\theta \cdot f(\gamma)}$ where $f(\gamma) = b(\gamma + a) \cdot \prod_{i=1}^{q-1}(\gamma + x_i)$. $\mathcal{S}$ sets the issuer public key $ipk = (\mathbb{G}_1, \mathbb{G}_2, \mathbb{G}_T, p, e, g_1', g_2, \mathrm{H}_1, \mathrm{H}_2, \mathrm{H}_3, \mathrm{H}_\alpha, \mathrm{H}_\beta, g_2^\gamma)$ and sends *ipk* to $\mathcal{A}$.

$\mathcal{O}_{\mathrm{Hash}}$: If the query string has been queried, $\mathcal{S}$ returns the previously queried result to ensure consistency. Otherwise, $\mathcal{S}$ chooses a value uniformly at random from $\mathbb{Z}_p^*$ (the result of $\mathrm{H}_1$, $\mathrm{H}_3$) or $\mathbb{G}_1$ (the result of $\mathrm{H}_2$) or $\{0,1\}^L$ (the result of $\mathrm{H}_\alpha$, $\mathrm{H}_\beta$).

$\mathcal{O}_{\mathrm{AddU}}$: Given a new signer with *ID* from $\mathcal{A}$'s query. $\mathcal{S}$ can freely choose a value from the set *X* as the signer secret key *sk* and removes the selected value from the set *X*. $\mathcal{S}$ generates the signing key $sigk_i = (g_1^{x_i \cdot \theta \cdot f_i(\gamma)}, g_1^{\theta \cdot f_i(\gamma)}) = (g_1'^{x_i/(\gamma+x_i)}, g_1'^{1/(\gamma+x_i)})$ where $f_i(\gamma) = f(\gamma)/(\gamma + x_i) = \prod_{j=1, j\neq i}^{q}(\gamma + x_j)$, stores $(ID,\ x_i, sigk_i)$ in $\mathrm{L}_j$ and adds $ID \rightarrow \mathrm{HS}$. At one point, $\mathcal{S}$ selects one query and sets $sk = a$ and signing key $sigk = (g_1^{a \cdot b \cdot \theta \cdot f'(\gamma)}, g_1^{b \cdot \theta \cdot f'(\gamma)})$ where $f'(\gamma) = \prod_{i=1}^{q-1}(\gamma + x_i)$, stores $(ID^*, sk, sigk)$ in $\mathrm{L}_j$ and adds $ID^*$ to HS.

$\mathcal{O}_{\mathrm{SndToI}}$: $\mathcal{A}$ requests for creating a new signer with *ID* and $x_i \in X$. $\mathcal{S}$ runs the Join/Issue protocol as the issuer by interacting with $\mathcal{A}$ as the signer, and generates the signing key $sigk_i = (g_1^{x_i \cdot \theta \cdot f_i(\gamma)}, g_1^{\theta \cdot f_i(\gamma)})$ as before. $\mathcal{S}$ stores $(ID, x_i, sigk_i)$ in $\mathrm{L}_j$ and adds *ID* to CS.

$\mathcal{O}_{SK}$: If a query is for a signer with $ID$, then $\mathcal{S}$ responds with the signer secret key corresponding to $ID$ in $L_j$ and moves $ID$ from HS to CS.

**Output.** Finally, $\mathcal{A}$ outputs a signer with $ID$, a message $m$, a basename $bsn$ and a DAA signature $\sigma$. There are two cases as defined by the user-controlled-traceability in section 2.2:

*Case* 1: If $\sigma$ can be successfully verified, i.e., Verify$(ipk,m,\sigma,$ RL$,bsn)=1 \wedge ID \notin$ CS, $\mathcal{S}$ can rewind $\mathcal{A}$ to extract the underlying signer secret key $sk^*=x^*$ and signing key $sigk^*=(g_1^{\prime x/(\gamma+x)},\ g_1^{\prime 1/(\gamma+x)})$ by making use of the forking lemma[29].

a).If $x^* \notin \{x_i,a\}_{i=1,\dots,q-1} \wedge sigk^* \notin \{sigk_1,\dots,sigk_{q-1},sigk\}$ ,$\mathcal{S}$ can compute $g_1^{\prime 1/(\gamma+x^*)}=g_1^{\theta\cdot f(\gamma)/(\gamma+x^*)}=g_1^{b\cdot\theta\cdot(C/(\gamma+x^*)+u(\gamma))}$ where $u(\gamma)=\sum_{i=0}^{q-1}c_i\cdot\gamma^i$ for $c_0,\dots,c_{q-1}\in\mathbb{Z}_p$ and $C\in\mathbb{Z}_p$ is a constant. $\mathcal{S}$ generates a SDH instance as follows: $D=((g_1^{\prime 1/(\gamma+x)})^{1/b\cdot\theta}\cdot\prod_{i=0}^{q-1}(g_1^{\gamma^i})^{-c_i})^{1/C}=g_1^{1/(\gamma+x^*)}$.

b).If $x^* \notin \{x_i,a\}_{i=1,\dots,q-1} \wedge sigk^*=sigk$ ,i.e., $g^{\prime b}=g_1^{\prime 1/(\gamma+x^*)}$, $\mathcal{S}$ can use the same method as the case a) to generate a SDH instance $(g_1^{1/(\gamma+x^*)},x^*)$.

*Case* 2. If $bsn\neq\perp$, $\mathcal{A}$ wins in this case if there exists another signature $\sigma'$ for $m'$ by the same signer using the same basename $bsn$ that Link$(ipk,m,\sigma,m',\sigma',bsn)=0$. Since the same $bsn$ is used, $J=J'$. However, two signatures are unlinkable, thus $K\neq K'$. This means $\mathcal{A}$ managed to create different $sk$ and $sigk$ for the same signer. $\mathcal{S}$ can use the same method as *Case 1*-a) to extract a different $sigk$ or as *Case* 1-b) to extract an expected $sigk$, thus obtain an extra SDH pair. $\mathcal{S}$ can also solve the $q$-SDH problem in this case.

In either of the above two cases, $\mathcal{S}$ can solve the $q$-SDH problem with a non-negligible probability if $\mathcal{A}$ can wins the game with a non-negligible probability.

### 6.2 Performance

In this section, we compare our DAA scheme with the existing DAA schemes in the signature length and the computational cost. At the beginning of the performance comparison of each scheme, we need to define the security parameters of different DAA schemes [4, 14, 17, 20, 21, 31] at the 128-bit security level.

The security parameters are defined as follows: 1) Bilinear groups. Our scheme makes use of the efficient BN elliptic curve algorithm [30], where the length of prime $p$ is $l_p=255$bits at the 128-bit security level. According to this, the length of element in $\mathbb{G}_1$ is 256 bits, and in $\mathbb{G}_T$ is 3072 bits, and the resulting length of the hash function is $l_H=255$. 2) RSA groups. At the 128-bit security, $l_n=2048$ and $l_\rho=208$. The corresponding lengths of parameters in [4] are $l_e=368$, $l_{e'}=120$, $l_v=2536$ and $l_H=160$ respectively.

For the computational cost: 1) For the ECC-based DAA schemes, we denote the cost of single-exponentiation and multi-exponentiation in $\mathbb{G}_1,\mathbb{G}_2,\mathbb{G}_T$ as $G_i^m\,(i=1,2,T)$ respectively where for single-exponentiation $m=1$, otherwise, $m>1$. In additions, we let $G_{i(L)}$ denote the cost of an exponentiation in the group $\mathbb{G}_i$ with the size of the exponent being $L$. Using BN elliptic curve [15], the computational cost in $\mathbb{G}_T$ is more than 13 times than that in $\mathbb{G}_1$, and the computational cost in $\mathbb{G}_2$ is more than 3 times than that in $\mathbb{G}_1$. In addition, we denote exponentiation computation of single pairing as P, and let $\mathrm{P}^m$ denote the cost of a batch pairing verification of $m$ pairings, as described in [18, 32]. Obviously, the computational cost of pairing is much more than that in the groups. 2) For the RSA-based DAA schemes, as above, we denote the computation of single-exponentiation and multi-exponentiation in $\mathbb{G}_N, \mathbb{G}_\rho$ as $\mathrm{G}_i^m$ $(i = N, \rho)$ respectively. Note that the cost of the exponent computation in the group $\mathbb{G}_N$ is almost the same as that in the group $\mathbb{G}_T$, see [15]. Besides, we denote the number of the entries in the rogue list RL as $n$.

Note that the computational cost of Join/Issue protocol is not compared in this paper, due to that the number of the executed Join/Issue protocol is much less than that of the Sign protocol. From the table 1, we can see that our scheme has lower computational cost than the existing DAA schemes. In the signing phase, for the TPM, when linkability is not requested (i.e., $bsn = \perp$) our scheme needs to perform only one exponentiation and when linkability is requested (i.e., $bsn \neq \perp$) it needs to compute just two exponentiations. We let $1\mathrm{G}_1 / 2\mathrm{G}_1$ denote the cost of this computation; For the host, our scheme needs to compute only three exponentiations (unlinkability) or nearly four exponentitions (linkability) in Sign protocol. We use $3\mathrm{G}_1 / 3\mathrm{G}_1 + 1\mathrm{G}_{1(L)}^2$ ($L < l_p$) to denote the cost of this computation. And compared with other DAA schemes in the computational cost aspect of the verification algorithm, our scheme is also better, due to our scheme only needs one pairing equation.

At the length aspect of DAA signature, from the table 1 we can observe that the signature length in our scheme is the minimum. When it does not request linkability, the signature length is just 1278 bits, and when it requests linkability, the signature length is just 1534 bits.

**Table 1.** The Comparisons between our DAA scheme and other DAA schemes in Computational Cost and Signature Length

| DAA Scheme | Sign(TPM) | Sign(Host) | Verify(Verifier) | Sig.Length(bit) |
|---|---|---|---|---|
| BCC Scheme[4] | $3\mathrm{G}_\rho + 1\mathrm{G}_N^3$ | $1\mathrm{G}_\rho + 1\mathrm{G}_N + 1\mathrm{G}_N^2 + 2\mathrm{G}_N^3 + 1\mathrm{G}_N^4$ | $1\mathrm{G}_\rho^2 + 2\mathrm{G}_N^4 + 1\mathrm{G}_N^6 + n\mathrm{G}_\rho$ | 20555 |
| BCL Scheme[14] | $3\mathrm{G}_T$ | $3\mathrm{G}_1 + 1\mathrm{G}_T + 3\mathrm{P}$ | $1\mathrm{G}_T^2 + 2\mathrm{G}_T^3 + 5\mathrm{P} + (n+1)\mathrm{G}_T$ | 7674 |
| CPS Scheme[17] | $3\mathrm{G}_1$ | $4\mathrm{G}_1$ | $2\mathrm{G}_1^2 + 1\mathrm{P}^4 + n\mathrm{G}_1$ | 2046 |
| Chen Scheme [21] | $2\mathrm{G}_1 + 1\mathrm{G}_T$ | $1\mathrm{G}_1 + 1\mathrm{G}_T^3$ | $1\mathrm{G}_1^2 + 1\mathrm{G}_2^2 + 1\mathrm{G}_T^4 + 1\mathrm{P} + \mathrm{n}\mathrm{G}_1$ | 2043 |
| BL Scheme[20] | $3\mathrm{G}_1$ | $1\mathrm{G}_1 + 1\mathrm{G}_1^2 + 1\mathrm{G}_T + 1\mathrm{P}$ | $1\mathrm{G}_1^2 + 1\mathrm{G}_2^2 + 1\mathrm{G}_T^4 + 1\mathrm{P} + n\mathrm{G}_1$ | 2043 |
| BCL Scheme[31] | $1\mathrm{G}_1 / 2\mathrm{G}_1$ | $4\mathrm{G}_1 / 4\mathrm{G}_1 + \mathrm{G}_{1(L)}^2$ | $1\mathrm{G}_1^2 + 1\mathrm{P}^4 + n\mathrm{G}_1$ | 1534/1790 |
| Our Scheme | $1\mathrm{G}_1 / 2\mathrm{G}_1$ | $3\mathrm{G}_1 / 3\mathrm{G}_1 + \mathrm{G}_{1(L)}^2$ | $1\mathrm{G}_1^2 + 1\mathrm{P}^2 + n\mathrm{G}_1$ | 1278/1534 |

## 7 Conclusion

In this paper, we have introduced the security model that contains two security notions for DAA, namely user-controlled anonymity and user-controlled traceability. And then by making use of 2PC protocol and complexity assumptions, we have also presented a new approach to construct a DAA scheme, which requires lower computational cost and less length of signature than other existing DAA schemes. Finally, we have proved the security of the new DAA scheme under the security notions.

## References


1. TCG. TPM Main Part 1, Design Principles Specification 1.2 (2003), https://www.trustedcomputinggroup.org/
2. TCG. Trusted Platform Module specification (TPM), version 1.2 (2003)
3. TCG. Trusted Platform Module specification (TPM), version 1.1 (2001)
4. Brickell, E., Camenisch, J., Chen, L.: Direct anonymous attestation. In: Proceedings of the 11th ACM Conference on Computer and Communications Security (CCS 2004), pp. 132–145. ACM Press, New York (2004)
5. TCG. TCG MPWG Mobile Trusted Module specification, version 1.0, Revision 1 (2007)
6. Bellare, M., Micciancio, D., Warinschi, B.: Foundations of group signatures: formal definitions, simplified requirements, and a construction based on general assumptions. In: Biham, E. (ed.) EUROCRYPT 2003. LNCS, vol. 2656, pp. 614–629. Springer, Heidelberg (2003)
7. Durahim, A., Savas, E.: A2-MAKE: An efficient anonymous and accountable mutual authentication and key agreement protocol for WMNs. Ad Hoc Networks 9, 1202–1220 (2011)
8. Bichsel, P., Camenisch, J., Groß, T., Shoup, V.: Anonymous credentials on a standard Java Card. In: Proceedings of the 16th ACM Conference on Computer and Communications Security (CCS 2009), pp. 600–610. ACM Press, New York (2009)
9. Bella, G., Giustolisi, R., Riccobene, S.: Enforcing privacy in e-commerce by balancing anonymity and trust. Computers & Security 30(8), 705–718 (2011)
10. Gummadi, R., Balakrishnan, H., Maniatis, P., Ratnasamy, S.: Not-a-Bot (NAB): Improving Service Availability in the Face of Botnet Attacks. In: Proceedings of the 6th USENIX Symposium on Networked Systems Design and Implementation, pp. 307–320. USENIX Association, Berkeley (2009)
11. Smyth, B., Ryan, M., Chen, L.: Formal analysis of anonymity in ECC-based Direct Anonymous Attestation schemes. In: Barthe, G., Datta, A., Etalle, S. (eds.) FAST 2011. LNCS, vol. 7140, pp. 245–262. Springer, Heidelberg (2012)
12. Greveler, U., Justus, B., Loehr, D.: Direct Anonymous Attestation: Enhancing Cloud Service User Privacy. In: Meersman, R., et al. (eds.) OTM 2011, Part II. LNCS, vol. 7045, pp. 577–587. Springer, Heidelberg (2011)
13. Dietrich, K., Winter, J., Luzhnica, G., Podesser, S.: Implementation Aspects of Anonymous Credential Systems for Mobile Trusted Platforms. In: De Decker, B., Lapon, J., Naessens, V., Uhl, A. (eds.) CMS 2011. LNCS, vol. 7025, pp. 45–58. Springer, Heidelberg (2011)
14. Brickell, E., Chen, L., Li, J.: A new direct anonymous attestation scheme from bilinear maps. In: Lipp, P., Sadeghi, A.-R., Koch, K.-M. (eds.) Trust 2008. LNCS, vol. 4968, pp. 166–178. Springer, Heidelberg (2008)
15. Chen, L., Morrissey, P., Smart, N.P.: Pairings in trusted computing. In: Galbraith, S.D., Paterson, K.G. (eds.) Pairing 2008. LNCS, vol. 5209, pp. 1–17. Springer, Heidelberg (2008)
16. Chen, L., Morrissey, P., Smart, N.: DAA: Fixing the pairing based protocols. Cryptology ePrint Archive. Report 2009/198 (2009), http://eprint.iacr.org/2009/198
17. Chen, L., Page, D., Smart, N.P.: On the design and implementation of an efficient DAA scheme. In: Gollmann, D., Lanet, J.-L., Iguchi-Cartigny, J. (eds.) CARDIS 2010. LNCS, vol. 6035, pp. 223–237. Springer, Heidelberg (2010)

18. Chen, L.: A DAA scheme using batch proof and verification. In: Acquisti, A., Smith, S.W., Sadeghi, A.-R. (eds.) TRUST 2010. LNCS, vol. 6101, pp. 166–180. Springer, Heidelberg (2010)
19. Chen, X., Feng, D.: Direct Anonymous Attestation Based on Bilinear maps. Chinese Journal of Software, China 21(8), 2070–2078 (2010)
20. Brickell, E., Li, J.: A pairing-based DAA scheme furhter reducing TPM resources. In: Acquisti, A., Smith, S.W., Sadeghi, A.-R. (eds.) TRUST 2010. LNCS, vol. 6101, pp. 181–195. Springer, Heidelberg (2010)
21. Chen, L.: A DAA scheme requiring less TPM resources. In: Bao, F., Yung, M., Lin, D., Jing, J. (eds.) Inscrypt 2009. LNCS, vol. 6151, pp. 350–365. Springer, Heidelberg (2010)
22. Brickell, E., Chen, L., Li, J.: Simplified security notions for direct anonymous attestation and a concrete scheme from pairings. Int. Journal of Information Security 8, 315–330 (2009)
23. Paillier, P.: Public-key cryptosystems based on composite residuosity classes. In: Stern, J. (ed.) EUROCRYPT 1999. LNCS, vol. 1592, pp. 223–238. Springer, Heidelberg (1999)
24. Camenisch, J., Shoup, V.: Practical Verifiable Encryption and Decryption of Discrete Logarithms. In: Boneh, D. (ed.) CRYPTO 2003. LNCS, vol. 2729, pp. 126–144. Springer, Heidelberg (2003)
25. Boneh, D., Boyen, X., Shacham, H.: Short group signatures. In: Franklin, M. (ed.) CRYPTO 2004. LNCS, vol. 3152, pp. 41–55. Springer, Heidelberg (2004)
26. Galbraith, S., Paterson, K., Smart, N.: Pairings for cryptographers. Discrete Applied Mathematics 156(16), 3113–3121 (2008)
27. Chase, M.: Efficient Non-Interactive Zero-Knowledge Proofs for Privacy Applications. PhD Thesis, Brown University, pp. 57-67 (2008)
28. Boneh, D., Boyen, X.: Short signatures without random oracles. In: Cachin, C., Camenisch, J.L. (eds.) EUROCRYPT 2004. LNCS, vol. 3027, pp. 56–73. Springer, Heidelberg (2004)
29. Pointcheval, D., Stern, J.: Security arguments for digital signatures and blind signatures. Journal of Cryptology 13(3), 361–396 (2000)
30. Barreto, P.S.L.M., Naehrig, M.: Pairing- friendly elliptic curves of prime order. In: Preneel, B., Tavares, S. (eds.) SAC 2005. LNCS, vol. 3897, pp. 319–331. Springer, Heidelberg (2006)
31. Brickell, E., Chen, L., Li, J.: A (Corrected) DAA Scheme Using Batch Proof and Verification. In: Chen, L., Yung, M., Zhu, L. (eds.) INTRUST 2011. LNCS, vol. 7222, pp. 304–337. Springer, Heidelberg (2012)

# Towards Internet Innovation: Software Defined Data Plane

Gaofeng Lv*, Zhigang Sun, Yijiao Chen, and Tao Li

School of Computer, National University of Defense Technology,
Changsha, Hunan, China 410073
{lvever,sunzhigang,yijiaochen,taoli}@nudt.edu.cn

**Abstract.** In order to support new network architectures, Openflow implements flows forwarding based on multiple tables via pipelines, which increases the difficulty of the implementation. With the advent of multi-core CPU, a software defined data plane, LabelCast, is proposed, which characterizes the ability of forwarding operations and processing services through the Label table and Cast table. Forwarding layer lookups based on fixed-length labels and schedules packets processing, including light-semantics action instructions of general process, which is easy to be realized and is denoted by the Label table, and protocol semantics or status-related service of special process, which could be enriched via opening resources within network devices and is arranged by the Cast table. LabelCast supplies a reliable and programmable data plane, and could load multiple network architectures, so as to facilitate Internet innovation.

**Keywords:** Processing in networks, network experiments, Labelcast.

## 1 Introduction

To promote network evolution, Stanford proposed Openflow protocol[1]. Openflow abstracts data-plane of networks, makes the control-plane programmable, and supports isolating experiment traffic from production traffic, which offers a powerful support for a new network protocol to be experimented in a real network environment. Openflow makes a compromise between academia and industry by abstracting the data-plane and opening the interface, so that it allows researchers to develop new protocols based on the unified interface. Openflow has been the de facto abstract layer of data-plane in the SDN (Software Defined Network)[2], and being applied to the WAN, like traffic optimization in Google's global data center and infrastructure construction of Internet2 etc.

Satisfying the vendor's demand for device closure and user's demand for isolation of packets promoted Openflow, which also placed restrictions on the Openflow's support for new network architectures. There are some network architectures which cannot run well based on the Openflow, especially which needs

* The work is supported by 863 project(2013AA013505) and NSFC project(61202485).

J. Su et al. (Eds.): ICoC 2013, CCIS 401, pp. 236–247, 2013.

to deal with packets one by one, like NDN[3] etc. Openflow provides two ways to deal with packets one by one. One way is sending packets to Openflow controller, which poses a great burden on Openflow controller and is also contrary to the architecture of separation between data-plane and control-plane. The other way is sending packets to intelligent data processing platform, which directly connects with Openflow switches. Due to the need of vendors for device closure emphasized by Openflow, it just provides the data-plane abstract but hides the implementation details in data-plane. It is not conducive for researchers to extend Openflow dataplane function to support per-packet processing.

In order to support the packet-by-packet processing of network architectures such as NDN and etc., researchers use programmable hardware to extend the network forwarding-plane like NetFGPA[4], NetMagic and etc., build a software virtual router[5][6] based on general multicore processors[7][8] and deploy Middleboxes[9][10] in networks so as to enable more functions of in-network processing. Processing in networks provides an efficient implementation of innovative network functions, but the lack of a unified abstraction and control interface is not conducive to the development and deployment of new network protocols. We further enhance the scalability of the network equipment to support new network architectures by lending the vendor's need toward the device closure of the resources, which lets device vendors provide intelligence processing resources and development interface based on the network equipment resources. At the same time, the isolation of experimental traffic and production traffic in Openflow is a kind of scheduling based on packet options, which is unable to meet the demand of dealing with special message options in new network architectures. We directly distinguish network architectures by labels, which simplify packets classification and forwarding. Inspired by opening resources and unified labels, we propose a software defined data-plane named LabelCast. LabelCast identify network architectures with labels at the protocol level, while only making abstraction for the ability of computing, storage and forwarding of network devices, so that could support new network architectures.

In Labelcast, by dividing the data plane of the network into fast forwarding plane and intelligence service plane based on semantics of processing in networks, and Label tables and Cast tables are proposed to abstract forwarding resources and the computation and storage resources separately. LabeCast has the following advantage: (1) Simplifying hardware implementation of forwarding lookup based on fixed-length labels, (2) Enabling multiple user-defined applications running concurrently controlled by multiple Cast tables, (3) Achieving the application isolation leveraging the extensible resource container, (4) Loading multiple network architectures via LabelCast abstraction layer.

The structure of the paper is showed as follows, section 2 introduces the evolution of network architectures, section 3 proposes a software defined data plane, LabelCast, and the key mechanisms, such as the mapping and allocation of labels, service atoms, section 4 provides the application of LabelCast, section 5 is the testing and analysis of the performance of the prototype, and the last section is the conclusion of the work.

## 2 Related Works

Openflow utilizes the three tuple <Matching, Instructions, Statistics> to denote the abstraction layer of network forwarding. In the evolution progress, the matching field extended from 12-tuples of Ethernet, IP and TCP in Openflow specification 1.0 to 15-tuples in Openflow specification 1.1, and from fixed length rules to the variable-length matching field based on TLV <Type, Length, Values> in Openflow specification 1.2. The complexity processing of matching implemented in Openflow switches try to support new network architectures. However, just enlarging the matching field would increase the difficulty of the implementation and could not satisfy unknown network protocols. The processing of Openflow extends from one stage process to multiple stage pipelines in order to solve the combination blast of multiple tables, which would increase the complexity of mapping the special processing of the content-centric or service-centric network architectures to the multiple pipelines of Openflow. The functions of Openflow switches are continuing to develop, but they are limited to the processing of packet basic options, such as modification and replacement, and still could not support the requirements of new network applications, such as data cache.

To solve the complexity of the implementation of Openflow multi-stage flow tables, based on current router functions of forwarding and controlling, Openflow+[15] made an extension of Openflow on the aspects of the interface between the forwarding and controlling layers and flow tables, and then proposed the presentation of openflow rules based on TLV and the mechanism of the mapping Openflow flow tables to ACL and FIB of routers. The scheme provides a simple method to implement Openflow on commodity routers, simplify the implementation of Openflow and enhance the deployment of Openflow.

Juniper enlarges the forwarding layer by customization services, and then proposes the service layer[16]. By integrating computing and storing resource with network elements Juniper service layer provides the platform and SDK for services from the third-party, which could support multiple services of network managements and has good scalability. Due to the capability of SDK Juniper service layer runs services mainly including network management, which could not support packets processing in depth in the key data path. On the other hand, Juniper service layer only admits authorized partners developing new network applications on their platform, which lacks of openness.

Middleboxes[11] provide a novel method of patching to add new functions to Internet, which could implement general packet forwarding and advanced packet processing, such as NAT, firewall, proxy, IDS, etc., in order to enhance the ability and security of Internet. On the other hand, the widespread deployment of middleboxes and other network appliances has primarily resulted in some challenges and criticism due to poor interaction with higher layer protocols.

Middleboxes also brought a lot of problems, which utilize the method of redirecting or DNS mechanism for targeting network traffic to Middleboxes. The method would increase the complexity of the network control, and add packet processing delay. On the other hand, Middleboxes are short of scalability, which could not meet the requirements of high-performance flows processing, and lacks of programmability, which could not support the new network protocol experiments, only act as the rapid deployment of mature network protocols.

Future Internet, such as XIA[12], NDN[13], Nebula[14], proposes different forwarding layer of networks. NDN abstracts the forwarding layer by the content store table(CS), the pending interest table(PIT) and the forwarding information table(FIB). CS provides the index of data storing, PIT records the pending interest packets to eliminate redundancy requests and the interest packets are forwarded according to FIB. Forwarding layer of NDN implements packets forwarding and supports data storing, which could not be implemented on Openflow switches. XIA adopts directed-graph to identify the path between the source and destination nodes, in which all elements are identifiers of entities (e.g., addresses, identifiers of services, identifiers of contents). The target contents could be retrieved at intermediate nodes of XIA when the present of the fallback path in the directed graph, which could support the end-to-end and non-end-to-end communication model and could not be realized in Openflow.

## 3 LabelCast: Software Defined Data Plane

With the development of microprocessors, the performance of CPU upgrades continuously and could implement more and more complexity processing in networks. At the same time, in the evolution of next generation architectures some new architectures are proposed, which requires high performance and more flexibility of network elements. To resolve the problem and extend the functions of forwarding layer of network platforms, a software defined data plane, *LabelCast*, is proposed based on network devices with multi-core processor.

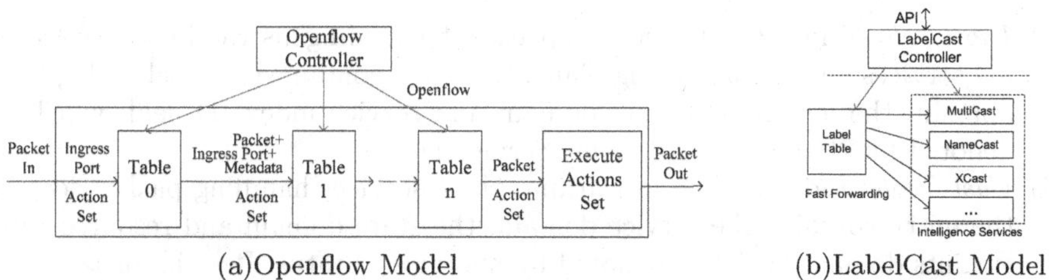


(a)Openflow Model (b)LabelCast Model

**Fig. 1.** Openflow vs. LabelCast

In LabelCast, services are running on the computing and storing resources within network elements to implement protocol-related special processing in data path, which could be added easily according to the requirements of new network experiments compared with mapping the special processing of new network protocols to multiple pipelines of Openflow, as illustrated in Fig.1(a), and could run concurrently via utilizing the parallelism of multicore processors, as illustrated in Fig.1(b). Logical central controller of Labelcast provides the running platform for network application controllers, maps the network protocols to labels and provides unified configuration interface of forwarding layer to support the designing and testing of new network experiments in future.

### 3.1 Labelcast Scheme

The abstraction layer of LabelCast provides five tuples <*Label, Instructions, Service, Status, Restrictions*> as a unified and simple management interface for LabelCast controller, which abstracts the forwarding operations and processing services of the forwarding layer. In rules the label field includes label value and options, which is the complementary of labels and indicates the method or precondition of packet processing. The instruction field indicates forwarding operations(e.g., lookup and modification of the base options of packets). The service field indicates the functions of processing packets including the sequence of service atoms(e.g., matching and modification of any packet fields, storing and loading data).

a) *Instructions*: Modifying basic options of packets, and controlling packet in/out( forwarding operations) in the fast forwarding plane.
b) *Services*: The network protocols semantics or status-related special processing functions in the intelligence service plane based on the computing and storage resources within network devices. Services abstract the characterizes of computing and storage resources and supply the development library for users to design applications, which is denoted by *atomService*, *atomService* = app (compResource, storeResource, pkt).

LabelCast utilizes *Label table* and *Cast table* to describe and manage packet forwarding operations and services of packets processing based on the computing and storage resources within network nodes.

c) *Label Table*: Indicates the index of packets forwarding instructions or processing services on the forwarding plane, the entry contains the label and option domain, the action command domain and service index ID field, which is denoted by <Labels, Instructions, ServiceID>.
d) *Cast Table*: Indicates the forwarding plane services handling packet deeply, the entry contains the service domain, the state domain and resource constraints domain, which is denoted by <Services, Status, Restrictions>.

After forwarding operations based on the Label table, packets could be redirected to the target Cast table to be further processed based on protocols and status of networks. Unlike Openflow model of pipeline, Labelcast adopts parallel processing model controlled by multiple Cast tables, which could utilize the ability of multi-core processors and exhibit the simplicity of run-to-completion model. Labelcast controller manipulates the behavior of forwarding layer by configuring the label table and the cast table with the rules.

In the rules, the label field is described by OLV <Offset, Length, Value>. The offset field is the offset of the fixed-length labels in packets. OLV could increase the flexibility of rules exchanged between the Labelcast controller and the forwarding layer of network devices.

### 3.2 Label Table

The label table includes labels, instructions and services. The matching field is labels of packets, and the instruction field indicates packets forwarding actions, and the service field indicates the index of the method to process packets.

Labels are allocated by the LabelCast controller. The first packet of flows are sent to LabelCast controller due to missing against the Label table. Labelcast controller analyzes the packet and dispatches it to the target network application, which registers to process the protocol type of the packet. The network application allocates the label from the subspace of labels and assigns the label to the flow, and make the process policy for the flow. Based on the label and the policy the Labelcast controller generates rules of Label table, and notify the rules to the upstream and downstream nodes, as illustrated in Fig.2. At the same time, the Labelcast controller notify the label to the source node of the flow. After the configuration, the host sends the following packets of the flow with the label, which are marked by the Labelcast adapter of hosts.

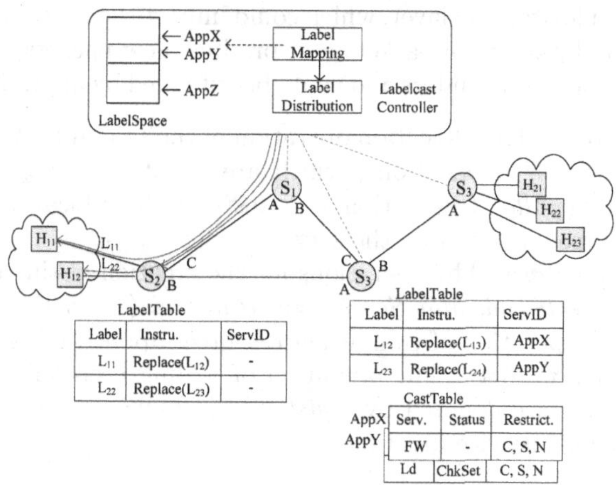


**Fig. 2.** Label Allocation and Distribution

In the forwarding layer lookup of the fixed-length labels of packets against the label table gets the method of packet processing, such as action instructions of light semantics or pointing to service atoms. The forwarding plane packet processing is usually implemented by multi-stage processing, including simple packet option modifications, such as TTL minus 1, look-up and output, as well as label replacement. Multi-stage processing are decomposed into the flow processing in the coarse-grained, firstly light semantics-related modifying options and matching against rules, then the semantics-related packet processing, and finally the light semantic output control. In Labelcast, modifying basic options and output control of packet forwarding are denoted by instructions and implemented by forwarding hardware, intermediate stage of packet processing as a network service based on the computing and storage resources. The instruction is constituted by a number of basic actions, such as output and drop action, which implement stateless packet forwarding operations.

### 3.3 Cast Table

Services are the sequence of service atoms and are scheduled by the Cast table. Labelcast could extend the service based on the resource of computing and storage. With the repaid increase of processors performance and memory capacity, network nodes has a strong ability of computing and storing in addition to the general forwarding hardware, which could provide the running platform for service to implement network protocol semantics and status-related services of packets processing in depth in the key data path.

Service atoms are implemented through application programs running on the platform, and provide advance functions related to network protocols, such as modification or replacement of any packet fields, forwarding based on rules and storing and loading of data. On the other hand, service atoms could modify the content of rules in forwarding layer, which could impact the process of subsequent packets, and could assimilate packets and produce new packets. Service atoms are developed by network vendors and could be extended by upgrading programs.

a) *Buffer primitives*: The allocation operation of the shared buffer or dedicated buffer memory for applications, which are denoted by *bufferAlloc*, *atomService* = *bufferAlloc* (restrictions) to abstract the allocation operation of storage resources required by the service applications.
b) *Threading primitives*: The operations for the creation of threads, which are denoted by *createThd*, *atomService* = *createThd* (restrictions) to abstract the allocation operation of computing resources applied by services.
c) *Registeration primitives*: The operation of adding user-defined function to a thread, which are denoted by *registerFun*, *atomService* = *registerFun* to dynamically load service functions.

Packets process involving a variety of services, for example, IP over MPLS process includes the options-specific modification of packets, in stack and out stack operations of labels, and the output control operations. Multiple service primitive perform in order, which constitutes a processing service, and pass the intermediate processing results through Metadata, which recorded in the state field of the Cast table entries, to implement more complex processing in networks.

Service atoms are application programs based on the computing and storage resources within network elements and implement protocol-related packet processing in depth on the key data path. Service atoms could be upgraded to implement new services and to support new network protocol-related packet processing, which could avoid the complex upgrade of hardware of forwarding layer and increase the flexibility of Labelcast. At the same time, network researchers could design new services of packet processing through reconfiguring the sequence of service and developing new service atoms, which could support new network architectures, based on opening resources within network devices.

### 3.4 LabelCast Processing

The Labelcast rules of five tuples include the restriction field of resources, which indicates the resources that network applications could use. Each LabelCast node allocates computing resource, storage and network bandwidth to network applications based on the LabelCast rules issued by LabelCast controller, which realize the resources sharing between network experiments. LabelCast nodes adopt eXtensible Linux Container to manage resources and allocate computing time, storage size and network bandwidth to the container based on the restriction field of rules, which provides the dedicated resources for network applications.

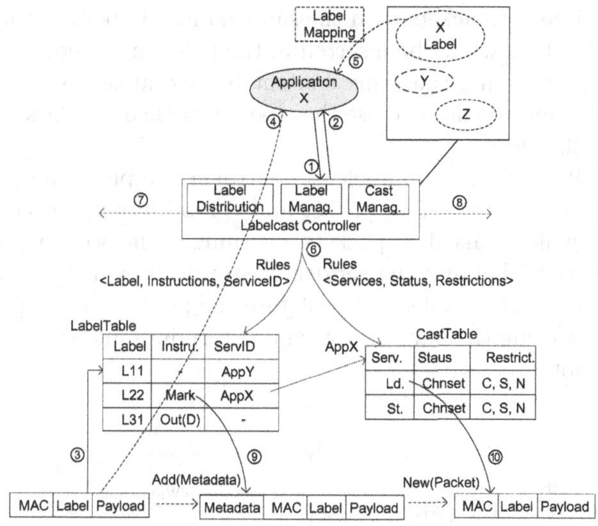


**Fig. 3.** Processing Model of Labelcast

The network application registers the network protocol of packets to the Labelcast controller firstly, and the Labelcast controller allocates the subspace of the label space to the application, as illustrated in Fig.3. When packets arrived at the Labelcast node, the Label table are lookup against the label in Labelcast options of packets. The first packet of flows with default label could be sent to the Labelcast controller due to unmatching against the Label table. The Labelcast controller dispatched the packet to the network application, which register the network protocol type. The network application allocates the label from the subspace and assigns the label to the flow, and make the process policy for the flow. Based on the label and the policy the Labelcast controller generates rules and configure the Label table and Cast table, and then notify the rules to the upstream and downstream nodes. At the same time, the Labelcast controller notify the label to the source node of the flow. After the configuration, the host send the following packets of the flow with the label, which are marked by the

Labelcast adapter of hosts. The following packets match the Label table and are modified according to the instructions, and then are forwarded to the Cast table and are processed by the target service.

## 4 NDN Based on Labelcast

We design NDN based on Labelcast, which demonstrate that processing in networks could be developed based on the software defined data plane efficiently.

For NDN, the prefixes of structural names are mapped to the fixed length label, so the interest packets for different chunks of the same content are assigned the same label, and are processed by the same method, which implements the aggregation of interest packets with the same names. Labelcast controller notify hosts the label, which would be inserted in the following interest packets for the content. Hosts requesting the same content behave alike, so they are assigned the same label, which could increase the characteristic of the flow and utilize the cache of data efficiently.

NDN controller running on Labelcast controller computes the path of interest packets, for simple, ingress data packet and egress interest packet are assigned the same label, which make data packets returning as the original path. Labelcast controller uses the label and the service of storing provided by the forwarding plane to configure Label table, and configure the policy of storage, which determines whether storing the data or not, and determines interest packet accessing data cache or not.

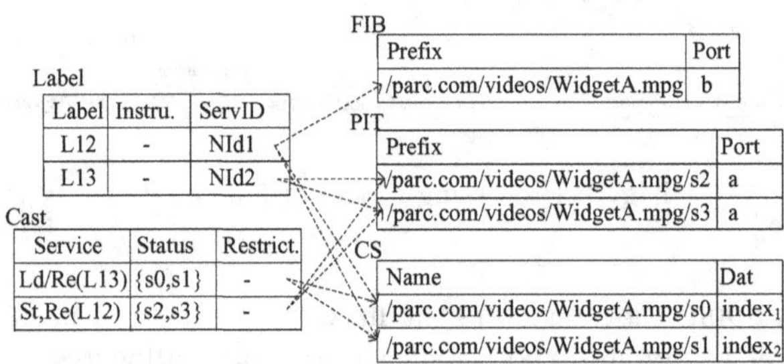


**Fig. 4.** Rules mapping between Labelcast and NDN

In NDN network, interest packets are forwarded based on FIB, while data packets are forwarded by PIT, which is generated according to the ingress port of interest packets. The lookup in NDN is longest prefixes matching, the publisher registers the name of content, and maintains the content on source nodes. In LabelCast, when interest packets arrive, the result of lookup based on the fixed-length labels indicates actions instructions of the general processing of the base options or services to process packets according to the name. Services update the status of storing by adding chunk number to the member set of labels and ports, which is implemented by Bloomfilter[17]. When data packets arrive, services modify labels, choose the output port, and delete the chunk number from the member set of labels and ports. The Label table and the Cast table implement the forwarding of interest packets and the generation of data packets together, which correspond the functions of PIT and CS in NDN, as illustrated in Fig.4.

## 5 Prototype of LabelCast

### 5.1 Implementation of the Prototype

Based on the general-purpose multi-core processor FT1000 and Network Processing Engine, NPE, we implement a prototype system to support LabelCast. The Label table is implemented in NPE to schedule packet forwarding operations and packet output control instructions in data plane. While taking the advantage of the computing and storage resources within FT1000 connected through the system bus PCI-E, we design the Cast table to implement a protocol and status related packet processing services.

In the prototype system, the eXtended Linux container, XLC, is designed to implement the virtualization and allocation of computing and storage resources, which simplify the development of user-defined services. Based on a scalable resource container, researchers could design and implement the custom packet forwarding and processing services, and in the development of services the application could call the system components and libraries provided by the Labelcast prototype system to accelerate applications development.

### 5.2 PacketDirect IO Performance

Labelcast data plane provides the basic operations of packet forwarding and services of packets processing. Basic forwarding operations in data plane are implemented in NPE, to provide the light semantics actions of general packet processing, including look-up table, modifying the basic packet options and output control. Packets processing are implemented by the services running on FT1000 being tightly coupled with the NPE, to implement network protocol semantics or the state-related deep packet processing services in data path, such as the replacement of specific fields of packets, packets caching and the calculation of route based on the matrix of the network layer reaching information. Therefore, in the prototype system the system bus between NPE and FT1000 becomes the key to improve the system performance.

In the design and implementation of the prototype system, an efficient PacketDirect mechanism was designed and implemented to improve system throughput of the transport mechanism between NPE and FT1000. In experiments network tester transmitting packets to NPE via two 10Gbps ports, testing the PacketDirect IO performance of the prototype in the case of different number of threads and packets size, the results are shown in Fig.5. With the number of forwarding threads increasing, the performance of processing has a certain upgrade under different packets size; 1 thread implements line-rate forwarding of

1024-byte packets, 3 threads arrive at the line-rate forwarding of 512 bytes packets, 4 threads reach the highest forwarding rate, the maximum bandwidth of the tester's ports, 20Gbps, for 256 bytes packets. 64 bytes packets forwarding rate is relatively high, because in the case of the same internal packet buffer size, the number of cached small packets is relatively high. For the system throughput, under the same number of threads the larger packet size is, the higher the throughput is, for the system throughput is proportional to the length of the packet under the same packet forwarding rate. For the packet size of 1024 bytes single-thread could achieve the maximum rate of the tester, and for other packets sizes as the increasing of the number of threads (processing power), the system throughput increases. The results show that the PacketDirect mechanism of the prototype meets the performance requirements of the system throughput.

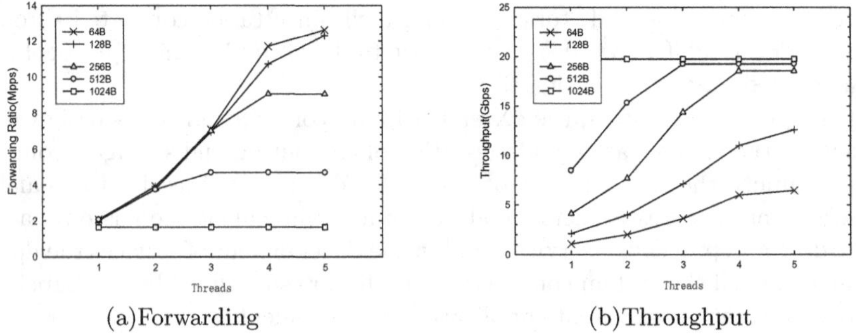


(a)Forwarding (b)Throughput

**Fig. 5.** PacketDirect IO Performance of Prototype

## 6 Conclusion

Labelcast provides and abstracts computing and storing resource within network devices for researches, and support running user-defined service based on extensible resource container, which provides a reliable and programmable data plane and support new network architectures. By dividing the data plane of the network into fast forwarding plane and intelligence service plane based on semantics of processing in networks, Label tables and Cast tables are proposed to abstract forwarding resources and the computation and storage resources separately. Action instructions based on fixed-length labels in Labelcast is easily to be implemented in hardware and service atoms of special processing could be dynamically extended compared with Openflow. NDN are designed on the NPE platform with Labelcast model, which support a large scale of parallel requests on the same content and packet by packet processing. The implementation of the prototype promotes the evolution of network architectures.

## References

1. McKeown, N., Anderson, T., Balakrishnan, H., et al.: OpenFlow: Enabling innovation in campus networks. ACM SIGCOMM Computer Communication Review 38, 69–74 (2008)
2. Gude, N., Koponen, T., Pettit, J., et al.: Nox: towards an operating system for networks. ACM SIGCOMM Computer Communication Review 38, 105–110 (2008)
3. Van Jacobson, Smetters, D.K., Thornton, J.D., et al.: Networking Named Content. Communications of the ACM 55(1), 117–124 (2012)
4. Naous, J., Gibb, G., Bolouki, S., McKeown, N.: NetFPGA: reusable router architecture for experimental research. In: Proc. of ACM PRESTO, NY, USA (2008)
5. Argyraki, K., Baset, S.A., Chun, B.-G., et al.: Can software routers scale. In: Proc. of PRESTO, Seattle, USA (2008)
6. Egi, N., Greenhalgh, A., Handley, M., et al.: Towards high performance virtual routers on commodity hardware. In: Proc. of ACM CoNEXT, Madrid, Spain (2008)
7. Dobrescu, M., Argyraki, K., Iannaccone, G., Manesh, M.: Controlling Parallelism in a Multicore Software Router. In: Proceedings of the ACM PRESTO, Philadelphia, USA (2010)
8. Guo-Han, L., Rui, M., Yong-Qiang, X., Chuan-Xiong, G.: Using CPU as a Traffic Co-processing Unit in Commodity Switches. In: Proc. of the HotSDN, Helsinki, Finland (2012)
9. Gibb, G., Zeng, H., McKeown, N.: Outsourcing network functionality. In: Proc. of HotSDN (2012)
10. Walfish, M., Stribling, J., Krohn, M., Balakrishnan, H., Morris, R., Shenker, S.: Middleboxes no longer considered harmful. In: Proc. of OSDI, NY, USA (2004)
11. Sekar, V., Egi, N., Ratnasamy, S., Reiter, M., Shi, G.: Design and Implementation of a Consolidated Middlebox Architecture. In: Proc. of NSDI, NY, USA (2012)
12. Anand, A., Dogar, F., Han, D., et al.: XIA: An Architecture for an Evolvable and Trustworthy Internet. In: Proc. of the Hotnets, Cambridge, MA, USA (2011)
13. Ghodsi, A., Koponen, T., Rajahalme, J., et al.: Naming in Content-Oriented Architectures. In: Proc. of SIGCOMM ICN, Toronto, ON, Canada (2011)
14. Ghodsi, A., Koponen, T., Raghavan, B., et al.: Information-Centric Networking: Seeing the Forest for the Trees. In: Proc. of the Hotnets, Cambridge, MA, USA (2011)
15. OpenRouter: OpenFlow extension and implementation based on a commercial router. In: Proc. of the ICNP, Vancouver, BC, Canada (2011)
16. Kelly, J., Araujo, W., Banerjee, K.: Rapid Service Creation using the JUNOS SDK. ACM SIGCOMM Computer Communication Review 40(1), 56–60 (2010)
17. Hao, F., Kodialam, M., Song, H.: Fast dynamic multiple-set membership testing using combinatorial bloom filters. IEEE/ACM Transactions on Networking 20(1), 295–304 (2012)

# Mining Network Behavior Specifications of Malware Based on Binary Analysis

Peidai Xie, Yongjun Wang, Huabiao Lu, Meijian Li, and Jinshu Su

[1] College of Computer, National University of Defense Technology, Changsha Hunan, China
peidaixie@gmail.com

**Abstract.** Nowadays, malware, especially for a botnet, heavily employs network communication to accomplish predefined malicious functionalities. The network behavior of malware attracts attention of researchers. However, the network traffic used for network-based signatures generation and botnet detection is captured passively from an execution environment, that there are several limitations. In this paper, we present a network behavior mining approach based on binary analysis, named NBSBA. Our goal is to accurately understand the network behavior of malware in details, capture the packets the malware sample under analysis launched as soon as possible, and extract network behavior of malware as completely as possible. We firstly give a network behavior specification and then describe the NBSBA. And we implement a prototype system to evaluate the NBSBA. The experiment demonstrates that our approach is efficient.

**Keywords:** Network Behavior, Binary Analysis, Malware.

## 1 Introduction

Malware is a generic term to denote all kinds of unwanted software that fulfills the deliberately harmful intent of attackers, such as computer virus, worms, Trojan horse, bot, etc. Malware is used by attackers to attack network infrastructure, steal important information and spam emails, that it is the main security threat of internet[1]. Nowadays, malware heavily employs network communication to accomplish predefined functionalities[2].

Remote Control is a dominating characteristic of malware. A representative process of a network attack activity performed by a malware sample like a bot is as following. Firstly, DNS-request packets are delivered for IP addresses, such as the IP address of a C&C server, a server for update of malicious executable, a spam email server, the bot agents for malicious purpose, etc., and then connections to those IP addresses are launched based on predefined protocols. Secondly, the malware sample will attack a target according to commands received from the C&C server. The attacking activities include collecting information of the victim, scanning the hosts in the victim's local area network, launching DDoS, pulling a spam template, etc. Finally, the malware sample may kill itself if the attacker asks for. Most of malicious functionalities of a

J. Su et al. (Eds.): ICoC 2013, CCIS 401, pp. 248–255, 2013.

malware sample are accomplished with the support of network communication. For those reason, to master network behavior of malware is very important for security analysts to malware detection.

The network behavior of malware can be classified into four categories according to their functionalities. The first one is scanning and propagating, it is means that an infected computer scans hosts in its local area network to propagate itself by exploiting vulnerabilities. The second one is DNS activities to locate the C&C server. The third one is interactive activities between a malware and its C&C server to get a command and return its results. The fourth one is the attacking activities, including DDoS, sending spam emails and phishing web pages.

The communications are obfuscated usually. For example, the Command and Control communication for a malware, especially for a bot, is crucial important to maintain the malicious network, so that it is necessary to hide the location of the C&C server. Malware makes use of domain-flux and ip-flux usually to protect the communication[3], which generate randomly many domains algorithmically and only registers several ones during a time interval. Those stealth methods make a great obstacle for reverse engineering of malware.

The existing researches on network behavior of malware mainly focus on the network traffic. The automatically signature generation techniques[4, 5] are used to extract signatures from labeled malicious traffic with statistical and machine learning for malware detection in IDS and IPS. The state of the art botnet detection and containment techniques[6, 7] include the botnet detection based on traffic analysis and the malicious domain identification based on DNS traffic analysis[8, 9]. Those approaches are efficient on detection and containment of malware based on the abstraction of a part of intrinsic characteristics of malware network behaviors. But there are several limitations that cannot be overcome. The first limitation is that it is a long time period to generate a network-based signature. The traffic data used for generating signatures is captured passively on an analysis environment in which the targeted malware instance is running. The time period usually is several days. The second limitation is that the capture cannot ensure if the packets are complete. A malware instance can launched many types of packets. It is possible that only a part of packets is launched during the period and the crucial packets with key features for detection may be not launched. The third limitation is that the encrypted communication traffic, which is prevalently used in modern malware, cannot be deal with for generating signatures. All of those limitations affect to be incomplete signatures and make a bad malware detection result. And also the understanding of malware is not accurate.

Even worse, the Advance Persistent Threat is prevalent and the network attack is not a toy any more. It is very important to understand the malware in details and accurately. A security analyst should figure out the communication patterns between malwares except the signature of its network traffic. To mine the network behavior of malware for understanding, detection and containment of malware is imperative.

In this paper, we present an approach to mine network behavior specifications of malware based on binary analysis. Our goal is to understand the network behavior of malware in details and accurately, capture the packets the under analysis malware sample launched as soon as possible, and extract network behaviors of malware as completely as possible. Firstly, we present a network behavior specification to describe the protocol information. And then we propose a malware analysis approach on the support of network behavior mining, and implement a prototype to evaluate it.

This paper makes the following contributions:

- A network behavior specification is proposed for the description of large part of aspects in network activities.
- A network behavior mining approach based on binary analysis is proposed, and its prototype system is implemented for evaluation.

The remainder of this paper is structured as follows. Section 2 gives the detailed description of network behavior specification. Section 3 describes the NBSBA approach detailed. Section 4 is an experiment. Finally, section 5 concludes the paper.

## 2 The Network Behavior Specification

This section describes the network behavior specification NBS. Our goal of proposing the NBS is to cover the information related to network behavior, such as the type of protocol, the functionality of the packets, the time elapse from the last packet, and the time period, as many as possible. Our NBS is different from protocol model based on state machine theory and can be used for the malware research area in view of network traffic.

A network behavior specification is a 3-tuple graph $<V,E,P>$. The $V$ is vertex set to denote the packet sent out from the executable under analysis. The $E$ is edge set to denote the packet received from network by it. The $P$ is the set of all packets related with the communication. A $p \in P$ is a 6-tuple $<dir, pinfo, dinfo, func, time, raw>$. The $dir$ denotes the direction of the packet, and it has two value $\{\text{IN}, \text{OUT}\}$, which means that this packet is received from network or sent to network respectively. The $pinfo$ denotes the protocol information, is a $<sip, dip, sport, dport, proto>$ structure, which is source IP address, destination IP address, source port, destination port and protocol, respectively. The $dinfo$ denotes the data information, the value of which is determined by the protocol type. For a DNS query packet, the $dinfo$ will include the domain name be queried, and its reputation is likely to be gained from public reputation system of the internet domain name. For a HTTP packet, the $dinfo$ will include the URL of a GET type http request packet, and all packets in this TCP session will be recorded. The $func$ denotes the functionality of this packet, such as DNS request, network scanning, spaming emails, propagating and attacking, etc. The $time$ denotes the time elaspse from the last packet received from or sent to. The $raw$ denotes the raw data of this packet.

A sample of the NBS is as shown in **Fig. 1**. The malware instance producing the NBS holds a MD5 value of 37b34239f524426c0c45c6292101e425.

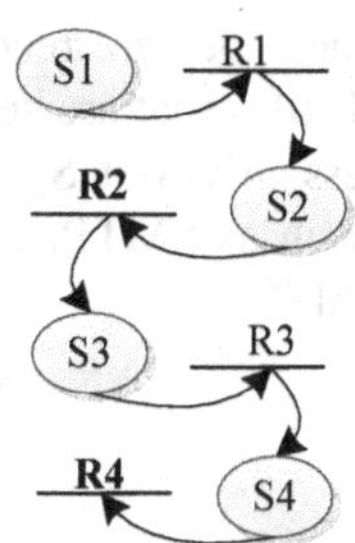


S1: DNS Request; www.google.com.br; Good
R1: DNS Response; Ip addr is x.x.x.x
S2: Http; GET / HTTP/1.1; web page
**R2**: 200 OK ···

S3: DNS Request; valehoje.com.br; Bad
R3: DNS Response; Ip addr is y.y.y.y
S4: Http; GET /winjar32T.dll HTTP/1.1; download exe
**R4**: 200 OK ···

**Fig. 1.** A sample of network behavior specification

In **Fig. 1,** the malware sample queries a DNS domain name *www.google.com.br* firstly, and then connects this IP address with HTTP GET request after a DNS response packet received. And then a DNS domain name *valehoje.com.br* is queried and its response packet is received successfully. The last domain name is malicious. The malware launches a HTTP GET packet to download a DLL file named winjar32T.dll. It received this binary file successfully. The *R2* and *R4* are italic notes with all packets in a TCP session respectively. All packets are delivered immediately and the malware sample quits its running after the network activity stopped, so we do not give the *time* information in this sample.

# 3 Mining NBS Based on Binary Analysis

In this section, we present the approach of mining NBS based on binary analysis, named NBSBA. The overview of NBSBA is as shown in **Fig. 2.**

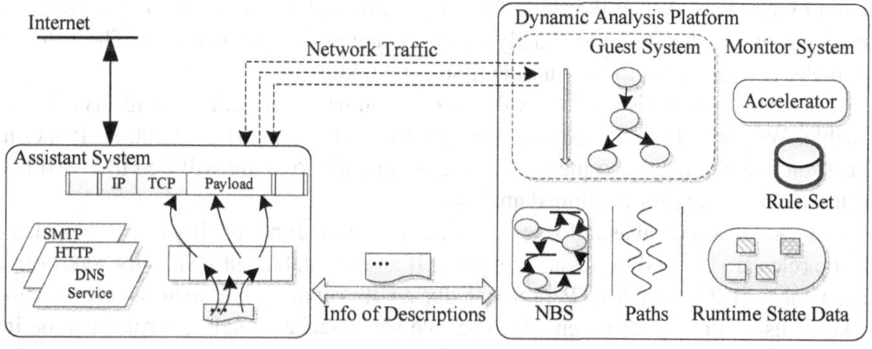


**Fig. 2.** The Overview of NBSBA

The basic mining process using NBSBA is as following. The executable under analysis is running in Guest System that is configured to communicate with the Assistant System. All execution activities will be recorded by Monitor System, including all packets received from or sent to network and instructions. The *recv* and *send* windows API are hooked in the Monitor System, and all messages are recorded. At the same time, some specific packets are descripted in XML files that are sent to Assistant System for a response packet to the running process in Guest System. The Assistant System also provides several network services, such as SMTP, HTTP and DNS, in order to support the running of the targeted executable.

### 3.1 The Guest System

The Guest System is a virtual execution environment for the running of a malware sample. In our dynamic analysis platform, the instruction-level analysis and memory space management are supported.

### 3.2 The Monitor System

This Monitor System is the kernel module of binary analysis that is used for dynamic analysis of the malware samples. There are several sub modules in it.

*Runtime State Data.* It is responsible for collection and maintain of the state data during the running of the malware instance under analysis, including the executed instructions, the data packet buffers, the elapsed time interval, etc. All of those data are used to construct the network behavior specification and explore execution paths for coverage. The other functionality of this module is to recombination of the sessions of network communication and record the elapsed time interval, which is calculated by gain the local time of Guest System when a packet is received or sent.

*Accelerator.* It is designed to accelerate the binary analysis for mining network behavior as soon as possible. In this component the windows APIs that are used for execution suspending are hooked, such as the sleep function, which is frequently employed by malware. When the sleep function is invoked, its parameter is recorded and the execution is returned immediately by the dynamic analysis platform. The value of parameter is transmitted to the runtime time data module.

*Paths.* This module is used to explore execution paths for path coverage as much as possible. We use a forced execution strategy for multiple paths exploration. If the inconsistent execution state in memory space occurs, this running will be killed and restart to a next running for continued analysis.

*Rule Set.* It is a database of rules which describe the functionality of some packets. All the rules are defined by security experts. If an executable automatically sends out a packet on port 25 with SMTP protocol during its running, we write a rule that the packet is used for spamming emails. The rule set is scalable and new rules can be inserted into it at any time.

*NBS.* It is the kernel module for mining network behavior. The network behavior specification is constructed by it. And it is performed to identify the type of a protocol in a packet by destination port and protocol signatures, unpack a packet to extract useful data, determine the functionality of a packet. An example of the function identification method is shown in **Fig. 3**.

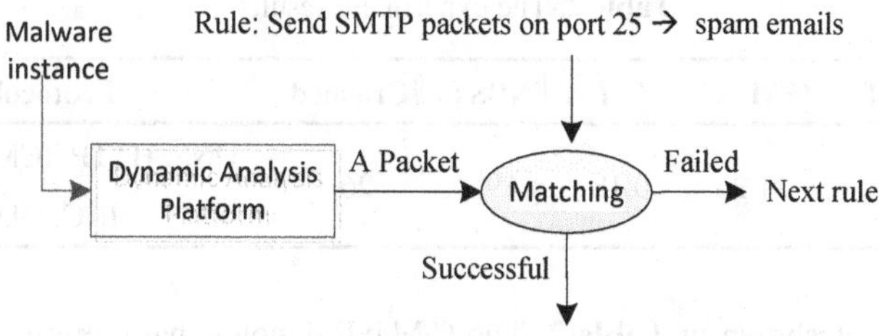


**Fig. 3.** Marking the functionality of a packet

In addition, the *NBS* module is also responsible for the construction of the expected packets and sends them to Assistant System for packets Guest System expected.

### 3.3 The Assistant System

The Assistant System is a network services supporting environment as well as a network behavior containment system. Several network services are installed in it. A traffic filter is running for network flow management. For example, if the malware instance under analysis asks for downloading files, this packet will be redirected to Internet. While, if a propagating packet is sent out, the packet will be discarded. In addition, this module also answers the Guest System according the packet description for triggering some stealing behaviors.

## 4 Experiment

In this section, we give a simple experiment to evaluate the NBSBA. We implement the prototype system in a roughly way because it is a very complex platform. The dataset of the experiment is as shown in **Table 1**. The samples indicated in the last row are included in the samples indicated in the first row, which is for a comparison.

**Table 1.** The dataset of malware samples

| | Viruses | Trojans | Worms | Bots |
|---|---|---|---|---|
| *Running in NBSBA* | 5 | 5 | 10 | 15 |
| *Running in a real system* | 2 | 2 | 2 | 2 |

We picked out 35 malware samples that consist of 5 viruses, 5 Trojans, 15 worms and 15 bots. Of course, the classification is not strict.

**Table 2.** The experiment results

| %MaxP | %P | %MaxT | %T | #NBSs | #Crashed | Protocols |
|---|---|---|---|---|---|---|
| 2.07 | 0.07 | 11.26 | 0.18 | 19 | 26 | DNS, HTTP, ICMP, SMTP, IRC, UDP |

The result is as shown in **Table 2**. The %MaxP denotes that there is a sample that we capture a 2.07 times amount of packets more than a regular capture in a real system. The %P is an average value of all samples. The %MaxT denotes that there is a sample that the analysis process is faster 11.26 times than a regular running. The %T is an average value. We got 19 NBSs and 26 samples crashed during running.

## 5 Discussion and Conclusion

The network behavior extraction of malware is a critical problem in malware analysis for malware detection and mitigation. In this paper we proposed a network behavior specification and a NBS mining approach based on binary analysis techniques. It is a challenge to figure out a detailed network behavior of malware. The limitations of the approach are that the evaluation is not enough and the NBSBA should be implemented in detail. Several problems related with NBS mining are studied for feature work.

**Acknowledgements.** This work was supported by the National High Technology Research and Development Program of China under Grant No. 2011AA01A103, the National Natural Science Foundation of China under Grant No. 61202482 and No. 61271252, PCSIRT(No.IRT1012), and Aid Program for Science and Technology Innovative Research Team in Higher Educational Institutions of Hunan Province: "network technology". The authors would like to appreciate anonymous reviewers for their valuable suggestions and comments.

## References

1. Egele, M., Scholte, T., Kirda, E., Kruegel, C.: A Survey on Automated Dynamic Malware Analysis Techniques and Tools. J. ACM Computing Surveys, 1–49 (2010)
2. Morales, J.A., Al-Bataineh, A., Xu, S., Sandhu, R.: Analyzing and Exploiting Network Behaviors of Malware. In: Jajodia, S., Zhou, J. (eds.) SecureComm 2010. LNICST, vol. 50, pp. 20–34. Springer, Heidelberg (2010)
3. Yadav, S., Reddy, A.K.K., Reddy, A.L.N., Ranjan, S.: Detecting Algorithmically Generated Domain-Flux Attacks with DNS Traffic Analysis. J. Transaction on Network. 20(5) (2012)
4. Krueger, T., Krämer, N., Rieck, K.: ASAP: Automatic semantics-aware analysis of network payloads. In: Dimitrakakis, C., Gkoulalas-Divanis, A., Mitrokotsa, A., Verykios, V.S., Saygin, Y. (eds.) PSDML 2010. LNCS (LNAI), vol. 6549, pp. 50–63. Springer, Heidelberg (2011)

5. Leita, C., Mermoud, K., Dacier, M.: ScriptGen: An Automated Script Generation Tool for Honeyd. In: Proceedings of the 21st Annual Computer Security Application Conference (2005)
6. Bilge, L., Kirda, E., Kruegel, C., Balduzzi, M.: Exposure: Finding Malicious Domains using Passive DNS Analysis. In: Proceedings of the 18th Annual Network and Distributed Systems Security Symposium (NDSS 2011), San Diego, USA (2011)
7. Stone-Gross, B., Cova, M., Cavallaro, L., Gilbert, B., Szydlowski, M., Kemmerer, R., Kruegel, C., Vigna, G.: Your Botnet is My Botnet: Analysis of a Botnet Takeover. In: Proceedings of the 16th ACM Conference on Computer and Communications Security (CCS 2009), Chicago, Illinois, USA, pp. 635–647 (2009)
8. Yadav, S., Reddy, A.L.N.: Winning with DNS Failures: Strategies for Faster Botnet Detection. In: Rajarajan, M., Piper, F., Wang, H., Kesidis, G. (eds.) SecureComm 2011. LNICST, vol. 96, pp. 446–459. Springer, Heidelberg (2012)
9. Shin, S., Xu, Z., Gu, G.: EFFORT: Efficient and Effective Bot Malware Detection. In: INFOCOM 2012 (2012)

# CoISM: Improving Security and Accuracy of BGP through Information Sharing

Ning Hu* and BaoSheng Wang

College of Computer National University of Defense Technology
ChangSha, Hunan, China
ning_hu@163.com, bsw@nudt.edu.cn
http://www.nudt.edu.cn

**Abstract.** Ensuring the authenticity of BGP routing information is a challenge problem of Inter-domain routing security. Due to lack of global information view, is it difficult to single autonomous system to detect bogus BGP routing information. A method for cooperative BGP validation based on self-organizing information sharing is presented in this paper. Cooperative validation gives a more comprehensive route view by sharing information among autonomous systems. It loosens the constraints from the autonomy and improves the security and accuracy of BGP. By leveraging the characteristics of locality and relativity, which is caused by routing policy, cooperative validation drives autonomous systems to cooperate independently and share information on-demand. More specifically, our method has incentive effect and supports incremental deployment.

**Keywords:** routing security, route validation, BGP monitoring, information sharing, coordination.

## 1 Introduction

Internet is comprised of thousands of Autonomous Systems (ASes), which exchange routing information with Border Gateway Protocol (BGP) and transmit traffic according to the routing information. Because it was designed for a trusted environment, BGP is vulnerable to routing attacks[1]. Recent studies and security incidents show that Inter-domain routing system is facing serious security challenges and the need to secure BGP has become increasingly pressing [2–4]. Many BGP security enhanced solutions based cryptographic authentications uses digital signatures and associated public key certificates to validate path attributes in BGP UPDATE messages passed among ASes[5–7]. All of these solutions provide an absolute security protection to routing information, but none of them has been deployed in Internet. The major obstacle includes: 1)lack of Internets global PKI infrastructure, 2)the high computational overhead caused

* Supported by Foundation of Science and Technology on Information As-surance Laboratory(No.KJ-12-07), Program for ChangJiang Scholars and Innovative Research Team in University(No.IRT1012), Light-weight algorithm and protocol for secure data transmission in RFID sensor networks(61070201).

J. Su et al. (Eds.): ICoC 2013, CCIS 401, pp. 256–265, 2013.

by calculating digital signatures, 3)the requirement to change BGP, 4) lack of incentive effect. Since there is no practically deployed security routing protocol, routing monitoring system is designed and deployed to offset the security vulnerability of BGP as a mitigation solution. BGP monitoring system improves the security and accuracy of routing information through collecting and validating BGP data from BGP router [8, 9]. However, most routing monitoring systems need a schedule or management center and do not consider the requirement of autonomy and incentive.

In this paper, we designed a cooperative method for BGP route validation which is based on information sharing. The basic principle of cooperative validation is as follows: multiple autonomous systems (ASes) deploy monitoring service and check the credibility of BGP route in a self-organized way to achieve the ultimate security together. By means of sharing the monitoring information among multiple autonomous systems, cooperative validating BGP provides a more comprehensive routing view, overcomes information unavailability and locality constraints and enhances the ability of autonomous system to detect false routing information. In this paper, we also consider two important factors which include incentive and deployment. For convenient, our method is names as CoISM.

This paper is organized as follows: Section 2 described our motivation and objectives. Section 3 describes the algorithm for cooperative route validation. Section 4 gives experiment and result analysis. Section 5 is an overview of related work. Finally, Section 6 concludes the paper.

## 2 Motivation and Objective

### 2.1 Motivation

Ensuring the authenticity of routing information is the key issue of routing security. Route monitoring system increase the security and accuracy of BGP routing information through route validation. But, due to lack of global information view, it is difficult to single BGP monitor to identity false BGP route. For example, due to lack of enough information about IP prefix ownership, single AS can not identify a prefix hijacking advertise. To implement cooperative BGP monitoring among ASes, we need more efficiency information sharing mechanism. Based on this purpose, we noticed two characteristics of monitoring information: local validity and relative validity.

When an AS (such as $X$) received a BGP route, it might do not select the route as the best route for some reasons. Hence, any monitoring information about this route is invalid to $X$. This characteristic is called local validity. Obviously, if a piece of monitoring information is invalid to AS $X$, it is not necessary to send this information to it. According to local validity, all of the internet ASes can be classified into three subsidiary sets which are infection set, immunity set and isolate set. For any AS node, if it selects the false route as the best one, it belongs to the infection set. If an AS node can identify the false route, it belongs to the immunity set. If an AS node does not receive or use the false route according to its routing policy even it is true, it belongs to the isolate set.

For an example, as shown in Fig.1, suppose AS $E$ is a malicious node and try to hijack prefix $P_1$ of AS $F$. When AS $E$ advertise a NLRI for prefix $P_1$ to AS $A$, both $A$ and $B$ will select this bogus route as the best route according to rule of shortest path first. In this case, AS $A$ and $B$ are infection nodes. AS $C$ is an immunity node, because $C$ is the owner of prefix $P_1$, when it receives NLRI advertised by AS $E$, it detects it is a prefix hijacking. At last, AS $D$ is $C$'s customer and $C$ will not advertise false routing information to AS $D$, so AS $D$ is an isolated node.

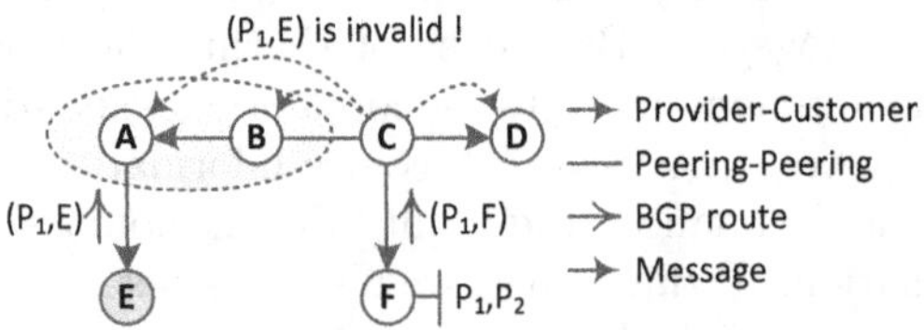


**Fig. 1.** Local validity of monitoring information

Most routing policies are designed oriented AS without diffusing prefixes owned by the same AS. Since routing hijacking attack is based on routing policy breaches, if an AS is under routing attack, all of its prefix might be under attack too. So, if monitoring information about prefix $P_1$ is valid to an AS (such as $Y$), information about prefix $P_2$ which is owned by the same AS is probably valid to $Y$. This second characteristic is called relative validity. According to relative validity, all of the monitoring information about prefix owned by the same AS might cause the same infection, immunity and isolation node classification.

Therefore, we realizes it is possible to implement monitoring information sharing on-demand.

### 2.2 Objective

For the sake of further argument, we explained the special meaning of some terms, which appeared in the following description.

**Term 1**: ***Monitoring Information***. Monitoring information refers to route validation request and acknowledge.

**Term 2**: ***Monitor***. Monitor collects BGP route from AS BGP router, validates the authenticity of BGP route according to local knowledge. To simplify description, we denote AS node as monitor. A monitor can be defined by a tuple $= (M_{ID}, I_M, K_M)$. $M_{ID}$ is a unique identity of monitor. $I_M$ represents set of local monitoring information which is produced or received by monitor. $K_M$ is the local knowledge database which is composed of BGP routing table, routing policy, prefix ownership, anomaly detection rules, blacklist of false route and so on. The local knowledge is used to produce, identify and deliver monitoring information.

**Term 3**: ***Information Coverage***. Given a monitor $M$ and a piece of monitoring information $I_i$, if $I_i$ is included in the $I_M$ of $M$, $M$ is covered by $I_i$.

**Term 4**: ***Effective Coverage/Ineffective Coverage***. Given a monitor $M_I$, and a piece of monitoring information $I$, if $M_I$ receives $I$ and benefits from it, it is an effective coverage, nor it is an ineffective coverage.

**Term 5**: ***Maximum Effective Coverage***. Given a piece of monitoring information $I$ and a monitor set $S = M_1, M_2,, M_n$, if and only if every monitor of $S$ is effective covered by information $I$, it is a maximum effective coverage.

**Term 6**: ***Routing Correlative***. Given two BGP routes $R_A$, $R_B$ and corresponding monitoring information $I_A$ and $I_B$, if any condition as follows is satisfied, $I_A$ and $I_B$ are routing correlated.

a) The IP prefix of $R_A$ and $R_B$ belong to the same AS;

b) The AS-PATH property of $R_A$ and $R_B$ share the common sub-path;

Being similar with the topology of Internet, all of the AS monitors are widely distributed and lacking of global view for information requirement, monitor only coordinates closely with a subset of the rest monitor.Considering these characteristics,the key issue of node coordination is how to share information. The objective of CoISM can be described as follows: For a given monitor set $S_M = \{M_1, M_2,, M_n\}$ and a series of information $S_I$=$\{I_1,,I_m\}$, how to realize maximum effective coverage for $S_I$ with low computing and communication cost.

## 3 Cooperative Validating BGP

### 3.1 Algorithm

Geoffrey G. proposed an origin and path validation method IRV [15]. In their study, BGP monitor sends query message to other ASes monitor one by one which are included in AS-PATH. Geoffreys method proposed a cooperative monitoring method but did not consider blind spot and linearity increasing communication cost.

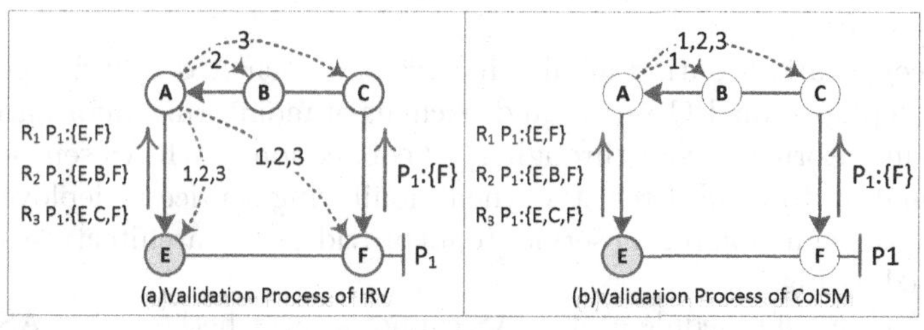


**Fig. 2.** Route validation process of IRV and CoISM

Fig.2 (a) demonstrates the validation process of IRV. The dotted line denotes validation message sent by AS $A$. In this scene, AS $A$, $B$ and $C$ deploy IRV services. These three ASes monitoring their native and customers IP prefix. $E$ is a malicious AS and advertises three false BGP routes $R_1$, $R_2$ and $R_3$ for prefix $P_1$ to AS $A$. In the first loop, AS $A$ sends a validation message to $F$ when it receives $R_1$ from AS $E$ because only AS $F$ is included in AS-PATH property of $R_1$. Unfortunately, AS $A$ does not get confirmation message because AS $F$ does not deploy IRV service. In the second loop, AS A will send validation message to $F$ and $B$ when it receives $R_2$ from AS $E$. Again, AS $A$ does not get confirmation message because AS $B$ cannot identify whether $R_1$ is a false route. Only when AS $A$ sends AS $C$ a validation message for route $R_3$, it will receive a notification because AS $C$ knows that AS $F$ is the actually owner of prefix $P_1$. In this example, AS $A$ is a blind spot for $R_1$ and $R_2$. In addition, IRV does not make use of relativity of monitoring message. For every BGP route, AS A sends message to all AS nodes included in AS-PATH. As the count of routing increasing, the communication cost increases linearly.

According to the analysis of local validity and relative validity, we propose a coordination model which is called CoISM. Fig.2 (b) demonstrates the route validation process of CoISM. When AS $A$ receives $R_1$, it sends validation request to AS $B$ and $C$ which has deployed BGP monitoring service. In the first loop, only AS $C$ replies a notification. In the second loop, AS $A$ does send request to AS $B$ because AS $B$ does not reply in the first loop. Instead, AS $A$ sends request to AS $C$, because these three routes are routing correlative. Contrasting with Fig.2 (b), our method removes blind spot and decreases communication cost. we designed CoISM algorithms which are described in algorithm1 and algorithm2.

### 3.2 Implementation

We implement a cooperative routing monitoring system which is composed of route monitor and CoISM registry. There are three functions of route monitor. First, monitor establishes dumb iBGP session with ASs router to collect BGP routing. Second, monitor exchanges routing monitoring information with other monitor. Last, monitor sends notification to other monitor when false route is detected. CoISM registry provides access information of AS which deploys monitor service.

In our cooperative routing monitoring system, each ASs routing monitoring service is deployed on PC server and exchanges monitoring information with other ASs monitoring service through TCP connection. Each AS sends registration information to CoISM registry when monitoring service is deployed. Small size AS can consign monitoring service to its provider. The architecture of CoISM is illustrated as Fig.3.

Due to lacking of schedule center, AS cannot sense whether other AS deploys monitor. Hence, an important issue of CoISM is how to locate monitor for AS. To resolve this question, we build a CoISM registry web site to store and provide all monitors contact information. CoISM registry only store monitor location

**Algorithm 1.** Produce and send route validation request

```
if Validate(R ,K_M) is VALID or INVALID then
    return;
end if
if Validate(R ,K_M) is UNCERTAIN then
    Initialize newM and add it into I_M;
    for I∈I_M do
        if I.Route is routing correlative with R then
            Add validator of I into authSet;
            Add producer of I into applicantSet;
        end if
    end for
    if authSet and applicantSet is NULL then
        Add monitor in R.AS-PATH into authSet;
    end if
    for all monitor in authSet and applicantSet do
        if newM.TTL equal THRESHOLD then
            break;
        end if
        Send newM to the monitor;
        emphnewM.TTL++;
        if ackM.result is VALID or INVALID then
            Update K_M and newM;
            return;
        end if
        if emphackM.suggestedList is not NULL then
            Add suggested monitor into authSet; goto 12;
        end if
    end for
end if
return;
```

**Algorithm 2.** Receive and reply route validation request

```
newM = Listen();
if Validate(newM.Route,K_M) is VALID or INVALID then
    Add newM into I_M;
    Update fields of newM and reply ackM;
    return;
end if
if auth(newM ,K_M) is UNCERTAIN then
    Search I_M for validation request which is routing correlative with R;
    Add requests validator into ackM.suggestedList;
    Add requests producer into ackM.suggestedList;
    Update fields of newM and reply ackM;
end if
goto 1;
```

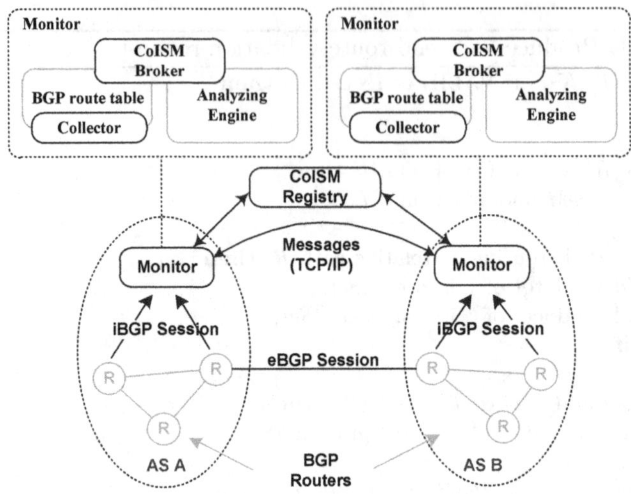


**Fig. 3.** Deployment and implementation of CoISM

information (e.g., IP addresses) for each AS. AS can get the monitor deployment view through CoISM. Be different from IRR, CoISM registry only provides the distribution view of BGP monitor and does not strive AS submit their monitoring information.

## 4 Simulations and Analysis

In this section, we define several indicators to evaluate the efficiency of CoISM.

1. **Effective Coverage Ratio**

Effective coverage ratio is used to assess whether CoISM implements information on-demand. In equation 1, function $Cover(I_i,\ M_j) \rightarrow \{0,1\}$ indicates whether monitor $M_j$ is covered by message $I_i$. Function Valid$(I_i,\ M_j) \rightarrow \{0,1\}$ indicates whether message $I_i$ is effective to monitor $M_j$.

$$\sum_{j=1}^{n}\left(\frac{\sum_{i=1}^{m}(Cover(I_i, M_j) * Valid(I_i, M_j))}{\sum_{i=1}^{m} Cover(I_i, M_j)}\right) \tag{1}$$

2. **Profit Ratio**

Profit ratio is used to indicate the incentive effect of CoISM. Function $Imp(I_i,M_j) \rightarrow \{0,1\}$ indicates whether message $I_i$ is received from other monitor. Function Exp$(I_i,M_j) \rightarrow \{0,1\}$ indicates whether message $I_i$ is exported by entity $M_j$.

$$\sum_{i=1}^{m}\frac{Import(I_i, M_j) * Valid(I_i, M_j)}{Exp(I_i, M_j) + Imp(I_i, M_j) * Valid(I_i, M_j)} \tag{2}$$

**3. Communication Cost**
To simplify analyze, we use count of information transmission to evaluate the communication cost when effective coverage ratio reach threshold value $t$.

$$\sum_{j=1}^{n}(Cover(I_i, M_j)) \tag{3}$$

To simulate the real inter-domain routing system, we select a BGP snapshot from RouteViews on May 20, 2012 [10]. In this experiment, we first construct a network according to BGP data of RouteView. Then we sorted AS node according to the degree in descending order and select the first $K$(K=200,400,600,800, 1000) nodes to construct monitor community $M$.

We adopt round-robin model to execute this experiment. In each loop, every monitor randomly received 10 hijacking route which shared prefix with one of other monitor. When any monitor receives a new BGP route, it produces and sends validation request according to algorithm1. This procedure repeats 10 loops. We calculate and record three indicators defined upon when every loop is finished and get the experiment result which are shown in Fig4.

In Fig.4(a), the horizontal represents the number of loop, and vertical represents the valid coverage rate. From Fig.3(a), we get following conclusions: For a specific AS set, valid coverage ratio approaches to 1 in a limited time. Due

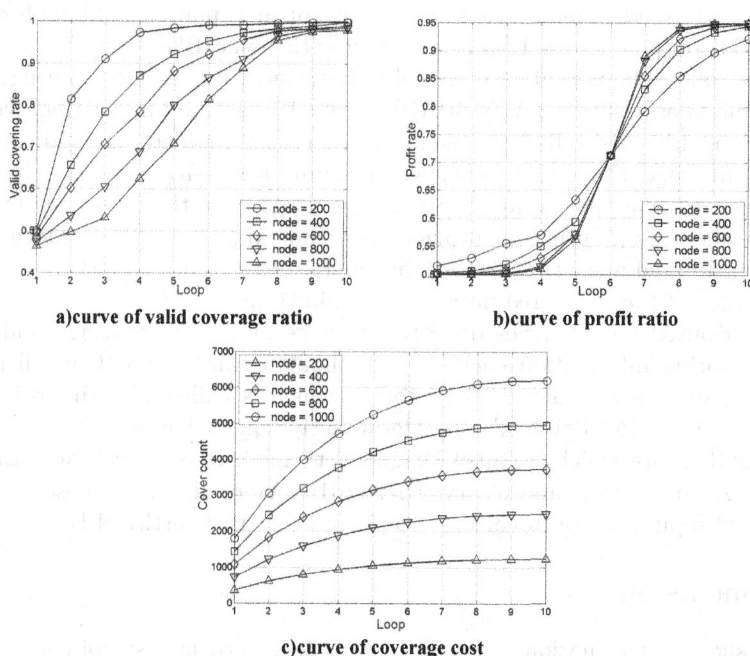


a)curve of valid coverage ratio

b)curve of profit ratio

c)curve of coverage cost

**Fig. 4.** Curve of valid coverage ratio

to lack of enough elicitation information in the initial phase, the valid covering rate increases slowly. This phenomenon is more obvious when the count of node is large.

Fig.4(b) shows the change of average reward. From this result we get following conclusions: The profit of monitor depends on valid coverage rate. At beginning, valid coverage rate is lower and profit rate of monitor increase slowly. Monitors profit rate increases quickly when the valid coverage is large than threshold value. This is because valid information causes more valid feedback. Due to transmission control and loops avoid mechanism, profit rate of monitor increases slowly when it approaches 1.

Fig.4(c) shows the change of communication cost when valid coverage arrives 0.9. From this result, we get two conclusions: The communication cost nonlinear increase with the iteration times and amount of monitoring information. This is better than IRV. After several loop iterations, CoISM slows down the increasing speed of communication cost. This is benefited from valid coverage increasing.

## 5 Related Work

Most route monitoring systems adopt two category information sharing model, which are centric model and distributed model.

In centric model, there is an information center which is in charge of collecting, storing and querying information from all the AS. For example, IRR (Internet Routing Registry) uses a centralizing model to store routing policy of AS. IRR allows ISPs to publish high-level specifications of their policies, and analyze the effects of their policies on Internet routing [11]. Some BGP routing monitoring project also adapts centralize model to implement information sharing, such as Looking Glasses [9], MyASN of RIPENCC [12] and Gradus of Renesys[13]. Centric model has some limitations. First, the cost of data storage and communication are huge. Second, the efficiency of information sharing is low, because every AS must search some information on demand from the massive database. Last, because the information provider does not know who their information customers are and what the purposes of them are. For protecting their security, the accuracy of the registered data is uncertain [14].

In distributed model, ASes directly exchange and share routing validating and monitoring information each other without a third party. Goodell et al. provide a solution to validate BGP routes which is called IRV (inter-domain route validation)[15]. Pei et al. provide an active query based method to validate a BGP route which is called Diagnosis through Root Cause Notification, topology Accumulation, and Query (DRAQ)[16]. Yu et al. [17] proposed a novel distributed reputation protocol to make assure the trustworthy of BGP route.

## 6 Conclusion

How to sharing information among AS nodes is the crucial issue of cooperative inter-domain routing monitoring. CoISM proposes a heuristic information sharing method which makes using the local validity and relativity of monitoring information. Being contrasted with flooding or IRV, CoISM has higher information transmission efficiency and lower communication cost. Additionally, CoISM is incentive and builds ASs reward on its invocation.

## References


1. Murphy, S.: BGP Security Vulnerabilities Analysis. RFC 4272, IETF (2006)
2. Ola, N., Constantinos, D.: Beware of BGP Attacks. Computer Communication Review 34(2), 1–8 (2004)
3. Butler, K.: A Survey of BGP Security Issues and Solutions. Proceedings of the IEEE 98, 100–122 (2010)
4. Rensys Blog, `http://www.renesys.com/2008/02/Pakistan-hijacks-youtube-1/`
5. Stephen, K., Charles, L., Karen, S.: Secure Border Gateway Protocol (S-BGP). IEEE Journal on Selected Areas in Communications (JSAC) 18(4), 582–592 (2000)
6. Cisco, `ftp://ftp-end.cisco.com/sobgp/presentations/BCR-soBGP.pdf`
7. Van, P.C.O., Wan, T., Evangelos, K.: On Interdomain Routing Security and Pretty Secure BGP (psBGP). ACM Transactions on Information and System Security 10(3), 1–41 (2005)
8. Yan, H., Oliveira, R., Burnett, K.: BGPmon: A real-time, scalable, extensible monitoring system. In: Cybersecurity Applications and Technologies Conference for Homeland Security (CATCH), pp. 212–223. IEEE Computer Society Press, Los Angels (2009)
9. Looking Glasses, `http://www.traceroute.org`
10. University of oregon route views project, `http://www.routeviews.org/`
11. Internet Routing Registry, `http://www.irr.net/index.html`
12. The RIPE NCC MyASN service, `http://www.ris.ripe.net/myasn.Html`
13. GRADUS, `http://www.renesys.com/index.shtml`
14. Georgos, S., Michalis, F.: Analyzing BGP Policies: Methodology and Tool. In: IEEE INFOCOM, pp. 1640–1651. IEEE Society Press, New York (2004)
15. Goodell, G., Aiello, W., Griffin, T.: Working around BGP: An incremental approach to improving security and accuracy of inter-domain routing. In: ISOC NDSS, pp. 75–85. National Security Agency Press, San Diego (2003)
16. Pei, D., Lad, M., Massey, D., Zhang, L.: Route Diagnosis in Path Vector Protocols. Technical Report TR040039, UCLA CSD (2004)
17. Yu, H., Rexford, J., Felten, E.W.: A distributed reputation approach to cooperative Internet routing protection. In: Secure Network Protocols, pp. 73–78. IEEE Society Press, New York (2005)

# Detecting Community Structures in Social Networks with Particle Swarm Optimization

Yuzhong Chen[1,*] and Xiaohui Qiu[1]

[1] Fujian Provincial Key Laboratory of Networking Computing and Intelligent Information Processing, Fuzhou University, China
yzchen@fzu.edu.cn

**Abstract.** Community detection in social networks is usually considered as an objective optimization problem. Due to the limitation of the objective function, the global optimum cannot describe the real partition well, and it is time consuming. In this paper, a novel PSO (particle swarm optimization) algorithm based on modularity optimization for community detection in social networks is proposed. Firstly, the algorithm takes similarity-based clustering to find core areas in the network, and then a modified particle swarm optimization is performed to optimize modularity in a new constructed weighted network which is compressed from the original one, and it is equivalent to optimize modularity in the original network with some restriction. Experiments are conducted in the synthetic and four real-world networks. The experimental results show that the proposed algorithm can effectively extract the intrinsic community structures of social networks.

**Keywords:** Community Detection, Particle Swarm Optimization, Modularity.

## 1 Introduction

In recent years, community detection in social networks has attracted a lot of attention [1] [2]. Informally, communities are groups of nodes that are connected densely inside the group but connected sparely with the rest of the network. Community structure is the key feature for uncovering the global property in social networks, which is very important for studying social networks. The community can represent special role, group or a substructure of certain function. For example, communities in World Wide Web are considered as thematic clusters [3], communities in biological networks are widely believed to have a close connection to biological function [4], etc.

As an important attribute of the social networks, community detection has attracted lots of people's attention from different fields, like sociology, biology, computer science, etc. Many classic methods have been proposed to detect community structures in social networks. They can be roughly classified into two categories. The first category employ heuristic strategies, such as Girvan-Newman (GN) algorithm [5], Wu-Huberman (WH) algorithm [6] and Hyperlink Induced Topic Search (HITS)

[*] Corresponding author.

J. Su et al. (Eds.): ICoC 2013, CCIS 401, pp. 266–275, 2013.

algorithm [7] etc. The secondary category choose optimization methods or approximation methods, such as spectral method [8], Kernighan-Lin algorithm [9] and Guimera-Amaral algorithm (GA) [10] etc. In recent years, with the widely application of computational intelligence, some global optimization algorithms have been used in detecting community structure with good results. In [11], particle swarm optimization (PSO) is used to optimize modularity[12] for community detection. However, global optimization process always has high computation complexity, and resolution limit problem[13]. There are also some multi-objective optimization algorithms for community detection [14] [15], these algorithms are flexible, but it is hard to design an effective strategy that can automatically selects a proper solution from Pareto front.

In this paper, community detection is considered as an optimization problem. An algorithm named SCPSO (Similarity Based Clustering and Particle Swarm Optimization) is proposed. The rest of this paper is organized as follows. Section 2 designs a similarity clustering algorithm and then the construction of new weighted network will be introduced in section 3. Section 4 depicts an improved PSO algorithm for community detection. In section 5, experimental results in synthetic network and four real-world networks are presented and analyzed. Finally, Section 6 draws the conclusion.

## 2 Clustering Based on Similarity

Many algorithms can discover core clusters (dense-linked areas) of the network. For example, DBSCAN is able to discover arbitrary clusters in any database and detect noise at the same time in one scan [16]. SCAN [17] is also a structural clustering algorithm for networks based on DBSCAN. SCAN is effective and fast, but it depends on a sensitive parameter: minimum similarity threshold $\varepsilon$. In the proposed algorithm, we aimed at finding the core areas effectively, so a similarity based clustering method is introduced.

### 2.1 Basic Concepts

Here, for simplicity and without loss of generality, we only consider simple, un-directed, and un-weighted networks. Let $N = (V, E)$ represents the network where $V$ is the set of nodes and $E$ is the set of edges. Some terms required for explaining the clustering algorithm is defined as follows [16][17].

- DEFINITION1 (NODE STRUCTURE)

The common neighborhoods of two connected nodes are important for measuring similarity. So in this paper, we define the structure of node $v$ as the node set including node $v$ and its neighborhoods , denoted by $\Gamma(v)$ as follows.

$$\Gamma(v) = \{\mu \in V \mid \{v, \mu\} \in E\} \cup \{v\} \quad (1)$$

- DEFINITION2 (NODE SIMILARITY)

Nodes in the same community share similar structure, the value of structural similarity metric will be large. The larger similarity value a pair of nodes have, the more likely they are in the same community. Here a normalized similarity function extended from Jaccard index is defined as follows.

$$sim(\mu, v) = \frac{|\Gamma(\mu) \cap \Gamma(v)|}{|\Gamma(\mu) \cup \Gamma(v)|} \quad (2)$$

- DEFINITION 3 ($\varepsilon$-NEIGHBORHOOD)

A minimum similarity threshold is used to be a cut to the similarity value. In other words, a node's $\varepsilon$-neighborhood is selected from its neighbors through threshold $\varepsilon$.

$$N_\varepsilon(v) = \{\omega \in \Gamma(v) \mid sim(v, \omega) \geq \varepsilon\} \quad (3)$$

- DEFINITION 4 (CORE NODE)

Core node represents a special node which have enough members in $\varepsilon$-neighborhood. Cluster(core area) are grown up from the core node. Here $\mu$ represents the minimum threshold of $\varepsilon$-neighborhood of the core node.

$$CORE_{\varepsilon,\mu}(v) \Leftrightarrow |N_\varepsilon(v)| \geq \mu \quad (4)$$

- DEFINITION 5 (DIRECT STRUCTURE REACHABILITY)

Core node is expanded to cluster(core area) according to the direct reach-ability rule formulized in the following definition. Node $v$ is direct-connected to node $\omega$ if and only if $v$ is a core node and $\omega$ is in the $\varepsilon$-neighborhood of $v$.

$$DirREACH_{\varepsilon,\mu}(v, \omega) \Leftrightarrow CORE_{\varepsilon,\mu}(v) \wedge \omega \in N_\varepsilon(v) \quad (5)$$

### 2.2 Clustering Algorithm

In this sub-section, a basic structural clustering algorithm that searches for core areas and isolated nodes in a network is discussed.

Firstly, all nodes are labeled as unclassified. For each node $v$ that is unclassified, if node $v$ is a core node, a new cluster_ID will be generated and all nodes which satisfy direct reach-ability rule will be inserted into a seed queue, otherwise node $v$ will be labeled as NOISE which means isolated node. Moreover, the cluster_ID will be assigned to all the nodes appeared in the seed queue.

Secondly, node $y$ is pick up from the top of the queue. If node $y$ is a core node, its unclassified neighborhood which satisfy the direct reach-ability rule will be added to the queue. Then remove node $y$ from the queue. The operation will be repeated until the queue is empty.

Finally, the network is partitioned into some clusters(core areas) and isolated nodes. The pseudocode of the algorithm is depicted as follows.

**Clustering Algorithm**

```
assign all nodes as unclassified;
for each unclassified node v
  if (CORE_{ε,μ}(v)) then
      generate new cluster_ID;
      insert DirREACH_{ε,μ}(v)  into queue Q;
      while(Q != 0) do
          y = first node in Q;
          assign cluster_ID to y;
          if (CORE_{ε,μ}(y)) then
              for each x ∈ DirREACH_{ε,μ}(y) do
                  if x is unclassified  then
                     insert  x into queue Q;
                 if x is NOISE then
                     assign cluster_ID to x;
        remove y from Q;
  else
     label v as NOISE;
```

# 3 Constructing New Weighted Network

After clustering process, now the original network consists of some core areas and isolated nodes. Meanwhile, in order to reduce the network scale, a new compressed weighted network will be constructed by abstracting each core area and isolated node in the original network as a super node in the new weighted network. For edges that are in the same core area of the original network, a self-join edge will be added to the corresponding super node in the new network. And for edges that are between core areas or isolated nodes in the original network, an edge between the corresponding super nodes will be added. Finally, a new weighted network is constructed. Fig.1 shows the conversion. Then the optimization based on modularity will be performed on the new constructed network which has a smaller scale than the original one.

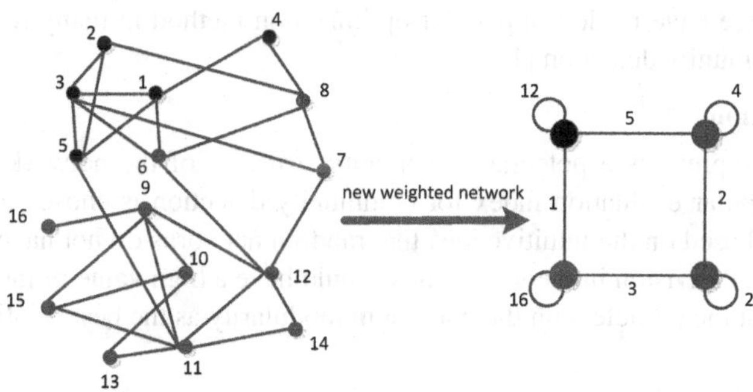


**Fig. 1.** Conversion from the original network to a new weighted network

Calculating modularity [12] in the new weighted network plays a significant role in community detection. Modularity has high computation complexity and is highly dependent on the scale of network. The optimization efficiency will be improved if we can prove that searching modularity optimum in the new constructed network and the original one is equivalent.

The equivalence here means optimization modularity in the new constructed network equals optimization in the original one with fixed combination of core areas. In another word, core area will not split when applying random optimization method. The proof of the equivalence of optimization modularity is presented briefly in the following paragraph.

Let $G$ denotes the original network and A=$(A_{ij})_{n\times n}$ denotes the adjacency matrix of $G$ where $A_{ij}$ is the weight of the edge from node $i$ to $j$. $k_i = \sum_{ij} A_{ij}$ is the degree of node $i$, and $m = \frac{1}{2}\sum_{ij} A_{ij}$ is the total of the edge weight of $G$, $c_i$ is the identifier of the community that node $i$ belongs to in certain iteration. If node $i$ and node $j$ are in the same community, $\delta(c_i, c_j) = 1$, otherwise 0. $Q$ denotes the modularity of $G$.

$$Q = \frac{1}{2m}\sum_{ij}\left(A_{ij} - \frac{k_i k_j}{2m}\right)\delta(c_i, c_j), 1 \le i, j \le n \quad \text{s} \tag{6}$$

Since all the edges in G are kept in the new constructed network. According to the definition of modularity, it is easy to find out that the modularity of the new constructed network equals $Q$. Therefore, searching modularity optimum in the new constructed network is equivalent to searching in the original one.

## 4 Modularity Optimization

Particle Swarm Optimization (PSO) is a computational intelligence algorithm proposed by Kennedy and Eberhart in 1995 [18]. It is a swarm intelligence algorithm that simulates the movements of a flock of birds which seek food. Its relative simplicity and fast convergence have made it a popular optimization method in many research fields including community detection [11].

**Fitness Function**

Each particle represents a potential community structure of the network. Modularity which is a popular evaluation index for community detection is chosen as the fitness function. It is based on the intuitive idea that random networks do not have community structure, a good division into communities should have a high value of modularity[12]. PSO will select the particle with the maximum modularity as the best solution.

**Particle Encoding**

A particle encoding scheme based on local neighbor list is adopted in the proposed algorithm. Such a particle encoding scheme does not require apriori knowledge of the number of communities.

Fig.2 shows an example of the particle encoding scheme based on the local neighbor list. Fig.2(a) is the topology of a constructed weighted network obtained by the framework, Fig.2(b) shows one possible particle encoding based on the local neighbor list. For a particle $P_i = (P_{i,1}, P_{i,2}, \ldots, P_{i,n})$, if $P_{i,k} = m$, it means particle $i$ represents that $V_k$ and $V_m$ are in the same community while m is chosen from the neighborhoods of particular k. Fig.2 (c) reveals how to convert a particle encoding into the community structure. Fig.2 (d) shows the community structure relevant to the particle encoding in Fig.2 (b).

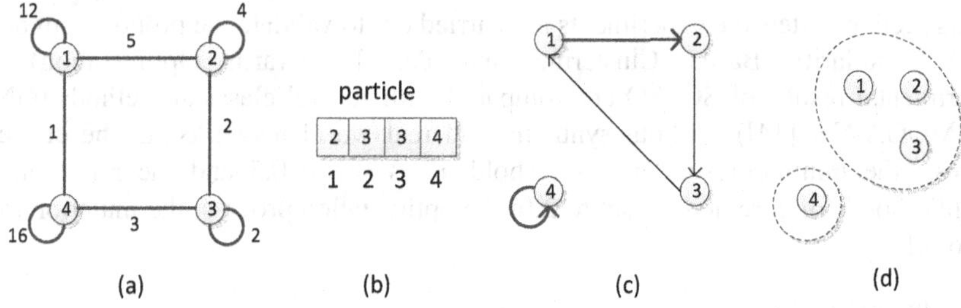


**Fig. 2.** Illustration of particle encoding based on neighbor list

**Update Strategy**

A potential solution is represented as a particle, each particle adjusts its trajectory based on the activities of its neighbor or the whole population. In each iteration, the particle adjusts velocity by the following formula (7) where $x_{ij}^{(p)}$ is the personal best position, $x_{ij}^{(g)}$ is the global best position of swarms, $\omega$ is the inertia weight, $c_1$ and $c_2$ are learning factors, $r_1$ and $r_2$ are random values in the region [0,1].

The update strategy in this paper refers to the update strategy of PSO in continuous space optimization [18]. However, an additional modular operation is added to ensure $x_{ij}(t)$ lies within $[0, \deg(v_j)]$, $x_{ij}(t)$ rounded upwards to the nearest integer. The resulting change in position is defined by formula (8).

$$v_{ij}(t+1) = wv_{ij}(t) + c_1 r_1 (x_{ij}^{(p)} - x_{ij}(t)) + c_2 r_2 (x_{ij}^{(g)}(t) - x_{ij}(t)) \tag{7}$$

$$x_{ij}(t+1) = (x_{ij}(t) + v_{ij}(t+1)) \bmod \deg(v_j) \tag{8}$$

**Algorithm Description**

The detail procedure of the optimization algorithm is shown as follows:

**Step1.** Build the local-neighbor-list based on the new constructed weighted network.

**Step2**.Set the parameters, and initiate each particle with a random value selected based on the local-neighbor-list.

**Step3**. For each particle, calculates its current fitness, copies its current position (fitness) to its local best position (fitness).

**Step4**. Perform the update strategy to each particle, if the fitness is better than its local best; update its local best,

**Step5**. Select the global best from the local best of each particle. If the fitness is better than the current global value, update current global value $gbest$.

**Step6.** If the stop condition is met, the community structure relevant to the global best particle is selected as the best partition of the network, otherwise go to step 4.

## 5 Experimental Results

In this section, extensive experiments are carried out to validate the proposed algorithm SCPSO(Similarity Based Clustering and Particle Swarm Optimization). The experimental results of SCPSO are compared with several classical methods (GN [5] and MOGA-Net [14]) on both synthetic and real world networks. In the clustering process, the minimum similarity threshold $\varepsilon$ is set to 0.5 and the minimum $\varepsilon$-neighborhoods of core node is set to 2.In the optimization process, the mutation rate is set to 0.1.

- Evaluation metric

In order to compare the performance of different solutions, two evaluation metrics are introduced.

One metric adopted in the experiments is Normalized Mutual Information (NMI) [19]. NMI is always used to calculate the similarity between two partitions. NMI is defined as follows. A higher NMI value represents a greater similarity between partition $A$ and partition $B$. When partition $A$ and partition $B$ are exactly the same, NMI will reach the max value of 1.

$$NMI(A,B) = \frac{-2\sum_{i=1}^{C_A}\sum_{j=1}^{C_B} C_{ij} \log\left(C_{ij}N / C_i C_j\right)}{\sum_{i=1}^{C_A} C_i \log\left(C_i / N\right) + \sum_{j=1}^{C_B} C_j \log\left(C_j / N\right)} \tag{9}$$

The other metric adopted in the experiments is modularity Q. Modularity Q is always used in estimating the quality of community structure discovered by different solutions if the community structure of a network is unknown. The community partition with a larger modularity usually indicates a better solution. Modularity and NMI are two commonly used metrics for evaluating the quality of community structure.

- Experimental results and analysis on synthetic network

The synthetic network is a benchmark proposed by Girvan and Newman [5]. The network consists of 128 nodes and is divided into four equally-sized communities, each with 32 nodes. Each node has $z_{out}$ links to nodes of other communities, $z_{in}$ links to nodes in the same community, and has an average degree of 16, namely

$z_{out}+z_{in} = 16$. When $z_{out} < z_{in}$, the network generated have relatively clear community structure while the community structure becomes obscure when $z_{out} \geq 8$. The benchmark networks are generated with $z_{out}$ varying from 0 to 8, each $z_{out}$ with 50 networks.

Fig.3 shows the distribution of NMI results of the three algorithms averaged over 100 runs for $z_{out}$ ranging from 0 to 8. The difference in the three algorithms increases when $z_{out}$ grows. Random optimization method like MOGA-NET become instable with the increase of $z_{out}$. The performance of GN drop rapidly when $z_{out} > 5$. On the contrary, SCPSO can always detect the community structure effectively when $z_{out}$ <=6, the NMI value is close to 1.0. When $z_{out}$ > 6 and even $z_{out}$ =8, the NMI value achieved by SCPSO is still close to 0.6. It indicates that SCPSO can still find out some high quality community structure even when the network structure becomes obscure.

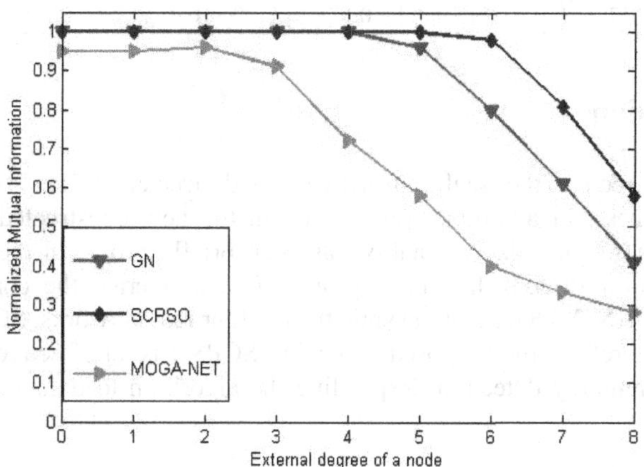


**Fig. 3.** The comparison of NMI in synthetic network

**Experimental Results and Analysis on Real Networks**

Four well studied real-world networks whose community structures are known in prior, including Zachary's Karate Club [20], Bottlenose Dolphins [21], the American College Football [5], and the Krebs' books on American politics [22], are selected as benchmark networks to verify the performance of SCPSO.

In the experiments on real networks, we run MOGA-NET 100 times over each real network and calculate the average value of modularity Q and NMI, since MOGA-NET are random optimization algorithms and the result of each run may be different. In addition, MOGA-NET is also a multi-objective optimization algorithm and returns a set of solutions called Pareto front. For the convenience of comparison, the solution with max modularity Q is selected as the single recommendation solution from the solution set of MOGA-NET and the corresponding Q and NMI are chosen as the final result.

Table1 illustrates the experimental results of three candidate algorithms. It is clear to find out that SCPSO outperforms the other three algorithms in most cases. In Karate network, SCPSO gets a little worse modularity Q than MOGA-NET. The reason is that clustering process in the framework has combine some nodes, SCPSO may not retrieval the global best modularity compared to random optimize in the original network. If splitting some core area increases the modularity index, SCPSO gets lower modularity index compared to optimize in origin network. In Dolphins, Krebs and Football, SCPSO outperforms its competitors in both modularity and NMI.

**Table 1.** Comparison of Modularity in Real Networks

| | MODULARITY COMPARISON | | | NMI COMPARISION | | |
|---|---|---|---|---|---|---|
| | SCPSO | MOGA-NET | GN | SCPSO | MOGA-NET | GN |
| **Karate** | 0.400 | 0.415 | 0.380 | 0.803 | 0.602 | 0.692 |
| **Dolphins** | 0.528 | 0.505 | 0.495 | 0.581 | 0.506 | 0.573 |
| **Krebs** | 0.521 | 0.518 | 0.502 | 0.549 | 0.536 | 0.530 |
| **Football** | 0.617 | 0.515 | 0.577 | 0.801 | 0.775 | 0.762 |

## 6 Conclusion

Our goal is to reduce the scale of network and accelerate the convergence in optimization process. In addition, optimization in the new constructed network has shown its advantage, and the rationality has been briefly proof. In the optimization process, a mutation strategy had been proposed to accelerate the convergence. In comparison with GN, MOGA-Net in synthetic and four real networks, SCPSO exhibits its advantage. Therefore, the proposed algorithm SCPSO is an effective optimization algorithm in community detection. Expanding the algorithm to dynamic networks is our next job.

**Acknowledgment.** The authors would like to thank the support of the Technology Innovation Platform Project of Fujian Province under Grant No. 2009J10027, the Key Project of Fujian Education Committee under Grant No. JK2012003, the Program of National Natural Science Foundation of China under Grant No. 60171 009.

## References

1. Fortunato, S.: Community detection in graphs. Physics Reports 486, 75–174 (2010)
2. Radicchi, F., Castellano, C., Cecconi, F., Loreto, V., Parisi, D.: Defining and identifying communities in networks. Proceedings of the National Academy of Sciences of the United States of America 101, 2658–2663 (2004)
3. Flake, G.W., Lawrence, S., Giles, C.L., Coetzee, F.M.: Self-organization and identification of web communities. Computer 35, 66–70 (2002)
4. Ravasz, E., Somera, A.L., Mongru, D.A., Oltvai, Z.N., Barabási, A.-L.: Hierarchical organization of modularity in metabolic networks. Science 297, 1551–1555 (2002)

5. Girvan, M., Newman, M.E.: Community structure in social and biological networks. Proceedings of the National Academy of Sciences 99, 7821–7826 (2002)
6. Wu, F., Huberman, B.A.: Finding communities in linear time: a physics approach. The European Physical Journal B-Condensed Matter and Complex Systems 38, 331–338 (2004)
7. Kleinberg, J.M.: Authoritative sources in a hyperlinked environment. Journal of the ACM (JACM) 46, 604–632 (1999)
8. Smyth, S., White, S.: A spectral clustering approach to finding communities in graphs. In: Proceedings of the 5th SIAM International Conference on Data Mining, pp. 76–84 (2005)
9. Newman, M.E.: Detecting community structure in networks. The European Physical Journal B-Condensed Matter and Complex Systems 38, 321–330 (2004)
10. Guimera, R., Amaral, L.A.N.: Functional cartography of complex metabolic network. Nature 433, 895–900 (2005)
11. Xiaodong, D., Cunrui, W., Xiangdong, L., Yanping, L.: Web community detection model using particle swarm optimization. In: IEEE Congress on Evolutionary Computation, CEC 2008, IEEE World Congress on Computational Intelligence, pp. 1074–1079 (2008)
12. Newman, M.E., Girvan, M.: Finding and evaluating community structure in networks. Physical Review E 69, 026113 (2004)
13. Fortunato, S., Barthelemy, M.: Resolution limit in community detection. Proceedings of the National Academy of Sciences 104, 36–41 (2007)
14. Pizzuti, C.: A multi-objective genetic algorithm for community detection in networks. In: 21st International Conference on Tools with Artificial Intelligence, ICTAI 2009, pp. 379–386 (2009)
15. Shi, C., Yan, Z., Cai, Y., Wu, B.: Multi-objective community detection in complex networks. Applied Soft Computing 12, 850–859 (2012)
16. Ester, M., Kriegel, H.-P., Sander, J., Xu, X.: A density-based algorithm for discovering clusters in large spatial databases with noise. In: KDD, pp. 226–231 (1996)
17. Xu, X., Yuruk, N., Feng, Z., Schweiger, T.A.: SCAN: a structural clustering algorithm for networks. In: Proceedings of the 13th ACM SIGKDD International Conference on Knowledge Discovery and Data Mining, pp. 824–833 (2007)
18. Kennedy, J.: Particle swarm optimization. In: Encyclopedia of Machine Learning, pp. 760–766. Springer (2010)
19. Danon, L., Diaz-Guilera, A., Duch, J., Arenas, A.: Comparing community structure identification. Journal of Statistical Mechanics: Theory and Experiment, 09008 (2005)
20. Zachary, W.W.: An information flow model for conflict and fission in small groups. Journal of Anthropological Research, 452–473 (1977)
21. Lusseau, D., Schneider, K., Boisseau, O.J., Haase, P., Slooten, E., Dawson, S.M.: The bottlenose dolphin community of Doubtful Sound features a large proportion of long-lasting associations. Behavioral Ecology and Sociobiology 54, 396–405 (2003)
22. Krebs, V.: Unpublished, `http://www.orgnet.com/`

# Author Index